M000240091

CONTINENTAL ACHIEVEMENT

KEVIN STARR

CONTINENTAL ACHIEVEMENT

Roman Catholics in the United States

Revolution and the Early Republic

IGNATIUS PRESS   SAN FRANCISCO

Cover illustrations by Matthew Alderman

Cover design by John Herreid

© 2020 by Ignatius Press, San Francisco
All rights reserved
ISBN 978-1-62164-263-3 (HB)
ISBN 978-1-64229-135-3 (eBook)
Library of Congress Control Number 2019947890
Printed in the United States of America ∞

For Sheila,
with love and gratitude for our partnership

CONTENTS

NOTE TO READERS

On the last day of his life, Kevin Starr prepared the preface, the table of contents, and the dedication. *Continental Ambitions* and *Continental Achievement* were hand-written, as were the volumes of his Americans and the California Dream series. He revised from printed transcriptions. He had completed ten of twenty chapters of *Continental Achievement* and had revised all of those chapters twice, save for the last, chapter 10.

In the unfinished chapters, he had envisioned first looking west, to Bardstown, Kentucky, reprising America as Holy Land, and to Cincinnati, Ohio, whose frontier diocese set the pace for midcontinental expansion into the Ohio and Louisiana Territories; then east, where Bishop John England of Washington, D.C., was struggling to keep alive a republican model of church governance. In Charlestown and Philadelphia, nativist fury destroyed a convent and two churches, and in Staten Island, a papal envoy fled for his life. Moving westward again, to Pacific shores, war with Mexico brought Texas, the Spanish Southwest, and California into the Union, and Rome established the first of two dioceses on the Pacific coast in Oregon City. Protestant writers embraced Catholic themes in the Oxford Movement in America, as a decade of religious ferment yielded conversions at Brook Farm, Massachusetts. Finally, in New York City, Archbishop John Hughes at some cost fashioned an identity of an immigrant church that would last for more than a century.

Kevin was intensely and happily absorbed in the research and the writing of this book. He once told me, "The book is practically writing itself, to the point that I sometimes wake up in the early morning with near-finished sentences running through my head."

Continental Ambitions and *Continental Achievement* remain his offering to the Church that raised him and sustained him throughout his life.

Sheila Starr
San Francisco
December 2019

PREFACE

The American Revolution allowed Roman Catholics of the English colonies of North America to earn a new and better place for themselves in an emergent American Republic. Roman Catholic Loyalists were few, for one thing, and mainly from Philadelphia (like New York, a noticeably Loyalist city). French forces tended to be Roman Catholic, and French military intervention on behalf of the Revolution was crucial to its military success. Every effort is made in these pages to keep in mind the pain and terror of the Revolutionary War as war, as combat, for each side over a period of eight years, with the death toll for Americans exceeding twenty-five thousand and that of the British forces exceeding fifteen thousand.[1] American Catholics did their fair share of the fighting and dying, and contemporary Catholic Americans can take note of this participation with controlled and proper pride as something commendable in itself as well as something that earned full citizenship for a previously disenfranchised sector of the American population.

The Franco-Spanish alliance of 1778—with Spain financing the rebellion in its part of Louisiana and France assuring a final victory at Yorktown through naval and siege deployments—formed a connection between the upper classes of the United States and Catholic France that lingered as a diminishing afterglow until relations between the United States and revolutionary France grew strained to the breaking point in the 1790s, although they did not disappear completely. The French Revolution, moreover, brought to the United States a generation of well-educated French priests, the society known in France as the Gentlemen of Saint-Sulpice, who played major roles in the establishment of Catholic institutions and significantly staffed the first generation and a half of the Catholic hierarchy.

While he remains relatively obscure in the Revolutionary War chapters of this narrative—aside, that is, from his brief participation in the ill-fated diplomatic mission to Canada, during which he formed a most fortuitous friendship with Benjamin Franklin—John Carroll makes frequent appearances in roles of increasing importance: missionary, constitution writer for his ex-Jesuit colleagues, prefect apostolic, controversialist and defender of the faith, bishop, founder of Georgetown, cathedral developer, archbishop and metropolitan, negotiator with the Court of Rome, patron and sponsor of the first American sisterhood, tireless correspondent, and, in all this, Founding Father in the matter of establishing the fullness of the Church in a new Republic to the benefit of each. In him, the Maryland ethos regarding Roman Catholicism reached a point of penultimate fulfillment. Devoted to his extended family and a few close friends, he was not overly friendly or familiar toward the general public. Belonging by birth to the leadership class, he governed, in great part, from a class perspective in the style of the eighteenth century. Yet he was no snob, remained approachable, and was ecumenical in his willingness to play a role in the larger institutions of society. His patience and capacity for conciliation, however—especially as far as his fellow clergy were concerned—further qualified the essential reserve of his personality, which seemed to lift entirely when he was keeping epistolary company with Charles Plowden, his good English friend from Jesuit times together on the Continent.

As founding bishop of Catholic America, Carroll had the goal of introducing Religion—by which he meant Roman Catholic belief and practice—as fully as possible into the United States without offending or confusing the reasonably well-disposed Protestant majority in whom he never ceased believing. Thus, he was scrupulous in keeping American ex-Jesuit property safe from any form of appropri-ation; he did not demand that such properties be forcibly yielded to the diocese he governed as bishop. Likewise was Carroll scrupulous in accepting the decisions of Propaganda Fide in spiritual matters and instructing its cardinals as to the limitations of their authority to this field alone. The patience Carroll demonstrated in dealing with ex-Jesuits who sought to circumscribe his episcopal authority, moreover, he extended equally to troubled priests and independence-minded lay church trust-ees, many of them hostile to episcopacy as it was now being introduced into the American church, some of them flirting secretly (or even openly) with the idea of a separate American Catholic Church modeled on events in Utrecht earlier in the century. There some elements of the local church insisted for a time that their bishop ought to be appointed by them, not by the Vatican.

Carroll showed the same patience in fostering the Catholic career of convert Elizabeth Bayley Seton as vowed religious and founder of the first American sis-terhood. Indeed, as bishop, Carroll made possible Seton's entrance into religious life while she saw to the rearing of her five children. As one of her trusted spiritual directors, moreover, Carroll also served as a steadying influence on her somewhat mercurial temperament as she adjusted herself to the religiously ambitious life that had been hers in one form or another long before her conversion.

John Carroll's death on 3 December 1815 did not end the Maryland era of Roman Catholic development in the new nation, but it did signal the transition that would take place, starting in the 1820s, as driven by two forces: immigration and lay trusteeism. Paradoxically, these dynamics were driven by each other in a negative manner, yet their combination resulted in the end of the Maryland tra-dition of confederated constituencies. These constituencies comprised laity (espe-cially upper-register laity), English, Irish, and German Catholics; clergy (particularly Sulpicians and ex-Jesuits); emergent sisterhoods; trustees; and, after 1790, a bishop (some forty bishops by midcentury)—each self-defining. The ex-Jesuits, for exam-ple, formed their own state-sanctioned corporation, which was interactive and interdependent. From this perspective, lay trustees were wary of bishops because bishops, by definition, usurped trustees' long-held power over Church properties, parish staffing, programs, and revenues. Anchored in a prior English identity of a church run of necessity by laymen and by a more recent exposure to Freemasonry, with its adherence to universal rights and opposition to arbitrary power, these trust-ees tended to consider bishops interlopers, not from the universal Church, but from a foreign power, the Court of Rome, and opposed them accordingly, with little interest in the historical development of the role of bishops in Church governance.

The Catholic population, however, was changing dramatically through immigra-tion, and bishops and clergy, not trustees, were accruing expanded status as leaders of immigrants (Irish immigrants especially), gathering in councils to legislate for the Church, and, increasingly, bypassing lay trustees while creating a clerically controlled system. In the 1820s and 1830s, Bishop John England of Charleston, South Carolina, made an honest effort to revive the best aspects of the Maryland tradition, with its emphasis on confederation and constitutionalism. Upper-class gentry trustees and survivors from the republican era of John Carroll, as well as friendly Protestants, approved of England's brilliant efforts, but as Irish Catholic immigrants continued to pour into the United States, England's campaign lost its base and had no lasting effect on an emergent Catholic polity whose paradigm was Archbishop John Hughes' governance of New York as shepherd in chief, tribune of the people, corporation sole, and political boss.

The Catholic peoples of the West, by contrast—Anglo-American Kentuckians, Irish and German immigrants, previously settled French—were slower perhaps to be consolidated under a militant episcopal leadership, although the same process was underway. Kentucky, for one thing, became even more Catholic than Maryland ever was; and the bishop of Bardstown, the French Sulpician Benedict Joseph Flaget, governed his vast region in an almost completely pastoral manner. The clergy of Bardstown, moreover—Dominicans, diocesan missionaries, Benedictines, Trappists—were accustomed to (and rarely, if ever, abused) a high degree of autonomy, as was a widely dispersed laity. German immigrants, moreover, obtained their own German-language parishes with greater ease and formed stabilizing connections to the German Benedictine communities being established in this region in the pre–Civil War era.

The Louisiana Purchase of 1803, however, brought New Orleans into American jurisdiction, including the ecclesiastical jurisdiction of John Carroll, and New Orleans featured the most resistant of cathedral *marguilliers* (church wardens), who literally forced the apostolic administrator of Louisiana, Louis William DuBourg, to remain outside the city for his own safety and later, as bishop, to govern from Saint Louis. Bardstown's most immediate creation, meanwhile, the Diocese of Cincinnati—established in 1821 and headed by the Dominican Edward Fenwick, who had introduced the friars into Kentucky—was serving the rise of Catholic society in Ohio, Michigan, and the eastern regions of the Old Northwest Territory in a manner that earned the praise of English travel writer Frances Trollope in her *Domestic Manners of the Americans* (1832). Trollope's evaluation of American Catholicism was followed by the even more extensive and flattering observations of French sociologist Alexis de Tocqueville in his *Democracy in America* (1835, 1840).

Yet the hopefulness of Mrs. Trollope's praise and de Tocqueville's complimentary, insightful analysis was offset by the parallel rise of an angry, abusive anti-Catholic nativism that would last until midcentury. Essential to this Protestant crusade were obsessively repeated descriptions of Catholic convents as brothels of the worst sort, with nuns murdering infants they bore their priest lovers. These charges and the lurid details that accompanied them constituted a form of pornography that had a powerful effect on young Protestant men as well as on some not so young male community leaders, who demanded the right to inspect the Ursuline convent in Charlestown, Massachusetts, where forty-seven female students, Catholics and Protestants alike from established families, were being educated. When this harassment proved insufficient, an organized gang of young men broke into and torched the convent, and the Ursuline sisters were barely able to get their charges safely out of the building.

Ten years later, in 1844, anti-Catholic rioting in Philadelphia cost twenty lives and two churches torched. When Italian archbishop Gaetano Bedini arrived in the United States in June 1853 as a papal envoy investigating anti-Catholicism in the United States, mobs harassed the archbishop or burned him in effigy as he toured the country on his fact-finding mission. Finally, on the advice of his host and escort, Archbishop John Hughes, Bedini secretly escaped from New York, leaving Staten Island in a rowboat to board his oceangoing vessel. Appointed secretary to Propaganda Fide and created cardinal, Bedini thus was able to bring to his assignment a firsthand impression of the violent and vulgar nativism gripping a nation still considered missionary territory.

War with Mexico, meanwhile, brought the Catholic peoples and societies of the Spanish Southwest, including Texas and California, into the fold of American Catholic jurisdiction as part of the Treaty of Guadalupe Hidalgo (1848), which ended that conflict. The Oregon Territory, jointly occupied by the United States and Great Britain since 1818, was, after some talk of war, diplomatically divided in 1846, and the American Territory of Oregon was created in 1848. Rome already had created the Archdiocese of Oregon City (later Portland) in 1846, and in 1853 Rome added the Archdiocese of San Francisco to the Diocese of Monterey, created in 1850. Thus, by the early 1850s, the Roman Catholic Church in the United States extended from the Atlantic to the Pacific, from Maine to the Mexican border. In slightly more than half a century, the Church had kept pace with the continental expansion of the nation itself.

In this national expansion, moreover, such major acquisitions as Florida, the Louisiana Territory, Texas, California, and the Spanish Southwest were historically Roman Catholic territories, with a rudimentary but time-tested Catholic population in residence. This linkage of English-, Spanish-, and French-speaking Catholic regions, along with the by now formidable presence of German Catholicism, conferred on American Catholicism a diversity increasingly necessary by midcentury, given the continuing surge of Irish immigration and the growing presence of Hibernian clergy. Maryland and Kentucky remained supportive of an ascendant Anglo-American Catholic population, but the dioceses then being created in the West—Cincinnati (1821), Saint Louis (1826), New Orleans (1826), Detroit (1833), Vincennes (1834), Nashville (1837), Milwaukee (1843), and Chicago (1843)—showed ethnic profiles reflective of the dioceses of the eastern states, with some lessening of the Irish factor, despite efforts to promote Irish settlement in the West.

The decades 1820 to 1850 also witnessed a replenishment of the Anglo-Catholic presence through conversion. Despite the rise of anti-Catholicism during this period, thousands of Americans converted to Catholicism. Married converts frequently converted because of their positive experience of the faith through their spouses. For some, rational analysis played a major role, especially among highly educated clergy. For others—John Thayer and Elizabeth Bayley Seton, for example— a personal crisis intensified an already active evangelism given further focus through an experience of Catholicism at home or abroad. West Point cadets converted, as did civilian students in Catholic and non-Catholic schools. Corresponding with the Oxford Movement in England, the American Anglo-Catholic movement brought many Protestant Episcopalians into the Church. Indeed, the most illustrious of the English Oxford Movement Catholic converts, John Henry Newman, would cite the influence of the Anglo-Catholic thinking of New York Episcopalian John Henry Hobart, later Protestant Episcopal bishop of New York, on his own efforts to come over to Rome. Vaguely anchored in German idealism, the transcendentalist movement of Boston helped a number of eminent converts of the era—Isaac Hecker and Orestes Brownson, to name two—to reach Rome and cross the Tiber.

As of the mid-1850s, in fact, the most prominent Roman Catholic intellectuals in the United States, including one former Protestant Episcopal bishop, were converts. In general, and a little begrudgingly, Archbishop John Hughes of New York approved of this acquisition of intellectual firepower through conversion. Hughes was himself a well-read man, whose ten-thousand-volume library of ecclesiastical studies was profiled in James Wynne's *Private Libraries of New York* (1860) as a model collection of its kind. But John Hughes had come up the hard way, working as an Irish immigrant groundsman at Mount Saint Mary's Seminary in Emmitsburg, Maryland, before, after repeated requests, being admitted to seminary studies. As bishop of New York, moreover, Hughes broke the power of the lay trustees and brought to perfection the model of the American diocese being governed in no uncertain terms by its bishop, who held the bulk of diocesan property in his own name as corporation sole and governed his flock without ambiguity or interference. Hughes also considered himself the chief policy maker of the New York Archdiocese and resented any incursions into this arena by Anglo-American converts. To Hughes' way of thinking, theological discourse or church polity discussions remained the prerogative of the bishop and his clergy. A half century before, the rebellious trustees of Saint Mary's Church had driven Franciscan Michael Egan, the first bishop of Philadelphia, to a mental breakdown and early death. Fracturing the power of the rebellious trustees of New York, Archbishop John Hughes returned the favor and thereby established the diocesan governance model for an immigrant church.

PART ONE

Revolution

Quebec City 1775

The Continental Congress proposes an alliance with French Canada

With the outbreak of hostilities in and around Boston in the spring of 1775—the skirmishes at Lexington and Concord in April, the battle of Bunker Hill in June—the thoughts of the Second Continental Congress almost automatically turned to an invasion of Canada by the United Colonies. New England and New York had been at war with French Canada in one form or another for the better part of a century before Great Britain defeated France on the Plains of Abraham, north of Quebec City, in September 1759. In 1763 France formally ceded Canada to Great Britain in the Treaty of Paris, which ended the Seven Years' War, known in North America as the French and Indian War. Victory in the Seven Years' War defined and solidified Great Britain as an imperial power with colonies, dominated dependencies, and fortified outposts scattered across the planet.

As of mid-1775, however, that nascent empire momentarily seemed vulnerable—in North America, at least—with the recent defeats in Massachusetts, especially on Bunker Hill, where the British had lost more than a thousand soldiers. At this point, British Canada appeared equally in jeopardy. Much to the distress of Commanding General Guy Carleton, two of the five British regiments stationed there had already been reassigned to Boston, as of September 1774, and had recently suffered heavy losses in the assault against Bunker Hill. Carleton, moreover—a professional solider who had served as a colonel in a battalion of the Royal Americans (Sixtieth Foot) on the Plains of Abraham—distrusted Iroquois auxiliaries, refused to recruit them, and was forced to defend the province of Quebec with the few troops under his command and wait for reinforcements. Nor did Carleton fully believe that he could depend on local militias other than the regiment of British colonists he had raised. The Quebecois were resisting muster; indeed, in June 1775 Carleton was forced to resort to martial law to raise a militia, given the lack of response he was encountering among rank-and-file French Canadians.

The collapse of royal governments in the colonies, meanwhile—Virginia in May and Massachusetts in October 1774, followed the next year by successive collapses or abandonments in New York, North Carolina, Georgia, New Hampshire, South Carolina, and New Jersey—ran concurrently with the launching of an American siege against British forces in Boston and gave rise to thoughts of a Canadian-oriented strategy among congressional delegates and George Washington (directing the siege of Boston from headquarters in Cambridge), whom Congress had recently placed in overall command of its military forces. Should Canada be taken, Congress and Washington reasoned, the British forces under the command of Sir William

Howe, now besieged in Boston, would be prevented from making an easy exit by sea to Halifax, Nova Scotia, as they obviously planned to do, if escape became necessary. Congress and Washington began to explore in November 1775 by dispatching commissioners (secret agents, in reality) Aaron Willard and Moses Child to Nova Scotia to ascertain the strength of the British military presence as well as to gauge the attitude of the French-speaking population regarding an American alliance. Returning to Cambridge from their mission, Willard and Child reported favorably: if the Nova Scotians could be assured of long-term protection, they would favor a United Colonies takeover of that strategic island.

On 15 June 1775, the Second Continental Congress commissioned as major general Philip John Schuyler, an upstate New York Anglo-Dutch landowner, businessman, diplomat, and veteran of the French and Indian War. Congress thereupon appointed Major General Schuyler commander of the Northern Department and directed him to prepare forces and supplies for the invasion of Quebec province. When it came to raising a militia, however, New England responded half-heartedly to Schuyler's effort, yet another instance of a long-standing New York versus New England rivalry recently exacerbated by opposing claims to the New Hampshire Grants (Vermont) and by Schuyler's aristocratic demeanor toward his troops. Still, an invasion force stood assembled, but Schuyler—his health broken by rheumatic gout (a hereditary malady and lifelong complaint) and the strain of organizing such a rapid and discordant mobilization—was in no shape to lead the invasion and turned field command over to the able and experienced brigadier general Richard Montgomery.

Montgomery takes command

Born the son of a prominent Parliamentarian in Dublin County, Ireland, in 1738 and educated at the University of St. Andrews and Trinity College, Dublin, Montgomery was yet another veteran of the French and Indian War. Following the war, he pursued an army career until, assigned to New York, he fell in love with the province and with farming. Cashing in his captaincy, he acquired a sixty-seven-acre farm at King's Bridge (today Kingsbridge, northwest Bronx), where he mastered the art and science of agriculture. Montgomery later put these newly acquired skills to use managing Grasmere, the estate of his wife, Jane Livingston, near Rhinebeck, on the Hudson. Thus, one landed gentleman, Richard Montgomery, a university man connected by marriage to a leading New York family, succeeded another landed gentleman, Philip Schuyler, connected by marriage to the Van Rensselaers, in the service of a rebellion led by and on behalf of an aggrieved colonial establishment.

By late August 1775 Schuyler and Montgomery's militia forces—largely New Englanders, poorly disciplined, given to desertion, ever on the edge of mutiny— were as ready as they would ever be and began the trek north to Quebec. Already, a vanguard of Green Mountain Boys from Vermont under the command of Colonel Ethan Allen had rendezvoused with New England militia under the command of Colonel Benedict Arnold and captured Fort Ticonderoga on 10 May, followed by a rapidly executed seizure and control of the Lake Champlain region. Moving north toward the border, Montgomery took Chambly and St. John's, where the invading

United Colonists captured the colors of the Seventh Fusiliers, the first British colors to be seized in what would turn out to be a protracted and precarious conflict. Entering Canada, Montgomery's force captured Montreal on 13 November 1775 and in December met with forces led by Arnold, whose men had invaded Canada by way of Maine. Each of them Connecticut-born and -raised, Ethan Allen and Benedict Arnold were similarly arrogant, impetuous, gifted, and on the make. In 1770 Allen had moved to the New Hampshire Grants. Elected colonel of the Green Mountain Boys militia, he linked his fortunes to the struggle to win for Vermont status as a separate colony. Physically imposing and charismatic, Arnold combined a perfervid Protestantism with a thin-skinned ambivalence toward authority and talent as a field commander, despite his lack of regular military service. Both Allen and Arnold, in fact, were militiamen, which throws into bold relief their jointly directed victory at Ticonderoga.

The siege of Quebec City

As of December 1775 Montgomery and Arnold were laying siege to Quebec. (Captured after a premature attack on Montreal on 25 September, Allen was by December a prisoner of war in irons en route to imprisonment in England.) Within Quebec, Governor Guy Carleton and his regulars commanded the defense of the city. Having failed to stop the United Colonies militia on its advance up the Richelieu Valley, the historic invasion route into Quebec province, Carleton knew that if the United Colonists, who now held Montreal, were to take Quebec as well, they would control the upper reaches of the Saint Lawrence Valley and hence control the heavily populated regions of Canada via Lake Champlain and the two major valleys and river systems of Quebec province. On his part, Montgomery, assessing the forlorn state of his militia forces—undisciplined, ill-armed, poorly supplied, liable to disease and desertion—realized that he could not sustain a siege throughout the long, brutal Canadian winter; and so, on 31 December 1775, Montgomery led an unsuccessful assault on the city and was shot and killed while leading the attack.

Between sixty and one hundred United Colonists were killed or wounded, as opposed to twenty British casualties. Some four hundred United Colonies militia were captured by British regulars in or around the city. Criticized for not launching an immediate counterattack, Carleton would nevertheless eventually receive a knighthood for his defense of the city and later be raised to the peerage. With Montgomery killed, command passed to Colonel Benedict Arnold, who continued the siege as best he could until he was replaced by Brigadier General David Wooster, a politically prominent Connecticut officer with extensive military experience in the French and Indian War. Now sixty-four, Wooster had remained in command in Montreal during the Quebec siege but outranked Arnold. In May 1776 Wooster was replaced by Brigadier General John Thomas, a fifty-two-year-old Massachusetts officer who had joined the British army as a surgeon in 1746, transferred to the line in 1747, risen to colonel of militia during the French and Indian War, and then returned to medical practice before rejoining the line, this time for the United Colonies. Thomas played a crucial role in fortifying Dorchester Heights on 4 March 1776 with British cannon captured at Fort Ticonderoga and heroically brought overland through New York and Massachusetts by Henry Knox, Washington's portly chief of artillery. The successful occupation of Dorchester Heights was a crucial factor in persuading the British to abandon Boston. Like Montgomery, John Thomas was a field general of great promise. Also like Montgomery, Thomas found his militia troops, now reduced to slightly less than a thousand, ill-supplied, undisciplined, dispirited, demanding discharge to go home, and—even worse—devastated by an epidemic of smallpox that would soon, on 2 June 1776, carry off Brigadier General Thomas himself, hero of Dorchester Heights.

A congressional delegation

By early 1776 the members of the Second Continental Congress were well aware that their military invasion of Canada was on the brink of disaster. Only a popular uprising of French Canadian *habitants*, they believed, could save the day. Given the nature of French Canadian society, moreover, such popular support would require the approval of the bishop, clergy, and seigneurial nobility of Quebec to be fully effective. And so, on 15 February 1776, Congress resolved that a committee of three, two of them current members of Congress, should repair to Canada on a diplomatic mission, seeking to persuade French Canadians that, like their English counterparts to the south, they should rise up and free themselves from the yoke of British oppression.

The importance accorded this mission by Congress was evident in the selection of its senior member, seventy-year-old Benjamin Franklin—scientist, inventor, philosopher, founder of institutions, social activist, and veteran diplomat—the single most prominent citizen in the North American English colonies before the rise of George Washington. Irascible Samuel Chase, the second congressional member, was an ambitious jurist from Maryland, not so accomplished or well known, but representing a colony with Roman Catholic origins and the largest Roman Catholic population in the United Colonies.

A well-known Catholic was the third member of the delegation: Maryland landowner, entrepreneur, and jurist Charles Carroll of Carrollton, thirty-nine, perhaps the wealthiest man in the colonies, famous for his brilliant and spirited opposition to taxation without representation three years earlier in the *Maryland Gazette*, writing under the name First Citizen. Charles Carroll, in turn, successfully nominated a fourth addition to the delegation, his distant cousin John Carroll, age forty-one, a Roman Catholic priest, formerly of the suppressed Society of Jesus, now on mission in Maryland, based out of Rock Creek Manor, his mother's home and estate in Prince George's County.

With the bold addition of the Reverend Mr. Carroll, the only Roman Catholic priest to support the Revolution openly, Congress was sending to Canada a most impressive delegation: the colonies' leading savant, an influential Maryland congressman, and the two Carrolls, layman and priest, each intellectually assured French speakers polished by European travel and sojourns, each markedly Catholic in culture and psychology.

After sixteen years of humanities and philosophy studies in three Jesuit colleges on the Continent and legal studies at the Inner Temple in London, Charles Carroll of Carrollton determined (so he informed his friends by letter) to come home and to live privately as a country gentleman, scholar, and agriculturalist. As a Roman

Catholic, he was barred from pursuing any form of public life, including voting, much less practicing law. Returning to Maryland in the fall of 1764, following the failure of negotiations for an engagement to Louisa Baker, the daughter of a retired Saint Croix planter of Irish descent, Carroll joined his father in the management of Doughoregan (House of Kings), the vast estate in Frederick County bequeathed to Carroll's father by his father, Charles Carroll the Settler, who in 1659 had emigrated from Ireland and begun the development of Carrollton Manor. From that point forward, Carroll signed his name Charles Carroll of Carrollton to distinguish himself from his father, Charles Carroll of Annapolis or Doughoregan (or both), the manor house and property Carroll would inherit in 1782 with the passing of his father.

During a winter visit to the Eastern Shore, Carroll met Miss Rachel Cooke, a direct descendant of the sister of his maternal grandmother and hence a cousin, and the two became engaged. A waiver of consanguinity was successfully requested of the Jesuit superior in Maryland. Rachel, however, fell ill and died shortly before the wedding. Carroll attended her in her last hours and later described her passing as that of a saint. In less than three years, he had lost two young women whom he loved, one to a protective mother and the other to death. For his third and successful attempt at marriage, Carroll turned to another cousin. (Nearly all upper-class Maryland Catholics were connected to each other by blood, marriage, business, or combinations thereof.) Eighteen-year-old Mary (Molly) Darnall was Carroll's first cousin, the daughter of his mother's sister, Rachel Brooke Darnall. Separated from her well-born but disgraced husband, Rachel in 1761 had nursed Charles' mother, Elizabeth Brooke Carroll, through her final illness and remained on in the Carroll household—along with her daughter, Molly—as housekeeper of Charles' father.

The return of John Carroll

The marriage of Charles Carroll of Carrollton to his cousin Molly Darnall on 5 June 1768, following the attainment of a second waiver of consanguinity from the Jesuits, provides dramatic evidence of the almost feudal nature of the Maryland Catholic elite: linked by land, family, and religion. Charles Carroll of Carrollton's distant cousin John Carroll was likewise responding to the power of this linkage when, in 1774, deprived of his identity and support after twenty-one years in the Society of Jesus, he contemplated his future as a secular priest. On the one hand, he could have remained in England as chaplain to Lord Arundell of Wardour Castle. John Carroll was, in so many ways, an ex-colonial near Englishman. As a Jesuit, moreover, he had renounced his patrimony in favor of his siblings, and now, for the first time in his life, he was faced with the challenge of organizing his personal support. The Wardour chaplaincy would provide him with a highly placed patron, Lord Arundell, his classmate from Saint Omer's College (a Jesuit school for English Catholics near Calais, France), a church—the most beautiful and commodious private Catholic chapel in England—a residence, a stipend, a flock running the gamut from aristocrats to farm folk, influence in an English Catholic community in the first stirrings of renewal, and, when required, the leisure and travel necessary to continue the intellectual life for which he had been trained as a Jesuit.

On the other hand, home beckoned: Catholic Maryland and his aged mother, who had not seen her son since he sailed for Europe in 1748 to attend Saint Omer's College in French Flanders. Securing faculties from Bishop Richard Challoner, vicar apostolic (missionary bishop) of the London District, to serve as a priest in Maryland, which was under Challoner's jurisdiction, the Reverend Mr. John Carroll sailed for Maryland in the early spring of 1774. Accompanying him was yet another distant cousin, the Reverend Mr. Anthony Carroll, likewise a former Jesuit, en route to Maryland to clarify matters of property ownership, now that he, too, faced supporting himself.

Reaching the mainland in the late spring of 1774 as the First Continental Congress met in Philadelphia, John Carroll's ship sailed up the Potomac and anchored off Bobby Brent's Landing on the shores of Richland, Virginia. Against a backdrop of white dogwood blossoms and shocking-pink Judas trees (so biographer Annabelle Melville tells us), John Carroll was greeted by his two sisters and their families: Eleanor, married to William Brent, and Anne, married to William's brother Robert, a classmate of Carroll's from their schooldays at Bohemia Academy and Saint Omer's. Virginia as well as Maryland Catholics in this era were linked by religion, land, and marriage. After two days of visiting, Carroll sailed or was rowed across the Potomac to Rock Creek, Maryland, where his mother, Eleanor Darnall Carroll, awaited the son she had not laid eyes on for twenty-six years.

Born in either 1703 or 1704, Eleanor Darnall Carroll grew up as a privileged daughter of the Maryland Catholic elite. Her home, Warburton Manor, was acquired by her father through his marriage to Anne Digges, a member of another prominent family, and was remembered by Eleanor as a spacious and beautiful residence. Like other similarly born Maryland daughters, Eleanor Darnall was sent to France for a convent education. Her husband, Daniel Carroll of Upper Marlborough in Prince George's County, whom she married in 1727, while not of such long-standing ancestry or wealth, was nevertheless a Carroll on the rise—land, slaves, tobacco, livestock, and a successful general store that specialized in imported goods. He was thus able to provide his wife with a good life, his daughters with proper tutelage, and his two sons with Jesuit educations at Bohemia Academy in Cecil County, on the Eastern Shore of Maryland, and across the Atlantic at Saint Omer's, from which John Carroll's brother Daniel returned to expand the family's fortunes even further, while son John became a Jesuit and remained in Europe.

John Carroll wrote to his English friend Charles Plowden, another former Jesuit, that, to return to his mother, he had "sacrificed the very best place in England". He said the same thing to the Reverend Mr. John Lewis, also a former Jesuit, now serving as vicar-general (deputy) to Bishop Challoner in London.[1] Lewis had aggrieved John Carroll by trying to assign him elsewhere, an assignment Carroll refused. Now that the Society of Jesus was suppressed and his vows of obedience to it were no longer in effect, Carroll felt in no way obliged to be moved from place to place, as in days of yore. Besides, Carroll argued, any effort such as Lewis' to carry on as if the suppression of the Society of Jesus had not been legally promulgated to the English province constituted a form of rebellion against the See of Peter, however misguided the suppression had been in the first place. Dated 28 February 1779, Carroll's first letter to Plowden, initiating a lifelong correspondence, teems with nostalgia for the Jesuit companions and institutional assignments he had been forced to leave behind by Ganganelli, rudely referring by his surname (as was common practice among former Jesuits) to Pope Clement XIV, the Conventual Franciscan responsible for the suppression of the Society of Jesus.

In its evocation of lost Jesuit life—companions in the Society, former students, friends and patrons of the order, many of them members of the nobility and upper-level savants—Carroll's letter reveals what a privileged expatriate he had become during those Jesuit years in Europe. But they were over. The late Clement XIV might be referred to as Ganganelli, a jumped-up, hostile Franciscan friar, but he had spoken as the pope. Hence, *finito*, goodbye, to the good old days: the dreams of the Society of Jesus, the thrill he felt as an eighteen-year-old novice when first clothed in the black cassock of the order, the years of education preparing for priestly and academic service, the grandeur of colleges across Europe, the sense of profession and purpose, the respect from laity, lowly and great alike.

Still, the Church was the Church; its decisions were final. *Roma locuta est, causa finita est.* Rome has spoken; the cause is finished. Returning to Maryland, John Carroll moved into his mother's home and began a freelance ministry. In time, his brother Daniel built for him St. John's Chapel in Rock Creek. (Daniel Carroll owned the chapel and, upon his death in 1796, left it to his brother.) Like the pious widows and deaconesses of the ancient Church and the recusant women of penal times in England, John Carroll's mother maintained home and chapel and supported her son in his ministry. The Reverend Mr. Carroll continued in this mode for some eighteen months before the call came from the Continental Congress.

Major obstacles to the mission

Aside from the deteriorating military situation in Canada, the delegation sent by the Second Continental Congress faced two further interrelated challenges working against success. First, in the aftermath of conquest and the Treaty of Paris, England had deftly brought about a rapprochement with the bishop, clergy, and seigneurs of Quebec. Second, the Quebec Act passed by Parliament in 1764 formally guaranteed the Quebecois freedom of religion, continuities of law and property, locally elected government, and exemption from military service should Great Britain ever go to war with France. Although the English-French rapprochements of 1760–1763 did not overly concern the English colonies to the south, the Quebec Act of 1764, conferring on French Canadians rights and privileges denied to English colonists, unleashed a tsunami of resentment south of the Canadian border and fanned even more—if that were possible—the pervasive anti-Catholicism of the Southern colonies.

In the course of the conquest of Quebec and its aftermath, England and French Canada achieved a surprising degree of mutual respect. This rapprochement was derived from and expressed itself through a regard on either side for the opposing general. The young British general James Wolfe, barely into his thirties, was tall, thin, and a lover of English poetry. He personally led the Louisbourg Grenadiers into the charge, wearing white military breeches and a bright red coat, waving a sword and cheering his men on: a perfect target, in short, shot three times, the third hit to his right breast proving fatal. And on the French line, Louis-Joseph de Montcalm-Grozon, age forty-seven, wearing a green coat embroidered with gold and a laced tricorn hat, the Grand Cross of Saint Louis on his chest, rode his charger at the head of the Languedoc Regiment and was shot in the abdomen, dying at dawn the next day. History (Francis Parkman) and literature (William Makepeace Thackeray) would remember and celebrate these men as paragons of their respective cultures. As if in an act of sacrifice made by them and the men who died with them, Wolfe and Montcalm laid the foundations of a future Canada, as the fifty-foot obelisk erected in 1828 in honor of the two generals verified via its inscription (in Latin): "Their courage gave them a common death, history a common renown, posterity a common monument."[2] Following the battle, wounded or sick soldiers from both sides were cared for by the nursing sisters of the Hôpital-Général. The wounded were crammed into the hospital proper and also into the chapel, the adjoining barn and stables, and other hospital buildings. Assured by a British brigadier that they would be respected and kept safe as they went about their tasks, Augustinian Canonesses Regular of the Mercy of Jesus did their best to care for their charges, regardless of rank or nationality. Paradoxically, the British victory had saved Quebec from an even worse fate: bombardment. Forty-nine men-of-war, three of them fire ships—one-quarter, that is, of the entire British navy—were in formation on the Saint Lawrence, ready to launch an all-out attack on the vulnerable city. Already, naval bombardment had killed a number of residents and destroyed hundreds of buildings. Had a full-scale siege been necessary, historic Quebec would have been reduced to rubble.

Following the British victory and the transfer of Quebec to British jurisdiction in 1763, a kind of enforced rapport emerged. Unlike Acadia in 1755, there was no mass expulsion—far from it. When the British gave the residents of French Canada permission to return to France, fewer than 300 of 150,000 exercised this option. French Canada, not France, was home to the majority of a new people in North America. Two successive English governors and military commanders, James Murray and Guy Carleton, pursued pacifying policies toward French Canadians, sometimes at risk to their careers. At the cessation of hostilities, British soldiers, with Murray's encouragement, gave up a day's rations per week to feed starving French in and around Quebec. From 1760 to 1763 Murray governed Canada as commanding general and chief administrator of Quebec, one of three military districts (the other two being Three Rivers and Montreal), and largely succeeded in keeping disgruntled British merchants and traders under control. In negotiations with Murray, Pierre de Rigaud, marquis de Vaudreuil-Cavagnal, the Canadian-born last governor of French Canada, had requested three points of agreement prior to formal surrender: neutrality for French Canadians in case of war with France, no new taxes, and a continuing Roman Catholic established church, with the king of France still empowered to name bishops. Murray had no authority to grant such stipulations, but he kept them in mind, and when the Treaty of Paris—which ended the French and Indian War—was signed in 1763 and Murray became governor and military commandant of an administratively reunited Canada, he fostered elected councils, brought French Canadians into the civil service, and sustained local laws and ordinances. In the matter of criminal law, Murray outlawed torture and established habeas corpus and trial by jury, among other reforms.

Achieving rapport with the bishop

Murray also wooed the clergy, quite effectively. Now that Canada was British, the king of France obviously could not continue to name the Roman Catholic bishop of Quebec, but Murray, an Anglican, volunteered to help out in this process and provided the terminology of paperwork and protocol to change the title "Bishop of Quebec" to "Superintendent of the Romish Religion". Murray thus recast this office as a civil-service appointment and hence avoided the implication that a papist hierarchy outlawed in Great Britain was being recognized in a British colony.

When Bishop Henri-Marie Dubreil de Pontbriand died on 8 June 1760, Quebec was left without a bishop for the three ensuing years of military government. With the reestablishment of Quebec as a unified province, the canons of Quebec cathedral named Étienne Montgolfier, Sulpician superior in Montreal, as bishop-elect. Governor-General James Murray, however, had another candidate in mind: Jean-Olivier Briand, vicar-general of Quebec. Over the past three years, Murray had been keeping a close eye on the parish priests of the province, rewarding those at peace with the British occupation with grants-in-aid to restore their churches if necessary. In gratitude for the bipartisan response of nursing sisters during and following the siege, Murray provided the nuns with food and fuel during the starving time after the fall of Quebec, endorsed claims of the Hôpital-Général against the French government, and supported the remission of outstanding debts still owed the French government by the Ursuline convent and the Hôtel-Dieu, the second and older (founded in 1637) hospital in the city. Murray also awarded Vicar-General Briand a gratuity of 480 pounds for his cooperative attitude ("good behavior", Murray put it) in the aftermath of the siege and the hostilities that continued. Bishop-elect Montgolfier was then in France for his episcopal consecration. Hearing of Murray's preference, the Sulpician graciously stepped aside in Briand's favor.

Born to a Breton farming family in 1715, Jean-Olivier Briand was by birth a solid, prosperous peasant, but a peasant nonetheless. At that time in France and its provinces, one had to be at the least minor nobility or, rarely, of an upper-middle-class background to be named to the hierarchy. Briand—intelligent, intuitive, pious, yet willful and shrewd—proved an exception to this rule. At age twenty-six, a mere two years after his ordination as a priest for the Diocese of Saint-Brieuc, he had earned an excellent reputation as an assistant parish priest working under the supervision of Abbé René-Jean Allenou de Lavillangevin, a well-connected cleric of prominent family and private means. That year, 1741, Henri-Marie Dubreil de Pontbriand, the newly consecrated sixth bishop of Quebec, made Abbé Lavillangevin and his assistant Jean-Olivier Briand an offer they did not—or could not—refuse. Come to Quebec, Pontbriand urged, and you, Abbé, will be my vicar-general for Quebec, and I will name you, young Briand, to the chapter of canons of my cathedral. A Breton himself, the nobly born Pontbriand—a graduate of the Jesuit college at La Flèche and the Seminary of Saint-Sulpice in Paris; a holder of a doctor's degree in theology from the Sorbonne; recommended for the See of Quebec by his maternal uncle the comte de LaGaraye and Jean Couturier, superior general of Saint-Sulpice, and no one less than Cardinal André Hercule de Fleury, the de facto prime minister of France from 1726 to 1743—had the confidence and the connections to make such generous, life-changing promises to his two fellow Bretons.

For nearly twenty years, the talented and discreet peasant Jean-Olivier Briand, dramatically promoted above his class, ministered side by side with his aristocratic bishop as bishop's secretary, cathedral canon, treasurer of the chapter, spiritual director at the seminary, confessor of the nuns of the Hôtel-Dieu and the Hôpital-Général, and traveler alongside the bishop as Pontbriand, an ardent and reforming prelate, tirelessly traveled his diocese. As Pontbriand's secretary and confidant, Briand grew increasingly acquainted with Quebec and its people: believing Catholics, true, but independent-minded and occasionally irascible, and frequently closefisted when it came to paying the tithes that supported parish and diocese. The priests of the diocese, moreover, shared those traits.

Unlike many bishops' secretaries, Briand did not develop the demeanor of a prelate in the making. On the contrary, he cultivated across these busy years a certain virtue marked by simplicity, caution, silence when required, and—this the most mysterious because it was so characteristic of the prosperous peasant—a refusal to be intimidated by higher authority. Coupled with that was the ability to deal with those higher authorities, the well-born and well-placed, not as an equal (that would be bad manners and, hence, self-defeating), nor as a sycophantic or a fearful inferior (equally disadvantageous), but as a person coming from a stratum of society whose support the higher authorities almost always needed and who thus was respected and offered the right to speak his mind, provided that protocols, deference, and good manners were observed. With the defeat of France and the death of Bishop Pontbriand happening almost simultaneously, Monsieur Briand, now vicar-general of Quebec, faced Governor (after 1763, Governor-General) James Murray and, later, Governor-General Guy Carleton, not as an equal—certainly not in civil terms—but not as an inferior, either. As bishop of Quebec (Superintendent of the Romish Religion, as far as the British were concerned), Jean-Olivier Briand entered into a contract with the new government. He would help keep the peace, provided that the Church not be interfered with; the British, in turn, were grateful for the arrangement, for it allowed them to consolidate their Canadian gains beyond military conquest and occupation. The Vatican, moreover, backed this concordat. Facing as it did the ferocious and near-universal anti-Catholicism of the British colonies south of Quebec, Rome had nothing to gain from a British declaration of war against the Church in Canada. Still, Briand's elevation to the See of Quebec—backed by Murray, unanimously voted by the canons of the cathedral on 9 September 1764—took eighteen months to wend its way through the process and through obstacles before Briand's consecration in Paris on 16 March 1766 and his departure on 1 May for Quebec, where he arrived on 28 June.

During the ten years that followed, Briand lived simply in a room in the Quebec seminary, eating with its faculty at a common table, with one part-time footman in his personal service. The bishop supervised his clergy, encouraging them to live in harmony with their parishioners and disciplining them when necessary; supported the four sisterhoods in the diocese; struggled with the lay churchwardens over governance of the cathedral (they said they owned it, but he disagreed); visited parishes to administer confirmation; and dealt successfully with Governors-General Murray and Carleton on a personal basis—no intermediaries allowed—in matters of church and state.

The Quebec Act

When the congressional delegation left New York City for Montreal on 2 April 1776, then, it faced the formidable obstacle of Bishop Briand's concordat with Great Britain. Despite the presence of a Catholic layman and a Catholic priest in the delegation, the long, outspoken legacy of anti-Catholicism in the English-speaking colonies to the south of Quebec likewise posed a problem. After all, for the previous one hundred years, the border between Canada and New York and New England had witnessed an almost continuous and violent struggle between French and English settlers that had expressed itself, in part, in religious terms. In the last third of the twentieth century, historians began to decode colonial anti-Catholicism from a number of secular perspectives. As of the American Revolution, it began to be argued, an eclectic pan-Protestantism had emerged in the English colonies: a generalized social sentiment and practice, that is, for which antipapism provided an almost folkloric expression. In the English colonies, churchgoers—an estimated 74 percent of the population by 1740—tended to attend the most attractive (or only) Protestant church in their locality. A much smaller number were willing to go through a process of formal church affiliation. In congregations practicing this rite, such self-selected attendance, devoid of formal membership, included the privilege of the Lord's Supper, if desired, at the conclusion of the sermon. Deprived as it was of bishops to offer confirmation, Anglicanism showed this eclectic inclusiveness, as did the Baptists and the residually traditional Lutherans, once German immigrants began to arrive in force. In frontier areas, Presbyterian, Lutheran, German Reformed, Huguenot, Moravian, and even Quaker congregations served their own congregants as well as a second informal membership. Jesuit missioners feared this inclusiveness, which helped keep them riding circuits; for there was some evidence, as well as a larger fear, that Catholics were known to drift into attending Protestant churches if Catholic services were unavailable.

Such eclecticism in church attendance, it can be speculated, strengthened a pan-Protestant identity among churchgoing people and can be considered a stepping-stone in the direction of a shared identity. The Great Awakening that swept the colonies in the 1730s and the early 1740s intensified an already flourishing Protestantism. The covenantal theology of the Great Awakening, as historian Alan Heimert has argued—its message of redemption for one and all through Jesus Christ—conjoined the colonies even further through an intensified experience of Christian community backed by doctrine and practice. In any event, church membership in the British colonies continued its inexorable march forward. Between 1700 and 1780, seven of the largest Protestant denominations increased by more than sevenfold. Truly a Protestant nation was on the verge of arriving.[3]

With this process of political emergence, the antipapal aspects of the preexisting anti-Catholicism became virulent as well as folkloric. In the English tradition of anti-Catholicism, the papacy, personified in the figure of the pope as an ogre, first proved its usefulness as a rallying cry when Pius V excommunicated Elizabeth on 27 April 1570, and a crusade against popery, as it was called, retained its usefulness to Protestant England down through the decades. Just as anticommunism emerged as a lingua franca of solidarity in the United States during the Cold War, antipopery—as policy, mantra, folklore—provided cohesion and purpose to Great Britain and its North American colonies as English Protestants battled Roman Catholic Spain and France for control of North America. The demotic, folkloric dimensions of this antipopery were expressed in celebrations on Guy Fawkes Day, commemorating the failure of the 1605 plot to blow up Parliament. Designated Pope's Day in New England, the most anti-Catholic region in colonial North

America, Guy Fawkes Day spread from New England to other colonies—Southern colonies especially—between 1700 and the 1740s and was characterized by bonfires, cannonades, speeches, sermons, and, in many cases, the hanging of the pope in effigy. Pope's Day, from this perspective, became increasingly linked to a defense of imperial Britain against French and Spanish encroachment. Much to the satisfaction of controlling elites, moreover, Pope's Day also created a sense of pro-British solidarity among ordinary folk, uniting them in a larger cause.

Imagine, then, the shock and anger that seized English colonials when in 1773 Parliament began to debate a Quebec Act designed to integrate French Canada further into the British Empire. Under the act, Catholics could hold office without swearing allegiance to Protestantism, as had been required since the Elizabethan era. Roman Catholics could sit on the legislative council advising a governor-general appointed by the Crown. French law, moreover, would continue to govern in such civil matters as marriage, inheritance, and related domestic issues. Authority over the distribution of land was restored to the seignorial system. Temporarily suspended following the conquest, tithes could once again be collected for the support of Catholic parishes, which constituted a legal establishment of Roman Catholicism in a British province. And finally, Quebec province was expanded to include what is now southern Ontario and the future states of Illinois, Indiana, Michigan, Ohio, Wisconsin, and parts of Minnesota. This threefold increase of Quebec province finalized the prior Royal Proclamation of 1763, which limited expansion of the English colonies beyond the Appalachian Mountains and established the five jurisdictions of the Hudson Bay Company grant, the province of Quebec, upper Illinois Territory, an Indian Reserve (formerly Louisiana), and the provinces of West and East Florida as further barriers to expansion from Atlantic coast colonies.

Facing the prospect of the Quebec Act, the English colonies had at their disposal a ready-made ideology to use as leverage against Great Britain. Parliament was on the verge of reversing three hundred years of English policy to make peace with Roman Catholicism—even worse, to establish a papal tyranny in North America! Contained within this was a second, equally important argument: Parliament and the Crown were on the verge of granting a measure of autonomy and traditional English rights to Quebecois that were simultaneously being denied to the English colonies on the Atlantic coast. Furthermore, by placing the trans-Appalachian region permanently off limits to investment and development, the act negatively impacted well-connected colonial land speculators and their hoped-for opportunities and profits in the West.

Parliament passed the Quebec Act, and King George III gave it his Royal Assent on 22 June 1774. In the outcry that followed from the pulpit, from state legislatures, and in newspapers and magazines, antipopery reached a fever pitch. "We may live to see our churches converted into masshouses", ranted one writer in the *Pennsylvania Packet* for 31 October 1774, "and our lands plundered of tythes for the support of a Popish clergy. The Inquisition may erect her standard in Pennsylvania, and the city of Philadelphia may yet experience the carnage of St. Bartholomew's Day."[4]

As part of this cascade of condemnation, the Second Continental Congress commissioned the fiercely Protestant John Jay, a delegate from New York, to compose "An Address to the People of Great Britain", protesting the act. The Congress, Jay wrote, did not believe that Parliament was authorized by the British Constitution "to establish a Religion fraught with sanguinary and impious tenets, or, to erect an arbitrary form of government, in any quarter of the globe". Jay also composed an open letter from Congress, an "Address to the People of Great Britain Hostile to the Catholic Church", protesting an act whereby "the dominion of Canada is to be so extended; modelled and governed, as that by being disunited from us, detached from our interests, by civil as well as religious prejudices, that by their numbers daily swelling with Catholic emigrants from Europe, and by their devotion to Administration so friendly to their religion, they might become formidable to us, and on occasion, be fit instruments in the hands of power to reduce the ancient free Protestant Colonies to the same state of Slavery with themselves."[5]

In addressing the people of Canada, however, Congress took another tack entirely. "We are too well acquainted with Liberality of Sentiment distinguishing your nation", Congress wrote, "to imagine, that Difference of Religion will prejudice you against a hearty Amity with us. You know that the transcendent Nature of Freedom elevates those who unite in her Cause, above all such low minded Infirmities. The Swiss Cantons furnish a memorable Proof of this Truth."[6]

Commanding the siege of Boston as of September 1775, George Washington likewise followed this irenic approach. Yet, in his case, a measure of sincerity was at work, for Washington, an aristocratic Anglican, loathed the virulent antipopery that characterized all classes and institutions of New England. On Sunday afternoon, 9 October 1774, for example, while attending sessions of Congress, Washington went to vespers at Saint Mary's Church in Philadelphia. While Washington merely noted the visit in his diary, his companion, John Adams of Massachusetts, took the occasion to share with his wife a typically New England response. He had "heard a good, short moral essay", Adams wrote to his wife later that evening, "upon the duty of parents to their children, founded in justice and charity, to take care of their interests, temporal and spiritual. This afternoon's entertainment was to me most awful and affecting; the poor wretches fingering their beads, chanting Latin, not a word of which they understood; their Pater Nosters and Ave Marias; their holy water; their crossing themselves perpetually; their bowing and kneeling and genuflecting before the altar. The dress of the priest was rich with lace. His pulpit was velvet and gold. The altarpiece was very rich, little images and crucifixes about, wax-candles lighted up." Adams concluded his letter with a flourish. "Here", he wrote, "is everything which can lay hold of the eye, ear, and imagination, everything which can charm and bewitch the simple and ignorant. I wonder how Luther ever broke the spell?" Adams' letter has become a classic of its kind. American Catholics remain grateful for Washington's silence.[7]

The commander in chief, in any event, was on more sincere ground when on 14 September 1775 he gave written instructions to Colonel Benedict Arnold (a fierce anti-Catholic in the New England style) on the eve of Arnold's taking his New England militia to Canada. "As the contempt of the religion of a country by ridiculing any of its ceremonies", Washington instructed Arnold (perhaps sensing Arnold's attitude), "or affronting its ministers or votaries, has ever been deeply resented, you are to be particularly careful to restrain every officer and soldier from such imprudence and folly, and to punish every instance of it. On the other hand, as far as lies in your power, you are to protect and support the free exercises of the religion of the country, and the undisturbed enjoyment of the rights of conscience in religious matters, with your utmost influences and authority."

That same day, Washington issued an "Address to the Inhabitants of Canada", in which he urged Canadians to join a contest that "has risen to such a height, that arms alone must decide it". The army he was sending into Canada, Washington promised, was coming, not to plunder or conquer, but to protect. "Let no man desert his habitation", Washington urged the Canadians. "Let no one flee as before an enemy. The cause of America and of liberty is the cause of every virtuous American citizen, whatever may be his religion or his descent. The United Colonies know no distinction but such as slavery, corruption, and arbitrary domination, may create. Come, then, ye generous citizens, range yourselves under the standard of general liberty, against which all the force and artifice of tyranny will never be able to prevail." A French translation of Washington's address was printed and distributed when the Americans reached an occupied Montreal.

A month and a half later, in Cambridge, Washington issued a general order on Pope's Day, 5 November, ending the traditional observance planned by his soldiers. "As the commander-in-chief has been apprised", the general order read, "of a design formed for the observance of that ridiculous and childish custom of burning the effigy of the Pope, he can not help expressing his surprise that there should be officers and soldiers in his army so void of common sense as not to see the impropriety of such a step." Now was hardly the time to ridicule Roman Catholicism, Washington's general order concluded. "At such a juncture and in such circumstances, to be insulting their religion is so monstrous as not to be suffered or excused; indeed, instead of offering the most remote insult, it is our duty to address public thanks to these our brethren, as to them we are so much indebted for every late happy success over the common enemy in Canada."[8]

First Citizen keeps a journal

Charles Carroll of Carrollton kept a well-written, detailed journal describing the journey to Canada of the congressional delegation, which departed 2 April 1776. (In 1876 the *Journal*, edited and annotated by Brantz Mayer, was published by the Maryland Historical Society.) The *Journal* gives evidence of Carroll's growth as a writer and documents an increasing knowledge of military matters that he would soon be putting to use when elected to Congress upon his return. Thirty-nine years old at the time of his departure for Canada, Charles Carroll of Carrollton had arrived at full maturity as a man, a writer, and—to his father's great satisfaction—a figure of political importance in Maryland, despite his Catholicism, enjoying the career and reputation not available to Carroll's father in years past because of his religion. The education in philosophy and law that Charles Carroll of Annapolis had provided for his son at the Jesuit colleges of France and the Inner Temple of the Inns of Court in London not only had given him a solid foundation in political theory but had also sharpened Carroll's analytical and debating skills. As early as 1764, in letters to his friends in England, Carroll showed himself a spirited opponent of the Stamp Act. The Townshend Acts of 1767 and the Tea Tax of 1770, likewise opposed in letters and conversations, afforded Carroll further opportunity to hone his arguments along trajectories being followed by a burgeoning group of colonial intellectuals.

Carroll, however, could not easily become a public spokesman. As a Catholic, he was banned from voting, holding office, and practicing law. An exchange of eight letters in the *Maryland Gazette* between 7 January and 1 July 1773, however, transformed him into a public figure. Three years earlier, on 26 November 1770, Maryland Governor Robert Eden had unilaterally issued a proclamation reinstating temporarily lapsed fees owed to officers of the colony—including tobacco inspectors and Anglican clergy—for their services. Eden did this, he claimed, because the lower house of the assembly had failed to set such fees. Besides, the fees had first been established by proclamation in 1733 and could thus be likewise adjusted. For three years, the controversy raged between a country party of tobacco growers who opposed the fees and a court party who upheld the right of a governor in a proprietary colony to govern by fiat.

On 7 January 1773, Daniel Dulany Jr., a leading lawyer and pamphleteer, writing under the name Antilon, published the first of four open letters in the *Maryland Gazette* defending the fixed and exclusive hegemony of the English Parliament over colonial affairs: the ultimate sovereignty of Parliament, in short, as established by the Glorious Revolution of 1688, and hence an authority to be exercised in the colonies as required. Nor could this authority be exported or franchised to the colonies beyond a partial authority in local matters granted to local legislatures. The British constitution, in short, was anchored in a sovereign Parliament and sovereign Crown, as established in the Glorious Revolution.

On 4 February 1773, Charles Carroll of Carrollton wrote a reply to Dulany under the pen name First Citizen. The Irish Protestant Dulanys and the Irish Catholic Carrolls had long since been at odds with each other as families, and this added a personal animus to the debate. In the course of four letters, Carroll put forth arguments reflecting his Jesuit education in philosophy and humanities and his English education in the common law. Neither Dulany nor Carroll argued in a linear manner. Each disputant, rather, advanced his case outward from a central point of view that was present from the beginning, increasingly engaged in the combat, point by point, adding new cases, citations, and arguments as the two went along.

Carroll's discourse reprised a growing colonial mind-set that was being expressed in many pamphlets and speeches. Like his Protestant and Enlightenment contemporaries, Carroll employed arguments based on natural law theory, empiricism, historical analysis, philosophical realism (Aristotle), the Scottish Enlightenment (Locke and Hume), and English common law. To these conventional sources, Carroll added Scholastic political theory, especially as represented in Aquinas, Francisco Suárez, and Robert Bellarmine. There is a natural law, runs a condensed and systematized version of Carroll's arguments. In terms of social and political arrangements, man possesses the ability to discern values fixed by this natural law. (In three years' time, Thomas Jefferson would be encapsulating these rights and values as life, liberty, and the pursuit of happiness.) Throughout history, successful societies evolved such arrangements or at least came close to them. *Senatus populusque Romanus*, the Senate and the Roman people. In each case, consent of the governed was present to one degree or another in any constitutional solution commensurate with natural law, reason, and human dignity (Aquinas, Suárez, Bellarmine)—the matter of slavery, of course, being conveniently put aside for the time being. Most successful constitutional solutions, moreover, were localized and remained under local control (Locke, Hume, and Montesquieu, the latter read by Carroll at the Inner

Temple or privately after his return to Maryland). English common law was replete with standing provisions and spot decisions ensuring as much consent of the people and local accommodation as possible. Originating with the people or legitimated by their consent, sovereignty percolated upward from the local and returned there for corroboration and assent.

How, then, Carroll argued, given these time-tested realities, could Daniel Dulany argue on behalf of the exercise of an exclusive legislative sovereignty by the English Parliament over British colonies in North America and elsewhere? Why, of course—and here Carroll, as a Catholic Marylander, comes closest to the white-hot emotional center of what was transforming him into an incipient revolutionary—in the Glorious Revolution of 1688, Parliament had removed one king by revolution and replaced him with William and Mary. Parliament had thus seized by revolutionary violence ultimate control of the realm and its empire in the making. At this point, Carroll edges near but avoids pro-Stuart Jacobinism. (Three years later, however, in writing the Declaration of Independence, Thomas Jefferson would personify George III as the tyrannical tool of a tyrannical Parliament.) This Glorious Revolution, it must be remembered, had permanently disenfranchised the Catholics of Maryland (of all the colonies, in fact) and had removed Carroll's grandfather Charles Carroll the Settler from office as attorney general and had so thwarted the political ambitions of his father, Charles Carroll of Annapolis, that he had seriously considered cashing out and moving to Louisiana.

Sensing the emancipative direction of Carroll's arguments, Dulany, in his fourth letter—at this point, the exchange had become an exchange of insults as well as arguments—questioned Carroll's right as a Catholic to enter this debate in the first place. How dare Charles Carroll use the term "we" in discussing the interests of Maryland! "This is rather too much in the imperial style", Dulany thundered. "We! It is as little my wish, as the Citizen's, to rekindle extinguished animosities; tho' I think his conduct, very inconsistent with the situation of a man, who owes even the toleration he enjoys, to the favour of government. His threats, of what the next assembly may do, as if his influence would sway, his assistance be sought, or his advice admitted, in the proceedings of the delegates, notwithstanding he is not even allowed by our constitution to vote for, or, in any manner, to interfere in the choice of, a delegate, are extremely impertinent."[9]

That final thrust by Dulany might very well have hit home and spurred Carroll to further action in the matter of independence for the colonies. Despite the acceptance and celebrity status—even fame—that the First Citizen letters had earned him as the exchange drew to a close, Charles Carroll of Carrollton remained in the eyes of Maryland law a disenfranchised Roman Catholic. No wonder, then, that shortly before his death in November 1832, looking back at the grand drama in which he had played such a conspicuous part, Founding Father Charles Carroll of Carrollton on 20 February 1829 wrote George Washington Parke Custis, the adopted son of the Father of His Country: "When I signed the Declaration of Independence I had in view not only our independence from England but the toleration of all sects professing the Christian religion and communicating to them all great rights. Happily this wise and salutary measure has taken place for eradicating religious feuds and persecution and become a useful lesson to all governments."[10]

At the time of this correspondence, Custis was serving as president of the Society of the Friends of Civil and Religious Liberty in Ireland. Carroll maintained a lively interest in Irish affairs. It took a revolution to emancipate the Roman Catholics of the United States. So, too, did a Carroll play a role in the later emancipation of Catholics in Great Britain. Married to Lord Richard Colley Wellesley, second Earl of Mornington and elder brother of the Duke of Wellington, Carroll's grand-daughter Marianne Patterson Caton, Lady Wellesley, served two terms as vice-reine of Ireland alongside her husband, the Lord Lieutenant (viceroy) of Ireland. Lady Wellesley kept in touch with her grandfather, who cautioned her against extravagance. In 1829, as prime minister, the Duke of Wellington, Lady Wellesley's brother-in-law, partially because of her persuasion (the duke adored his American-born Catholic sister-in-law), reluctantly but effectively sponsored a bill emancipating Roman Catholics in Great Britain.

A futile mission

If one is to judge from his *Journal*, the most educational and enjoyable aspect of Charles Carroll's journey to Montreal in April–May 1776 was not the congressional mission, which failed, but the journey itself: the dramatic scenery, the people, and, most important to his impending career as a member of Congress, the opportunity for an education in fortifications, defensive strategies, and related military matters. As a Marylander, Carroll knew the Chesapeake region: Maryland, Virginia, southern Pennsylvania, and Delaware. Sailing up the Hudson, he had the chance further to expand his North American horizons by experiencing another great river and the valley through which it flowed: a region guarded by densely forested riparian highlands nurtured and celebrated in later decades in the literature and art of a new nation. Transferring to wagons at Albany, Carroll temporarily returned to horse-back six miles outside the city for a side excursion to Cohoes Falls on the Mohawk River. Ninety feet high and one thousand feet wide, Cohoes Falls was the second-most famous cataract in New York, after Niagara. "The foam," noted Carroll, "the irregularities in the fall broken by projecting rocks, and the deafening noise, presented a sublime but terrifying spectacle."[11]

The Anglo-Dutch ascendancy that Carroll encountered on this first Hudson River phase of the journey—Dutch patroons such as the Van Rensselaers, hold-ers of a grant of some twenty miles on each side of the river; Anglo-Dutch gentry such as the Livingstons, masters of a 300,000-acre estate—by and large favored the Revolution, although Carroll does go out of his way to mention one Tory family manor that the delegation sailed past en route. These were Carroll's class of people: landed aristocrats in favor of the Revolution commanded in the field by His Excellency George Washington, one of their own. From this perspective, Major General Philip Schuyler, the Albany-born Dutch patroon commanding northern New York, emerges as a leading figure in the *Journal*. Meeting the delegation at Albany, Schuyler accompanied the congressional party to Cortlandt Manor, his estate on the Mohawk River, thirty-two miles north of Albany, taking time from the journey to escort Carroll on the side trip to Cohoes Falls. Then in his early forties, raised at the heart of the Dutch ascendancy, married to Catherine Van Rensselaer, Schuyler belonged to Carroll's genre of wealthy revolutionary. Like Carroll, Schuyler prized the intel-lectual life. Schuyler read widely, spoke fluent French, and excelled in mathematics. Like Carroll and so many other Revolutionary leaders, Schuyler practiced advanced agriculture and business entrepreneurship—in Schuyler's case, lumbering (pine and hardwoods) processed in his own water-driven sawmills, the lumber and agricultural products transported to market via the Hudson on Schuyler's private fleet of a schooner and three sloops. While entertained at the Schuyler estate, the congressional party was charmed by Schuyler's daughters. One of these young ladies, Elizabeth Schuyler, later married Alexander Hamilton.

Above Saratoga, Carroll's eye for scenery remained keen and appreciative as the party journeyed north toward the border through the lake country en route to Montreal. Yet, at this point, military fortifications—Fort Miller, Fort Edward, Fort George, Fort William Henry—also began to attract Carroll's attention. He noted their histories and their present condition. Forts Edward, George, and William Henry remained in ruins from the French and Indian War, and Carroll's mind turned by implication to thoughts of invasion and defense. The party, still under Major General Schuyler's personal escort, crossed Lake George in military transports recently in use by United Colonies militia for the invasion of Canada: a route that could serve as a retreat from Canada into upstate New York, should the fortunes of the Revolution meet reversal. Entering Lake Champlain, the transports drew seven or eight inches and thus scraped the rocks at the bottom of the ripple between the two lakes. Brought ashore, the transports were emptied and then dropped onto four-wheeled carriages for hauling, six oxen to a carriage, three and a half miles inland to Fort Ticonderoga, the Gibraltar of the New York–Canada border. Built by the French in 1755 as Fort Carillon, it had fallen to Lord Jeffery Amherst in 1759 and had been renamed. In this new war, taken the previous year by Benedict Arnold and Ethan Allen, it had been stripped of its cannon for Washington's army to use in besieging Boston.

At this point, Carroll's interests, as reflected in his journal, focused on military matters as he assessed the condition of Fort Ticonderoga, estimated the costs of rebuilding it, and carefully reconnoitered the water and land routes remaining on the journey. Gauging all of this from a strategic perspective, Carroll noted the need for armed vessels on Lakes George and Champlain to carry troops and supplies to United Colonies forces in Quebec—or for defensive purposes "should we unfortunately be driven out of Canada".[12]

Evidence of divided loyalties

In Quebec City, meanwhile, Bishop Jean-Olivier Briand was doing his best to keep French Catholics loyal to a British government still on the defensive militarily. Serious signs had already been noted in the province of pro–United Colonies sentiment. French Canadians were neutral, by and large, as John Dugnia, a former resident of Quebec, informed Congress on 2 August 1775, and neutral was better than hostile. When Governor-General Guy Carleton attempted to raise a French Canadian militia, some three thousand *habitants* rose up in a body and drove the recruiting officer and his staff back to Montreal. Even the violently anti-Catholic Colonel Benedict Arnold was optimistic. "Great numbers of the Canadians have expected us at Montreal for some time and are impatient for our delay, being determined to join us whenever we appear with a sufficient force to support them", Arnold wrote to Governor Jonathan Trumbull of Connecticut on 13 June 1775 from Crown Point on the west shore of Lake Champlain in northern New York while en route to Canada. "This I am confirmed in by many of the Canadians themselves, having just returned from an excursion down the Lake, where I saw numbers of them, who offered to join us." The theater commander, Major General Philip Schuyler, nurtured similar hopes. "The Canadians are friendly", Schuyler wrote to the provincial Congress of New York on 29 September 1775, "and join us in great numbers." The British were discerning the same possibility of an alliance. "The Canadians' minds are all poisoned by emissaries from New England and the damned rascals of merchants here and at Montreal", English merchant Thomas Gamble wrote to General William Howe, the British commander at Boston, on 6 September 1775. "General Carleton is, I believe, afraid to order out the Militia, lest they should refuse to obey. In short, the Quebec Bill is of no use; on the contrary, the *Canadians* talk of that damned absurd word, Liberty."[13]

Among the merchant classes, such pro–United Colonies sentiment was centered upriver from Quebec in Montreal and Three Rivers. Perhaps expected, Bishop Briand might have thought, was Montreal merchant Thomas Walker's show of support for the United Colonies. The English-born Walker was literally a *Bostonnais*, the generic French Canadian name for English colonists. Migrating from Boston in 1752 to Montreal—where he prospered in the western trade and was already a well-known troublemaker to the British—Walker had long been agitating for an elected assembly in Quebec province, going so far as to travel to London to lobby William Legge, second Earl of Dartmouth, on its behalf. Walker vehemently opposed the Quebec Act and in April 1775 had been part of a group of United Colonies sympathizers who met and talked of sending delegates to the next Continental Congress. When the invasion of Canada was launched, Walker supplied military information to Benedict Arnold and Ethan Allen and promised support if and when a pro–United Colonies militia could be organized. When United Colonies forces crossed the border, the British arrested Walker and shipped him to Quebec. The vessel carrying him was captured by United Colonies forces. Freed, Walker returned to his stone mansion on the rue Saint-Paul, Montreal, in which he housed Franklin, Samuel Chase, and the two Carrolls upon their arrival.

Thomas Walker, in short, represented a small but influential fifth column. Yet his being a *Bostonnais* and Protestant probably made his support unsurprising. Another ardent backer of the United Colonies, however, Christophe Pélissier, director of the ironworks at Saint-Maurice, seven miles northwest of Three Rivers, was French-born and Catholic and in charge of a foundry explicitly authorized and regulated by the Crown. Betting on a United Colonies victory, Pélissier met with Major General Richard Montgomery and supplied him with a written memorandum of military information in exchange for a promise that, once victory was assured, Montgomery would call for an election throughout the province preparatory to choosing delegates from Quebec to the Continental Congress. Even more dramatically, Pélissier supplied Montgomery's invading army with bombs and bullets, forged in the royal foundry that he directed, for use against the British forces besieged in Quebec.[14]

Bishop Briand regulates the clergy

In this war of persuasion, so intensified following the invasion by the United Colonies, the Quebec clergy were crucial to the outcome. Confirmed in their place and role by the Quebec Act, the Canadian nobility remained secure in the

British scheme of things, in which aristocracy was solidly established. Ordinary French Canadian Catholics (the habitants), by contrast, less secure in their political preferences, could—or so it seemed as of late 1775 and early 1776—be won over to republicanism. Thus, Bishop Briand turned to his diocesan clergy as the best means of ensuring habitant loyalty to Great Britain in the civil sphere. Close to the people, parish clergy wielded primary influence over their flocks. Opposition to British rule had already arisen among some of the regular clergy; for Great Britain's stated policy was that, while the locally controlled diocesan clergy as well as nursing and teaching nuns might remain in place, priests and brothers belonging to religious orders—Jesuits, Sulpicians, Paris Foreign Missions Society, Recollects, and Capuchins, international orders controlled from Rome or Paris—would gradually be phased out of service. Members of these orders found this policy unfair. Their orders, after all, had played key roles in the founding of New France and, before the establishment of a secular clergy, had ministered to its people and in many instances—the Sulpicians of Montreal, for example, a community of diocesan priests who did not take vows of obedience or poverty (community property)—continued to do so. Sulpician Pierre Huet de La Valinière, pastor of the parish of Saint-Sulpice near Montreal, had already gained a reputation for resistance to British rule before the United Colonies invasion, a suspicion compounded by the fact that La Valinière was friendly with Montreal merchant Thomas Walker and, more recently, had personally negotiated with the invaders for the release of two priest prisoners, a feat that earned one priest his freedom and La Valinière the sobriquet *Bostonnais*.

Former Recollect Eustache Chartier de Lotbinière took resistance to greater levels. A troubled friar who found celibacy and sobriety special challenges, Lotbinière—a onetime military chaplain before deserting his post—had been placed under interdict and suspension from the active ministry around 1756 and returned to his family in France, where he temporarily shifted his Franciscan allegiance to the Friars Minor of the Observance (Cordeliers), suffered a serious illness, and went apostate for two years, leaving both his new order and the Church. Recovering his faith and his vocation, Lotbinière became affiliated with the Order of Malta and emigrated to Martinique, where once again he was expelled—this time by the Capuchins and the governor—for disorderly conduct. Returning to Quebec in 1768, Lotbinière served briefly as a lay brother in the Order of Malta before being restored to priestly status in 1772 by Bishop Briand. Two years later, Lotbinière was suspended once again for the same familiar offenses. The American invasion offered him the opportunity of a lifetime. Declaring himself pro-rebellion, the cleric set himself up as a chaplain to Canadians who chose to join the United Colonies; he was given £1,500 and promised a bishop's miter. On 26 January 1776, Benedict Arnold confirmed Lotbinière's appointment as a chaplain to French Canadian militiamen in the United Colonies forces.

Father Augustin-Louis de Glapion SJ saw the Society of Jesus through its twilight prior to suspension. French-born, prepared for the Society of Jesus at the Collège de La Flèche and Collège Louis-le-Grand in Paris, Glapion was sent to Canada in 1758 to serve as minister and procurator of the College of Quebec, the Jesuits' flagship institution in North America. The very next year, however, the British vacated the college and converted it into a military storehouse. The college was partially restored in 1761, and in 1763 Glapion was named Jesuit superior in Canada. That August, London issued orders that no new members be admitted to the Society of Jesus in Canada. Bishop Briand agreed to ordain three Jesuit seminarians, however, and Glapion managed to postpone the inevitable. When the Society of Jesus was suppressed in 1774, Governor-General Carleton refused to enforce the order, and the Society of Jesus survived (as it did in Prussia and Russia), although its Canadian properties remained hotly claimed and contested; the claims of General Sir Jeffery Amherst, the overall commander of British forces during the conquest of Canada, were the most insistent.

Thus, one quasi-former Jesuit, Pierre-René Floquet, sustained as a Jesuit by British civil power, invited to dinner at the Jesuit residence one John Carroll, a fully suppressed Jesuit from Maryland, currently serving as a delegate from the United Colonies, now rebelling against British authority and doing its best to bring French Canada into the conflict on its side. Floquet was already under suspicion for associating with the occupying forces of the United Colonies in Montreal. Indeed, writing from Montreal on 15 November 1775, General Montgomery informed General Schuyler that Father Floquet had proven quite friendly. "I have had some conversation with Pere Flacquet [Floquet]," Montgomery informed his commander, "a Jesuit at the head of the society here and esteemed a very sensible fellow. He complained of some little indignities shown their order, particularly in making part of their house the common prison, by His Majesty's Governours. I promised redress and hinted, at the same time, the great probability of that Society enjoying their estate, notwithstanding Sir Jeffery Amherst's pretensions should this Province accede to the general union. I hope this hint may be of service; the Priests hitherto having done us all the mischief in their power; in many parishes they will not yet give the people absolution. However, I have shown all the respect in my power to religion, and have winked at this behavior in the Priests for fear of having malice to handle."[15] Bishop Briand knew of Floquet's prior friendliness to Montgomery as well as his ministry to United Colonies French Canadian militiamen raised by Colonel Moses Hazen, who called Floquet "my Chaplain".[16]

All this made Floquet's hospitality toward John Carroll the last straw, as far as Bishop Briand was concerned. The resentments of suppressed Jesuits in Maryland, Briand feared, could very well be further fueled by the resentments of Canadian Jesuits forbidden to add to their membership. The bishop himself was a pro-Jesuit prelate who went into shock when the Society was suppressed. Nevertheless, here was a Canadian Jesuit entertaining a Maryland ex-Jesuit, and that could be dangerous. Briand suspended Floquet from exercising his priestly functions, summoned him to Quebec, and kept the Canadian Jesuit under interdict for six months, releasing him only after he received a letter of apology. "My Lord," Floquet wrote, "to satisfy my conscience, I the undersigned, confess that the grievous circumstances in which I found myself last Winter in Montreal, have been to me the occasion of many faults of which I sincerely repent. I humbly supplicate your Lordship to pardon me, and to remove the interdict which my misdoings have drawn down on me. If I obtain this favor of your goodness, my Lord, I hope that my conduct will convince my Superiors and the public that I wish to yield and to endeavor in my sphere to make others yield to Caesar that which is Caesar's and to God that which is God's."[17]

Bishop Briand's deployment of clergy to quell rebellious sentiment began to take effect. The campaign was backed by penalties: suspension for clergy, exclusion from the sacraments for laity, and excommunication for an egregious offender, whether clergy or laity. The lead enforcer in this effort was the French-born Sulpician Étienne Montgolfier, vicar-general for the district of Montreal. Montgolfier drew up and disseminated talking points reprising Bishop Briand's pro–British point of view for sermons to be delivered by the clergy and kept a sharp eye out for possible transgressors.

Over before it starts

The most effective talking point for the bishop and his vicar, however, was provided by the First and Second Continental Congresses: the rabid anti-Catholicism expressed by Congress in opposition to the Quebec Act and the conciliatory attitude toward Catholicism expressed in Congress' communications with Canada. Translated into French and compared side by side, the disparity between these official statements—which surfaced as early as March 1775, according to one report from Montreal that castigated a "perfidious, double-faced Congress"—continued to do its work on Bishop Briand's behalf among Canadian opinion makers and also corroborated preexisting Catholic sentiment on the part of the general population.[18]

No United Colonies delegation, not even one that contained two such prominent Catholics as Charles and John Carroll as well as the renowned Doctor Franklin, could counter the self-defeat of the United Colonies themselves when its Congress had issued such blatantly anti-Catholic statements. Nor did invading forces do their cause much good when, in the aftermath of their defeat at Quebec and the smallpox epidemic that followed—freezing, starving, ill-supplied by Congress—they turned to plunder and confiscation to survive.

And so, the work of the United Colonies delegation was over almost before it began. Benedict Arnold and his staff met the delegation in Montreal on 20 April, John Carroll told his mother in a letter of 1 May. A cannonade and other military honors greeted the party. Given the recent defeat of Montgomery at Quebec, however, followed by the smallpox epidemic and Arnold's withdrawal of forces to Montreal, these ruffles and flourishes masked a deteriorating military situation. Taken to Arnold's headquarters, the delegates enjoyed a glass of wine, followed by a tea party in the company of several French ladies, followed by an elegant supper at which the ladies serenaded delegates with their singing. The following day, the delegates received visitors in the forenoon, followed by another elegant meal in large company. John Carroll never finished this letter to his mother, perhaps because he had little else to report. Presenting a letter of introduction from Father Ferdinand Farmer of Philadelphia, Carroll said Mass and dined at the Jesuit residence (once! Floquet would soon be pointing out), resulting in his host Floquet's suspension *a divinis* and summons to Montreal.

In the days that followed, Carroll found it next to impossible to reconcile the virulent anti-Catholicism of Congress' "Address to the People of Great Britain" and "Petition to the King", written and submitted in October 1774, with the more recent and respectful "Continental Congress to the Inhabitants of the Province of Quebec". At one meeting, while making his argument, Carroll was confronted

by an Irish-born, Gaelic-speaking diocesan priest by the name of John Mac-
Kenna. Ordained for the Scottish Mission, MacKenna in 1773 had accompanied
his Highland Catholic congregation from Scotland to Albany, New York, where
Sir William Johnson, superintendent of Indian affairs there, helped the emigrants to
acquire land and establish a community in the Mohawk Valley. Technically, Mac-
Kenna was in violation of the 1700 New York statute that prohibited the entrance
of Roman Catholic priests into the province; Sir William Johnson ruled his domain
as a law unto himself. The Scots Catholic community was, however, MacKenna
informed Carroll, loyal to the Crown and thus had been harassed and was forced
to move to Montreal rather than come under the yoke of the anti-Catholic New
Englanders dominating the United Colonies invasion. A large and imposing man,
MacKenna forcefully made his anti–United Colonies case to Carroll. MacKenna
had already taken to the field as chaplain to the Canadian forces, including Scots
Catholics from the Mohawk Valley, who had resisted Montgomery's advance north
into Quebec province, and within the year, MacKenna would be back in the field
as an active-duty chaplain to Loyalist forces.

Confronted by MacKenna (a good priest, loyal to Crown and parishioners), Carroll sensed the futility of the mission to which he had been recruited. The Catholics
of Maryland might very well have everything to gain from independence—most
dramatically, religious freedom and political enfranchisement—but there was no
way that even such a learned and patriotic priest as John Carroll could persuade
French Canadian or Scots Highlander Catholics that the Revolution of the United
Colonies was in their best interest.

Benjamin Franklin, suffering from boils and swollen legs, was coming to the
same conclusion. And so, less than two weeks after the congressional delegation's
arrival in Montreal, Franklin departed for Philadelphia on 11 May 1776, and John
Carroll—"seeing that it was out of my power to be of any service", as he later
wrote—accompanied Franklin as friend and caretaker.[19]

As Franklin and John Carroll traveled south to Philadelphia, the military situation in Quebec took a dramatic turn for the worse when a British fleet arrived off
Quebec and landed a thousand-man force. Leaving some two hundred smallpox
victims behind, as he had to do, General Thomas ordered a retreat, dying of smallpox himself on 2 June. Charles Carroll spent the remaining days of May in the
field with Samuel Chase, assessing the increasingly chaotic military circumstances
preparatory to their report to Congress. On 31 May, the pair attended a council
of war at Chambly, which decided on an orderly retreat from Canada. The next
day, Carroll and Chase departed for Philadelphia. Now in command, following
the death of General Thomas, Benedict Arnold conducted a masterful retreat in
force from Canada.

On 31 December 1776, Bishop Briand conducted a service in the Quebec cathedral, commemorating the defeat of General Montgomery's forces one year earlier.
The ceremony began with a Pontifical High Mass before a packed congregation,
during which a choir accompanied by the cathedral organist sang the Te Deum, an
ancient fourth-century canticle of joy and praise. To prepare for the commemo-
ration, Briand issued a pastoral letter chronicling the expulsion of *Bostonnais* from
Canada and thanking God for this victory. As part of the ceremony, eight Canadians found guilty of helping the American invaders stood before the altar with halters

around their necks and begged pardon from God, the Church, and King George for their disloyalty. Bishop Briand thereupon assigned them a penance, pardoned them, and admonished them to go and sin no more. Thus, a Breton peasant bishop and his clergy saved Quebec province—and hence Canada—for the British empire in the firm belief that British rule in the aftermath of the passage of the Quebec Act was best for his flock, lest it be subjected to the anti-Catholicism of the *Bostonnais*.

Loyalist French Canadians

French Canada was Catholic in religion and British in the civil sphere and would stay that way. The majority of clergy and all but one documented seigneur assented to a détente fusing religion, social identity, and self-interest. Forming a Seigneurial Guard under the command of Colonel Baron de Longueuil, Canadian nobility and their retainers fought and delayed the American invasion along the Richelieu River and helped defend Quebec during the American attack. Roman Catholic Highlanders living in the back settlements of upstate New York, having had their fill of harassments from anti-Catholic New England and New York, migrated en masse to French Canada and—their faith trumping their Stuart loyalties and dislike of Hanoverians on the throne of Scotland—fought with the Seigneurial Guard and the Eighty-Fourth Royal Yorkers, with John MacKenna serving as chaplain.

Born in 1742 in Glenaladale, Scotland, John MacDonald, a graduate of the Jesuit University of Ratisbon, Germany, migrated to Canada when his relative and laird married a Protestant, converted, and tried to force his tenant farmers to convert to Protestantism. With the help of Bishop Alexander John Grant, vicar apostolic of the Highlands, and Bishop Challoner in London (who took up a collection in the Catholic embassies of that city), MacDonald migrated with these recusant tenant families, more than two hundred in all, to St. John's (later Prince Edward) Island. During the American Revolution, MacDonald organized the defense of St. John's Island and Nova Scotia by Scots Catholic militia and won accolades from the British government. Out on the frontier, the *coureurs des bois* and their leadership also seemed to support the British. Critically important was the Loyalist orientation of such frontier leaders as the French-born Charles Michel de Langlade of Baie des Puants (Green Bay), later known as the Founder and Father of Wisconsin. Saved from the horrors of war, the habitant majority backed the British as well.

Joining the Revolution

Notwithstanding this overall acceptance of British rule, a number of Canadians acted on their republican leanings despite the anti-Catholicism of the English colonies (now self-declared independent states) in rebellion. Born and raised in Montreal to New York parents living in that city, twenty-eight-year-old James Livingston rallied to the cause of the then United Colonies when Montgomery's forces besieged Quebec, and he quickly raised a regiment of some three hundred French Canadians. This unit would soon be called the First Canadian Regiment or Congress' Own, because it belonged to no one state and instead reported directly to Congress. The First Canadians fought with Montgomery at Quebec. The Continental Congress later commissioned Livingston a colonel of the New York Line in the Continental Army, and in September 1780, he played a key role in uncovering Benedict Arnold's treasonous plan to surrender West Point to the British.

Like Livingston, Moses Hazen had connections on both sides of the border. Born in Massachusetts, Hazen retired to Quebec on half pay after serving as a commissioned officer in the British army during the French and Indian War. When the Americans invaded Canada, Hazen—after momentary indecision—joined Montgomery's forces during the siege of Quebec. In 1776 he organized and became colonel of the Second Canadian Regiment, raised in Canada and among Canadian refugees in upstate New York. Hazen's Own, as the regiment was called, fought ably for the United States throughout the war, up to and including the decisive siege of Yorktown. Members of Hazen's Own—Captain (later Major) Clement Gosselin, Lieutenants John Goulet and Amable Boileau, and enlisted soldier Pierre Cadieux—went separately and secretly to Canada up to four times each to gather intelligence for a possible second invasion of Canada to be commanded by the marquis de Lafayette. Numerous French Canadians joined other units or served in various capacities. On 29 July 1776, Congress appointed Christophe Pélissier, former director of the Three Rivers Iron Works, an engineering officer with the rank of lieutenant colonel, at a compensation of sixty dollars per month. Former Recollect and Knight of Malta Eustache Chartier de Lotbinière never received the bishop's miter the Americans had promised him, but Congress did ratify his appointment as military chaplain with Hazen's Own and kept him on salary until February 1781.

Tenuous connections

The first phase of the Revolutionary War, ending with the American retreat from Canada, did at least bring Americans into contact with Catholic French Canadians. For New Englanders, this encounter could have been dramatic, given the intensity of Protestantism in New England, its overt and virulent anti-Catholicism, and the century of murderous border warfare that preceded the American Revolution. Yet the two French Canadian regiments that were brought into congressional service suggested a measure of accommodation that would be confounded when France entered the war on behalf of the United States, although in time these regiments enrolled more and more Americans, and French Canadian officers frequently found themselves at a disadvantage regarding promotion. Nevertheless, Congress explicitly directed that French Canadian prisoners of war taken during the invasion were to be treated humanely. Some of these prisoners, accompanied by their wives and children, were relocated to Reading and Bristol, Pennsylvania, and Trenton, New Jersey, where they were supported by weekly allowances from Congress. One prisoner, a certain Major Regonville, being kept in Trenton, on 21 December 1775 applied directly to Congress for permission to travel to Philadelphia and fulfill his Easter duty by going to confession. Congress granted the required permission.

The importance of such accommodations should not be exaggerated. Yet, given the ingrained and pervasive anti-Catholicism of the English colonies now in active rebellion, they do (however slightly) suggest the accommodations that would soon, as of July 1776, be sending Charles Carroll of Carrollton—up to now a disenfranchised Roman Catholic—to the Continental Congress as a duly elected member.

Diaries kept by certain New England militiamen reflect a similar note of hope. Being in Canada gave some New Englanders their first positive encounter with Catholic people. Captured in the course of Arnold's desperate last effort to take Quebec, Francis Nichols, a second lieutenant, contracted scarlet fever and, on 10 March 1776, was transferred to the care of the nursing sisters of the Hôtel-Dieu. The mother superior took personal charge of his case. "I had fresh provisions and good attendance", Nichols later remembered. "For several nights the nuns sat up with me, four at a time, every two hours. Here I feigned myself sick after I had recovered, for fear of being sent back to the Seminary to join my fellow-officers, and was not discharged until I acknowledged that I was well. When I think of my captivity I shall never forget the time spent among the nuns who treated me with so much humanity."[20]

Valley Forge 1777–1778

Colonial and European Catholics rally to the Revolution

British and Hessian forces under Sir William Howe entered and occupied Philadelphia on 27 September 1777. Philadelphia was the third important American city the British occupied, following Boston and New York. Only Boston had returned to American hands. After two failed attempts to dislodge the British from Philadelphia by force—the Battles of Brandywine on 11 September 1777 and Germantown on 4 October 1777—followed by a series of skirmishes and standoffs, George Washington, on 21 December, took his 11,000-man army (8,200 fit for duty) into Valley Forge, which was not a valley at all. It was, rather, a range of wooded hills two miles long and a mile and a quarter wide, set between Valley Creek and the Schuylkill River. The iron forge that once operated there had long since been abandoned. Yet Valley Forge was near enough to Philadelphia for renewed campaigning (when the time came) and remote enough to prevent a surprise attack. In this place, through a harsh winter—a starving time for soldiers; a time of congressional inquiry for Washington; and, with the coming of spring, a time for the recovery and rebuilding of the army with the help of European professionals—the Revolution faced transformative challenges and prevailed.

The army that straggled into Valley Forge on 21 December—cold, hungry, ill-clothed, exhausted—was coming in from seventeen months of campaigning that had kept the Revolution alive through a few victories, true, but many more partial defeats and standoffs, yet no annihilating catastrophes. The Battles of Lexington, Concord, and Bunker Hill managed to launch the war in 1775, but the invasion of Canada that same year ended in defeat. The retaking of Boston constituted a recovery. American forces besieged the British in Boston and with the decisive assistance of cannons seized from the fall of Fort Ticonderoga in May 1775—transported overland from northeastern New York under the supervision of Henry Knox, Washington's chief of artillery, and emplaced on Dorchester Heights overlooking the city—the British were forced to evacuate Boston and sail to Halifax, Nova Scotia.

On 3 July 1776, British forces under Howe, having driven the Americans from Canada, landed on Staten Island and dug retrenchments as reinforcements arrived from Nova Scotia, England, and South Carolina: thirty-two thousand in all by mid-August, including eight thousand Hessians. Their objective: the annihilation of the American army under Washington now occupying the southern portion of Manhattan. Driven from New York in November 1776 following defeats, near defeats, and standoffs in Manhattan, White Plains, and Long Island, Washington masterfully evacuated his two thousand troops across the Hudson to Fort Lee, New Jersey. Four days later, on the morning of 20 November, four thousand British regulars under the command of Major General Charles Cornwallis crossed the Hudson to a site six miles north of Fort Lee and began to move against Washington. The Revolutionary War now shifted to New Jersey and Pennsylvania for the next year and more, as Washington, pursued by British and Hessian forces, moved his army southward, fighting when forced to do so but avoiding a pitched battle that could destroy his army and end the Revolution.

The war of posts, as Washington described it—moving, that is, from one defensible location to another—included victories based on initiative, surprise, and attack at Trenton (26 December 1776) and Princeton (3 January 1777); indeed, the victory at Trenton, with Washington moving his army by night across an ice-choked Delaware River to surprise Hessian forces sleeping off their Christmas celebrations, remains—like the earlier Battle of Bunker Hill—an iconic event, celebrated, among other places, in Emanuel Leutze's panoramic painting *Washington Crossing the Delaware* (1851). In the Battle of Princeton eight days later, Washington confronted Cornwallis' forces by direct attack and, leading from the front on horseback, drove the British northward to New Brunswick.

Washington's maneuvering and countermaneuvering in an effort to block a British entry into Philadelphia and the two remaining battles that followed the British occupation—Brandywine (11 September 1777) and Germantown (4 October 1777)—while not resulting in victories, did once again, as was the case at both Trenton and Princeton, show the Revolutionary forces' developing ability to attack directly and withstand direct attacks from the British and to withdraw when forced to do so, in contrast to the disorderly withdrawals—routs, really—of the Long Island and Manhattan campaigns.

Still, there was much to learn: to establish security at night, for one thing, as troops under the command of Brigadier General Anthony Wayne failed to do on the night of 21 September 1777, when, exhausted by several small-scale battles and pelted by heavy rains, they failed to post sentry guards at the settlement of Paoli, twenty-five miles west of Philadelphia, as they wrapped themselves in their blankets and fell into a deep sleep. Under the command of Major General Charles Grey, a master of surprise attacks, a superior force of British grenadiers—bayonets at the ready, flints removed from muskets so that no grenadier would accidentally discharge his weapon and break the silence—crept into the impromptu, unguarded bivouac of the Americans and, given the order, began to bayonet sleeping soldiers, killing or seriously wounding more than three hundred of them and taking another hundred into captivity. In the attack, sword-wielding officers slashed fleeing Americans to the ground, where the grenadiers would finish them off.[1]

Multiple ordeals

Truly, as the psalmist sayeth of another valley, Valley Forge represented a valley of shadows, death, and betrayal. The place was harsh and cold, for one thing. For shelter, both Continentals and militia had little more than fourteen-by-sixteen-foot split-slab huts housing twelve men to a cabin. Laid out in regimented order, these cabins were sealed with clay and heated with clay fireplaces. An absence of rations for up to three days at a time was not uncommon in the first phases of the encampment. The only food consisted of firecakes, thin bread made of flour and water and baked over a campfire. Men died of hunger, as did some five hundred horses. No greatcoats were available for use against freezing temperatures. Men wrapped themselves in the blankets in which they slept at night, and many were forced to tie rags around disintegrating footwear or, worse, around their bare feet.

A year earlier, Congress had replaced Washington's choice for quartermaster general, the Irish Catholic Philadelphia merchant Stephen Moylan, with its own man, Brigadier General Thomas Mifflin, who was not personally loyal to Washington as commander in chief.[2] In any event, whether through incompetence, deliberation, or a mixture thereof, commissary support of Washington's army was at a low point. Two further developments, moreover—the victory at Saratoga of American forces led by General Horatio Gates over invading British forces led by General John Burgoyne and the appointment of a congressional committee to investigate the state of Washington's army and, by implication, Washington's conduct of the war—cast a shadow on Washington's leadership, favoring those opposed to Washington's continuing appointment as commander in chief.

A hero of the English campaign in Portugal during the Seven Years' War, a member of Parliament, and a popular London playwright and man-about-town, Gentleman Johnny Burgoyne had witnessed the earliest phases of the Revolutionary War in Massachusetts and Canada, after which he returned to England to sell to Lord George Germain, cabinet secretary for North America, a plan to invade New York via Canada and then, linking up with British forces marching north from New York City, isolate upstate New York and New England from the rest of the United States.

Poorly organized and understaffed, Burgoyne's invasion was in a state of collapse as it approached Saratoga. American forces under Gates' command, maneuvered in the field by Benedict Arnold, Daniel Morgan, Thaddeus Kościuszko, and other talented senior officers, attacked and defeated Burgoyne's foundering invasion, which British forces marching north from New York failed to reach. On 17 October 1777, Burgoyne surrendered an army of 5,700 to Gates and accepted the draconian and humiliating Convention of Saratoga, whose demands included that the surrendered British forces return to England and never again be used against Americans.

Coming in the aftermath of the British occupation of Philadelphia and the apparent American defeats at Brandywine and Germantown, the Saratoga victory propelled Horatio Gates into congressional prominence. A retired British officer and a veteran of the French and Indian War, Gates had been living in the American colonies only since 1772. Yet, in the aftermath of Saratoga, Gates' more-than-residual Englishness was part of his appeal. The capture and neutralizing of an entire British army! Here was an alternative to the homegrown leadership of Washington, a self-taught general fighting a war of posts and strategic retreat. Certain congressmen's fear of provincial amateurism on the battlefield had previously worked in favor of another British army veteran, Charles Lee—a permanent resident of Virginia only since 1773—whom Congress had almost instantly appointed major general when war broke out. Overtly eager to replace Washington, whom he was serving as second-in-command, Lee had repeatedly disobeyed Washington's orders to cross the Hudson following the battle of White Plains. When he did cross, Lee was captured and, as subsequently discovered documentation indicates, most likely offered treasonous advice to General Howe as how best to capture Philadelphia.

Resistance to Washington was centered in New England and was most fervent in that veteran polemicist of revolution Samuel Adams, who, like Brutus toward

Caesar, resented what he considered Washington's Caesar-like status as His Excellency the commander in chief. That dislike must have intensified and spread to others when Congress, fleeing Philadelphia, extended even further—albeit temporary (sixty days)—powers to Washington, to direct affairs in the civil sphere if and when necessary, until Congress reestablished itself in another location. Anti-Washington congressmen, in any event, dominated the process leading to the reorganization of the Board of War and Ordnance following Congress' flight from Philadelphia and staffed the board's membership with either themselves or similarly inclined congressmen, such as Jonathan Trumbull and Timothy Pickering. Brigadier General Thomas Mifflin, an anti-Washingtonian, remained on the Board of War and Ordnance as quartermaster general. Pointedly, Washington's personal friend and strong supporter Charles Carroll of Carrollton was not reappointed.

In November 1777 Congress appointed Horatio Gates president of the Board of War and Ordnance—the chief executive, that is, of the committee charged with overseeing the conduct of the war, hence putting Gates in a direct and quasi-supervisorial role over Washington. Congress named Thomas Conway as inspector general. Washington had opposed Conway's promotion to major general on the grounds that Conway, an Irish-born officer on leave from the French army, had not particularly distinguished himself as a brigadier, was something of a braggart, and had been in the country only eight months. Silas Deane, a congressman then serving as a diplomat in France, had recommended Colonel Conway to Congress, which promoted Conway to brigadier general a month after his arrival. When Washington openly opposed Conway's promotion to major general, Conway offered his resignation. The anti-Washington faction in Congress, seeing an opportunity, leveraged his threat to resign to promote Conway to major general and on the same day, 14 December 1777, named him inspector general of the army.

Fortunately for Washington, just before a congressional Committee of Inquiry left for Valley Forge, pro-Washington congressmen managed to add to its membership Charles Carroll of Maryland and Gouverneur Morris of New York. Building on his experiences in New York and Canada in 1776, Carroll had been developing his skills in military matters as a member of Congress specializing in supply and staffing. Scandalized by Congress' failure to equip Washington's forces, Carroll had written the commander in chief on 27 September 1777, urging him to use his temporarily expanded powers to launch a counteroffensive of punishments against the quartermaster and commissary general for nonperformance of duty. "Nothing but severe punishments", Carroll wrote Washington, "will, in my opinion, make the Commissaries and Quartermasters attentive to their duty! Your Excellency has the power, and I hope will not want the will, to punish such as deserve punishment. I hope your Excellency will excuse the freedom of this letter. My zeal for our country and my wishes for your success have impelled me to write thus freely on a subject which claims all your attention—the reformation of the army and the abuses prevalent in the two important departments of the Quarter Masters and Commissary General."[3]

Another Irish Catholic on staff

Charles Carroll of Carrollton was not the only Irish Roman Catholic openly to support Washington. Prior to Valley Forge, a number of Roman Catholics, colonials and Europeans alike, had responded to Washington's need for specialized staff. On 11 August 1775, for example, while headquartered in Cambridge outside Boston, Washington appointed Stephen Moylan of Philadelphia, a veteran of Bunker Hill, to serve as muster-master of the Continental Army. Later that year, on Washington's recommendation, Congress named Moylan commissary general with the rank of colonel. As muster-master, Moylan bore the primary responsibility for recruiting, retaining, accounting for, and supplying the Continental Army troops, without whom Washington would have had only militia under his command.

Born in Cork, Ireland, in 1734, at a time when Catholics still lived under serious penal-law restrictions and penalties, Moylan, the son of an ambitious Cork merchant, nevertheless belonged to an assertively Catholic clan. One uncle became a Jesuit. Of Moylan's eight siblings, his brother Francis was ordained a secular priest after studies at Paris and Toulouse, named bishop of Kerry in 1774, and transferred to Cork in 1786. Two sisters became Ursuline nuns. Like his brother Francis, the future bishop, Moylan was smuggled out of Ireland for an education, most likely to Lisbon, where the Moylans had business interests and where, in time, Stephen began his own business career shipping merchandise to Philadelphia and other New World ports via a hundred-ton brigantine the Moylan family had built and maintained in the Quaker city.

In 1768, Moylan himself relocated from Lisbon to Philadelphia. Within two years, six ships involved in import-export trade were registered with the port of Philadelphia as being wholly or partially owned by the Moylan family interests that Stephen was managing. Like the Catholic landowners of Maryland, the Catholic merchants of Philadelphia, while banned from politics, were otherwise permitted to flourish. Urbane, genial, knowing the larger world, and speaking three languages, Moylan rose in social circles. The prominent Philadelphia lawyer John Dickinson became a close friend and mentor, and, through Dickinson, Moylan expanded his friendship circle to include other prominent Protestants in the city.

Philadelphia was a clubbable city, to use C. S. Lewis' phrase. As early as 1727 Benjamin Franklin formed the Junto Club, oriented around serious reading, discussion, and self-improvement. Since 1751 leading merchants in Philadelphia, Protestant Scots-Irish and Catholic Irish alike, had been enjoying the camaraderie and sociability of the Hibernia Fire Company, a club organized around a volunteer firefighting company. In 1766 the Gloucester Fox Hunting Club was founded by a predominantly Protestant elite. Moylan was elected a member in 1770, thereby joining the company of such prestigious Protestants as John Dickinson, author of the *Letters from a Farmer in Pennsylvania* (1767–1768), opposing British taxation, and Robert Morris, soon to earn a place in history as the financier in chief for the Revolution. Moylan also belonged to the Irish Club, established in 1765 by Irish merchants of the city, a more informal group that met weekly in Burns' Tavern for backgammon or whist and mercantile gossip, followed by supper and a rum punch.

The Friendly Sons of Saint Patrick

When on Saint Patrick's Day, 17 March 1771, the Friendly Sons of Saint Patrick was formally organized, it perhaps came as no surprise that Stephen Moylan was announced as founding president of what was in many ways an umbrella organization enfolding the membership of a half dozen or more Irish societies. Like all these clubs, the Friendly Sons of Saint Patrick was ecumenical, with Catholic merchants such as Moylan, Thomas FitzSimons, and George Meade (while in the minority) standing alongside the Scots-Irish Protestant elite of the city. This elite was already opposed to Great Britain's stranglehold on colonial trade: such soon-to-be Revolutionary notables as financier and future congressman Morris, merchant activists such as FitzSimons and Meade, future pamphleteer and congressman Dickinson, and future Revolutionary general John Cadwalader.

For the time being, the Friendly Sons of Saint Patrick might appear to have had clubbable fun as their main interest: the dinners at Burns' or Mushatt's Tavern, the talk and laughter, the flowing rum punch over business gossip, the stories and memories connected to Ireland. Yet behind the camaraderie was a more serious purpose. The American Revolution was most overtly over economic matters—taxation without representation, an enforced mercantilism implemented through restraint of trade—and these Friendly Sons of Saint Patrick were successful businessmen, merchants and shippers in the main, and hence directly affected by these restrictive policies. On one side of the official Friendly Sons of Saint Patrick medal the word *Hibernia*, guarded by an Indian armed with a bow and a quiver of arrows, was linked by the word *Liberty* and supported from below by the word *Unite*. (On the reverse side stood Saint Patrick himself in full episcopal regalia.) When the city of Philadelphia established a Committee of Correspondence on 20 May 1774, four Friendly Sons were named to the committee. Six Friendly Sons participated in a Committee of Forty-Three formed on 18 June to select delegates to the Second Continental Congress. When a unit designated the Light Horse of the City of Philadelphia (later designated First Troop, Philadelphia City Cavalry) was created on 17 November 1774, ten of its first twenty-eight volunteers were Friendly Sons. Soon-to-be general Anthony Wayne of Chester County joined the Friendly Sons as a guest at a dinner at Thomas Mushatt's Tavern on Saturday, 17 September 1774, and was admitted to membership on 17 December.

Word of the Battle of Lexington reached Philadelphia around five o'clock on the afternoon of 24 April 1775. For some months before the news arrived, a number of Friendly Sons had been drilling as members of the Quaker Greens, commanded by John Cadwalader, who set out Madeira for his men, seventy in all, to refresh themselves after their twice-daily drill. Now forty-one, Stephen Moylan sought an appointment in Washington's army. John Dickinson wrote Washington on 25 July 1775 to introduce Moylan to His Excellency. "As he resided some years in this City", wrote Dickinson, "and was much esteemed here, I sincerely hope he will be so happy to recommend himself to your favor." Within a month, Washington had interviewed and appointed Moylan commissary general of musters, as Washington so informed Congressman Dickinson by letter on 30 August.[4]

Among Moylan's first assignments from Washington, drawing upon his background as a shipper, was the staffing of officers and crew for two (later seven) armed privateers authorized by Congress to intercept and seize supply ships en route to the colonies from England, Ireland, Nova Scotia, or the West Indies. With the success of this program, Moylan handled the correspondence related to the disposition of seized cargoes. Pleased with Moylan's work as well as his military bearing and cooperative attitude, Washington appointed Moylan secretary and aide-de-camp to the commander in chief with the rank of lieutenant colonel.

To run his headquarters, write his orders and letters, and troubleshoot military matters, Washington needed men of background, education, and practical ability. Writing to Congressman Richard Henry Lee on 29 August 1775, Washington outlined the difficulties he faced in selecting and promoting effective line and staff officers. (Congress had granted Washington authority to make spot brevet appointments up to and including the rank of colonel.) In this letter, Washington allowed himself to be candid with his fellow Virginian, who had served with John Adams and Edward Randolph on the three-man committee that recommended Washington to Congress for appointment as commander in chief. The officers of the Massachusetts militia, Washington complained, were little (if at all) better than the private soldiers who elected them and whom these officers must please to remain in their positions. Even worse were instances of cowardice, incompetence, and criminality. Already, Washington noted of militia officers from Massachusetts, he had been forced to break a colonel and two other captains for cowardice on Bunker Hill and two other captains for submitting false pay and provision requests, and he had at this time a colonel, a major, a captain, and two subalterns under arrest and awaiting trial on similar charges. "There has been so many great, and capital errors", Washington concluded, "& abuses to rectify—so many examples to make—& so little Inclination in the Officers of inferior Rank to contribute their aid to accomplish this work, that my life has been nothing else [since I came here] but one continued round of a[nnoyance] & f[at]igue . . .; in short no pecuniary r[ecompense] could induce me to undergo what I ha[ve espe]cially as I expect, by shewing so little Co[unte]nance to irregularities & publick abus[es to] render myself very obnoxious to a gre[ater] part of these People."[5]

Stephen Moylan, Esquire, by contrast (Washington always used "Esquire" after Moylan's name during Moylan's civilian service as muster-master), came from a background Washington recognized, trusted, and required for his immediate staff. "Aid de Camps", Washington wrote to John Hancock on 23 April 1776, apropos of Moylan's appointment, requesting from Congress salary and rank for this assignment, given its long hours and heavy workload, "are person's in whom entire Confidence must be placed—It requires Men of abilities to execute the duties with propriety and dispatch where there is such a multiplicity of business as must attend the Commander in chief of such an army as ours; and persuaded I am that nothing but the zeal of those Gentlemen who live with me and act in this capacity for the great American Cause and personal attachment to me, has induced them to undergo the trouble and confinement they have experienced since they have become Members of my Family."[6] Congress responded with a salary of forty dollars per month for Moylan and the rank of lieutenant colonel.

Yet another trusted secretary

As secretary to the commander in chief, Stephen Moylan shared duties with another Roman Catholic born in Ireland, John Fitzgerald, whose rise in the world paralleled Moylan's. Born in County Wicklow (most likely) around 1739, Fitzgerald grew up in a Catholic family that may have been able to send him to the Continent for an education, or he may have served there as a soldier or an apprentice merchant shipper, one of the few roles then available to an ambitious young Irish Catholic of good family. In any event, by the time Fitzgerald arrived in the port town of Alexandria, Virginia, in 1769, age thirty or so, and entered mercantile trade, the handsome young man spoke perfect French, had impeccable manners, and displayed a warm Irish charm that soon won him acceptance in select social circles. Anglican and tolerant in its religious preferences, the Virginia elite had long since accepted accomplished Catholics living in or near Virginia: the Brents, for example, or the Diggeses of Warburton Manor in Maryland, directly across the Potomac from Mount Vernon. Shortly after his arrival in Virginia, Fitzgerald met Washington at an all-night ball honoring Washington's election to the House of Burgesses. Washington loved to dance and stayed at the ball until dawn. However brief his introduction to Fitzgerald might have been, it must have left the master of Mount Vernon with a positive impression of the young Irishman, who would become his wartime secretary, aide-de-camp, and lifetime friend.

Fitzgerald did well in the West Indies and British trade and prior to the Revolutionary War was able to build and maintain his own wharf operation. He formed a partnership with Major Valentine Piers, a Scots veteran of British military service married to the daughter of Washington's close friend and neighbor, Colonel Dennis McCarthy. Fitzgerald's connection to Washington was enhanced when Fitzgerald married Jane Digges, a daughter of Washington's friend Doctor William Digges of Warburton Manor. Like Roman senators, Washington and Digges would visit back and forth across the Potomac on Doctor Digges' barge.

Aside from achieving yet another connection to Washington, Fitzgerald now enjoyed membership in one of the leading Catholic families of Maryland, which dated back to the founding of the colony. Fitzgerald shared the Whiggish point of view of the majority of Virginia and Maryland landowners, Protestant and Catholic alike, in regard to the worsening relations between the colonies and the mother country. As armed conflict grew more probable, Fitzgerald joined his business and social peers in drilling with the Fairfax Independent Company, soon to be absorbed into the Buffs and Blues, a volunteer regiment that selected George Washington as its commander. Fitzgerald dined with Washington at Mount Vernon at least twice in 1774. On one of these occasions, John Carroll's brother Daniel was at the table as well, testimony to Washington's familiarity and ease with Catholic company. When Washington assumed command of the Continental Army on 3 July 1775, Fitzgerald was on hand to offer his congratulations and was named aide-de-camp by the newly installed commander in chief. On 5 March 1776, Washington named Fitzgerald secretary as well as aide-de-camp, to serve alongside Stephen Moylan.

A brief assignment

When Stephen Moylan accepted the promotion to quartermaster general offered by Congress on 5 June 1776, he left behind the security of his headquarters appointment for a job that was both political and military: political in that Moylan now reported directly to Congress in addition to Washington and was dependent on civilian suppliers as well as the fortunes of war. Moylan lasted a mere four months in office until military reverses forced an evacuation from Long Island, which led to the abandonment of military property, a loss that, in turn, caused problems in resupplying an army in strategic retreat. The trouble led to the appointment of a congressional committee to "inspect the state of the army at New York", and this committee persuaded Moylan to step aside so that Congress might reappoint the more experienced Brigadier General Thomas Mifflin to that position. Rather than take the matter personally, Moylan resigned for the good of the army and rejoined Washington's staff as a volunteer aide-de-camp. Congress thereupon, on 1 October 1776, voted the new quartermaster general, its chosen candidate, a sum of $300,000 to resupply Washington's army, now in New Jersey—money that had not been forthcoming to Moylan. Moylan, however, suffered no loss of prestige. Washington welcomed him back to his staff on 8 January 1777 and formally ordered him to organize and take command of a regiment of mounted dragoons.

Military engineering

In his efforts to develop the Continental Army as a competent and up-to-date force, Washington required the services of trained and experienced officers who could at once lead and instruct. Experts in large-scale military engineering for siege operations, artillery emplacement, and the construction of earthworks and ambitious fortifications were not readily available in either the Continental Army or the colonial militias. Thus, the Board of War and Ordnance of the Continental Congress proved grateful when a brilliant young Polish Catholic military engineer by the name of Tadeusz (Thaddeus) Kościuszko, currently employed as a civilian directing the fortification of the Delaware River to prevent a British attack on Philadelphia via naval and marine action, appeared before it. Born in 1746 to a family of minor nobility in the Polish-Lithuanian Commonwealth, the son of a Polish army colonel, Kościuszko entered the family profession as a cadet at the Royal College in Warsaw and, upon graduation, was promoted to captain of artillery in recognition of his academic performance. He was also granted a scholarship for further academic study as a guest auditor at the École Militaire in Paris and the engineering and artillery school at Mézières. While in France, Kościuszko read widely in Enlightenment authors, most notably Montesquieu and Locke, from whom he absorbed a passionate commitment to liberty as an abstract ideal and a localized opposition to the enforced reduction and division of his native Poland by Prussia, Russia, and Austria. Failing to secure a position in the highly reduced Polish army, Kościuszko left for the United States to join its struggle against Great Britain, armed with a letter from his mentor, Prince Czartoryski, to Major General Charles Lee, who had served in the Polish army from 1765 to 1770.

Impressed with his work as a civilian along the Delaware and Philadelphia waterfronts, as well as by his education in philosophy and military engineering and his dashing demeanor, Congress, in October 1776, commissioned Kościuszko colonel of engineers and named him chief engineer for the Northern Department, which was soon to face invasion by Gentleman Johnny Burgoyne from Canada and Sir Henry Clinton, moving north from New York. Brilliantly, Kościuszko conceived of, organized, and supervised a defensive plan for Fort Ticonderoga based on a command via artillery of the high ground on Sugar Loaf Hill and interlocking fields of fire from surrounding high points. Major General Philip Schuyler, however, canceled the plan. But when Burgoyne closed in on Ticonderoga, Gentleman Johnny reprised Kościuszko's strategy for Sugar Loaf Hill and established his artillery atop that same height and thus enjoyed a direct line of fire into the fort. The Scottish-born American commander, Major General Arthur St. Clair, had no choice but to withdraw stealthily by night from Ticonderoga without firing a shot and later faced a court-martial for doing so. Narrowly acquitted, St. Clair never again held a field command in an engagement against the British.

In contrast to Schuyler, Colonel Kościuszko's next commanding officer, Major General Horatio Gates, heeded his engineer's advice, and thereby the military and public-relations disaster of Ticonderoga was followed by the military and public-relations triumph of Saratoga. First of all, to delay the southern advance of Burgoyne's column, Kościuszko diverted a river and created a lake-size barrier, made even more impassable by emplacements of fallen, tangled trees. That done, Kościuszko led a force of one thousand men to a preselected site near Saratoga and rapidly constructed a defensive barrier of entrenchments, redoubts, and overlapping fields of fire dominated by artillery atop Bemis Heights, overlooking all avenues of approach. Virginia sharpshooters under the command of Daniel Morgan established firing positions throughout this defensive network.

Burgoyne attacked twice. He had to. His initial force of seven thousand now stood at five thousand soldiers, exhausted by the march from Ticonderoga and dwindling even further from desertion by regular soldiers and Indians alike. On 19 September 1777, the British seized the American position on Freeman's Farm, but Morgan's sharpshooters took a terrible toll on British officers and artillerymen. On 7 October, in the Battle of Bemis Heights, Burgoyne tried a direct attack on that fortified height. Some four hundred British soldiers were lost as, for the first time in the war, Americans prevailed in a set-piece battle. In a burst of generous honesty, General Gates gave Kościuszko full credit for the part the young Polish engineer had played in securing the victory.

Named chief engineer of the Middle Department, Kościuszko began work on the fortification of West Point and the lower Hudson just as the Valley Forge winter encampment was drawing to a close. Kościuszko's fortifications for West Point remain in use, and parts of the great chain he designed to be lifted by hoist above water level across the Hudson so as to block invading ships are on view at the United States Military Academy. For private amusement as well as in tribute to the beauty of the site, Kościuszko built a flower garden in a rocky declivity, watering it with spouting jets and cascades.

An engineering contretemps

During this West Point sojourn, Kościuszko crossed swords, however briefly, with Brigadier General Louis Lebègue Duportail. Recruited by Benjamin Franklin and sent secretly to the United States in March 1777 to serve as chief engineer for the Continental Army, Duportail—likewise a graduate of the engineering school at Mézières—was at the time a lieutenant colonel of engineers in the French army; his secret dispatch to the United States was, to Franklin's way of thinking, phase one of a larger French involvement. When Duportail, however, sent to West Point a French engineering officer of lesser rank than Kościuszko and expected Kościuszko to report to him, the usually mild-mannered Pole refused, confident, perhaps, that he too had friends in high places, such as Major General Gates, now serving as president of the Board of War. Thus, two French Catholic military engineers—a member of the first generation of European Catholic volunteers and an officer sent by the government of King Louis XVI as an advance guard of a larger French commitment—foreshadowed the difficulties that arise when a great power enters a war on behalf of a lesser power and expects to be deferred to.

For Revolutionary War leaders, West Point—fifty or so miles upstream from New York on a narrow gorge cut by the Hudson River as it proceeds south through the Highlands mountain range—was the Gibraltar of the American North. At West Point, the Hudson becomes narrow enough for ships seeking passage to be fired upon from the Highland Heights or blocked by a great chain at water level. Thus, either West Point could keep the Hudson free of British men-of-war and troop transports moving north and isolating New England, or, if left inadequately fortified, it could facilitate such an invasion. As a graduate of Mézières and a regular officer in the Royal Engineer Corps of France, Duportail had been formed by a school of interpretation of the military engineering doctrines and practice of Sébastien Le Prestre de Vauban, *commissaire-général des fortifications* for Louis XIV. Vauban favored large, unified, and commanding defensive fortifications, such as the great European fortress Louisbourg, built by the French between 1720 and 1740 on Cape Breton Island, Nova Scotia. Kościuszko, by contrast, an experienced combat engineer recently engaged in improvised forest warfare, preferred a more diversified network of fortifications, which he proceeded to design and build at and around West Point. He and Duportail were perhaps destined to meet in a kind of representative conflict over European doctrine and American improvisation. (Ironically, Marshal Vauban approved of both alternatives, depending on circumstances.) In any event, the report that Duportail filed to Washington on 13 September 1778 regarding Kościuszko's scheme favored further construction as well as the deployment of the great chain three feet below the water (rather than at water level) and was treated by Kościuszko as a standoff or partial victory. "Conclusion was made", Kościuszko wrote to Gates following Washington's inspection of the fortifications, "that I am not the worst of Inginier."[7]

Duportail, however, now took his case directly to Congress, writing its president, John Jay of New York, on 11 May 1779, to inform him that West Point was vulnerable to British attack if and when the British were reinforced and moved north from New York. Kościuszko, moreover, continued to refuse to submit monthly reports to Duportail regarding construction progress. On 1 June, the British did move out of New York and easily captured Fort Stony Point and Fort Lafayette on Verplanck's Point. By the fall of 1779, however, Kościuszko's sixteen-sited defensive complex at West Point was completed or near completion. For the rest of the war, the British were unable to move troops farther up the Hudson than Stony and Verplanck's Points, thanks in great measure to the dissuading presence of Kościuszko's defensive fortifications.

The Conway Cabal

George Washington's army survived the ordeal of Valley Forge because of Washington's leadership and the resilience of his men. Crucial to this survival were Washington's supporters in Congress, the release of an indiscreet letter, the revitalization of supply following the reorganization of the quartermaster department, the drill mastery of a German baron, and—to a lesser, perhaps even minor, degree, but not irrelevant to the process—the continuing loyalty to Washington on the part of influential Catholic supporters from Philadelphia and Maryland. That a certain faction, particularly the New Englanders, had it in for Washington personally was evident in Massachusetts Congressman James Lovell's remarks to Samuel Adams that the Congressional Committee of Inquiry was going to Valley Forge "to rap a Demi-G—over the Knuckles". Washington, however, hardly considered himself either a demigod or a demagogue when committee president Francis Dana of Massachusetts ran into the commander in chief as he was pacing late at night outside his farm cottage headquarters and, putting aside his customary reserve, confessed to Dana, "Congress, sir, does not trust me—I cannot continue thus."[8]

Yet outside this open and rare expression of political vulnerability, Washington's customary reserve served him well as he maintained proper boundaries between himself and the Committee of Inquiry. He did not hide the lack of food, winter coats, and shoes; the dirty faces of soldiers who lacked soap; the lethargic demeanor of hungry, exhausted men; the sick, lying on blankets spread over earthen floors. Washington served his Committee of Inquiry visitors wineless dinners of parsnips, cabbage, and turnips on a torn tablecloth in the stone farmhouse that functioned as his headquarters. Politely, Washington answered their queries, allowed them access to his accounts and papers, and refused to play the victim in any manner.

Washington had a political dynamic working in his favor. At some point in the aftermath of the victory of Saratoga, Major General Thomas Conway wrote a letter to Major General Horatio Gates, congratulating him on his victory at Saratoga. "Heaven", Conway wrote, "has been determined to save your Country; or a weak General and bad councellors would have ruind [sic] it." By "weak general", Conway obviously meant George Washington, under whom he was serving at the time. Gates sent Brigadier General James Wilkinson to make the official report on the Saratoga victory, not to Washington, his military superior, but to Congress directly. Stopping off at an inn in Reading, Pennsylvania, Wilkinson imbibed too freely and began to talk indiscreetly of Conway's letter, specifically referring to this disrespectful and revelatory sentence. Hearing of Wilkinson's remarks, Major General William Alexander Stirling reported them to Washington. Secretary and aide-de-camp John Fitzgerald, meanwhile, secured an especially offensive extract from the letter from Henry Laurens, president of the Second Continental Congress, and forwarded it to Washington at Valley Forge.

On 5 November 1777, Washington wrote a terse letter to Conway: "Sir, a Letter which I receivd last Night, contained the following paragraph." At this point, Washington quoted verbatim the offending sentence and signed off "I am Sir Yr Hble Srvt." The very same day, Conway replied with a letter denying that he used this sentence in his letter to Gates. Two months later, Gates himself wrote Washington on 23 January 1778, denying that Conway's letter contained the sentence in question. It must have been a forgery, Gates argued. And as far as General Conway was concerned, Gates concluded, "I never wrote to him in my Life, but to Satisfy his doubts Concerning the Exposure of his private Letter, nor had any Sort of intimacy, nor hardly the Smallest acquaintance with him, before our Meeting in this Town. With Great Respect I am, Sir, Your Excellency's Most Obedient Humble

Servt." Nine months later, on 4 September 1778, at West Point, Gates fought an inconclusive duel with Wilkinson—pistols, three firings, no hits, stopped by seconds before a fourth firing—as testimony of the bad blood that remained between him and his bibulous, talkative subordinate.[9]

Even before going into winter quarters at Valley Forge, then, Washington and his supporters had damning evidence in hand of what history would later remember as the Conway Cabal. Conway's letter also provided conclusive and forewarning documentation of the hostility toward Washington seething beneath the surface among the majority of members of the Committee of Inquiry. Unfortunately, Charles Carroll of Carrollton was away in Maryland for the first phase of the board's visit. His wife, Mary (Molly) Darnall Carroll—worn down by multiple pregnancies, a miscarriage, and the loss of children in their early years—had developed an addiction to opium-derived laudanum and had fallen desperately ill. With Molly's temporary recovery, however, Carroll reentered the fray at Valley Forge in partnership with Gouverneur Morris. Carroll and Morris exercised persuasive influence on Committee of Inquiry president Dana, who began to edge away from the anti-Washington faction and consider matters from the perspective of His Excellency the commander in chief. By the time the Committee of Inquiry was preparing its final report to Congress, the Conway Cabal—which had no contemporary name, left behind no documents, and accomplished little but the formation of the Committee of Inquiry itself—had vanished back into the thin air from which it had emerged.

Washington's longtime nemesis Thomas Mifflin, moreover, found himself criticized by the very committee of which he was a member for the appalling conditions at Valley Forge. Mifflin had seen the handwriting on the wall as early as October 1777 and had submitted his resignation as quartermaster but had remained on the Committee of Inquiry. By April, a reorganized quartermaster department had appreciably improved supply to Valley Forge. Soldiers were issued shoes, clean uniforms, and rations and began to regain the weight they had lost over the winter.

A Catholic-friendly Calvinist

Of equal importance, a Prussian officer named Friedrich Wilhelm von Steuben was by April drilling Continentals and militia on the parade ground and instructing them in the school of the soldier, thereby bringing them to a new level of professionalism, esprit de corps, and capacity for maneuver. Von Steuben, a Calvinist, did not come from a Catholic nation. Yet Frederick the Great pursued Catholic-friendly policies. In 1745, after two wars, Austria formally ceded Catholic Silesia to Prussia, and Frederick the Great did all that he could to accommodate his newly acquired Catholic population, including building for them Saint Hedwig's Cathedral in Berlin. (Frederick would later refuse to allow the suppression of the Jesuits in Prussia.) When von Steuben's father, an engineering officer, was stationed in Silesia following its conquest, young Friedrich grew up in that Catholic province and received his high school education at the Jesuit college in the fortress town of Breslau (present-day Wrocław, Poland) before entering the army at age sixteen as an infantry cadet. The grandson of theologian Augustin von Steuben, court preacher to the king of Prussia, Friedrich von Steuben nurtured a lifelong interest in biblical study and Roman Catholic theology, a legacy from his boyhood in Silesia and high school years with the Jesuits. Following his release from the Prussian army, moreover, von Steuben spent a decade as *Hofmarschall* (court chamberlain and chief administrator) of the small Catholic principality of Hohenzollern-Hechingen. Denounced in an anonymous letter for overly familiar behavior with young men while serving as *Hofmarschall*, von Steuben resolved to acquire an appointment to the American army before the allegations in the letter became public and ruined his chances of a career as a retired Prussian officer, still employable in the freelance military market of the mid- to late eighteenth century. Overwhelmed with applications for high-ranking appointments to the American army, Franklin recommended von Steuben to Congress as a volunteer only, despite the baron's impressive experience.

Disembarking from the frigate *Flamand* in Portsmouth, New Hampshire, on 1 December 1777, von Steuben and his entourage—an aide-de-camp, a military secretary, two manservants, and von Steuben's great dog, Azor (variously described as an Italian greyhound, a mastiff, and an Irish wolfhound)—were feted in Boston. A habitué of the theater, the baron played his part magnificently before an admiring American audience, thrilled to have such a celebrity rallying to its cause. Elegantly uniformed, armed, and superbly mounted, von Steuben and his entourage proceeded histrionically, operatically, four hundred miles south by horseback to York, Pennsylvania, where Congress had taken refuge. Azor rode with the baggage wagon.

Congress greeted von Steuben respectfully and granted captaincies to his two aides-de-camp, Augustin François des Epiniers and Louis de Ponthière, as well as appointments for two unemployed French officers whom the baron had met in Boston, one of whom, Pierre Charles L'Enfant, would in time design the capital city of the nation now struggling to win its independence. Von Steuben and his entourage reached Valley Forge on 24 February 1778, reporting for duty as commissioned volunteers. (Von Steuben had, somewhat reluctantly, accepted a temporary captaincy from Congress so as to legalize his presence with the Continental Army, should he fall into British hands.) Washington himself, then enduring the full onslaught of the Conway Cabal, rode out in the company of a uniformed honor guard to greet von Steuben as he approached Valley Forge and escorted him and his aides into camp with full military honors.

Launching an inspection tour of the camp, von Steuben made recommendations on siting and sewage flow. Bypassing senior officers, he interviewed (with the help of translators) key junior officers, noncommissioned officers, and enlisted men, speaking to them with that mixture of authority, empathy, and respect characteristic of company-grade Prussian officers. Enlisted men enjoyed von Steuben's theatricality as he made his rounds of their log and clay cabins in his military greatcoat and three-cornered hat, an ivory-topped black cane in hand. "Never before or since", remembered sixteen-year-old private Ashbel Green, later president of the College of New Jersey at Princeton, "have I had such an impression of the ancient fabled God of War as when I looked on the baron. He seemed to me a perfect personification of Mars. The trappings of his horse, the enormous holsters of his pistols, his large size, and his strikingly martial aspect, all seemed to favor the idea."[10]

Recommendations poured into headquarters from the baron regarding better ways to organize and account for troops—this from an experienced former adjutant. The former quartermaster von Steuben also looked into the woeful problems with supply and suggested improved procedures of distribution and accountability. But it was in the matter of drill, musketry, and the bayonet that von Steuben sensed the most pressing need for these American soldiers, once problems of sanitation and supply were solved.

Under the Prussian system, cadets were required to serve in the ranks as non-commissioned officers before receiving commissions so as to better understand, sympathize with, and lead enlisted soldiers. When commissioned, moreover, officers were expected to drill their troops personally, a task most European armies left to noncommissioned officers. Even the king himself, Frederick the Great, wearing his famed three-cornered black hat and an unadorned regimental coat, would drill troops on the parade ground at Potsdam as part of his duties. Drilling, Frederick believed, taught precision, awareness, and solidarity and came into practical use when units maneuvered on the battlefield.

Drill, disciplined firing and reloading of muskets, the bayonet: herein lay the difference between an irregular force and an effective eighteenth-century army. From drill came the mindfulness of movement of soldiers organized into intermeshed squads, platoons, companies, and battalions of infantry, each element—from individual soldier to maneuvering battalion—moving in concert with the others to form the whole. Drill fostered a capacity for unified forward movement and a capacity for deploying columns into battle lines, unified regroupings, and lateral movement—and retrograde movement as well, without such withdrawal turning into a rout. Because reloading a musket was an intricate process, it had to be practiced again and again to ensure as much speed as possible, and it was best done behind the firing line moving forward, which involved passing and repassing firing lines, loading lines, and refiring lines through each other in an orderly fashion.

And the bayonet! So ancient and simple a weapon, yet so effective for closing with the enemy when firing, reloading, and refiring became difficult. American soldiers, however, tended to regard the bayonet as a cooking spit—until, that is, it was used devastatingly against them at Paoli by troops led by British Major General Charles Grey. So Americans had to master the bayonet through a rehearsal of drilling, beginning with the individual soldier and deployed down the line of an attacking company.

Forming a model company of 120 specially selected soldiers, von Steuben taught these things, demonstrating and drilling them personally—as was the Prussian style, holding drilling exercises twice a day. Thus, he established norms for the rest of the army, as adept sergeants from the model company drilled other units. Their work was supervised by chosen colonels reviewed by von Steuben, the baron wearing his full dress uniform, giving orders in French for English translation, swearing in German, French, Russian, and the one English profanity—*Goddam!*—he had managed to master. His multilingual profanity when his instructions were not carefully followed became a popular form of entertainment for enlisted men. Von Steuben recognized the theatrical value of his cursing and (frequently feigned) temper tantrums, yet he maintained a Prussian-style distance from enlisted men, who could not speak to him directly unless he spoke to them first. The men responded to this baron turned drill sergeant, and he, in turn—having previously served as adjutant of a Prussian Free Battalion of scouts and raiders (white Indians, as he described these men to his new American colleagues)—instinctively understood the American soldiers he was now drilling. They were independent-minded, true, and anything but servile, these citizens who were not serfs. Still, the men were highly teachable, provided the reason for a particular drill was given, and capable of discipline as long as they believed themselves to be respected.

Through March and April 1778 the soldiers of the Continental Army rapidly absorbed the maneuver and firing drills of a European-style army. On 28 March 1778, Washington named von Steuben acting inspector general of the army, to replace Major General Thomas Conway, who had requested a transfer from the position. Learning on 1 May 1778 of the newly finalized alliance with France, Washington ordered von Steuben to prepare a grand military review in honor of the alliance. Von Steuben planned a feu de joie: a traditional European military salute in which two double lines of troops marched into interface with each other and then, following the firing of a cannon, discharged their loaded but blank muskets one by one at regular intervals, fire running up and down the assembled lines. Held on 6 May 1778, the Grand Review demonstrated the Continentals' newfound maturity in drill, maneuver, and firing. Even as the army rehearsed the review, Congress was busy responding to Washington's letter of 2 May requesting a permanent appointment for von Steuben. On 5 May, Congress appointed von Steuben as inspector general of the army with the rank and pay of major general. Washington kept the news to himself until he announced it at a reception held on the night of the Grand Review.[11]

A need for dragoons

Infantry, artillery, engineering, and cavalry constituted the basic components of an eighteenth-century military land force. Through drill, von Steuben was raising the American infantry to a new level of maneuver. Boston bookseller Henry Knox had mastered artillery through self-instruction via manuals and experience and was performing credibly as chief of artillery. Thaddeus Kościuszko and Louis Lebègue Duportail brought a European art and science of military engineering to the Revolution. Yet Washington also required horse soldiers, and for these mounted troops he turned to, among others, Colonel Stephen Moylan of Philadelphia.

Having resigned as quartermaster general in September 1776, Moylan returned to Washington's staff as a volunteer aide-de-camp in a variety of field assignments throughout the New Jersey campaign. During this time, Washington felt a lack of mounted soldiers for reconnaissance, screening, patrolling, and prisoner-of-war escort. Just before January 1777 he made up his mind to ask Colonel Moylan to recruit and organize a light horse regiment. Washington informed Congress of this intention on 21 January 1777 by letter from his headquarters at Morristown. Between 26 February and 30 May, Congress authorized warrants totaling $62,000 to finance this new branch of the Continental Army. Similar outlays were expended to create light horse regiments under separate commands in Connecticut, Maryland, and Virginia. When these units were raised, Congress and Washington would take up the appointment of a general of horse.

These horse soldiers were to be dragoons, lightly armed soldiers capable of dismounted deployment as infantry. In European armies, dragoons or hussars were elite troops, elaborately uniformed; Moylan designed for his men an Irish-themed uniform of green coats trimmed in red, red waistcoats, buckskin breeches, and black leather helmets trimmed with bear fur. The garb was very Philadelphian, which is to say, appropriately stylish as befitting the congressional seat of the newly declared nation and the city's wealthy citizens who supported Washington, as did those of Maryland and Virginia. Dragoon regiments were being raised in three colonies in which the gentry rode for sport and could be expected to transfer to military service their equestrian skills along with some of their light horse volunteer units, especially in Philadelphia. One local unit, the Philadelphia Light Horse, organized before hostilities broke out, had already been serving with the Continental Army. In effect, each region would be expected to muster and adopt a regiment, which were not regiments in the full sense of the term but, rather, two or three companies with a headquarters.

By May–June 1777 Moylan's Dragoons, recruited and organized in Philadelphia and elsewhere in Pennsylvania, were screening the advance of two thousand British in the general direction of Princeton, part of a larger land and sea movement south to Philadelphia under the command of General Sir William Howe. The war was moving southward. After some hesitation, the British had decided to occupy Philadelphia and its immediate environs so as to deprive the Revolution of its greatest port and provide a base for the subdual of the greater Chesapeake region (southern Pennsylvania, Delaware, Virginia, Maryland) by blockade and coastal sorties, as well as to set the stage for taking the war farther south.

Roman Catholic Loyalists

As the largest city in the United States, Philadelphia featured a variety of sentiments and allegiances regarding the Revolution. Observant Quakers sustained their commitment to nonviolence and remained neutral. A number of prominent Tories maintained a quiet presence in the city that had been an important imperial port as well as a center of humanistic learning, medicine, and science oriented toward the intellectual and literary life of Great Britain. Yet the very presence of the Revolutionary government in Philadelphia, before Congress fled to Lancaster as Howe approached the city, resulted from the predominantly Whig sentiment among the maritime and commercial elite. Roman Catholics were few among this pro-independence elite, but, in addition to Stephen Moylan, it included Thomas FitzSimons, who had seen action at the Battle of Princeton as captain of a militia company; FitzSimons' brother-in-law George Meade, a member of the home guard Associators (also known as the Public Defense Association); and the veteran merchant sea captain John Barry, on active duty since 1776 as commander of the *Lexington*, the first American ship to capture a British vessel, who was now organizing the naval defense of the city as senior commander of the navy in the port of Philadelphia. With the exception of the Philadelphia-born Meade, all of these prominent Roman Catholic Patriots were Irish-born, as were many members, officers, and rank-and-file of the city and state militias as well as some three hundred members of the Pennsylvania Line (regiment) of the Continental Army. Add German and Anglo-American Catholics to this mix, historian Charles Metzger points out, and you have Roman Catholics numbering between 33 and 50 percent of Pennsylvania's Revolutionary forces.

Still, nineteenth-century historian John Gilmary Shea (and others) grew defensive when it came to the issue of Catholic Loyalists, whether in Philadelphia or elsewhere. Such anxiety ignores the fact that the Revolutionary War represented a species of civil war between the American colonies and Great Britain as well as an internal civil war on a smaller scale between Loyalist and Patriot. Isolated by language and the lack of Anglo-American political traditions, moreover, the German Catholics of Pennsylvania cannot be faulted for keeping a low profile on one side or another of the conflict in comparison with Irish and Anglo-American Catholics. Even New England Yankees living in Nova Scotia maintained neutrality during the conflict. Nor can the Roman Catholic clergy of the Chesapeake region—all but a few of them English-born and, until recently, members of the English Province of the suppressed Society of Jesus as well as clergy under the jurisdiction of Bishop Richard Challoner, vicar apostolic of the London District—be blamed for lying low during the war, favoring an apolitical pastoral practice anchored in discretion. One notable exception, of course, was Father John Carroll, a former Jesuit of Maryland who sided openly with independence. After debating whether to return to England, Jesuit Joseph Mosley swore his allegiance to Maryland in 1779.

During the occupation of Philadelphia, Father Ferdinand Farmer (originally Steinmeyer) witnessed the weddings in Saint Mary's Church of at least five Hessian Catholic soldiers and their brides. Farmer was not making a political statement. After all, an estimated 5,500 Catholic soldiers were serving with the 30,000 German soldiers attached to the British forces. Only one Hessian Catholic chaplain makes an appearance in Martin Griffin's three-volume anthology of primary sources, *Catholics and the American Revolution*—and he is writing to request permission to be discharged from active duty and accept a parish in Albany![12] During the occupation, then, Father Farmer functioned as an equal-opportunity, equal-access pastor for Hessian Catholic soldiers and their brides (and perhaps the less explicitly documented baptisms of their offspring as well); no opprobrium was ever attached to him for these ministries.

When the record shows that General Howe wanted to raise a regiment of Roman Catholic Loyalists in Philadelphia, however, and Father Farmer was tentatively listed as chaplain, John Gilmary Shea dealt with this challenge by ignoring it. "The Catholics spontaneously, universally, and energetically gave their adhesion to the cause of America", Shea told the United States Catholic Historical Society in 1884, "and when the time came, to American Independence. There was no faltering, no division, every Catholic in the land was a Whig. In the list of Tories and Loyalists, in the volumes written since about them, you cannot find the name of a single Catholic. There were no Catholic Tories."[13] Eager to refute claims by historian George Bancroft in his *History of the United States* (1875) that most Roman Catholics in the colonies were either indifferent or hostile to the independence movement, Shea in the 1870s and 1880s repeated this assertion a number of times in a number of venues.

Each of Shea's statements, Martin Griffin was arguing as of 1909, was in error. There were Catholic Loyalists and Tories, Griffin contended, pages of them, whom Griffin listed by name. Given the discrimination Catholics endured in the colonies, that loyalty to England is not surprising. Philadelphia, in fact, was an epicenter of Toryism, if one is to judge from how gleefully Quakers and Tories cheered when, on 26 September 1777, British troops under the command of Major General Lord Charles Cornwallis marched smartly into the city and the eminent Tory lawyer Joseph Galloway—a believer in self-governance but not independence for the colonies—assumed the direction of civil government. In his catalogue of Catholic Loyalists, Griffin went on to name at least a dozen Tories of the artisan class, followed by a listing of former Jesuits Robert Molyneux and Ferdinand Farmer as Loyalist sympathizers: Molyneux because he never wrote or said anything in favor of the Revolution and, when offered in 1779 a trusteeship of the newly organized University of Pennsylvania, refused it in favor of Farmer rather than take an oath of allegiance (Griffin suggests) to Pennsylvania; and Farmer because the German priest called personally on General Howe and later wrote appreciatively of the chaplaincy in the Catholic volunteer unit Howe had offered him.

Like Lieutenant Colonel Alfred Clifton, to whom Howe offered the command of the new unit, a number of the Loyalists connected or sympathetic to the Roman Catholic Volunteers were parishioners of Saint Joseph's or Saint Mary's and, hence, ministered to by Father Farmer. That evidence, however, argues historian Charles Metzger, does not constitute Farmer's formal acceptance of a chaplaincy. Still, Griffin makes a convincing case in refuting Shea's claim, as across twelve closely printed pages Griffin lists an array of documented Loyalists of the Roman Catholic persuasion, most of them with Philadelphia connections. Lieutenant Colonel Clifton was able to enlist 180 men for the Roman Catholic Volunteers from Philadelphia itself and another 151 members when the unit took to the field. Yet the majority of these new enlistees were deserters from other militias and Valley Forge, so their long-term allegiance was unstable. Membership shrank to 80 or so as of May 1778, the same month the Supreme Executive Council of Pennsylvania proclaimed Clifton guilty of treason. This remnant of Roman Catholic Volunteers was later absorbed into the Volunteers of Ireland, a less Catholic and more regularized regiment also founded by Howe, which was deployed from New York in late 1779 or early 1780 to Charleston, South Carolina, as the war moved south. Tory Catholic Lieutenant Colonel Alfred Clifton died in exile in London in 1783.

Germantown

While the Battle of Germantown on 4 October 1777 was technically a victory for the British, Howe and his army had taken such a beating—the Americans had maneuvered well and come close to winning—that Howe curbed his ambitions and remained close to home for the remainder of the fall and winter, happy to enjoy life in the company of his mistress in former governor Richard Penn's stately home on Market Street. Hearing in France of Howe's occupation of Philadelphia, Benjamin Franklin remarked that it was debatable whether Howe had captured Philadelphia or Philadelphia had captured Howe. Less commodiously quartered, of course, were the five hundred American prisoners crammed into two city prisons and kept alive, barely, on near-starvation rations, which they supplemented with boiled leather, rats, and whatever handouts they received in buckets they lowered by rope to Walnut and Third Streets.

In the weeks leading up to the Battle of Germantown, Colonel Stephen Moylan and his dragoons had been employed as scouts, as military police rounding up stragglers or deserters, and as a parade unit when Washington marched his men through Philadelphia to show force against the invading British; they also escorted stores and supplies to the front at Brandywine and Germantown and removed these stores when threatened by capture. At the Battle of Germantown, Washington specifically charged Moylan's dragoons to screen the front for intelligence regarding the British order of battle as well as to keep American troops aligned and advancing in the right direction through the heavy fog that was proving so challenging to Washington's four-column plan of attack. During the battle itself, Moylan's dragoons directly engaged the enemy and took prisoners, earning the praise of Washington, who was struggling with the belief that at Germantown he had withdrawn his men from victory.

A legendary cavalryman

At this time, an antagonism developed between Moylan and the Polish Catholic nobleman Casimir Pulaski. The quarrel reflected the larger resentment of American officers, including Catholics such as Moylan, toward titled Catholic Europeans who were given higher rank and placed over them; language barriers (Pulaski spoke next to no English) and differences over tactics also contributed to bad feelings. Born in Warsaw in 1745 or 1747 (records differ), Pulaski was educated by the Theatines, an order of clerics regular founded in Rome in 1524 as part of the reforms of the Counter-Reformation. Pulaski originally intended to pursue a career in law, like his father, but in the early 1760s he switched to a military career and acquired his skills as a horseman and cavalry tactician while on active duty with the Bar Confederation of nobility, which was opposed to Russian domination of the Polish-Lithuanian Commonwealth. Through a decade on the battlefield, Casimir Pulaski came of age as a cavalry officer of intrepid, headstrong bravery: a Roman Catholic, to be sure, as were nearly all Poles, but a Freemason as well, at a time when prominent Roman Catholics of an Enlightenment orientation, including some members of the hierarchy, held dual citizenships in Catholicism and Freemasonry.

Pulaski showed an early tendency to self-assignment on the battlefield as he rose to preeminence as a Bar Confederation cavalry officer with a preference for bold maneuver and frontal attack. In May 1772, feeling squeezed out of the Bar Confederation leadership and seeking better military opportunities, Pulaski exiled himself first to Prussia and then to the Ottoman Empire, in the throes of the Russo-Turkish War. Following a Russian victory in that conflict, Pulaski barely escaped to France, where he sought another military assignment. He had a Polish-Lithuanian death sentence attached to his name as a rebel and would-be regicide, however, which led to his rejection by the French army.

Down and out in Paris from 1775 to 1777, Pulaski was at least on one occasion thrown into debtors' prison before coming to the attention of the marquis de Lafayette. The marquis introduced him to Benjamin Franklin, who recommended him to a Congress by now growing resistant to an oversupply of European officers. Like von Steuben, Pulaski agreed to come to the United States as a volunteer and prove himself worthy of a formal appointment in the Continental Army. Pulaski arrived in Marblehead, Massachusetts, on 23 July 1777 and within the month presented himself as a volunteer to Washington at his headquarters outside Philadelphia.

At the Battle of Brandywine, Pulaski rode with Lafayette as a member of Washington's personal guard of thirty cavalrymen (six of them Irish Catholics), specially selected for their height (a minimum of five foot nine), riding skills, upright personal habits, and proven bravery under fire. Accounts vary as to Pulaski's contribution that day, but all agree as to his courage on the battlefield as well as to his superb horsemanship. One veteran later remembered the dramatic sight of Pulaski rearing his horse upward on its hind quarters to get a better view of the opposing British forces. It was as if "some warlike creature had come up out of the solid earth", this eyewitness recalled. A cannonball hit the very spot where Pulaski had made this reconnaissance and only seconds earlier vacated. Unsheathing his saber, Pulaski led a small group of cavalrymen to a higher elevation for a more accurate view of the Hessian and British advance and rushed this intelligence back to Washington. The sight of Pulaski standing in his stirrups to see the advancing enemy better before leading a charge, urging his men on, and pointing the way with his saber doubly, triply confirmed other reports of Pulaski's bravery and panache under fire.[14] The Polish count could certainly ride. And he was fearless in the face of an oncoming enemy. Pulaski's reconnaissance of the front, it was later asserted, prevented the British from cutting off Washington's line of retreat: a claim that Pulaski saved the day for the Continental Army and prevented the possible—indeed, probable— capture of Washington on the battlefield.

On 15 September 1777, Congress named Pulaski brigadier general of cavalry in the Continental Army. In the United States less than two months, capable of giving orders only in French for translation, Pulaski now outranked all four dragoon colonels on active duty, including Stephen Moylan. Washington placed the Polish nobleman in command of all four light horse regiments. Not surprisingly, Moylan was restive under Pulaski's command. It was a case of longtime resident versus recent arrival, Friendly Son of Saint Patrick versus arrogant Polish count, traditional Irish Catholic with Philadelphia attachments and Masonic Catholic committed to an Enlightenment and pan-European point of view.

Following the Battle of Germantown, Pulaski brought charges against Moylan on grounds of disobedience to orders, disrespectful language to a commanding officer, and striking Polish volunteer Lieutenant Ignacy de Zielinski, a member of his staff and a cousin of Pulaski. A court-martial hearing acquitted Moylan of all charges. A month later, however, the affronted Lieutenant Zielinski unhorsed Moylan, riding up against him and pushing him to the ground with his lance—a particular form of contempt in European cavalry circles—but Zielinski claimed it was an accident. Nothing came of the matter, perhaps because an embarrassed Moylan did not wish to dwell on the incident, so damaging to his reputation as a colonel of light horse when Pulaski brought it to Washington's attention.

The antipathy between Moylan and Pulaski was also animated by differing opinions as to what could be accomplished through mounted forces. Limited in their support from Congress, the four Continental Army regiments—oversize companies in reality, not regiments—were mounted troops, useful as scouts, guides, military police, or infantry, depending on need. So Moylan saw them. Pulaski, by contrast, wanted to develop a more ambitious force modeled on the Bosniaken, the corps of light lancer troops that Frederick the Great created in 1745, designed to close with the enemy with speed and force, their lances deployed as bayonets. Stationed with his mounted troops at Trenton through the winter of 1777–1778, Pulaski wrote (in French) two memoranda to Washington, dated 23 November and 19 December 1777, outlining a program to establish such a force, which in some respects paralleled the program for infantry soon to be enacted at Valley Forge by Baron von Steuben. Pulaski requested permission to form a company of 120 specially chosen dragoons, whom he would personally train as lancers. Like von Steuben's model company, this elite squadron would set standards and serve as a training cadre for the mounted service. Pulaski would likewise train promising dragoon officers to staff the squadron. Two hundred mounted militia soldiers, meanwhile, would be trained as a support force for elite lancer cavalry oriented toward rapid maneuver and attack.

Frustrated in his efforts to win Washington's approval of his lancer program; dissatisfied with the small-scale skirmishes and constant patrolling and foraging of his winter assignment at Trenton; weary of the resentment and pay disputes coming his way from American officers, Pulaski resigned his command of the Continental dragoons in early March 1778. At the same time, he won the praise of New Jersey governor William Livingston for his service in that state. "I am pleased with the favorable account you give of Count Pulaski's Conduct while at Trenton", Washington replied. "He is a Gentleman of great activity and unquestionable bravery and only wants a fuller knowledge of our language and Customs to make him a valuable Officer."[15]

Returning to Valley Forge with a new idea—an independent legion of cavalry under his command, for which he would report directly to Congress—Pulaski presented this proposal to Major General Horatio Gates, hero of Saratoga, president of the Board of War and Ordnance of the Continental Congress, and no particular friend of George Washington. Gates approved the proposal, as did Congress on 28 March 1778, authorizing the unit and placing Pulaski in command under the newly created title "Commander of the Horse". Thus, Pulaski achieved an end run around Washington—and Moylan, for that matter. Pulaski had in mind a foreign legion: 68 lancers and 200 dragoons, leavened with (if not dominated by) experienced European professionals. Named captain of dragoons, Pulaski's cousin Ignacy de Zielinski joined the command, as did the Hungarian hussar (light horse cavalryman) Michael Kovats de Fabriczy, a decorated veteran of Hungarian and Prussian service, whom Congress commissioned colonel commandant of the Legion on 18 April 1778 (yet another European Catholic recruited to American service by Benjamin Franklin). Taking immediate charge of training while Pulaski concentrated on recruitment, Kovats created a legion of 330 officers and men organized and trained on a European model. Until he was ordered not to do so by Washington, Pulaski went so far as to enroll deserters from the British army, provided they possessed cavalry skills.

Back in Valley Forge, meanwhile, Washington, on 28 March 1778, returned Colonel Stephen Moylan to command of the four light horse regiments now stationed in New Jersey. The urgency of an impending campaign pervaded Washington's letter reappointing Moylan as well as the letters he sent to dragoon colonels Theodorick Bland, Elisha Sheldon, and George Baylor regarding Moylan's reinstatement. "You will use your utmost endeavours", Washington wrote Moylan, "to have the Cavalry belonging to the four Regiments (now in

N. Jersey) put in the best order possible, that they may take the field with some degree of eclat."[16]

Further Irish connections

As important and strategically placed as Stephen Moylan, John Fitzgerald, and John Barry were, they should not be seen in isolation. They were, rather, part of a larger pattern of Irish Catholic support for the Revolutionary cause, including support in Ireland itself, England's first colony. The people of Ireland responded to the American Revolution as a mirror image of their own conditions and hence divided themselves into opposing and supporting camps. Under the system set up in 1494 by Sir Edward Poynings, Henry VII's lord deputy, Ireland had a Drogheda (parliament), but this body remained under the control of the English Crown. Since Roman Catholics remained disemancipated under Poynings' Law, as it was called— and most support for the American Revolution could be expected to come from this quarter—the Lord North administration was able to keep the all-Protestant Irish parliament generally in line regarding sympathies for the Americans, as such luminaries as Edmund Burke were showing support in the English Parliament. Still, the eloquent and perfervid Irish nationalist Henry Grattan, the predominant Irish parliamentary leader of this era (known today as the Grattan Ascendancy in his honor), used the American war to leverage English acceptance of Irish trade with the colonies, pointing out to the North administration just how disastrous restraint of trade against America had proven thus far.

When the British government was forced to withdraw four thousand or so troops from Ireland for service in America, the Castle—meaning the lord lieutenant— raised a force of some thirty thousand volunteers to resist, if necessary, a French invasion. Thanks to Grattan's insistence, this volunteer army included Catholics, long excluded from such service, so as to make it, Grattan argued, a force for unity. At the same time, this volunteer force represented a form of autonomy for Ireland, which now had its own army, which it could raise in support of a French invasion and a Stuart restoration as well as a defense of the Crown. Grattan skillfully used this subliminal threat to negotiate further trade leverage and bring about the suspension of the restrictions of Poynings' Law.

Ireland, in short, had the American Revolution on its mind during the second half of the 1770s. The British government, sensing the parallels between Ireland and the colonies, was fully aware of what might very well be on Ireland's mind and thus, after much debate, took the first small (and, alas, temporary) steps—Catholic membership in the volunteer force and a measure of autonomy for the Irish parliament—in the direction of Catholic emancipation and limited home rule. From this perspective, the Irish Catholics fighting for American independence were establishing one paradigm of resistance and liberation; and the Grattan Ascendancy was establishing another.

Fifteen or so years later, under the influence of the French Revolution, the Irish patriot Theobald Wolfe Tone would replace Henry Grattan's affinity with Edmund Burke (reform in order to preserve) with a more disruptive program (invade Ireland with the help of France and declare independence), which resembled the program put forward in 1778 by the Franco-American Alliance when an entire generation of

Irish American and French Catholics went into harm's way on behalf of American independence. In Ireland, Catholic men were in general reluctant to enlist in the British army for American service and had a reputation for having a high rate of desertion once they arrived. Contemporary testimony, by contrast—Loyalist lawyer Joseph Galloway, for example, testifying before Parliament after his repatriation to England—estimated that as many as 50 percent of those in the Revolutionary forces were Irish in origin.[17] In *Catholics and the American Revolution* (1962), historian Charles Metzger convincingly discounts any such claim. After all, the colonies contained only twenty-five thousand or so Catholics when the Revolution broke out, and a good percentage of these Catholics were Anglo-Americans from Maryland. Besides, the surge in immigration to the colonies from Ireland just before the Revolution contained a large number of Scots-Irish Presbyterians.[18] Yet many Irish Catholics did serve, and in his classic anthology, historian Martin Griffin provides documentary profiles of a number of them.

John Barry, Father of the American Navy

Second only to Charles Carroll of Carrollton in reputation in American Roman Catholic remembrance as a prominent Roman Catholic Revolutionary War leader remains the Irish-born John Barry, today considered the cofounder, with John Paul Jones, of the United States Navy. Daring, flamboyant, the Scottish-born Jones has been subsequently more vividly celebrated for his brilliant handling of the outgunned *Bonhomme Richard* in battle against the *Serapis* and his reply to the commander's query "Has your ship struck?" with the eminently quotable "I have not yet begun to fight!" Barry—an experienced Philadelphia-based merchant-ship captain before the war—while less quotable, was equally impressive as a maritime leader with a roll call of victories to his credit by 1783, including his prevailing as commander of the *Alliance* over the British ship *Sybil* in the last naval action of the Revolutionary War.

Born in 1745 in County Wexford, Ireland, to poor but self-respecting parents and raised in the port city of Wexford, Barry went to sea as a cabin boy. At the early age of fifteen or sixteen, while working his way steadily up the ranks of merchant seamanship, he chose to make his permanent home in Philadelphia, where he joined Saint Mary's parish and alternated his spare shore time with visits back to Wexford. By twenty-one, the very tall (six feet four, by one report) and forceful young veteran of eleven years of seamanship had command of his own ship, the sixty-ton schooner *Barbadoes*, active in West Indies commerce. In 1767 Barry married the Irish-born Mary Clavy, age twenty-two, and the young couple moved into a home in the South Ward of the city. In the winter of 1768–1769 Barry was elected to membership in the elite Charitable Captains of Ships Club—five future captains of the Continental Navy likewise belonged—officially incorporated in 1770 as the Society for the Relief of Poor, Aged, and Infirm Masters of Ships and Their Widows and Children. By the eve of the Revolutionary War, then, John Barry belonged to the same clubbable Philadelphia and Saint Mary's parish world that produced at least a half dozen Irish Catholic Revolutionary War leaders.

On 9 February 1774, Mary Barry died from a sudden illness while her husband was at sea. Father Ferdinand Farmer of Saint Mary's offered the Requiem Mass, and

Mary was buried in Saint Mary's churchyard; Barry later placed over her grave a simple headstone that bore her name, date of death, and age (twenty-nine years, ten months). John Barry's brother Patrick, also a Philadelphia-based ship's captain, and his wife saw Mary Barry through her final illness and death and John Barry through two months of intense grieving.

The following year, the English-born Robert Morris, merchant prince of Philadelphia, having monitored Barry's rise in maritime circles, offered the young sea captain the command of the two-hundred-ton merchant ship *Black Prince*, on which, on a return voyage from England, he set a record of traveling 237 miles in twenty-four hours by dead reckoning. Thus, the future Father of the American Navy entered the employ of the future superintendent of finance for the war effort in the brief period before the Revolution debuted at Lexington and Concord on 19 April 1775. *Lexington* was also the name of the fourteen-gun brigantine John Barry took command of on 14 March 1776 and in which he shortly thereafter, on 7 April, captured the British tender *Edward* off the Capes of Virginia after a fierce engagement, bringing her into the port of Philadelphia—the first prize of Barry's military career and the first captured British ship to be brought into Barry's home city.

In December of that year, as General Sir William Howe's twelve-thousand-strong army was advancing across New Jersey and threatening Philadelphia, Barry volunteered for shore duty in a hastily organized volunteer artillery company attached to the right wing of Washington's army on the Pennsylvania side of the Delaware River. Attached to Colonel John Cadwalader's staff, Barry helped coordinate artillery defenses along the Delaware and saw action at the Second Battle of Trenton, on Assunpink Creek, and the Battle of Princeton. Washington personally selected Barry to deliver to Princeton the medicines and a surgeon for the wounded requested by the British under a flag of truce and to escort back to Philadelphia Hessian prisoners, along with baggage and supplies, captured at Trenton.

Now ranked seventh on the seniority list of Continental naval captains, Barry returned to Philadelphia to serve as senior captain of the port. During this period, at age thirty-two, he courted the prosperous Sarah Austin, age twenty-three, whom he married on 7 July 1777 in an Episcopalian ceremony at Old Christ Church. Was there also a Roman Catholic blessing for this union? Perhaps. In that time, such couples—Roman Catholic men who married Protestant women, especially Episcopalian women—frequently went through two ceremonies: a formal Book of Common Prayer ceremony followed by a less conspicuous Catholic blessing in another location. In any event, John Barry continued to attend Mass at Saint Mary's before and after the British occupation, eventually in the company of his wife, who, two years later, on 21 July 1779, was received into the Catholic Church.

Other Catholic officers

Many of the Catholic Revolutionary servicemen cited by Griffin are officers, who tended to come from more prominent backgrounds and hence were easier to document: figures such as Colonel Morgan Connor of the Seventh Pennsylvania Regiment and the Dublin-born Colonel John Moore of the Pennsylvania militia, who was elected to Congress in 1790. (In 1853 Moore's grandson Father George Carrell would become bishop of Covington, Kentucky.) Another Irish Catholic

Pennsylvanian, Major Michael Ryan of Bucks County, served as adjutant to Colonel (later Brigadier General) Anthony Wayne, another Pennsylvanian, dubbed "Mad Anthony" for his sangfroid under fire. Prior to the war, all three children of Michael and Elizabeth Ryan were baptized by the itinerant Father Ferdinand Farmer. Other Irish Catholic officers—Captain Thomas Doyle, for example, who also served under Wayne, and Lieutenant Samuel Brady, who was with Wayne as well and a survivor of the horrendous British nighttime bayonet attack at Paoli—were likewise southern Pennsylvanians, as was Captain Anthony Selin, a Swiss Catholic immigrant.

Although his father was a Loyalist, Alsatian Roman Catholic Joseph Cauffman of Philadelphia—a graduate of the Jesuit college at Bruges, with a degree in medicine from the University of Vienna—joined the American privateer *Randolph* and lost his life at sea in the company of his captain, Nicholas Biddle, an even more prominent Philadelphian, when the British cruiser *Yarmouth* broadsided the *Randolph* in battle and set off an explosion, sending all hands but four to the bottom of the Atlantic. Another Roman Catholic physician in military service was Jacob Durang, a native of Strasbourg and a veteran of the French army, who in 1762 immigrated to Pennsylvania with his newly married wife and set up practice in York. Following his Revolutionary War service, Durang reestablished his family in Philadelphia, where he and his wife belonged to Saint Mary's parish. Durang lived until 1822 and was buried in the Saint Mary's graveyard.

Not every Roman Catholic officer was a saint. Take the case of Captain Patrick Duffey, a member of the independent artillery regiment raised in Pennsylvania (sixty-seven Irish, twenty-two German, thirteen English, four Scots) by the Irish-born (County Longford) Thomas Proctor, a unit later absorbed into the Pennsylvania Line. Enlisting in June 1776 as a corporal and company clerk, Duffey earned promotion to officer rank and fought a long, hard war from the Battle of Long Island to Yorktown. A month before the siege of Yorktown ended, however, Duffey experienced what in retrospect appears to be a psychotic breakdown, compounded by battle fatigue and alcohol. The charges leveled against Duffey—being drunk and disorderly in a public manner, rioting in the streets, quarreling and drawing a sword on a fellow officer, trying to stab said fellow officer and firing a pistol at him, snapping a loaded pistol at another officer, who was trying to make peace, verbally abusing a French soldier stationed as a guard at the hospital—constituted an egregious breach of discipline. Found guilty on all counts, Duffey was dismissed from the Continental Army on 12 October 1781. Returning to Philadelphia, he opened a brokerage business (general merchandise as well as real estate transactions and land transfers) on Chestnut Street, joined the local militia, and regained his captain's rank.[19]

Roman Catholic enlisted men

Cardinal Newman once remarked that clergy would look rather foolish without a laity. It would have been equally foolish had Griffin confined himself to documenting only Catholics who held officer's rank. Who, after all, would fight the war? Or do the bulk of the dying? Thus, Griffin documents the long, battle-tested career of Andrew Wallace, a Scots Catholic immigrant who served as sergeant in the

Pennsylvania Line throughout the war in units commanded by General Anthony Wayne. Born in 1730 in Inverness, Scotland, gateway to the Highlands, Wallace reportedly fought with the clans against the British at Culloden Moor on 16 April 1752. He subsequently saw militia service in Virginia during the French and Indian War. When the Revolution broke out, Wallace, now in his mid-forties, enlisted in the Fourth Regiment of the Pennsylvania Line, Colonel Anthony Wayne commanding. Sergeant Wallace was reputed to have seen action in the Battles of Three Rivers, Iron Hills, Brandywine, Paoli (where his brother was killed), Germantown, Monmouth Courthouse (where he was taken prisoner and later exchanged), Stony Point, Cowpens, Eutaw Springs, Camden, and Yorktown.

Wallace returned to Philadelphia after the war, but military life called him back, and he reenlisted in 1785 and served—again, under Wayne, now a major general—on the western frontier. Multiple legends grew up around him—some true, no doubt, others more dubious—for Griffin quotes letters from the Bureau of Pensions that indicate that Wallace remained on military duty in one form or another until retiring on disability at age eighty-one. He lived on as a pensioner in Upper Oxford, Chester County, Pennsylvania, until his death in 1833 at the age of 103 and was buried from Old Saint Patrick's Cathedral in New York with a Requiem Mass and military honors.[20]

Although he remained a civilian, Delaware River ferryman Patrick Colvin likewise made a major contribution to the war effort and, like Sergeant Wallace, lived long enough to enjoy iconic status. An Irish Catholic belonging to Father Ferdinand Farmer's far-flung flock, Colvin owned 264.5 acres on the New Jersey side of the Delaware River, which he developed as Colvin's Ferry and from which he ran a ferry service. As might be expected from someone in his profession, Colvin knew the intricacies of the Delaware River down to the last details of tides, flow, fords, crossings, and serviceable points of entrance and exit. He also knew every boat owner in the region. This knowledge became especially useful to George Washington and his staff and commanders when, on Christmas night 1776—having consulted Colvin and other boatmen—they organized the crossing in a sleet storm of the ice-choked Delaware River from Pennsylvania to a site eight miles above Trenton, New Jersey, and early the following morning fell upon its Hessian garrison. Colvin played an equally important role in mustering and organizing boats and men to ferry the 4,500-strong American forces back across the Delaware to defensive positions preparatory to an attack against British forces in Princeton.

Twelve years later, when Washington was en route to New York for his inauguration, Patrick Colvin, now an elderly man, personally ferried the president-elect and his staff across the Delaware and organized the ferrying of his closed carriage and carriage horses. Revolutionary veterans lined the shore and cheered their onetime commander in chief as his barge progressed across the river. Two years later, on 16 November 1792, Colvin sold his Colvin's Ferry property to Robert Morris, financier of the Revolution. Morris developed the site as Morrisville, and the Colvins moved to Trenton, where he became active in its Catholic community and enjoyed legendary status as the Charon turned consultant and commodore of that crucial Delaware crossing.[21]

In terms of George Washington's elite personal guard—composed of carefully selected tall, physically fit soldiers—the roll call of such names as Dougherty,

Hennessey, Driskell, Barry, Danagh, Griffin, O'Neill, Reilly, Whelan, Leary, and others of a similar vein suggested the presence of soldiers of Irish descent and Catholic background and practice among the three hundred or so men who, over the years, served in this praetorian cadre. It is difficult, of course, to ascertain the level of Catholic instruction or practice of any one soldier with an unmistakable Irish surname; yet two factors—birth in Ireland and enlistment from either Maryland or Pennsylvania in the Continental Army lines of those Catholic-rich and clergy-served states—improve the probability of a Catholic connection. In the case of James Blair of Londonderry, New Hampshire, for example, evidence exists of his birth in Ireland in 1763 and his death in Mill Village, Pennsylvania, in 1822. Similar evidence shows that Robert Blair of Burlington, New Jersey, was born in Ireland in 1762 and died in Newburgh, New York, in 1840. Guard members with Irish surnames recruited from the Maryland and Pennsylvania Lines are even more documentable and probably Catholic: enlisted soldiers such as Thomas McCarthy, Dennis Moriarity, Hugh Hagerty, and (most likely) Andrew O'Brien, all recruited from the Pennsylvania Line (McCarthy's family are recorded as practicing Catholics in Haycock and Nockamixon Townships, Pennsylvania), as well as Jeremiah Driskell.

Time and again in Revolutionary War battles, American sharpshooters proved decisive, whether in victory or in forestalling disastrous defeat. This fact may explain why Griffin, assembling the third and final volume of his documentary history (published in 1911), very much wanted the illiterate but deadly accurate Timothy Murphy—so obviously Irish—to be Roman Catholic, even if only in a vestigial way. Griffin openly expressed his disappointment that such a connection could never be proven. He took consolation in the possibility of Murphy's Roman Catholicism, given his Irishness, and countered that Murphy's non-Catholicism could not be proven, either. Tall, handsome, black-haired (in the mien of Black Irish, with a genetic connection to survivors of the Spanish Armada who were washed ashore on the Emerald Isle in 1588), catlike in his capacity for rapid movement, and preternaturally accurate in musket fire, Timothy Murphy emerges from Griffin's brief selection of histories, reminiscences, and oral traditions as the iconic American sharpshooter of the Revolutionary War. Murphy served with Colonel Daniel Morgan's riflemen and reputedly felled British Brigadier General Simon Fraser during the Battle of Saratoga. Following Saratoga, Murphy served with a detachment of Morgan's riflemen in upstate New York in campaigns against pro-British Iroquois.

Maryland and the Revolution

The war, meanwhile, brought statehood and independence to Delaware, Virginia, and Maryland. On 15 June 1776, a constitutional convention meeting in New Castle voted to declare that the three counties on the eastern edge of the Delmarva Peninsula—New Castle, Kent, and Sussex—now constituted the free and independent state of Delaware, affiliated with the United Colonies. While Sussex County to the south supported a significant Loyalist resistance, the Catholics of New Castle and northern Kent Counties supported the Oath of Fidelity to the new state and rapidly enlisted in local militias, including highly mobile Flying Camp units (assisted whenever possible by American privateers), designed to counter British attacks against the extensive Delmarva coastline.

On 8 November 1776, after long discussion by its constitutional convention regarding the form of government it should adopt and a bill of rights, Maryland ratified a constitution and reconfirmed its earlier declared independence. The heavily Catholic St. Mary's County busily raised two militia battalions, prompted by— among other factors—British raids on the Jesuit manors of St. Mary's and Charles Counties, now held under private names since the suppression of the Society of Jesus three years earlier. Thus, Flying Camp tactics characterized the Maryland militia as well. (Pennsylvania followed suit, and Washington later brought Flying Camp rapid response units north to New Jersey.) Altogether, historian Metzger points out, Maryland sent to the Revolution, either to militia units or to the Maryland Line of the Continental Army, at least 130 Roman Catholic soldiers. The prevalence of the first name Ignatius among these fighting men reflected the enduring legacy of Jesuit formation in the newly declared state. So, too, does the roll call of last names on surviving rosters—Fenwick, Spaulding, Neale, Plowden, Digges, Mudd, and other similar names from longtime Maryland families—offer solid evidence of Roman Catholic support of the Revolution.

Mary Digges Lee, a Catholic, and her husband, Thomas Sim Lee, an Anglican, concentrated their efforts on fundraising, recruitment, and supply for the Revolutionary cause. Mary's father, Ignatius Digges, had allowed her marriage to Lee only on the basis of his promise that their children would be raised Catholic. Following a period of militia service, Thomas Sim Lee entered public life in 1777 as a member of the provincial council. In 1779 he began the first of three one-year terms as governor of Maryland, which now had a Catholic first lady. Lee himself converted to Catholicism after the war. Mary Digges Lee made it her task to rally the women of Maryland behind the cause and to raise funds on its behalf. Working with Continental Army commissaries, Governor Lee concentrated on supplying Washington's armies, north and south, from the abundance of the Chesapeake, lest they face another starving time, as in Valley Forge.

Upper Marlboro merchant Daniel Carroll, brother of the priest John Carroll, was elected to the council of state in 1777—yet another Roman Catholic entering public life—and served until 1781. Under the new form of government, members of the council of state served alongside the governor as heads of executive departments and exercised authority in military matters, including recruitment, supply, and finances. Daniel Carroll proved particularly useful to Governor Lee in locating clothing, blankets, and foodstuffs—meat, flour, salt, rum—for the military via a network of agents at work throughout the region. In 1781, upon his resignation from the council, Daniel Carroll was elected to the Continental Congress, where Thomas Sim Lee joined him in 1783, following the completion of his third term as governor.

Catholics' election to public office or to militia commands must be seen in a Maryland context. Of the thirteen colonies, Maryland joined the independence movement with the most trepidation. The culture of Maryland was wealthy, aristocratic, Anglican, and pro-proprietary. After flourishing for decades in trade, enjoying extensive London connections, and basing their economy on the British pound sterling, the planters of Maryland, as of 4 July 1776, had trouble envisioning a future through the dark glass of an ambiguous independence built on rebellion and military victory. Anglican Maryland, in short, had its doubts. Roman Catholic

Maryland, by contrast, was fully confident that it would be far better off in the new dispensation.

Into this picture entered recently enfranchised Catholics capable of leadership and public life, beginning with the debut of Charles Carroll of Carrollton as First Citizen in the 1773 controversy with Daniel Dulany Jr. in the *Maryland Gazette*. Now the niece of a priest, Mary Digges Lee, married to a governor with Catholic tendencies, and the brother of a priest, Daniel Carroll, had joined Charles Carroll of Carrollton in public life, a mere four years from the time that Dulany was taunting Charles Carroll regarding his noncitizenship. Independence had its opportunities as well as its dangers, especially for re-enfranchised Catholics, and they were seizing the day in the struggle for independence that had brought them these new possibilities.

Charles Carroll of Carrollton, meanwhile, continued to serve the Revolution as state convention delegate, diplomat on mission to Canada, member of the Continental Congress, signer of the Declaration of Independence (the only Catholic to have this privilege), and member of Congress' Board of War and Ordnance and its Committee of Inquiry to Valley Forge. In 1777, as a member of the Maryland Senate, Carroll expressed preliminary support for a Tender Bill authorizing the acceptance in Maryland of paper currency issued by the Continental Congress for purposes of payment, including payment for public and private debt. In this program of support, Carroll was joined by Samuel Chase, a veteran of the diplomatic embassy to Canada, now a member of the Maryland House of Delegates. Hearing of the bill, Carroll's father, Charles Carroll of Annapolis—more correctly these days, Charles Carroll of Doughoregan (House of Kings) Manor, since his son Charles Carroll of Carrollton was now living with his wife and family at the Annapolis Manor—went into a distemper verging on rage. To accept Continental paper of dubious value for debts made in pounds sterling, Carroll senior argued, resembled the double tax levied on Catholics in the proprietary era. The money that would be inevitably lost constituted a form of double taxation. In person and through a number of letters, Charles Carroll resisted his father's arguments by appealing to classic Catholic values regarding the common good and the need for sacrifice in times of peril, but Papa was buying none of it. It was a difference of generations. The older Carroll was showing the scar tissue of an earlier anti-Catholic era, while his son—who respected wealth and fair dealing as much as his father did—had psychologically crossed over into another territory. Religious freedom had liberated the younger Carroll from corrosive resentment. The free state of Maryland had restored his citizenship. Maryland and the United States had seated him in its Senate and Continental Congress, respectively. The Tender Bill was necessary to keep this new order. The Catholics of Maryland were doing their part to assist in the survival of this new common good.

And yet, Papa was Papa the patriarch, Papa the domineering, Papa accusing his son of being overly desirous of public approval, yet a father, father-in-law, and grandfather generous and affectionate toward his family. And so, when it came time to vote, Maryland Senator Charles Carroll of Carrollton argued on behalf of an adjustment he knew had no chance of passing: henceforth to require that prior debts be paid in pounds sterling, while Continental paper would be required from this time forward but not in retrospect. No Maryland senator supported this idea.

Charles Carroll of Carrollton was the only Maryland senator to vote against the Tender Bill—a vote he cast out of respect for his father. But he never spoke a word against the bill once it passed.

A Marylander abroad

In terms of policy and strategy, wars are usually directed by elites. The American Revolution was no exception. But the military and diplomatic intelligence required by war frequently has establishment origins as well. George Washington understood this perfectly and, as spymaster in chief, authorized and sponsored a first-rate intelligence network. The longer Benjamin Franklin remained in France, moreover—from September 1778 onward (Lafayette brought his appointment from Congress to Paris), as minister plenipotentiary presenting his credentials to the king on 23 March 1779—the more dependent he became (as do all diplomats) on inside, frequently secret information. Crucial to Franklin's intelligence network was a Catholic Marylander by the name of Thomas Attwood Digges, who, for a number of years, served as Franklin's secret (or semisecret) agent in England. No historian has ever claimed that Digges was a pious Catholic. Indeed, in a landscape of the upright American Catholic clergy and laity whom historians prefer to chronicle, the sometimes roguish Digges—an heir apparent, whom a misappropriation of funds or other form of financial irregularity drove into exile; an American agent living in England during the war, passing for a Loyalist but also suspected by some as being a double agent—offers a welcome version of the prodigal son, antihero of one of the most psychologically realized parables in the New Testament.

Like the prodigal son, Digges came from the heart of the Maryland Catholic elite, born in 1742 to William and Ann Attwood Digges of Warburton Manor, Prince George's County, across the Potomac from their good friends George and Martha Washington. The two families kept in touch with each other via the Diggeses' barge, manned by six African American rowers who wore, according to Washington Irving, a livery of checked shirts and black velvet caps. Thomas Digges' English ancestry included Queen Elizabeth's muster-master general; an ambassador to Prussia; a commissioner to Holland, Lord Petre, Baron of Writtle, a leading Catholic peer; and Edward Somerset, Earl of Worcester. His Maryland ancestry included members of the Calvert family in times past and, more recently, such iconic Catholic families as the Sewalls, Darnalls, and Attwoods. Of the original thirteen states in the mideighteenth century, Maryland alone could produce such Anglo-Americans: wealthy, landed, socially prominent, Roman Catholic, and, because of their religion, kept from public life. No wonder the upwardly mobile and ambitious Lieutenant Colonel John Fitzgerald, Washington's secretary and aide-de-camp, was happy to have married Thomas Digges' sister Virginia; and Daniel Carroll of Rock Creek, brother of the priest John Carroll and distant cousin of Charles Carroll of Carrollton, believed himself equally fortunate to have married Digges' sister Elizabeth.

Under the terms of his father's will, Thomas Attwood Digges, as the oldest surviving son, should have inherited Warburton Manor, as well as his mother's separately held properties; but by the time of his father's passing, Digges had long since—in 1766, when he was in his mid-twenties—fled Maryland for Lisbon, Portugal, most likely (records and other references are vague) due to financial irregularities and a scandalous attachment to a married woman of equal social standing. Nine years later, then living in London, Digges published a novel based on this earlier period of his life, *Adventures of Alonso* (1775), which some literary historians consider the first published novel written by a native-born American.

If, indeed, *Adventures of Alonso* is truly the first published novel by a native-born American—and a Roman Catholic native-born American, at that!—it merits redactive honors in these pages, given Digges' contribution to the Revolution as a secret agent. Set in Maryland, Portugal, and Brazil, *Adventures of Alonso* (by a Native of Maryland, the title page notes) reprises in a displaced fictive format Digges' disruptive early love affair, which Digges recasts in rather Catholic terms. Alonso, runs the story line, the son of Alvaris, a wealthy Portuguese merchant, is educated in England in his teens so as to master English and enter the Anglo-Portuguese trade. Returning to Lisbon, he falls in love with Eugenia, a married woman, only to discover that she has been forced into this marriage with a much older man whom she does not love. Such a forced marriage, of course, provides no barrier for the young couple to fall in love, which Alonso and Eugenia proceed to do. Disguised as a man, Eugenia elopes with Alonso to Cádiz, where Alonso learns of a business opportunity in Brazil that will support the couple in the years to come. Reluctantly, Eugenia takes refuge in a Cádiz convent while Alonso goes to Brazil, where he has many adventures in the diamond mines and as a prisoner of Barbary corsairs. Years later, returning to Cádiz, where he hopes to be reunited with Eugenia, Alonso finds that she has taken the veil in a Lisbon convent following the death of her aged husband. Alonso arrives at the Lisbon convent chapel only to find a Requiem Mass in progress for the deceased Eugenia. Reuniting with his father, Alonso sees him through old age and, upon his death, inherits his father's fortune. Thus, Digges fictionally reprises his own career, including a period of education in England as a teenager. Filling out this theatrical plot of lost love found too late, however, are pages and pages of fictionalized current affairs, discussions of Portuguese, Spanish, and English politics—featuring a brief digression on Sebastião de Carvalho, marquês de Pombal—a scandalous intrigue by a corrupt Franciscan friar, and other topics of the day. Like Pierre-Augustin Caron de Beaumarchais, Digges loved melodrama, behind-the-scenes maneuvering, and role-playing: all this suggesting the temperament of an effective secret agent.

Falling in love (yet again!) with an older woman—Elizabeth Tyler, thirty-four, beautiful, intelligent, strong-willed, visiting Lisbon from England to secure a small inheritance—Digges pursued her back to England in 1774. Thomas Attwood Digges, poet Robert Southey would later write in his journal, was an American adventurer to whom Southey's aunt Elizabeth Tyler "gave more encouragement than was prudent"; and when his pursuit of Miss Tyler came to naught, Digges found himself an unemployed American adventurer in London. What to do?

At this point, Digges wrote *Adventures of Alonso*, which took him into *annus mirabilis* 1775 of the United Colonies' revolt in North America. Certain sections of Digges' novel as well as passages in surviving letters by him during these London years underscore his skepticism regarding the treatment of the American colonies by the Crown and the Lord North administration. He shared these sentiments with other Anglo-American friends he made in London, along with Benjamin Franklin and John Adams. Indeed, it is through his surviving letters, more than two hundred of them—a trickle from 1767 to 1778 and a torrent after 1779, beginning with forty-five letters to Benjamin Franklin in 1779 alone—that we can reconstruct Digges' extraordinary activities on behalf of the United States during the Revolutionary War and the peace negotiations that followed. Digges' half-hidden life reads like a John le Carré novel two centuries ahead of its time. Parliamentary maneuvers (Digges had pro-American sources in each house), possible military movements, public opinion regarding the war, relief for American prisoners of war being held in England, the best escape routes for American prisoners of war who regained their freedom: Digges employed some thirty aliases in the torrent of letters he sent across the Channel to keep his clients, Franklin and Adams especially, up to date on what they needed to know. He also acted as a diplomatic courier for Franklin when necessary, and in 1782 he did some reverse couriership, carrying a peace feeler from Lord North to John Adams, which gave rise to Digges' shadow reputation as a double agent. Yet Digges pledged his allegiance to the United States in the presence of Franklin in Paris in 1779 and at one point had his papers seized and was interrogated by British authorities.

As early as December 1775, moreover—a full three years before his torrential correspondence with Franklin and Adams got underway—Digges had come under scrutiny by the British treasury office for shipping saltpeter and other military stores to the United Colonies via Nova Scotia, which he was most likely doing, given his Beaumarchais-like love of politics, intrigue, patriotism, and profit. In early 1777, Digges was still in the smuggling business: musket locks, this time, hidden in nail casks, shipped to the United States out of Bilbao, Spain.

Meschianza

After the long ordeal and recovery in Valley Forge, Washington knew that spring 1778 demanded a resumption of campaigning. Having been so surprisingly confronted by Washington at Brandywine and Germantown, General Sir William Howe and his men had enjoyed a comfortable and merry winter in Philadelphia. Genial, sportsmanlike, strikingly handsome, pleasure-loving Howe expressed a liking for Americans before the Battle of Bunker Hill; and when he found himself isolated in that battle, caught in the open while trying to rally his troops—so London's *Town and Country Magazine* reported regarding the battle—the Americans returned the favor and did not fire upon such an easy target.[22] When Howe's pet hound, identifiable by the "Howe" on its collar, wandered into American lines prior to the Battle of Brandywine, the dog was returned to the British under a white flag of truce. Now the popular Howe was to be replaced by General Sir Henry Clinton. This shift could be interpreted as a sign of weakness; and so the British decided to throw themselves a party, as if to assert to themselves that all was well with their effort to subdue the American rebellion. The proximate cause of this party—a *Meschianza*, a medley of entertainments, it was dubbed by its officer in charge, the bright young adjutant Captain John André—was to put the best possible face on a change of command that could signal trouble for the British.

When General Clinton arrived in Philadelphia on 8 May 1778 to relieve Howe as commander of British troops in North America, Howe viewed the change-of-command ceremony later that month as an occasion for celebration, not disgrace.

After all, he reasoned, he had resigned his command voluntarily. In honor of Howe's departure, Captain André—a devotee of opera and theater who had an antiquarian's fascination with the elaborate masques written by Ben Jonson for the court of James I—organized an all-day, all-night festival to be held on 18 May. André later documented this fête champêtre in detail in an article published in the *Gentleman's Magazine* of London for August 1778. Prudently, he made sure to note that the Meschianza was privately financed through donations and the sale of tickets of admission to its main events.

The Meschianza began with a regatta on the Delaware River, led by Admiral Lord Richard Howe, commander of British sea forces in North America; his brother, the departing commander, Sir William Howe, Knight of Bath; Sir Henry Clinton, the new commander in chief; the English general Lord Francis Rawdon; and the German general Wilhem von Knyphausen. Each of their launches was gaily decorated and was followed by columns of smaller craft. Onshore, crowds watched the procession upriver and the landing of the principal worthies from their launches as men-of-war, anchored at a distance, fired salutes.

Next, those in possession of an elegantly engraved ticket proceeded past files of grenadiers and light horse dragoons to decorated pavilions. Thereupon ensued mock tournaments of light tilting between mounted officers dressed in Turkish attire, each proclaiming allegiance, via a printed program distributed to spectators, to one or another young Philadelphia woman of social standing. These honored young ladies and others, likewise attired in Turkish-themed costumes, sat or stood together in two designated groups—Ladies of the Blended Rose and Ladies of the Burning Mountain—each of which featured a distinctive headdress and costume color. Military bands played martial music to accompany the tournament. There followed speeches, poetry recitations (verses by John André were read), and a grand procession to the nearby Wharton Mansion for refreshments, a ball, fireworks, a midnight supper, and then more dancing into the wee hours of the next day. The ballroom of the Wharton Mansion was decorated with drapes, ribbons, and mirrors borrowed from Philadelphia families. The midnight supper was served in an equally decorated space adjacent to the ballroom. "Towards the end of the supper", writes André in *Gentleman's Magazine*, "the herald of the Blended Rose, in his habit of ceremony, attended by his trumpets, entered the saloon and proclaimed the king's health, the queen's, and the royal family; the army and navy, with their respective commanders; the knights and their ladies in general. Each of these toasts was followed by a flourish of music. After supper we returned to the ball-room, and continued to dance till four o'clock."[23]

What was the purpose and meaning of this Meschianza, this festival fantasy in the midst of war? In one sense, it testified to the Loyalist sentiment that survived in the congressional seat of the rebellious United States. Crowds of cheering civilians lined the shores of the Delaware as the festive regatta approached the city. Soon some three thousand civilians would take ship with the British fleet or otherwise flee to New York when Sir Henry Clinton ordered the return of all forces to that city— a decision that had already been made at the highest levels in London. Nonetheless, even Loyalist lawyer Joseph Galloway, civil administrator of the city under Howe, found the Meschianza a scandalous exercise in vanity on Howe's part. Howe was accepting a Roman triumph, Galloway complained, when he had failed to conquer.

Far from conquering, he was being edged out of command for accomplishing so little. This was a time for war, not for celebration. Soldiers were dying and would continue to die, and the outcome remained uncertain. From Howe's perspective, the
festival told the ministry in London in no uncertain terms that his officers and men
still believed in him. The Meschianza represented a vote of confidence, a welcomed
recreation, an instance of English sangfroid as well as an assurance of final victory.

One hundred five years later, Philadelphia historians John Thomas Scharf and
Thompson Westcott published in their monumental three-volume, densely printed
history of the city the names and short biographies of the twenty-plus young women
of Philadelphia who had attended the Meschianza in Turkish dress. The group
included one Englishwoman and one New Yorker. The roll call of names, fathers'
occupations, and subsequent marriage history of these young women testifies to
the mixed and uncertain outcome—as far as the Philadelphia establishment was
concerned—of the rebellion still underway. The sole New Yorker at the festival
was a Van Cortlandt on her mother's side, and hence related to Continental Congressman John Jay of New York. The majority of the young women ultimately
married Americans, citizens of the new Republic, of their own social standing.
Two married American generals. Miss Margaret Chew of Germantown married
American colonel John Eager Howard of Maryland. In the Battle of Germantown,
Colonel Howard commanded the Americans opposing the British Fortieth Regiment, with whose bachelor officers his wife had been dancing at the Meschianza
ball. Indeed, Miss Chew attended the Meschianza as the chosen favorite of adjutant
captain John André, coordinator of the festival, who drew a portrait of the charming Miss Chew for his article in *Gentleman's Magazine*. At least three of the young
women, however, sooner or later left for England. Miss Becky Bond died there
unmarried. The solitary English girl, a Miss Auchmuty, married Guards officer J. F.
Montresor. Miss Mary (Polly) Franks, an American, married British officer Henry
Johnson, who years later retired from the army as a knighted lieutenant general.

From Valley Forge to Monmouth Courthouse

The day following the Meschianza, as Philadelphia rested from the celebration,
the British learned that the marquis de Lafayette had crossed the Schuylkill River
on the western edge of the city with a force of 2,500 men and eight cannons and
had taken up positions. Marching hastily, a force of 5,300 British soldiers advanced
in two columns—grenadiers and light infantry in one, Hessian troops in the other—
and almost succeeded in surrounding the Americans and thereby cutting off their
escape across the Schuylkill. Learning of this pending envelopment with a mere
hour left to spare, Lafayette reacted adroitly by sending a small force forward to
feign an attack, thus forcing the British to halt their envelopment and go into
defensive positions. At the same time, Lafayette rapidly returned his men across the
Schuylkill, including the mock attack force, and took up defense on the opposite
riverbank before retreating. When the two British columns reached their scheduled
rendezvous at Barren Hill Church, they discovered that the Americans had made
good their escape back to Valley Forge.

On 24 May 1778, General Howe sailed for England. The next day, General
Clinton called for a council of war at the British Tavern (formerly the Indian King),

to which he invited his commanders and their staffs and the civilian leaders of Philadelphia. Following the surrender of the British at Saratoga on 17 October 1777 and the announcement of a Franco-American Alliance on 6 February 1778, the British realized that they had lost an opportunity for victory in the northern colonies and would soon lose their monopoly over naval blockade when a French fleet arrived off North America. Already, Clinton had been briefed in London by Lord George Germain, the British secretary for North America in the administration of Lord Frederick North, as to what form the new British strategy would take.

With the British fleet and army safely concentrated in greater New York, Clinton was to organize and carry out seaborne coastal bombardments and landings on the New England coast, continue such attacks on the Chesapeake region, and take the main British effort to the Carolinas and Georgia. France would soon be declaring war on the United Kingdom, and England would hence be facing formidable foes, France and Spain, across the Channel as well as on the Atlantic coast of North America and in Florida and the Caribbean. (Clinton was ordered to dispatch as soon as possible 5,000 troops to the West Indies for the seizure of French-held islands there.) With this new New York–based strategy, Clinton informed the gathering at the British Tavern, Philadelphia ceased to be of major importance. The city was too difficult to defend from the sea, too close to the Americans at Valley Forge—now numbering some 13,000—and (as Benjamin Franklin had already noted) too capable of capturing its captors in comfortable circumstances and active social life.

So then: Philadelphia must be evacuated. Great Britain would fight the American Revolution from New York. In less than a month, Clinton arranged the exodus of troops and 3,000 Loyalist civilians to New York, courtesy of the Royal Navy, and prepared his remaining 10,000 troops for an overland march through New Jersey to New York. This land convoy included 1,500 wagons loaded with military services and supplies as well as officers' baggage wagons teeming with acquisitions bought or appropriated in the City of Brotherly Love. (Having been quartered in Benjamin Franklin's home during the occupation, John André was bringing along a selection of books borrowed from Franklin's library on a nonnegotiable, long-term basis.) Private carriages and humbler wagons serving the haut monde, demimonde, and camp followers were incorporated into the column, which extended twelve miles when on the road.

The British caravan left Philadelphia at three o'clock in the morning of 18 June 1778 and took hours to clear the city. Washington heard the news later that morning and called a council of war for his general officers. Their advice: do not launch a major attack. Returned from his long captivity and possible treasonous submittal to Howe of a plan for British victory, British army veteran Major General Charles Lee—five years in the country, nearly a year and a half of that in comfortable British captivity, and a chronic critic of Washington's skills as a general—spoke strongly against any sort of attack and convinced the council, including Washington, who also had reservations regarding a pitched battle. Nevertheless, Washington decided to move out of Valley Forge with what was left of his 13,500-man army, between 11,000 and 12,000 men. Crossing the Delaware, Washington's army marched fifty-seven miles in six days to Hopewell, New Jersey, fifteen miles west of Cranbury. At this point, Generals Anthony Wayne and Nathanael Greene, the marquis de

Lafayette, and Baron Friedrich von Steuben urged attack, with von Steuben and Lafayette recommending an assault against the vulnerable baggage train. Once again, Lee argued against attacking the British. Sir Henry Clinton, meanwhile, veered his men to the northeast to avoid crossing the Raritan River, leaving his second-in-command, Lord Charles Cornwallis, in charge of a rear guard.

On 26 June the British reached Monmouth Courthouse, nineteen miles from Allentown. Washington's vanguard (advance elements) reached a point a mere five miles from the English, and, leaving his baggage behind, Washington pushed the remainder of his force to join them. A battle had become inevitable. Lee kept expressing doubt, yet Washington offered Lee command of the vanguard closest to the British. Lee refused. It should go to Lafayette, he maintained. Why should a senior major general, a veteran of long service in the British Army, defer to a twenty-one-year-old Lafayette? one can legitimately ask. And why did Lee then change his mind and accept Washington's offer, even as he continued to argue against an attack? Certainly, Washington must have remembered how, despite repeated orders, Lee had delayed and delayed crossing the Hudson and joining him following the Battle of White Plains in December 1776; and when the recalcitrant Lee did at long last cross, he was captured by the British, and Washington assumed control of his forces.

In any event, there was Lee in command of the American troops facing Cornwallis' rear guard on the morning of 28 June 1778 near Monmouth Courthouse on the edge of a sandy-bottomed, creek-crossed pine barrens cut through by three large ravines running east-west. Washington had given Lee two options: engage Cornwallis, the preferable option, or merely stand your ground. Lee did neither. He organized no plan of attack. When Cornwallis' rear guard began to follow the British main column, Lee's cavalry made contact, and by midmorning, in one-hundred-degree heat, a confused, directionless battle ensued, absent clear or effective orders from Lee. When militia forces started to withdraw, Lee established no clear line of defense to the rear of his position, and the withdrawal devolved into a confused retreat.

The retreating militia ran into Washington near the west ravine. Washington and his aides queried militia officers about what was happening. Riding forward, Washington found Lee and—in the heat of battle, for Washington rarely lost his composure—gave him a tongue lashing, "poltroon" being among the milder epithets he employed. Drawing his sword, Washington rallied and re-formed his fleeing, disorganized troops. Coming upon the scene, Colonel John Fitzgerald saw the commander in chief shouting orders as he organized a defensive line. A volley of British musket fire filled the scene with noise and smoke. Fitzgerald closed his eyes momentarily at the shock. Opening them, he expected to see Washington's horse riderless. Yet the commander in chief was unscathed and still mounted, rallying the men. Fitzgerald, however, was not to be so fortunate, and later in the battle—which lasted inconclusively into the late afternoon—he was seriously wounded. That night, as the exhausted Americans rested, Clinton withdrew his troops and resumed the trek to New York. Washington decided against pursuit. The British convoy reached New York on 6 July.[24]

The Southern strategy now being launched by the British—seaborne assaults on coastal objectives, including the port cities of Charleston and Savannah—had already been underway for some time against coastal Maryland, Delaware, and

Virginia. On the extensive shores of this region (bounded and configured by the Atlantic Ocean, Chesapeake Bay, and the Delaware and Potomac Rivers) were cities and settlements reachable by maritime attack as well as scores of private wharfs that fronted slightly inland manors. Safely returned to New York, British forces were fully capable of conducting such a land-and-sea campaign.

3

Camden, South Carolina 1780

War rages in the South and enters the West as France and Spain join the cause

At a council of war in Philadelphia on 24 May 1778, prior to the British evacuation of the city on 18 June, General Sir Henry Clinton outlined a Southern strategy to British officers and Loyalist civilian leaders. The army would return to New York. The Royal Navy and the army would increase raids on the coastal regions of the Chesapeake and lay siege to the Southern port cities of Savannah and Charleston. Initially, this Southern strategy enjoyed great success. Savannah fell to the British on 9 December 1778. After a long, hard-fought siege, Charleston surrendered on 12 May 1780. On 16 August 1780, in the Battle of Camden, South Carolina, a force of 2,400 veteran troops under the command of General Lord Charles Cornwallis forced 2,000 militiamen under the command of Major General Horatio Gates—the hero of Saratoga—into a panicked retreat at first contact, leaving the Continentals under Gates' command to face all but certain annihilation.

Gates had been given this Southern command of Continentals and militia (a "Grand Army", Gates called it, erroneously believing it to number more than 7,000 men) precisely because his victory over the British at Saratoga had proved to be the turning point of the war. New England had escaped being cut off from the rest of the colonies. Saratoga was proof that Americans could defeat British regulars in a pitched battle: proof that accelerated a French alliance in the earliest, still hesitant stages. Following the loss of Savannah and Charleston, as well as the inability of Washington's army to do much against Clinton's army safely ensconced in New York, Congress wanted a second Saratoga in the South. Instead, Congress received a stunning defeat at Camden, with the hero of Saratoga fleeing the field in disgrace and Lord Cornwallis subsequently making plans to advance into North Carolina.

In the course of these three defeats—Savannah, Charleston, and Camden—the Southern colonies witnessed the eruption of a cruel civil war between pro-Revolutionaries and the Loyalist populations of Georgia and the Carolinas. Animosity against Loyalists existed in New England and the Mid-Atlantic states, yet Loyalists there were basically a persecuted minority. In Georgia and the Carolinas, by contrast, Patriots and Loyalists were more evenly balanced in number. Furthermore, Loyalists elsewhere in the colonies tended to be shopkeepers, small-business owners, professionals, and Anglican clergy. In Georgia and the Carolinas, Patriots and Loyalists came from all sectors of society, including the most violent. The best of each persuasion served in militias and were hence restrained by a modicum of military or semi-military discipline, or both. Loyalist militia units, moreover, possessed an instinctive attraction to British military discipline, rarely broke ranks under fire, and tended not to be chronic deserters, as was too often the case in Patriot units.

Bitterness between the two factions ran deep as frontier Americans resorted to nonmilitary violence off the battlefields—raids, murders, rapes, thefts, burnings, and cruelties of every sort. This sheer criminality tore apart the fabric of society, left scars for generations to come, lowered the moral tone of the Revolution, and asserted a fundamental social instability and taste for violence that did not bode well for the future of the southern American states.

All this, then—the sieges and seizures of cities by the British, the humiliation of Camden, the backcountry mayhem—led Washington to recommend, and Congress to approve, the sending of Major General Nathanael Greene to the Carolinas to assume the Southern command, literally abandoned by Horatio Gates. A Rhode Islander, the thirty-eight-year-old Greene was then serving as quartermaster general of the Continental Army, despite his proven combat record as a troop commander at Trenton, Brandywine, Germantown, and Monmouth. Prior to Camden, Washington had needed Greene at the critical post of quartermaster general, but now nothing less than Georgia and the Carolinas was at stake. They were on the verge of being permanently occupied and cut off from the rest of the states, as Burgoyne had hoped to do to New England before his defeat at Saratoga. In the South, Washington required the presence of the general whom historians today rank second only to Washington himself.

Greene takes command

Greene reached Southern command on 27 November 1780, having stopped off in Philadelphia to request further funding for his troops, now reduced to 1,400 or so ill-supplied and demoralized men, many of them shoeless and near naked.

To counter a repetition of Valley Forge, Greene needed supplies and the bracing presence of at least some of the 6,000 French troops under the command of Lieutenant General Jean-Baptiste Donatien de Vimeur, comte de Rochambeau. (Only Washington held comparable three-star rank in the American army.) From July 1780 to July 1781, however, Rochambeau kept his men on bivouac in and around Newport, Rhode Island, following its evacuation by the British. For a year, the campus of the College of the Colony of Rhode Island and Providence Plantations (today Brown University) was transformed into a French military garrison as the French intervention went into remission. Not until July 1781 did Rochambeau—reluctant as he was to leave the French fleet while it was being blockaded in Narragansett Bay—feel it safe to join Washington's army encamped in Mount Kisco on the Hudson River, north of New York City.

As commander in the South, Nathanael Greene confronted a seemingly insurmountable challenge: regain as much of the South as possible with a small, battle-weary force of 1,400 facing three times that number of battle-tested British troops. Greene chose a tactic of divide and conquer, dividing his troops into two separate units and, while keeping them moving, forcing the British to divide their forces as well and give chase. At the same time, Greene mobilized even more separately functioning partisan (guerrilla) units under such able commanders as the legendary Swamp Fox, Francis Marion, plus Thomas Sumter, Andrew Pickens, and Elijah

Clarke. Thus, the British had six mobile American commands to face, not to mention the mobility of two cavalry units under the commands of Henry (Light-Horse Harry) Lee and William Washington.

Greene kept these units in constant motion through a tactic of ambush and retreat. He applied this stratagem to the two militia columns as well, augmented by whatever Continentals had survived the debacle at Camden. In short, Greene did not seek victory on the battlefield against the British. He employed, rather, maneuvers of march and countermarch, engagement, damage, and strategic withdrawal, moving from South into North Carolina, then back into South Carolina, then northward once more, keeping the British divided and off-balance. The first two battles of this campaign—the ferociously fought King's Mountain (6 October 1780) and Cowpens (17 January 1781)—were clear-cut victories: a cruel victory in the case of King's Mountain, with Patriot militiamen bayoneting fallen Loyalist militiamen lying on the field after the battle and hanging three Loyalist officers. The following battles, however—Guilford Courthouse (15 March 1781), Hobkirk's Hill (25 April), the siege of Ninety Six (22 May to 18 June), and Eutaw Springs (8 September)—ended inconclusively at best for the American forces. At least, no American army was destroyed while the British forces under Cornwallis were gradually driven back to the safety of the coast, and American forces increasingly controlled the interior.

Land and sea

The coast! The Chesapeake coast! This meant the offshore protection of the Royal Navy. The British strategy depended on coordinated sea-land, land-sea operations, and Lord Cornwallis had been trapped inland, forced to maneuver on multiple fronts into what had devolved into a retreat north into Virginia. Joining Benedict Arnold, now a brigadier general in the British army following his defection from the American cause, Cornwallis merged his three thousand men with Arnold's five thousand and with this combined force drove Lafayette's force of some three thousand—and very green—militia from Richmond before moving southeast through Williamsburg to the tip of the Yorktown Peninsula, where the York River flows into lower Chesapeake Bay, which in turn opens onto the Atlantic. There, at Yorktown, Cornwallis awaited the arrival of a Royal Navy squadron under the command of Admiral Thomas Graves. His Majesty George III's land forces were now bottled up in New York, Savannah, Charleston, and Yorktown. The Royal Navy had become more critical than ever.[1]

France dreams of a North American comeback

To understand French involvement in the American war of rebellion, it is necessary to go back nearly two decades. As minister of foreign affairs, Étienne François, duc de Choiseul, participated in negotiations with Great Britain leading to the Treaty of Paris (1763), which ended the Seven Years' War. It was a humiliating experience for Choiseul—a career army officer before being sponsored by the marquise de Pompadour, longtime mistress of Louis XV, to serve as French ambassador to Rome—to preside over the forfeiture of Quebec and Louisiana and the long-term curtailment of French ambitions in Europe and abroad in favor of a triumphant British empire. The situation was especially galling since, when previously serving as ambassador in Vienna, Choiseul had done so much to promote the Franco-Austrian alliance that had failed to bring victory. And so, as foreign minister Choiseul pursued the king's policies—the acquisition of Corsica, the expulsion of the Jesuits from France (joined in this regard by the other Bourbon power, Spain), the marriage of Marie Antoinette to the dauphin—he continued to brood over France's loss of its North American empire and diminished status in Europe.

The resistance of the English colonies of North America to the Stamp Act (1765) and the Townshend Acts (1767) captured Choiseul's attention, and he began to ask himself questions. How strong was the North American colonies' resistance to the mother country? Might the English colonies of North America break into open rebellion, thereby creating an opportunity for France to ally itself with such a rebellion and regain Quebec and Louisiana?

To that end, Choiseul retained the services of Johann von Robais de Kalb, a Bavarian-born (yet Huguenot) lieutenant colonel in the French army, winner of the coveted Order of Military Merit in 1763. Subsequently raised to the nobility with the title of baron, de Kalb was now married to a wealthy heiress (cloth manufacturing) and living comfortably in retirement. Choiseul asked the baron to travel to the American colonies under the guise of a retired German colonel traveling on business (de Kalb spoke French, German, and English) and ascertain the depth and extent of colonial resistance to the British. De Kalb at first demurred, but Choiseul persisted, and de Kalb, sensing an opportunity to return to active duty as a brigadier general following the successful completion of this mission, accepted it with some misgiving.

The twelfth of January 1768 found the baron in Philadelphia at the start of what would turn out to be four months of travel, conversation, and reconnaissance. On the first leg of his journey, from Philadelphia to New York, de Kalb's ferry, crossing from New Jersey past Staten Island, got caught in a violent squall. Crew and passengers were marooned on a tiny, treeless, shelterless island—little more than a sandbank—where two passengers succumbed to the freezing wind before rescue arrived the next day.

The dispatches that de Kalb sent Choiseul from Philadelphia, New York, Boston, Newport, and Edenton, North Carolina, throughout the remaining months of his mission teem with good reporting and prescience. Resistance to the Crown, de Kalb stated, would not have developed had the king merely observed the protocols employed when taxing the colonies during the Seven Years' War: to wit, requesting the tax from the colonial assemblies instead of directly imposing it. New England, moreover, presented a paradox. It was at once the center of resistance (as in the Boston Tea Party) and the most English of the colonies in terms of population and sentiment. Paradoxically, New Englanders' sense of themselves as English, and hence entitled to English rights, drove their resistance. Yet this sense of being English would prevent New Englanders from accepting assistance from France should an open rupture occur. "In fact," de Kalb commented, "they are so well convinced of the justice of their cause, the clemency of the King, and of their own importance to the mother country, they have never contemplated the possibility of extreme measures." Yet de Kalb also noted another paradox, this time regarding the colonies as a whole. "All people here", de Kalb observed, "are imbued with such a spirit of independence and even license, that if all the provinces can be united under a common representation, an independent state will certainly come forth in time."

As for Choiseul's pet project—the fomenting of resistance in Canada preparatory to a French effort to regain that lost province through a combination of revolution and intervention—de Kalb was skeptical. "There are at this day", de Kalb observed of French Canadians, "but few persons in those immense provinces in sympathy with France. Those most devoted to our government have left the country since the close of the war, and those who remain are satisfied with their present government, or expect no improvement in their condition from a change in rulers. Their lands have risen in value, they pay but trifling taxes, enjoy unqualified freedom of conscience, as well as all the privileges of the English people, and take part in the management of public affairs. Besides, they have become closely allied with the inhabitants of the neighboring provinces by intermarriages and other ties."

Choiseul needed to be aware of the French Canadian acceptance of British governance, de Kalb reported—rather courageously, given Choiseul's preference. "I regard it as my duty", de Kalb wrote, "to speak candidly on all these matters, because I will not deceive you, and do not wish to be deceived by others. In case of a war with our neighbors beyond the channel, it would be difficult, therefore, to make a diversion in this part of their possessions. I always recur to my belief that the quarrels of the English with their colonies will terminate to the satisfaction of the latter. A war with us would only hasten their reconciliation, and on the footing of restored privileges, the English court could eventually direct all the troops, resources and ships of this part of the world against our islands and the Spanish Main."[2]

Discovering that several of his letters had been opened in transit, thus compromising the secrecy of his mission, de Kalb cut short his visit and by 12 June 1768 was back in Paris, where Choiseul—ostensibly busy with the Corsican venture but also no doubt disappointed by the drift of de Kalb's reports—refused to receive and debrief the baron. De Kalb nonetheless submitted detailed reports to the foreign minister, who sent six thousand francs for expenses incurred on the mission. Choiseul kept his word regarding de Kalb's promotion and on 4 June 1770 placed the baron's name on a list of officers to be promoted to brigadier general. By the Christmas season, however, Choiseul was out of office, fired by the king for refusing to support the promotion of Madame du Barry, Louis XV's charming and popular new mistress (and introduced to the court as such), given her low origins and earlier profession. (She made him forget that he would soon be sixty, the previously depressed and gloomy king noted of his twenty-three-year-old consort.)

Despite Choiseul's rejection of an interview and subsequent fall from power, the baron's mission to America had not been a waste of time, nor were his final reports irrelevant. As of 1768, the Baron de Kalb had sorted out the dynamics—the obtuse intransigence of Parliament and the king, a taste for independence in the American character, as well as a drift toward nationhood—that in a few short years would surface. He was correct, moreover, regarding French Canadians' satisfaction with the status quo, made even more satisfactory in 1774 with the passage of the Quebec Act. De Kalb would eventually change his mind about the value of France's interposing itself once again into the American equation; indeed, past the age of sixty, the baron would introduce to American service the marquis de Lafayette and would himself achieve the generalship he so desired, wearing, like Lafayette, an American uniform.

A Franco-American alliance

Into this temporarily interrupted but still unfolding drama now enter two crucial players. Charles Gravier, comte de Vergennes, foreign minister of France after 1774, and polymath Benjamin Franklin, American envoy to France since 1776, were both masters of diplomatic policy and practitioners of realpolitik. A professional diplomat, Vergennes had spent the bulk of his career in foreign postings—Portugal, the Rhineland-Palatinate, Hanover, the Ottoman Empire, Sweden—before being named secretary of state for foreign affairs in June 1774 by the nineteen-year-old Louis XVI, grandson of the recently deceased Louis XV. Although on a less grand scale, Franklin served diplomatic stints in London, negotiating in 1757 and 1764 for Pennsylvania—where he served twelve years in the assembly, followed by an appointment as deputy postmaster general for the colonies—along with (in 1764) Georgia, New Jersey, and Massachusetts. Yet while Vergennes did one thing, diplomacy, very well, the achievements of the polymathic Franklin ranged across a diversity of fields—printing, journalism, institutional development, colonial administration, invention, scientific research, literature, education, diplomacy—and his writings and correspondence with fellow savants gained him an international reputation.

With thirty years of service in European postings, the comte de Vergennes did not harbor the same dreams of revenge and reconquest that motivated Choiseul, a career army officer before entering diplomacy. Vergennes, by contrast, saw the French-English rivalry in terms of the balance of power in continental Europe in the aftermath of the Seven Years' War. During the seventeenth century and in the first half of the eighteenth, France, under the Bourbons and the allied Bourbon monarchy of Spain, held the balance of power in Central and Western Europe. Under the Treaty of Paris, however, France lost its empire in North America, which Great Britain gained, while Austria, Prussia, Great Britain, Russia, and the Ottoman Empire emerged as coequal powers on the Continent. The recent (1772) partition of Poland by Russia, Prussia, and Austria—a partition that France did its best to oppose—provided Vergennes with a chilling case in point of a future in which these post–Treaty of Paris powers, in one combination or another, could almost at will redraw the map of Europe in their favor, leaving France a second-tier state.

Austria and Prussia held hegemony in German-speaking Europe. The Ottomans ruled the Balkans, much of Eastern Europe, the Greek peninsula, and North Africa. And the great landmass of Russia was an empire unto itself. France, by contrast, had only a handful of islands in the West Indies and mere footholds in Asia and Africa. Of all these powers, moreover, Great Britain was the most threatening because it was capable of waging commercial as well as military warfare against France and of ending France's waning spheres of influence on the Continent.

So, when the United Colonies began its revolt in 1775 and declared independence in 1776, Vergennes reopened a modified version of the Choiseul initiative. France had a stake in the outcome of this rebellion. If the Americans could carry it off, the British Empire would suffer a serious military and economic setback.

Vergennes dispatched to Philadelphia a secret envoy, Julien-Alexandre Achard de Bonvouloir, who arrived in December 1775 and informed a hastily convened secret nighttime meeting at Carpenters' Hall with three Committee of Correspondence members—Benjamin Franklin, John Jay, and Franklin's translator-librarian, Francis Daymon—that France would be willing to sell military supplies to the Americans.

A de facto American embassy was opened in Paris in July 1776, three days after Congress approved the Declaration of Independence, with the arrival of Silas Deane, a Yale-educated Continental Congressman from Connecticut empowered to seek French support and to negotiate on behalf of Congress. In December Deane was joined by Benjamin Franklin and Continental Congressman Arthur Lee, of the famed Virginia family, a British-trained physician and lawyer. Their assignment: purchase military supplies on behalf of Congress and seek a more ambitious alliance, bringing French military assistance. Franklin brought with him a Model Treaty written by John Adams, setting forth the nonnegotiable requirements of any future treaty with France. In keeping with American caution as well as suspicion of an alliance with a Roman Catholic power, the Model Treaty abounded in prohibitions. No political connections. No involvements in foreign wars. No French control of American military. No efforts by France to regain lost North American territory—in fact, a formal renunciation of such ambitions. (By contrast, France was free to regain lost West Indies territories by military action.) No agreements by either party to a separate peace without formal notification given six months in advance. And finally, no effort by the United States ever to use its participation in an Anglo-French war as a bargaining chip with England.

Rather rapidly, as such matters went in the eighteenth century, the young King Louis XVI—following heated debate in the Royal Council of State that pitted the pro-alliance Vergennes against the anti-alliance finance minister, Anne Robert Jacques Turgot—in May 1776 decided to make available on credit to the Americans a million livres of arms via the creation of Roderique Hortalez et Cie. This dummy company was to be organized and administered by the businessman and advocate of the American Revolution, celebrity playwright, and polymath Pierre-Augustin Caron de Beaumarchais, remembered today as the author of *Le Barbier de Séville* (1775) and *Le Mariage de Figaro* (1784) but at the time a leader in avant-garde Enlightenment circles. (Among Beaumarchais' many ventures was the publication of a seventy-volume edition of Voltaire.) Thanks to the immediate and extensive popularity of Benjamin Franklin among the French, moreover, this line of credit and arms shipments by Beaumarchais' fictive company continued through the next two years as Franklin employed his renown and negotiating skills to achieve an even more binding alliance.

The Franklin phenomenon

Setting himself up in a comfortable home in Passy, a village on the outskirts of Paris, Franklin received and entertained on behalf of his mission and moved easily in court and ministerial circles. The French considered Franklin a new kind of savant: unpretentiously New World in his fur hat worn over a wigless balding pate, unfashionable rimless glasses, a plain broadcloth coat; a play of wisdom and innocence darting across a grandfatherly mien; pithy wisdom and good humor; a love of company, conversation, and the good life. A lifelong admirer of the opposite sex, Franklin—despite his age, his gout, and his cane—enjoyed playing the charmer when in the company of attractive women. The leading women of France, in turn, adored Franklin's company and felt it a privilege to fuss over the celebrity savant (*mon cher papa* to the younger set) on social occasions.

Franklin was a friend of Charles Carroll and his cousin John Carroll the priest, Franklin's roommate and youthful escort on their recent mission to Canada, a savant who enjoyed social connections with many prominent Irish Catholics of Philadelphia. Though a deist, Franklin had by now overcome an earlier tendency toward anti-Catholicism and (if only from enlightened self-interest) had tried to understand the established nature of Catholicism in France and to appreciate the pan-European diplomatic network centered in Rome. The United States' reputation for anti-Catholicism, Franklin had learned in Quebec, stood in the way of any Franco-American détente. It was time to put such self-destructive biases aside. Franklin cultivated connections with the French hierarchy and corresponded with curial cardinals, who were already assembling a file dealing with the American Revolution and were now opening one on Franklin.

Of the three Americans representing the United States in Paris as of January 1777, Benjamin Franklin stood in a class by himself and maintained a semi-independent center of influence. The Virginian Arthur Lee was socially connected and highly educated (Eton, an M.D. from Edinburgh, followed by legal studies in London). Lee's social network enabled him to move easily in the same circles as Beaumarchais and to assist in the creation of the cover company Hortalez et Cie. As a diplomat, however, the irascible, impulsive, opinionated Lee proved a liability to Deane and Franklin, with whom he quarreled constantly. Worse, Lee acted independently, to the detriment of the mission. Silas Deane had a habit of lining his pockets by misreporting French funds or other means of leverage, for which Lee denounced Deane to Congress in separate reports, forcing Deane's eventual recall to Philadelphia to explain himself. Even more troublesome, Deane had in his employ Edward Bancroft, a secret British agent who was funneling information to London. Also, through Bancroft, Deane entered into correspondence with another British agent, contact that might legitimately be considered treasonable.

But all this, as of 1777, was a matter either of future action or of present actions not yet come to light. In the first months of the American mission, Deane (and Franklin, to a lesser degree) entered the eighteenth-century free market of military recruitment and sent nearly a hundred French officers to the United States—junior officers in the main, yet a colonel or lieutenant colonel or two as well—recommending them for commissions in the Continental Army. The goal of these officers was future promotion in the French army through American service at a time when the war ministry of France, downsizing its forces, was forcibly retiring officers or leaving those who survived dead-ended in their present rank.

The Lafayette phenomenon

The nineteen-year-old Gilbert du Motier, marquis de Lafayette, was one such officer whose military career had been brought to a halt. This stoppage constituted a shock to the young captain of dragoons, whose military career up until that point had—despite the young marquis' lack of combat experience—seemed assured, given his birth, wealth, and social connections. One of Lafayette's ancestors had commanded Joan of Arc's army. Another had recently served as commander of the king's musketeers. Lafayette's father, a colonel of grenadiers, died on the field of battle a month before Lafayette's birth, cut down by cannon fire while fighting against a British-led force at the Battle of Westphalia during the Seven Years' War. Commissioned a sous-lieutenant of musketeers when barely into his teens, Lafayette continued his education at the Collège du Plessis of the University of Paris and the Académie de Versailles, where he also enrolled in the famed riding academy of that all-powerful royal court palace suburb. His personal wealth, meanwhile, was yielding an income of 120,000 livres a year and was increased even further through an arranged marriage to Marie Adrienne Françoise, daughter of Jean-Louis-Paul-François de Noailles, duc d'Ayen, to whose Noailles Dragoons Lafayette transferred his commission in 1773 and in which he was promoted to captain in 1775.

At this point, the marquis de Lafayette fits all too easily into an all-too-common collective profile of young (and not so young) officers of his background and wealth during the final years of ancien régime France: a noble promoted because of class and social connections, a creature of court rather than regiment, a carouser and womanizer, spoiled, impulsive, and not overly bright or battle-tested. Much to the distress of his father-in-law, the duc d'Ayen, Lafayette was guilty of much of this, to which should be added a lax (if not lapsed) relationship to the Catholic tradition and practices of his ancestors.

Yet other forces were at work as well in this young man. The death of his father at the hands of the British, for one thing: a residual influence, true, but as powerful in its way as was his widowed mother's tendency to raise her fatherless son as a child of destiny who would one day distinguish himself. Promoted beyond his ability to a captaincy, Lafayette made every effort to gamble, drink, and wench according to the rakehell norms of his contemporaries. He became a peripheral member of the circle of Bright Young People surrounding Queen Marie Antoinette at court, drawn into *les liaisons dangereuses* labyrinth of sexual intrigue evident in his public but failed seduction of Aglaé, comtesse d'Hunolstein—losing out in this regard to the duc de Chartres, a relative of the king, and thereby making a fool of himself in the eyes of his ducal father-in-law.

Despite such gaucheries and mistakes of youth, the marquis de Lafayette did realize that his life as a back-bench courtier at Versailles, a young man no one took seriously, was heading in the wrong direction. He became a Freemason, which exposed him to such Enlightenment ideals as reason and a reason-based effort to expand the perimeters of personal liberty and improve society along more rational lines. Versailles became a distraction, a dead end for chances at a serious military career. When Lafayette's ever-hopeful father-in-law arranged an appointment as a lord-in-waiting to Monsieur, comte de Provence, the king's younger brother, the young captain deliberately sabotaged the appointment by being rude—twice!—to Monsieur and happily rejoined his regiment at Metz. The garrison town of his regiment on the Moselle River, in northeastern France, Metz now emerged as the site of Lafayette's half-perceived but fully desired destiny.

A revelation

The military commander at Metz at the time was Charles-François, comte de Broglie, a fifty-six-year-old professional soldier promoted to lieutenant general in 1760

and a leading member of the Secret du Roi, Louis XV's private undercover diplomatic service. On 8 August 1775 the well-connected de Broglie hosted a dinner
at Metz for the Duke of Gloucester, brother of King George III, then en route to
Italy. At the dinner, the marquis de Lafayette listened attentively as the duke, no
friend of his brother, defended the resistance of the English colonies in North
America against the ill-advised policies of Parliament and the king. The outspoken
defense of the American rebellion made a deep impression on Captain Gilbert
du Motier, marquis de Lafayette, now in the process of trying to reorient his life.
America! Here was a cause to support: a defense of liberty commensurate with the
effort he was currently making to pursue a military career animated by Masonic and
Enlightenment ideals.

The host of the dinner, the comte de Broglie, was also listening closely to his
royal Highness the Duke of Gloucester's remarks; in the general's mind, they reinforced the probity and probable success of the effort he was making in the company
of the playwright-entrepreneur Pierre Beaumarchais and the retired lieutenant colonel Johann de Kalb to secure aid for the American insurgency. What de Kalb had
informed the foreign minister Choiseul in 1768 would never happen, an American
rebellion, was now happening—indeed, it had even gained the support of King
George III's brother. As this scenario unfolded, the comte de Broglie speculated,
France would intervene, and a French general (meaning himself) would be placed
in overall command of the war effort. Following victory—who knows?—an American crown might be in the offing. On his part, de Kalb saw a general's commission
in the American forces as well as an opportunity to reclaim that promotion to brigadier in the French army once offered him by Choiseul but never given.

On 11 June 1776, the marquis de Lafayette found himself and a number of other
courtier officers placed on the inactive list by the new minister of war, Claude-
Louis, comte de Saint-Germain, who was eager to introduce Prussian discipline in
the French army by ridding it of officers, however noble in origin, whose services
were not needed. Even worse: Lafayette's influential father-in-law had done little
if anything about the listing. The nineteen-year-old Captain Gilbert du Motier,
marquis de Lafayette, was now yet another French officer in search of employment.

Negotiating commissions

As aide to Lieutenant General the comte de Broglie, Baron Johann de Kalb organized the application process being orchestrated out of Silas Deane's office for congressional commissions in the American army for a dozen or more French officers
associated with the comte's American ambitions. On this list, Lafayette represented,
literally, the marquee candidate in terms of noble rank and personal wealth. Initially, Lafayette's brother-in-law Louis-Marie, vicomte de Noailles, wished to go
to America as well; but their mutual father-in-law, the duc d'Ayen, forbade them
both. Lafayette, however, informed de Broglie that he had his father-in-law's
approval. Furthermore, de Kalb and Lafayette failed to notify Deane of this prohibition as de Kalb negotiated a contract: the appointment of each of them as major
general in the American army, no charges for transportation to the United States,
and no salary required for their volunteer services. Deane and the French officers
were in violation of French law, moreover, for following the arrival in France of

news of American forces' defeat at the Battle of Long Island in August 1776, the French government had forbidden further volunteering of French officers to the United States.

As the negotiations were being pursued, Lafayette kept his plans secret from his wife. Having been confronted by the prince de Montbarrey of the war ministry, who had learned of Lafayette's intentions, the marquis planned and executed a deceptive maneuver: a pleasure trip in the company of another young in-law, Philippe-Louis-Marc-Antoine de Noailles, prince de Poix, to London, where another member of the Noailles family was serving as French ambassador. Lafayette had already promised the prince de Montbarrey that he would abandon his plans to go to America. Montbarrey's knowledge had most likely come from the French secret police. There was no better way for Lafayette to conceal his intentions than to visit London; and thanks to his Noailles connections, be personally presented (along with the prince de Poix) to King George III; attend a dinner dance given by Lord George Germain, minister for the American colonies, where Lafayette sat next to General Lord Francis Rawdon, a first-rate field commander freshly returned from the English victories in New York; and be introduced at the opera to General Sir Henry Clinton, whom Lafayette would one day face at the Battle of Monmouth Courthouse.

Thus, a petted, spoiled, conniving nineteen-year-old wanting to be something more was, thanks to his wealth and social status, able to beard the British Lion itself in its London den and thereby deceive his family, the war ministry, and the secret police as to his intentions, while he turned down an offer to tour the Royal Navy docks at Plymouth because it felt too much like spying. Yet even after he had returned to France and secretly purchased with his own funds the ship *La Victoire* and had sailed from Bordeaux with his companions for the New World, Lafayette read letters from his wife imploring him not to leave her and their two daughters and go to America but to return home. Lafayette decided to comply and abruptly ordered *La Victoire* back to Bordeaux.

At this point, Lafayette came close to abandoning the entire American enterprise. A chain of contingencies, though, worthy of a novel by Alexandre Dumas—including encouragement from General de Broglie to carry on the American mission, brought to him by de Broglie's hard-riding chief aide as Lafayette was en route to Paris—turned Lafayette back to his original purpose. Reversing direction, Lafayette rejoined *La Victoire* as it lay at anchor at Los Pasajes near San Sebastián on the Bay of Biscay, having sailed from Bordeaux just ahead of the arrival of an order from the king himself forbidding the ship's departure. Lafayette and his companions thereupon embarked upon a voyage of fifty-four days: the vanguard, they believed, of a triumphant return by France to the North American empire.

A rude awakening

Having sailed into Georgetown Bay, South Carolina, on 13 June 1777, the French officers arrived in Philadelphia on Sunday, 27 July. The eleven men were in for a jolt. Walking as a group to the house of John Hancock, president of the Continental Congress, with military credentials and letters of introduction from Silas Deane in hand, they were coldly received and told to report on Monday to Robert Morris, the rebellion's financial expert and a member of Congress. The next morning, the officers were kept waiting on the street outside Independence Hall until, finally, Morris emerged along with Congressman James Lowell of Massachusetts. Briefly introducing Lowell, Morris reentered Independence Hall. Lowell addressed the French officers in excellent French. Sorry, gentlemen, no new French officers were required, Lowell informed the shocked officers. Silas Deane had no authority to sign employment contracts or offer commissions in the American army. Turning as abruptly as Morris had, Lowell went into Independence Hall.

What Lafayette, de Kalb, and the others did not realize at the time was two-fold. Word of the comte de Broglie's ambition to assume command in America had reached Congress through French officers already in American service. Furthermore, complaints had been growing among American officers that too many French officers of dubious ability were being promoted over their heads. Just how knowledgeable about or committed to de Broglie's intentions Lafayette was remains a matter of conjecture. De Kalb, not Lafayette, had been the driving force behind recruitment. And yet it strains credulity to believe that de Kalb and the others had kept Lafayette in the dark regarding the comte de Broglie's long-term plans for a Franco-American alliance, an eventual appointment to overall command, and a victory over Great Britain, followed by proconsular (even royal) governance of an independent American nation.

Whatever his degree of complicity, however, Lafayette, once rejected, acted independently and effectively by having his credentials and letters of introduction personally distributed to key members of Congress. A marquis? these gentlemen now learned. A marquis, moreover, of immense wealth who had already retained Robert Morris as his private banker? Here was a French celebrity too important to be kept waiting on the street and to have his desire to serve the Revolution as an unpaid volunteer so rudely dismissed! Thus, Congressmen James Lowell and William Duer were personally apologizing to Lafayette by Tuesday. It had all been a mistake!

Sensing his advantage, Lafayette suggested a compromise: either an appointment as major general or the payment of his travel expenses back to France. Lowell and Duer returned to Congress and later that day came back with an offer: a commission as the most junior major general on the major generals' list, but more in the nature of an honorary appointment, with no promise of a command. Confident that he could maneuver his way to a command, Lafayette accepted. By 31 July 1777, four days after his arrival in Philadelphia, three days after being rebuffed by John Hancock, two days after being dismissed on the street before Independence Hall by Morris and Lowell, Gilbert du Motier, marquis de Lafayette, was commissioned major general by Act of Congress, taken to General Washington's headquarters, and invited by Washington to join his staff and take up residence at headquarters as a member of his military family.

Washington and Lafayette

For Washington, the pragmatic and the personal were converging. The siege of Boston had ended well, yet the invasion of Canada had been a disaster. Driven from Long Island and Manhattan, Washington had kept his army alive through

September 10, 2020

Kathryn Jean Lopez
National Review Online
19 West 44th Street, Suite 1701
New York, NY 10036

Dear Kathryn Jean,

There are few accomplished historians and writers in the Catholic space as the late Kevin Starr. With degrees from the University of San Francisco, Harvard University and UC Berkeley as well as multiple awards, Starr leaves a rich legacy of knowledge to generations left behind in the closed copy of his new book, ***CONTINENTAL ACHIEVEMENT: ROMAN CATHOLICS IN THE UNITED STATES – REVOLUTION AND THE EARLY REPUBLIC.***

Starr's widow, Sheila Starr, writes in a note to readers how happy and absorbed Kevin was when researching and writing this book. Starr passed away in 2017 after having nearly completed his work and Sheila tells readers that *"**CONTINENTAL ACHIEVEMENT** remains his offering to the Church that raised him and sustained him throughout his life."*

FOR IMMEDIATE RELEASE

For More Information:
Kevin Wandra, 404-788-1276 or
KWandra@CarmelCommunications.com

What roles did Catholics play in America's early history?

New book gives interesting historical account of Catholic influence on our country's founding

SAN FRANCISCO, Sept. 15, 2020 – Marrying the study of America's early history and founding with the influence of Catholics in the same time period is at the heart of the new book by the late Kevin Starr, *CONTINENTAL ACHIEVEMENT: ROMAN CATHOLICS IN THE UNITED STATES – REVOLUTION AND THE EARLY REPUBLIC.*

Starr received a B.A. from the University of San Francisco, an M.A. and a Ph.D. from Harvard University, and a Master of Library Science from U.C. Berkeley. He served as the City Librarian of San Francisco and the State Librarian of California. Starr also was a university professor and a professor of history at the University of Southern California. Starr passed away at age 76 on January

CONTINENTAL ACHIEVEMENT follows Starr's *Continental Ambitions: Roman Catholics in North America*, and focuses on the participation of Catholics, alongside their Protestant and Jewish fellow citizens, in the Revolutionary War and the creation and development of the Republic.

With his characteristic honesty and rigorous research, Starr gives readers an enduring history of Catholics in the early years of the United States. John Carroll makes frequent appearances in roles of increasing importance: missionary, constitution writer for his ex-Jesuit colleagues, prefect apostolic, controversialist and defender of the faith, bishop, founder of Georgetown, Cathedral developer, archbishop and metropolitan, and negotiator with the Court of Rome. In him, the Maryland ethos regarding Roman Catholicism reached a point of penultimate fulfillment.

"Kevin Starr's ***CONTINENTAL ACHIEVEMENT*** is itself a glorious achievement," said John T. McGreevy, Francis A. McAnaney Professor of History, University of Notre Dame. "Starr's narrative turns the early years of Catholicism in the United States into a riveting story of rivalry, piety and ambition. It is a superb introduction to how a global religion made itself in a deeply Protestant republic. It will also stand as an appropriate valedictory for one of our era's most gifted historians."

For more information, to request a review copy or to schedule an interview Sheila Starr, the widow of Kevin Starr, please contact Kevin Wandra (404-788-1276 or KWandra@CarmelCommunications.com) of Carmel Communications.

###

John Carroll, the founder of Georgetown, is prominently featured in the book, as is Charles Carroll, the only Catholic signer of the Declaration of Independence and who just had terrible luck with women he loved.

The book is divided into two parts: Revolution and Diocesan Formation in the Republic. *CONTINENTAL ACHIEVEMENT* covers the years 1775 through 1821 and takes readers through the Continental Congress, the Revolutionary War, and key moments in the spread of Catholicism in Baltimore in the early 1800s.

"Kevin Starr's final work displays the magnificent abilities that marked his entire career," said Robert M. Senkewicz, Professor Emeritus of History at Santa Clara University. "This deeply researched and eminently readable volume demonstrates how an unlikely group of former Jesuits, French Sulpicians and an indomitable woman laid the foundations for American Catholicism. Starr shows how the American Church, equally distrusted by American Protestants and Vatican officials, managed to demonstrate that Catholicism and republicanism could enrich each other."

We will be in touch soon to answer any questions. We are happy to coordinate interviews with Sheila Starr, and will assist in your coverage in any way we can.

Respectfully,

Kevin Wandra

a long war of posts (some were saying a disguised retreat) southward down New Jersey. Victories at Trenton and Princeton signified a recovery, but these wins were followed by defeats at Brandywine and Germantown, and British general John Burgoyne was advancing south through upstate New York with a force of 5,700, seeking to link up with General Howe's forces, advancing north from New York City. Already, on 5 July 1777, facing Burgoyne's artillery atop nearby Sugar Loaf Hill, American general Arthur St. Clair had abandoned Fort Ticonderoga without firing a shot. A number of congressmen were beginning to listen to Washington's critics—such as the outspoken brigadier general Thomas Conway, an Irish-born French army professional now in American service—and, privately at least, were thinking the unthinkable: replacing His Excellency the commander in chief with a more experienced professional. Washington knew this, and following the victory of former British officer Horatio Gates over Burgoyne at Saratoga and the surrender on 17 October 1777 by Burgoyne of his entire force, he would be even more aware of the Conway Cabal.

Thus, the presence on his staff of a wealthy French marquis would not only please Congress but would also suggest continued French financial support of the Revolution and perhaps even the possibility of an open, articulated Franco-American alliance that would bring to the American war effort even more substantial support by land and sea.

Between Washington and Lafayette, moreover, there almost immediately developed a personal relationship that—while sometimes challenged by Lafayette's impulsiveness and requests for high command—touched depths in each man's psychology. For the twenty-year-old Lafayette, the forty-five-year-old Washington—tall, commanding, majestic in mien and demeanor, respected by his troops—constituted the reprise of the father who had died on the field of battle before Lafayette was born. Soon, in the style of gentlemanly discourse in the eighteenth century, Lafayette would directly and unabashedly profess in letters (Lafayette was a compulsive letter writer) his love and adoration for this all-powerful father figure and man of destiny.

Washington returned Lafayette's affection, albeit in more restrained terms. The Frenchman's nobility, wealth, and aristocratic connections spoke to Washington's lifelong desire as a Virginian to transcend the merely provincial. Washington respected rank and what Edmund Burke would soon be calling "the unbought grace of life" that Lafayette embodied. Washington was delighted when the young major general proved to be fearless on the battlefield on 11 September 1777 during the Battle of Brandywine, rallying under heavy fire the men of the Third Pennsylvania Brigade (commanded, no less, by Brigadier General Thomas Conway) in the face of an overwhelming British and Hessian attack and being shot and seriously wounded in the lower leg in the process. Had Lafayette remained merely an honorary major general, he would have perhaps proven useful to Washington, but after Brandywine and Valley Forge, Washington gradually advanced the young marquis into increased responsibilities of combat command, although he never placed him on the same level as, say, Nathanael Greene, nor did he give the persistently requesting Lafayette what he most wanted, command of a reinvasion of Canada.

Yet, having witnessed Lafayette's bravery, the sonless Washington could now release fatherly feelings of affection and approval toward the fatherless Lafayette. As a boy of eleven, Washington had lost his own father, and between Washington and his mother there had always been (and continued to be) a mutual reserve edging into an open rift. Washington's beloved older half brother, the English-educated Lawrence, had served Washington as a second father, and so Washington knew and revered this role of father surrogate and easily assumed it toward Lafayette. Returning to France as a celebrity hero in February 1779 to lobby successfully for French troops to be sent to the United States, Lafayette was reunited with his wife, Adrienne, and in December the couple named their newborn son Georges Washington Lafayette.

The bonds of Freemasonry

The Masonic bond fed the relationship between Washington and Lafayette. Freemasonry had introduced the college-deprived but ambitiously reading Washington into wider vistas of thought when he was a young surveyor and planter. Freemasonry helped put a measure of serious thought and ambition into the previously distracted brain of Lafayette. Baptized and confirmed a Catholic and married in a Catholic ceremony, the marquis de Lafayette otherwise neglected the practice of his faith until he confessed and received the last sacraments on his deathbed.

France was a Catholic nation, even more so after 1685, when Louis XIV, persuaded by Catholic zealots, revoked the Edict of Nantes (1598) through which Henri IV established the rights and privileges of the Huguenot (Protestant) population. The revocation of the edict drove one million or so Huguenots from France, some to the English colonies of North America. Yet no sooner had the Huguenots been expelled in the name of a purified Catholicism than the European Enlightenment took hold among French intellectuals and was advanced as a body of thought by such philosophers as Rousseau, Voltaire, and Montesquieu. So, too, did Freemasonry enter upper-class European Catholic life, lay and clerical, as part of the Enlightenment legacy.

From the eighteenth-century perspective, Freemasonry did not formally stand in contradiction to Catholic belief or values. It represented, rather, an accommodation by elites to Enlightenment thought as well as a mode of service to the betterment of society. Thus, Mozart could in good faith belong to the Masonic lodge of Vienna (along with the archbishop of that city) without forsaking his Catholic heritage and the Catholicity of his genius. In the nineteenth century, this détente between Catholicism and Freemasonry broke down, but for the time being, Enlightenment Catholicism and Freemasonry remained in a state of truce.

The American Revolution embodied Enlightenment and Masonic ideals that French Catholics did not find alien or threatening. Indeed, in 1781 the nuns of a convent in Nantes—at the request of two patrons of the convent who were Masons—prepared a Masonic apron for Washington cut from excellent cloth and embroidered with entwined French and American flags. "May the Grand Architect of the universe be the Guardian of your precious days for the glory of the Western Hemisphere and the entire universe", stated the letter of transmittal. To which George Washington, a practicing Episcopalian, replied on 10 August 1782: "If my endeavors to avert the evil with which the country was threatened, by a deliberate plan of tyranny, should be crowned with the success that is wished, the praise is due the GRAND ARCHITECT of the universe Who did not see fit to suffer

His superstructure of justice to be subjected to the ambition of the Princes of this world, or to the rod of oppression in the hands of any power upon earth."[3]

Given the American Revolution as, in part, a fight for such Enlightenment and Masonic ideals as liberty and the rights of men and the iconic reputation that Washington personally enjoyed in Masonic circles, and given as well the acceptability of Masonic membership and practice in advanced European Catholic circles, it is not surprising that so many European Catholics who volunteered to travel to North America and serve in the Revolution had strong Masonic affiliations (the marquis de Lafayette comes immediately to mind) or were highly influenced by Enlightenment and Masonic values (Thaddeus Kościuszko, the marquis de Lafayette, and Casimir Pulaski, for example), while remaining culturally Catholic.

Franco-American alliance

On 4 May 1778, the Continental Congress ratified the two treaties with France—a treaty of friendship and commerce and one of military alliance—that Franklin, Deane, and Lee had successfully negotiated the previous February. Initially in these negotiations, the foreign minister Vergennes, waiting to see how the war was going in North America, practiced a strategy of delay, but two developments—the American victory at Saratoga and the fact that Franklin and Deane were meeting with peace commissioners from London—prompted Vergennes and the king to finalize the agreement. The treaty of military alliance passed by Congress on 4 May reprised the Model Treaty drafted by John Adams, approved by Congress on 17 September 1776, and brought to Paris late that year by Benjamin Franklin.

Article 1 of the Treaty of Alliance promised a joint effort between France and the United States should a war between France and Great Britain break out (which happened within a matter of weeks). Article 2 guaranteed the liberty, sovereignty, and independence of the United States. Articles 3 and 4 dealt with wartime arrangements. Articles 5, 6, and 7 handled territorial arrangements, freeing France to expand its possessions in the West Indies and allowing wiggle room for a reentrance into North America via Newfoundland fishing rights. The highly important Article 8 declared that neither party could lay down its arms until American independence was fully assured by treaty. Articles 9 through 13 (13 explicitly stated that the official language of the treaty was French) dealt with the diplomacy deadlines as well as other technical and administrative matters relating to the ongoing relationship. Nothing in either treaty, however, made reference to the eight-hundred-pound gorilla in the room. With laws banning or otherwise seriously circumscribing the practice of Roman Catholicism on the books of nearly all states; indeed, with its very Revolution taking some of its earliest energies from violent opposition to the pro-Catholic provisions of the Quebec Act, anti-Catholic America was now the ally of France and would soon be the ally of Spain, the two most powerful Catholic powers in Europe.

Loyalist fears amplified

Loyalists made much of this Franco-Spanish-American alliance in their objections to the Revolution. The Loyalist *Pennsylvania Ledger* asked on 13 May 1776,

Is it possible we can *now* wish for a final separation from Britain, the ancient and chief support of the Protestant religion in the world, for the sake of upholding a little longer, at the expense of our own lives and fortunes, the arbitrary power of that Congress, who without even asking our consent, have disposed of us, have mortgaged us like vassals and slaves, by refusing to treat with Britain and by entering into a treaty with that ambitious and treacherous power whose religious and political maxims have so often disturbed the peace and invaded the rights of mankind? The Congress have wonderfully altered their tone of late. The time was when the bare toleration of the articles of capitulation, was treated as a wicked attempt to establish "a sanguinary faith, which had for ages filled the world with blood and slaughter." But now the Congress are willing to make us the instruments of weakening the best friends, and of strengthening the most powerful and ambitious enemies of the Reformation to such a degree as must do more than all the world besides could do, towards the universal re-establishment of Popery through all Christendom. Judge then what we have to hope or expect from such an alliance! We not only run a manifest risk of becoming slaves ourselves, under the treacherous title of independency but we are doing everything in our power to overturn the Protestant religion, and extinguish every spark, both of civil and religious liberty in the world![4]

In August 1778 rumors swept the Loyalist community that French admiral Charles-Hector, comte d'Estaing, had transported to the United States a papal nuncio and a representative of Prince Charles Edward Stuart, "the Pretender" (then living in Rome), for secret negotiations with Congress, bringing with them "offers of Assistance Offensive and Defensive", as wrote a correspondent to the Loyalist *New York Gazette* for 8 August 1778. "On this being declared", continued the letter, "numbers cried out that they now only waited one from the Prince of Darkness to make the Alliance complete. Congress in order to appease the People gave out that they did not expect these gentry, and that an Alliance of this Nature has not been sought after. But I am well informed by a Gentleman who has had a sight of the Treaties formed with the French King that he guarantees the Assistance of these two Powers; the other follows of course. O poor Britain, you have now to fight against the French King, the Pope, Pretender and Congress."[5] Later that month, on 29 August, Johann Heinricks, a captain in the Hessian Jager Corps, conveyed the same rumor in a letter to his brother-in-law, with the added news that Catholic chapels were being designed in Philadelphia and Boston for the recent arrivals.[6] On 16 January 1779, the *Royal Gazette* magazine of New York reported that the Loyal Ladies of New York were in the process of equipping a privateer called the *Fair American* "for the very laudable purpose of cruising against the detested Rebel Corsairs and their new Popish Allies, the perfidious French".[7]

Once war broke out, wherever opportunity arose, the English returned to this theme of France and Spain as Catholic aggressors. In advising William Eden, for example, one of the peace commissioners sent to America in 1778, the Earl of Carlisle wrote to him on 20 September 1778 that a possible line of argument might very well be the opportunity the French alliance "will give to the introduction of the Popish religion".[8]

Then there was the question of France's return to North American empire—a possibility not fully laid to rest in the articles of the two treaties approved by Congress on 4 May 1778. Prior to that signing, on 28 March, the admiral the comte d'Estaing printed for distribution aboard the French ship *Le Languedoc*, then anchored in the port of Boston, a lengthy appeal he had personally composed in the name of King Louis XVI to the Ancient French in North America. D'Estaing's letter was an extended plea for French Canadians to rise and support the American Revolution now that France had entered the war as an ally of the United States. "Can the Canadians who saw the brave Montcalm fall in their defense," d'Estaing asked the laymen of French Canada on behalf of the king, "can they become the enemies of his nephews? Can they fight against their former leaders, and arm themselves against their kinsmen? At the bare mention of their names the weapons would fall out of their hands." And as far as the Catholic clergy of Canada were concerned, they were even more crucial to the uprising d'Estaing was calling for. "I shall not observe to the ministers of the altar", the comte addressed the clergy, promising them a return to their former status among the people, "that their evangelic efforts will require the special protection of Providence to prevent faith being diminished by example, by worldly interest, and by sovereigns whom force has imposed upon them, and whose political indulgence will be lessened proportionably as those sovereigns shall have less to fear. I shall not observe, that it is necessary for religion that those who preach it should form a body in the state, and that in Canada no other body would be more considered, or have more power to do good than that of the priests, taking a part in the government; since their respective conduct has merited the confidence of the people." If any French Canadians questioned to what d'Estaing was alluding, the comte concluded with an indirect but urgent summons to action. "I shall not urge to a whole people", he concluded coyly, "that to join with the United States is to secure their own happiness, since a whole people, when they acquire the right of thinking and acting for themselves, must know their own interest: But I will declare, and I now formally order in the name of His Majesty, who has authorized and commanded me to do it, that all his former subjects in North America, who shall no more acknowledge the supremacy of Great Britain, may depend upon his protection and support."[9]

Translated into English, d'Estaing's expression of renewed continental ambition on the part of France appeared in the *Massachusetts Spy* of Worcester on 10 December 1778 and played into the prejudices and fears of American Protestants, Loyalists and Patriots alike. Even George Washington, so fair to and supportive of Catholics in his dealings, was at the time discounting (if not actively resisting) calls for a second invasion of Canada, led by no less than the marquis de Lafayette, on the basis of his fears that the French, once they regained French Canada, would hold on to it until the United States paid off its war debt.

When the French army and navy sojourned in and off Newport, Rhode Island, throughout 1780, the Loyalist *Royal Gazette* of New York reported on 2 August 1780, they took possession of the city in the name of King Louis XVI. Rochambeau, moreover, flew only the French flag. Earlier that year, the *Royal Gazette* ran a futuristic scenario of the Roman Catholicization ("shackles of Popish superstition") of the United States that could develop as a result of the French connection. By November 1789, the *Royal Gazette* predicted, a decade into the future, Dominican and Franciscan friars have converted the majority of Americans to Catholicism. In Boston, the Old South Meeting House has been refashioned as a Roman Catholic cathedral, the prediction went on, and rebel leader Samuel Adams has read a public recantation of his former heresies, has attended Mass, and is reported to be willing to be ordained a Catholic priest and be appointed to the American Sorbonne. On 16 November 1789, a cargo of rosaries, Mass books, and indulgences will arrive in Philadelphia on the *Saint-Esprit* out of Bordeaux. A Te Deum will be sung in Philadelphia celebrating the victory of France over the Dutch in Flanders. ("It is hoped that the Protestant heresy will soon be extirpated in all parts of Europe.") The Philadelphia Inquisition, meanwhile, is planning a grand auto-da-fé for Wednesday next: burning to death an old man, age ninety, "convicted of Quakerism and of reading the Bible, a copy of which in the English Language was found in his possession". The king of France, finally, has directed his viceroy for North America to gather together and send over "500 sons of the principal inhabitants of America, to be educated in France, where the utmost care will be taken to imbue them with a great regard for the Catholic faith and a due sense of subordination to Government".[10]

Native American loyalties

While many Native Americans took the British side during the Revolutionary War, or sought to remain uninvolved in the struggle, some groups, such as the Six Nations of the Iroquois, were divided in their loyalties. Led by the Mohawk Chief Thayendanegea (English name Joseph Brant), the Mohawk, Cayuga, Onondaga, and Seneca fought for the British. Then in his early thirties, Joseph Brant was a graduate of Dartmouth (opened as a school for Indians in 1755 in Connecticut and later moved to New Hampshire) and the brother-in-law of the late Sir William Johnson, who paid for his education. Brant was also a devout Anglican and an honorary colonel in the British forces and, as such, epitomized the possibilities of that Anglo-Indian détente to which Sir William had devoted his remarkable career. When the Revolution broke out, Brant was brought to England by the Lord North administration and—handsome, educated, well-mannered, bicultural in demeanor and dress, as the great portrait by Gilbert Stuart would later attest—took London by storm. He toured the city in the company of James Boswell, among others, and promised Iroquois support against the United Colonies in exchange for the guarantee of a Six Nations homeland on the Canada–New York border following the successful conclusion of hostilities.

Not all Iroquois, however, agreed with Brant's plan. The Oneida and the Tuscarora, for example, Catholic Iroquois evangelized by the French, tended to favor the United Colonies/United States, as did the Eastern Tribes—specifically, the Saint John's, Mi'kmaq, Penobscot, Stockbridge, and Passamaquoddy—Catholic Indians of Maine and Nova Scotia, also evangelized by the French (in the case of the Mi'kmaq, nearly 150 years earlier). Indeed, a chief of the Saint John's tribe came into George Washington's headquarters in Cambridge in mid-August 1775 to promise military assistance. Interviewed at Washington's request by selected representatives from the Massachusetts House of Representatives as to why the Saint John's people wished to come to the assistance of the Americans, the chief replied, "As our ancestors gave this country to you, we would not have you destroyed by England, but are ready to afford you our assistance."[11] Altogether, the chief told the legislators, the pro-American tribes had some two thousand men in their ranks capable of bearing arms.

For various reasons, such an impressive force of Eastern Indians never materialized for the invasion of Canada, although a number of Eastern Indians did join the campaign. The majority of Mi'kmaq remained neutral throughout the conflict. Yet on 2 December 1775—with the invasion of Canada underway—the Continental Congress voted for a resolution stating that, in case of necessity, these Eastern Indians would be called upon; in the interim, gifts should be sent to them in recognition of and thanks for their friendship. During the siege of Boston, therefore, the American army did not have to deal with hostile Indian action to the north. Indeed, during the siege itself, on 31 January 1776, a delegation of Saint John's and Passamaquoddy told Washington in a "Talk" (powwow) that they had been requested by the Caughnawaga and four other Canadian tribes to inform the general that these Canadian Indians wished to sign treaties of peace with the Americans—specifically, General Schuyler in New York and General Washington in Massachusetts—so that they, too, could consider themselves a free people, like their New England brothers.[12]

Helping to motivate these professions of friendship, historian Francis D. Cogliano points out, was a drawn-out effort by the Catholic Indians of eastern Maine and Nova Scotia to secure for themselves a resident priest, along with supplies and other gifts, in return for their loyalty to the American cause. As of 1775–1776, these protestations of friendship were being made most vigorously by the Penobscot and Passamaquoddy of eastern Maine and the Saint John's and Mi'kmaq of Nova Scotia. The very idea that Massachusetts would support a Catholic priest in eastern Maine, part of Massachusetts at the time, ran contrary to the deepest convictions of the citizens of the most anti-Catholic region in North America. Receiving such requests for a priest in the 1760s and early 1770s, Royalist governors Francis Bernard and Thomas Hutchinson ignored them on general principle, forcing the Penobscot and Passamaquoddy to travel north to Nova Scotia, where the British government allowed the free practice of Catholicism, including Mass and the sacraments. The Revolution, however, opened up a new line of thought among the legislators of the Massachusetts General Court. The Eastern Indians' continued friendship was essential to the safety of the Massachusetts frontier, especially since Nova Scotia had not joined the Revolution. These tribes were capable of fielding five to six hundred warriors of fighting age if they joined the British; and even if they did not, could Massachusetts afford three thousand hostile Indians massed on its eastern border? Was not the safety of Massachusetts worth a Mass in a faraway forest? No! remained the answer to this question. Fearing the reaction of the populace, the General Court refused any form of papist aggression, however necessary such cooperation might seem.

To prompt the Massachusetts leadership to consider and (insincerely) promise to send a Catholic priest and more supplies to its Indian allies took two years and a number of factors: the prohibitive expense of defending its eastern frontier; the Penobscot's growing insistence, edging into hostility; the participation of Saint John's and Mi'kmaq warriors in an invasion of Nova Scotia that ended in failure and embarrassment for Massachusetts; pressure on Massachusetts from the Continental Congress to secure the active support of the Maine tribes and at least the neutrality of the Catholic Indians of Nova Scotia. Still, the anti-Catholic attitudes of Massachusetts were so fundamental and persistent that, by the fall of 1778, when Congress again pressured the General Court to act, nothing had yet been done about sending a priest to the Eastern Tribes; their loyalty to the American cause was showing signs of stress, according to Indian agent Colonel John Allen, sent by Congress to the Eastern Tribes in the spring of 1777.

The military implementation of the Franco-American alliance, however, prompted Congress itself to act. On 5 December 1778, Congress wrote to the General Court of Massachusetts, directing it to send a Catholic priest to the Eastern Tribes. Congress would pick up the bill for his salary and expenses. The French admiral comte d'Estaing approved the selection of naval chaplain Hyacinthe de La Motte for the post. An Augustinian friar who had spent a short time as a prisoner of war before being exchanged, Father La Motte arrived in Maine on 18 May 1779 and began his ministry.[13]

A frontier priest

The Revolutionary states aligned on the trans-Allegheny frontier, meanwhile, continued to consider their western borders an open-ended question to be settled at a later date. Even Massachusetts and Connecticut, for that matter, had trans-Allegheny claims. For Virginians, at least—if one may judge from Thomas Jefferson's *Notes on the State of Virginia* (1784)—the western boundary of the Commonwealth of Virginia extended indefinitely into the interior of the North American continent. This sense of western extension most likely fed into the thinking of Patrick Henry, the first elected governor of the state of Virginia, when in 1777 he commissioned veteran frontier surveyor George Rogers Clark as a lieutenant colonel of the Virginia militia and sent him at the head of a force of 175 men into the Illinois Country of the northern Mississippi Valley. Their mission: to drive the British from French settlements in this region and, whenever possible, have these French residents swear allegiance to the United States.

Watered by the Mississippi, Missouri, Illinois, Wabash, Arkansas, and other river systems, the Illinois Country of the upper Mississippi Valley south of Lake Michigan would in time comprise the American territories (later states) of Illinois, Indiana, Iowa, and Missouri; but as of a census taken in 1767, it was a British-held region of some two thousand French settlers and their African and Indian slaves. Explored and evangelized by French Jesuit missionaries over the past century, the area represented a tenuous projection southward of frontier Quebec and the Great Lakes region into the heart of the continent by hardy French settlers and their families, who were increasingly gathering themselves into villages as farming replaced fur trapping. By 1767 the aging Jesuit missionary Sebastian Meurin remained the sole Roman Catholic priest assigned to the Illinois Country. That only one priest was serving all French Catholics who lived between Michilimackinac and the Arkansas River worried Bishop Jean-Olivier Briand of Quebec, concerned as he was with rebuilding the Catholic Church and servicing its far-flung flock under the new British administration. And so, Briand sent Pierre Gibault, a recently ordained priest of his diocese, to the Illinois Country to assist Father Meurin.

Born in 1735 in Montreal, Pierre Gibault did not fit the mold of the average Quebecois priest. He was older at the time of his ordination, for one thing, having entered the seminary in his late twenties. He was considerably educated, if one is to judge from the 243-book library he had accumulated by the end of his life: theology in the main (dogmatic, moral, practical), biblical commentaries, patristics, Church history, French Christian classics, a five-volume set of Latin classics (Ovid, Cicero, Juvenal), fine and practical arts (agriculture, cooking). The large number of Latin texts in the collection suggests that Gibault might have spent time earlier in his life at the Jesuit college in Quebec, obtaining competency in the language in which he celebrated Mass and read daily his breviary of Scripture, psalms, and prayers.

Yet here was a priest who in his years as a frontier pastor loved to hunt and fish, wear pistols in his belt when on long journeys, play in competitive sports with the younger men of his parishes, and join parishioners for a friendly glass or two (or three or four) on a cold winter's night while being openly boastful of his capacious avoidance of drunkenness, which would be unseemly in a priest. Just as his Latinity suggested a stint at the Jesuit college in Quebec, Gibault's love of the outdoors, sport, and conviviality suggested (and reprised) time he might have spent as a young man among the *coureurs des bois* and rustic habitants of the frontier. After all, one has to have done something during one's pre-priestly life when (like Gibault) one entered the seminary at the advanced age of twenty-eight and spent only two years there studying theology before ordination.

The fact, moreover, that Gibault's first assignment following ordination was to the Notre Dame Cathedral of Quebec suggests a certain gentlemanliness and refinement of manner, as do his beautifully composed letters to Bishop Briand written in the years to come. Cathedrals are at once the province of the poor and of the bon ton. Gibault appreciated women and enjoyed their company. When he left Montreal in July 1768 for the Illinois Country, he brought his widowed mother and single sister along with him and was delighted when his sister found a suitor, married (Gibault most likely performed the nuptial Mass), and brought his nephews and nieces to him for baptism. Never once in his church career was there any evidence, or accusations, of unpriestly sexual behavior, although he was criticized for kibitzing too much with the ladies of this or that parish while obviously enjoying their company. Monsieur Pierre Gibault, in short, did not follow the usual pattern for diocesan priests in Quebec: early entrance into the ecclesiastical estate, rigid formation, and adherence to a clerical life apart from the laity as a member of the priestly caste.

As a priest on the frontier, Pierre Gibault might have lacked typical clerical formation and personal style; yet he was meticulous in the exercise of his pastoral duties, as the surviving records of baptisms and marriages he administered attest. (Documentation of the funerals he conducted show gaps and are on the laconic side.) In the first years of his ministry, based out of the township of Kaskaskia (Illinois), he seemed happy enough, given the presence of his expanded family (mother and sister, followed by brother-in-law, nephews, and nieces) and the robust frontier people he served: the French, the Christianized African and Indian slaves and their families, the British officers and Catholic Irish soldiers of the Eighteenth (Royal Irish) Regiment stationed at Kaskaskia, the sparse number of Atlantic coast colonial Catholics migrating into the territory. All of them required the Mass and the sacraments, which only he and the increasingly failing Sebastian Meurin could administer.

Over time, however, Monsieur Gibault began to suffer from a number of interrelated problems. Sebastian Meurin's advancing age meant that Gibault was the

only effective priest in the region. Gibault was forced to travel vast distances as
he covered the villages and settlements under his jurisdiction—Michilimackinac,
Saint Joseph, Vincennes, Sainte Genevieve, Cahokia, Saint Louis, Peoria. After
Meurin's retirement to Prairie du Rocher, Gibault became vicar-general of the
Illinois Country as well as its sole active priest. The French laity in these various
locations, meanwhile—especially at the larger settlements of Kaskaskia, Cahokia,
and Vincennes—were growing weary of paying tithes to support a frequently
absent priest.

As of the 1760s the Paris Foreign Missions Society, a society of secular priests,
ran the Quebec seminary and supported Gibault during his two years of theological
education. While not a member of the society, Gibault was formed in its missionary
ethos and thus was willing to take to the circuit by horse, foot, or canoe—a flint-
lock pistol or two tucked into his belt for protection—to serve the people of his
vast territory. At the same time, as a diocesan priest supported by tithing, Gibault
was expected to cultivate the laity of each congregation and to win their approval
before they, in turn, willingly paid their tithes. Gibault's Jesuit predecessors in this
region had been self-supporting from a farm worked by slaves, had served a smaller
population of settled laity, and mainly had ministered peripatetically to the Native
American peoples who were themselves on the move.

By the time Colonel Clark and his Virginia militia entered the Illinois Country
in 1778, serious tension had developed between Gibault and his far-flung flock,
resentful of his absences. This trouble offended Gibault's amour propre and acti-
vated his sense of not being appreciated, which led to his request that Bishop Briand
allow him to return to Quebec. Written at Michilimackinac and dated 9 October
1775, this letter contains a level of alienation as high as alienation can get between a
priest and his flock. It opens with a reprise of his ministry. "For the last eight years",
Gibault begins,

I have obeyed you, firmly believing that in doing so I was obeying God himself.
This is my fourth expedition, the shortest of which is 500 leagues in length, visiting,
exhorting, reforming, as best I can, the people you have confided to me, employing
not only what the writings of the missionaries taught but reminding the long-time
residents of the customs they instituted at each place. I tried to conform to those uses
in each place in so far as I could discover them. Nothing deterred me from my duty:
neither suffering nor illness nor fatigue nor rain nor snow nor ice nor heat nor winds
nor storms nor hunger nor danger from the Indians. I have never complained to you
even though for four years I have not had so much as a bottle of wine for my table
or any of life's other small comforts. Furthermore, I have never been envious of the
lot of others.

From there, Gibault launches into a description of his weakening condition. "By
now", he laments, "my body is weakened by these sufferings and I can no longer
accomplish what both you and I would wish. I am now forty years old. Never spar-
ing myself, I have often had poor food and frequently went hungry, traveling on
foot day and night, exposed to all sorts of weather and in every season."

Now ensues a bitter denunciation of the people he served and the psychological
stress they have caused him. "Worst of all", Gibault bemoans,

is the mental anxiety [of] being a stranger in a country of libertines, exposed to all the calumnies which the irreligious and impious could invent, having my every action, even the most well-intentioned, misinterpreted and misrepresented to you. In spite of my care [of them]; my weariness, my solicitude and even the 4,000 livres, and more, I contributed toward building a new church, which I never made the least effort [to have erected], but which was [built after a vote of a] general assembly. Yet I am in debt to the amount I mentioned. But I encounter such ingratitude that, for the most part, no one offers to contribute, even those who daily squander [money] for drink and debauchery. For all of these and other reasons, I ask you to let me leave the Illinois.... The people have lost what they had when M. Forget and the Jesuit Father Aubert thought they had never seen a better place. After the suppression of the Society [of Jesus] Father Meurin suffered and is still suffering a veritable martyrdom. It would be sinful on my part if I did not tell you ... that I cannot any longer condone that Babylon.[14]

And so a correspondence continued for the next three years of complaint by Gibault and countercomplaint against Gibault from other sources. Through it all, Bishop Briand turned down Gibault's emotional pleas for a reassignment to Quebec province. Briand refused to grant Gibault's request not only because of a shortage of priests, but also because he felt Gibault—given his personality and abbreviated seminary preparation—was better placed as far from Quebec as possible. In short, Gibault was a maverick, and mavericks did best, Briand believed, as missionaries on the frontier. Neither Briand nor his successor, Jean-François Hubert, ever authorized Gibault to return to Quebec—except once, and that was to go home to face charges of treason, which, of course, Gibault refused to do. In 1778, however, Briand did dispatch his vicar-general Hubert to the Illinois Country to investigate Gibault's complaints and the criticism reaching Briand regarding Gibault himself.

The Clark expedition

Yet before Hubert could reach Illinois, history—in the form of George Rogers Clark and his men—raised the entire situation to a new level of drama. For two years before he received the approval and support of expansionist Governor Patrick Henry, Clark was already planning nothing less than the conquest on behalf of Virginia of the lands between the Ohio, the Mississippi, and the Great Lakes west of Lake Ontario: the Old Northwest, as it was called. Clark first encountered this region in 1772 as a young surveyor, and in 1777, just before launching his June 1778 entry into this British-held territory, he sent two undercover agents disguised as hunters to assess British defenses there and ascertain any pro-American sentiment among French settlers. Clark's agents found only limited pro-American sentiment, but they did report back on the sketchy military hold the British had on the region and the unpopularity of the regional governor at Kaskaskia, Philippe-François de Rastel, chevalier de Rocheblave, a Frenchman who was now a British subject.

Aided by inside information provided by five or more American traders living at Kaskaskia, Clark and his men marched into the town on the rather symbolic day of 4 July 1778 without firing a shot. Throughout the following day, the population of Kaskaskia fearfully pondered scenarios ranging from slaughter, to plunder, rapine, expulsion, or all of the above. A delegation of Kaskaskians, including

Gibault, called on Clark, and—half believing but hopeful that the least damaging scenario, expulsion, would be their fate—Gibault requested that the townspeople might congregate at his church and share with each other their farewells.

In the course of a second discussion on 6 July, the French leaders informed Clark that they were unfamiliar with the causes of the current conflict between Great Britain and the American colonies, but had they been informed of the causes, they most likely would have sympathized with the American point of view. In any event, they accepted their conquest and were prepared to cooperate. Sensing the extent of his victory over the hearts and minds of the citizens as well as the town itself, Clark consolidated his win with an onslaught of magnanimity. "I asked them very abruptly", he later wrote of this next phase of the conversation, "whether or not they thought they were speaking to savages that I was certain that they did from the tenor of their conversation did they suppose that we meant to strip the women and children or take the Bread out of their mouths or that we would condescend to make war on the women and Children or the Church that it was to prevent the effution of innocent blood ... that caused us to visit them, and not the prospect of Plunder ... that the King of France had joined the Americans ... as far as their church all religions would be tolerated in America ... and to convince them that we were not savages and Plunderers ... they Might return to their Families and inform them that they might conduct themselves as utial [before]."[15]

With Kaskaskia out of danger, Gibault had the church bells rung in thanksgiving, and the men of Kaskaskia, abjuring their loyalty to George III, swore an oath of allegiance to the sovereign state of Virginia and the Continental Congress of the United States. Moreover, the French volunteered to send a delegation to nearby Cahokia and persuade its citizens to take the same oath. Clark took them up on this offer. To show his trust, he allowed them to accompany his deputy, Major Joseph Bowman, and a small detachment of Virginia militia as armed militia in their own right, now loyal to Virginia and the United States. The townspeople of Cahokia took the oath of allegiance on 8 July 1778.

The oath of Vincennes

Next on Clark's agenda: Vincennes on the Wabash River, the oldest settlement (1702) in present-day Indiana. The settlement was important for Clark, since it led to his ultimate goal 150 miles to the northeast, Detroit, which came under Gibault's jurisdiction as a regional vicar-general. George Rogers Clark consulted Gibault at length regarding his plans to take Detroit. By now, Clark trusted Gibault as an advisor on matters pertaining to the French people of the region, and, as Clark informed the Kaskaskians, the Franco-American alliance was aligning the king of France behind the American cause. The very length of the interview between Clark and Gibault—during which Clark gave Gibault the impression that he had a larger force in reserve—underscores the fact that Clark seriously considered as an advisor the only Roman Catholic priest in the region.

In the interview, Gibault advised against military action toward Vincennes. It would cost lives, Gibault argued. Besides, it was not necessary. Like the citizens of Cahokia, the citizens of Vincennes could be persuaded to sign the oath of allegiance to Virginia and the United States voluntarily. In point of fact, so Clark later wrote, Gibault volunteered to be part of this effort—its spiritual aspect—and recommended that physician Jean-Baptiste Laffont be named head of the mission and chief spokesman. Clark agreed and proceeded to have composed a grandiloquent letter to the citizens of Vincennes, offering "assistance and protection to all the inhabitants against all their enemies and promising to treat them as citizens of the Republic of Virginia (in the limits of which they are) and to protect their persons and property, if it is necessary". The oath itself opened with a reference to taking the oath on the Holy Evangel (Bible) of Almighty God "to renounce all fidelity to George the Third, King of Britain, and to his successors, and to be faithful and true subjects of the Republic of Virginia as a free and independent state; and I swear that I will not do or cause anything or matter to be done which can be prejudicial to the liberty or independence of the said people, as prescribed by Congress, and that I will inform some one of the judges of the country of the said state of all treasons and conspiracies which shall come to my knowledge against the said state or some other of the United States of America; In faith of which we have signed. At Post Vincennes, July 20, 1778. Long live the Congress."[16] "The French of the oath", noted Catholic historian Clarence Walworth as long ago as 1907, "is barbarous. The pronoun is three times changed."[17] No matter: one catches echoes of Gibault in parts of the oath, especially its theological opening. At the least, he was consulted regarding it as well as the proclamation itself, which contains a mixture of prior writing and current update.

On 14 July 1778, Gibault, Laffont, and party (which included a secret plant by Clark to make sure Gibault and Laffont stayed on message) left by horseback for Vincennes, which they reached on the 17th and immediately entered into discussion with its inhabitants. Within a week, 180 householders signed or made their mark on a written version of the oath. Just as George Rogers Clark had planned, he and his men had advanced Virginia and the American Revolution into the heart of the continent without firing a shot. A small force of Virginians now stood, however briefly, in control of a sizable frontier portion of Britain's North American empire.

Aftermath and reconquest

Word of the taking of Kaskaskia, Cahokia, and Vincennes reached Virginia by late fall. Militarily, 1778 had been a meager year for the United States. Clark's victories in the Old Northwest offered welcome encouragement. By the time Governor Henry sent formal congratulations to Clark on 15 December 1778, Henry Hamilton, a retired brigade major serving as lieutenant governor and military commandant of the territory with the rank of lieutenant colonel, was in the process of recapturing Vincennes on 17 December with a force of 180 against an American force of thirty. Hamilton gathered residents into the settlement's church and upbraided them for taking the American oath, which violated their duty to God and man. At the same time that Governor Henry was praising Gibault ("the Priest to whom this country owes many thanks for his zeal and services") and enlisting Gibault's support in the liberation of Detroit, Lieutenant Governor Hamilton was denouncing Gibault as "the priest, who had been an active Agent for the Rebels whose vicious and immoral conduct was sufficient to do infinite mischief in a Country where ignorance and bigotry give full scope to the depravity of a licentious ecclesiastic". Hamilton was condemning Gibault in the classic anti-Catholic invective of the period, which is to say, as a treacherous and intemperate priest. Even worse, Hamilton was soon to level charges of treason against Gibault and most likely would have hanged him if he had been apprehended. Gibault knew full well the lieutenant governor's intentions in mid-January 1779, when rumor had it that Hamilton was approaching Kaskaskia with a large force. Gibault persuaded Clark to send him to Spanish Louisiana on a mission, which shortly ended with the hapless priest stranded for three days on an island in an ice-blocked Mississippi.[18]

On 6 February 1779, Gibault—returned to Kaskaskia from his hypothermic flight—was sermonizing, blessing, and giving absolution to a French militia who were part of a force of 130 being led by Colonel Clark against Vincennes, now being held by Hamilton. After a long march and a short siege, Clark forced Hamilton's unconditional surrender on 24 February. Clark dispatched Hamilton and his officers back to Williamsburg, Virginia, as prisoners of war but allowed the French militia under Hamilton's command to go free on parole. Pierre Gibault returned to his priestly duties. On 12 June 1780, Bishop Briand wrote Gibault to suspend him from these priestly duties, with the exception of saying Mass. On 29 June, Bishop Briand wrote Gibault, requesting him to return to Quebec to answer charges of treason. There is no record of Gibault's having received or answered these letters, which were most likely sent in one package. Gibault took his ministry to Sainte Genevieve on the west side of the Mississippi. As part of Spanish Louisiana, Sainte Genevieve was under the governance of Spain, now an ally of the United States and under the ecclesiastical authority of the bishop of Santiago de Cuba.

A fateful minute

When Doctor Benjamin Rush of Philadelphia—who held degrees from the College of New Jersey at Princeton and from Edinburgh, signed the Declaration of Independence as a member of Congress, and served thereafter as surgeon general of the Continental Army—received an invitation to the Requiem Mass to be held on 8 May 1780 at Saint Mary's, Philadelphia, sponsored by the French envoy Anne-César, chevalier de la Luzerne, in honor of the recently deceased Don Juan de Miralles, agent of the king of Spain to the United States, Rush declined the invitation, so he wrote on it, "as not compatible with the principles of a Protestant".[19] The violently anti-Catholic Benedict Arnold, however, soon to be secretly plotting against the Revolution he had served with such distinction in its earliest phases, was invited to the same Requiem Mass and reluctantly attended it in his capacity as military governor of Philadelphia. Following his changing of sides, the now British brigadier general Arnold issued an open letter "to the Officers and Soldiers of the Continental Army who have the real Interest of their Country at Heart and who are determined to be no longer the Tools and dupes of Congress or of France". "Do you know that the eye which guides this pen", Arnold wrote, "lately saw your mean and profligate Congress at mass for the soul of a Roman Catholic in Purgatory and participating in the rites of a Church against whose anti-Christian corruption your pious ancestors would bear witness with their blood?"[20]

It is perhaps not too surprising that Benedict Arnold, now wearing a British uniform, should be playing the anti-Catholic card so egregiously. A Connecticut man, Arnold had always been fiercely anti-Catholic, and dealing with Catholic French Canadians throughout 1776 must have constituted a great strain. Arnold was looking for any reason to justify his betrayal of the American cause, and the Miralles funeral offered yet another excuse for going over to the British. Doctor Rush's regrets, by contrast, were kept civil, documented only in a handwritten note on the back of the invitation. Yet Rush's education, scholarship, long scientific service, and medical distinction in the Revolutionary cause underscores the grave reservations many Americans of all social classes had regarding the French and Spanish alliances. Certainly Rush, the most prominent scientist in North America now that Franklin was in Europe, was aware of how crucial French and Spanish assistance was proving to the Revolutionary effort—whether in the form of material aid from France via Hortalez et Cie or in the financial support from Spain being organized by the Irish-born Oliver Pollock. Appointed commercial agent of the United States to New Orleans in 1777, Pollock—a New Orleans–based entrepreneur and self-made man of wealth with excellent Spanish contacts—had most recently used both his own money and funds borrowed from Bernardo de Gálvez, governor of Spanish Louisiana, to finance the successful American campaign against the British in the Mississippi Valley led by Virginia militia colonel George Rogers Clark.

Bourbon Spain remained cautious regarding an open alliance with and outright military aid to the United States. While Spain, for example, might employ warfare to regain Florida and Louisiana, lost in the Seven Years' War, it feared the future expansion of a victorious United States into these two recovered territories. Still, when Spain did enter the war in April 1779 as an ally of France, its military involvement, like its previous three years of financial and supply support, proved indispensable. Spain's four-year siege of Gibraltar, while unsuccessful, kept British naval resources occupied in a sector far from the rebellious United States, as did Spain's prevailing two-year effort to recover the Balearic Islands, especially Mallorca, with its capital city of Palma de Mallorca. Likewise did Spain's efforts to recover Florida from the British prevent British military resources from being used farther north, as did Spanish Louisiana governor Bernardo de Gálvez's triumphant campaigns to recapture Baton Rouge, Natchez, Mobile, and Pensacola. Spanish army operations in the Mississippi Valley as far north as present-day Michigan proved equally distracting to the British and their Indian allies.

To monitor this somewhat indirect but valuable alliance, the Havana-based merchant and businessman Don Juan de Miralles was dispatched to Philadelphia in early 1778 as an unofficial Spanish agent (or resident), not formally accredited by Congress but charged nevertheless with reporting on American affairs and establishing connections with the American leadership. (The respected but anti-Catholic nineteenth-century historian George Bancroft describes Miralles as a spy.) After living on High Street for a year, followed by a period on Fourth Street below Walnut, Miralles took up residence at Mount Pleasant, a Philadelphia mansion and grounds. He lived there until General Benedict Arnold, military commander of the city— grown rich from kickbacks and related schemes—purchased the estate in March 1779 as a gift for his Loyalist fiancée, Miss Margaret (Peggy) Shippen, in honor of their forthcoming marriage.

Miralles moved easily in congressional and commercial circles, a Beaumarchais-like figure for Philadelphia—rich, assured, exuding an ambience of impending importance connected to a forthcoming Spanish alliance. Yet the Havana don also went out into the field, as on the two occasions when he visited Moravian settlements north of Bethlehem, Pennsylvania. When George Washington stayed in Philadelphia for two weeks in January 1779, Miralles entertained His Excellency at Mount Pleasant and ordered for distribution in Cuba and Spain five copies of the portrait that Charles Willson Peale had painted of Washington during this visit at the request of the Supreme Executive Council of Pennsylvania. Miralles' purchase of the copies of Peale's painting was indeed fortunate, for in September 1781 Loyalists broke into the chambers of the council and destroyed the original.

A pleasant association developed between Washington and Miralles. In late February, for example, Miralles notified the quartermaster department in Philadelphia that he had a crate of oranges at his home for shipment to the general. Writing to Don Diego Joseph Navarro, governor of Cuba, on 4 March 1779, Washington praised Miralles for the courtesies Miralles had extended to him on his recent sojourn in Philadelphia. "His estimable qualities", Washington wrote of Miralles, "justify your recommendation & concur with it to establish him in my esteem. I doubt not he will have informed you of the cordial and respectful sentiments, which he has experienced in this Country. On my part I shall always take pleasure in convincing him of the high value I set upon his merit, and of the respect I bear to those who are so happy as to interest your Excellency's friendship."[21]

The next month, on 28 April 1779, in the company of the French minister the chevalier de la Luzerne, Miralles made the first of two visits to Washington at his headquarters in New Jersey, where the French and Spanish envoys reviewed troops and were entertained by the commander in chief. A year later, Luzerne and Miralles returned. Miralles fell sick "of a pulmonic fever" (pneumonia) and took to bed. On 23 April 1780, Miralles summoned to his bedside the chevalier de la Luzerne, the baron von Steuben, Alexander Hamilton, and a few others and dictated his will in their presence. Its provisions included repayment of itemized debts, ratification of previously made provisions for his wife and daughters in Havana, payment of all physicians' fees, a new coat for each of his servants, freedom for his African slave Rafael and Rafael's wife and children, and the manumission of any time left on the contract of his indentured servant, a Scots boy named Angus.

Miralles passed away on 28 April. The next day, his corpse went on view at Washington's headquarters, in a coffin with the top half opened and the bottom half draped in black velvet, according to Spanish Catholic custom. The deceased was formally dressed in a scarlet suit with gold lace and embroidered decorations. A gold-laced three-cornered hat was laid beside the decorations. At the funeral, on the late afternoon of 30 April, Miralles was accorded full military honors. As chief mourners, Washington, other general officers, and several congressmen walked behind the casket, which was borne on the shoulders of artillery officers in full uniform. As the procession wended its way to the Presbyterian cemetery at Morristown for temporary interment, Continental Army artillerymen fired cannon salutes at the stately pace of one per minute. At the cemetery, a Spanish priest in vestments conducted the traditional Roman Catholic ceremonies and Latin prayers of interment, including the sprinkling of the coffin with holy water as it was lowered into the earth. Later that day, Washington dictated a letter to Cuban governor Don Diego Joseph Navarro, expressing his regret at the passing of Don Juan de Miralles. Once again, Washington expressed his respect for this gentleman and the pleasure Washington took "in performing every friendly office to him during his illness and that no care or attention, in our power, was omitted towards his comfort or restoration".[22]

The Requiem Mass celebrated at Saint Mary's in Philadelphia on 8 May 1780 constituted a second round of funereal honors accorded Miralles within a fortnight by American civil and military authorities out of respect for the Franco-Spanish alliance that had internationalized the American Revolutionary War, to the benefit of the United States. One attendee, Ebenezer Hazard of Philadelphia, writing to the famed New England historian the Reverend Jeremy Belknap, provided Belknap with a detailed description of the ceremony. The congregation, Hazard reported, was a blend of Papists, Presbyterians, Episcopalians, Quakers, and others. The two chaplains of Congress, an Episcopalian and a Presbyterian, were in attendance. The Papists followed the proceedings with all due solemnity. Most Protestants were respectful, although several did edge into irreverence during the ceremonies. And no wonder, given the full display of the rites of a religion they had been taught to revile from childhood. Conducted before an altar ablaze in candles, beneath an oversize painting of the Crucifixion, with two rows of candles aligned on an empty casket, incense, sprinklings of holy water, the stately Latin prayers of a full-length Requiem Mass being intoned by the celebrant, praying for the release of the souls of the departed—that of the late Don Juan de Miralles, in particular—from Purgatory: such a liturgy quite naturally tested the sensibilities of the more intensely Protestant members of the congregation.

Yet this largely Protestant congregation attempted to be on its best behavior. When the celebrant of the Mass—the Recollect Franciscan Seraphin Bandol, chaplain to the French delegation, who preached that day as well—finished sprinkling the chevalier de la Luzerne with holy water during the asperges (a ceremony that dated back to the ninth century), he dipped his aspergillum into a pail of holy water and offered to sprinkle Samuel Huntington of Connecticut, president of the Continental Congress. The president of Congress paused for some time—perhaps as long as a minute, according to one report—thinking it over before he nodded assent, and Father Bandol liberally sprinkled the Congregationalist congressman. By the end of the Mass, ran this same report, every congressman in the chapel was carrying a lit taper in his hand and had, presumably, been sprinkled with holy water as well.

The Loyalist *Royal Gazette* of New York carried this report on 20 May 1780, and it was reprinted by the London *Chronicle* and the *Scots Magazine* of Edinburgh. Not only Benedict Arnold but American Loyalists and Britons alike were leveraging accounts of Don de Miralles' Philadelphia funeral as proof positive that the rebellious Americans were willing to allow a papist takeover of their country in exchange for French and Spanish assistance. Lost in a sea of hate for the cause he had betrayed for money, Benedict Arnold wrapped himself in detestable Protestant rectitude. Loyalists and Britons were seeking some kind of argument, intellectual and emotional, to deal with the dawning recognition that two Catholic powers were now all but certain to play crucial roles in bringing a primarily Protestant nation to full, secure independence. Congressman Huntington and his congressional colleagues, by contrast, accepted the asperges and held the lit tapers, in a spirit of realpolitik and diplomacy. France and Spain were transformative allies in the American struggle, and for these Protestant Patriots, the independence of the United States was well worth a Mass.[23]

4

Yorktown 1781

French arms bring about an American victory

In the first phase of the Battle of Yorktown, British forces under Lord Cornwallis, emerging from North Carolina into Virginia, performed with notable efficiency. Cornwallis' force rendezvoused with five thousand additional troops under the command of Benedict Arnold, who now held a permanent commission in the British army as a colonel of cavalry and a temporary commission as brigadier of provincial troops. The combined British and German forces numbered as many as nine thousand troops. On 28 May 1781, the Queen's Rangers, a Loyalist legion under the command of Lieutenant Colonel John Simcoe, drove from the field at Point of Fork, at the juncture of the Rivanna and Fluvanna Rivers, American militia units under the command of Baron von Steuben. On or about 18 June Cornwallis reached Richmond. Earlier, the approach of Cornwallis had forced Lafayette's outnumbered troops to abandon the city and sent the Virginia government fleeing west to Charlottesville. Continuing on to Charlottesville, the Queen's Rangers compelled the Virginia legislature to flee for a second time and came within ten minutes of capturing Governor Thomas Jefferson.

French naval power, however, and the indecision it was causing General Sir Henry Clinton in New York were complicating matters. Thus far, the British had controlled the Atlantic coast and kept it under effective blockade. But Clinton learned that on 22 March a fleet of twenty French ships of the line under the command of Admiral François Joseph Paul de Grasse had sailed from Brest. De Grasse's arrival, Clinton realized, would give France naval superiority in North America. (The comte d'Estaing had sailed his fleet to the West Indies in 1778, but a squadron under the command of Jacques-Melchior Saint-Laurent, comte de Barras, remained off Newport.) New York City stood in danger from land and sea.

While the British still held Charleston and Savannah, the ports of these cities were minor operations. Given the buildup of French ships and troops in the West Indies, within striking distance of the South and the mid-Atlantic coast, the English fleet required a developed port on the Chesapeake. Clinton thus sent Cornwallis three separate orders: (1) dispatch troops to Virginia for the defense of New York (later modified to strengthen the defensive lines along the Delaware); (2) select a site and develop a naval station on the Chesapeake; (3) take up a defensive position in Virginia, but do not launch any major campaigns against the Americans.

Cornwallis would have preferred to continue his string of victories, but orders were orders. And so, on 4 July he began a withdrawal from Williamsburg, in the course of which he dealt the Americans yet one more defeat: on 6 July, he once again targeted Lafayette, who sent Anthony Wayne against what Lafayette believed to be the British rear guard but turned out to be a full-force ambush, costing the Americans 145 dead. After a short stay at Portsmouth, Cornwallis decided to postpone sending troops to Clinton, and on 2 August he began to take up a defensive position on the site he had selected for a Chesapeake naval station: Yorktown, east of Williamsburg on a low plateau on the west side of the navigable York River as it flowed into open sea.

A brilliantly executed forced march

Since July, Washington and Rochambeau had been operating around New York City to little effect. Learning by 14 August of two major developments, however—Cornwallis' defensive position at Yorktown and the departure of Admiral de Grasse' fleet (twenty-nine ships, three thousand troops) from the West Indies for the Chesapeake—Washington, Rochambeau, and their respective staffs and commanders almost instantly beheld a dazzling prospect: a land-sea envelopment of British forces at Yorktown. This was provided, of course, that Franco-American land and naval forces could convene, on and offshore the Yorktown Peninsula, swiftly, efficiently, in sufficient numbers, and in secret, lest the forces of Sir Henry Clinton dash or sail forth from New York, cross over to New Jersey, and block their way. To maintain secrecy, Washington kept a small number of his troops busy probing and harassing British lines around New York City as if in preparation for a siege of that city. Washington went so far as to have an oversize oven for baking bread constructed where the British or British spies could see it, as proof positive that a long-term siege of New York City was in the offing. Calling upon Admiral de Barras at Newport, Rhode Island, where de Barras was preparing for an invasion of Newfoundland, Rochambeau persuaded de Barras to postpone the Newfoundland expedition in favor of a rapid deployment of his fleet south to Yorktown. On 27 August de Barras departed Newport with eight ships of the line, four frigates, and eighteen troop transports.

Next, French and American troops—as secretly as possible!—embarked upon a 450-mile forced march to Yorktown. By early September 1781, with the arrival of Rochambeau, de Barras, and de Grasse, 20,000 French sailors, soldiers, and mariners in two fleets had joined a land force of 7,500 Americans and 4,000 French for the naval Battle of the Chesapeake (also known as the Battle of the Virginia Capes) and the siege of Yorktown.[1]

An era of good feeling

In terms of sheer numbers, the American Revolution had become—by the time of its two final battles—significantly Catholic in its military presence, especially if Spain is brought into the equation. Indeed, one of its principal commanders, Admiral de Grasse, was a Knight of Malta, a professed religious under vows. De Grasse entered the Order of Malta in 1734 as a boy of eleven and served successively as page to its Grand Master and as an ensign in one of its Mediterranean galleys before entering the French navy at the age of nineteen. Each French ship of the line, moreover, had an ordained military chaplain, which brought some ninety French priests to the United States, including two otherwise undocumented American secular priests. These naval chaplains serving in American waters tended to focus their ministries on the officers and men of the ships they served. Still, crews and chaplains did come ashore, and hence, these French naval chaplains constituted a new priestly presence in the emergent nation and occasionally made their presence known. The same is even more true of the ten French army chaplains whose names have come down to us, for their ministries were by definition more directly connected to the immediate American environment. Still, whether navy or army, glimpses and vignettes of French priests serving as chaplains do emerge in the annals of the Revolutionary War. "The Catholic priests hitherto seen in the colonies", notes John Gilmary Shea, "had been barely tolerated in the limited districts where they labored; now came Catholic chaplains of foreign embassies; army and navy chaplains celebrating Mass with pomp on the men-of-war and in the camps and cities. The time had not yet come for complete religious freedom; but progress was soon made. Rhode Island, with a French fleet in her water, blotted from her statute-book a law against Catholics."[2]

Regarding pomp and circumstance, the first of two Requiem Masses and Te Deums sponsored by the Continental Congress was the funeral for French artillery officer Philippe Charles Tronson du Coudray in Saint Mary's Church on 18 September 1777, followed by burial in the church's cemetery, with expenses paid for by a Continental Congress preparing to evacuate Philadelphia as the British approached. Recruited by Silas Deane in November 1776, General du Coudray arrived in the United States in May 1777, along with twenty-eight other officers and twelve sergeants of artillery to bolster this essential sector of battlefield service, and drowned in the Schuylkill on 16 September 1777, when the horse he was sitting on bolted into the river.[3]

When Admiral Charles-Henri-Louis d'Arsac de Ternay was buried at Newport on 16 December 1780, twelve French Catholic chaplains in liturgical vestments attended the solemn services. The ceremony was at twilight, an eyewitness reported, and following the Requiem Mass with military honors, the vested priests preceded the coffin with lighted tapers in hand. Reaching the gravesite at Trinity churchyard, they chanted the prayers and hymns of the Roman Catholic burial rites. The eyewitness was impressed by the event's stateliness and solemnity.[4] Protestant Rhode Islander Solomon Southwick was likewise impressed by the Catholic ceremonial. "The Catholic King of France", Southwick later wrote, "took part with the Protestant rebel, and his Catholic subjects at home were taught to reverence our cause. We found that Roman Catholics were not monsters, for these very Frenchmen who came to fight our battles were Roman Catholics. The soldiers of the Catholic king, and those of the rebellious Protestant provinces, went hand in hand together in worshipping their common Creator. I saw the whole French army under Rochambeau go to a grand Mass in a body: and never did I behold a more sublime spectacle."[5] At noon on 4 July 1779, His Excellency Conrad Alexandre Gérard, minister plenipotentiary of France to the United States, sponsored a chanted Te Deum in the Chapel of Saint Mary's, Philadelphia, to celebrate the third anniversary of the signing of the Declaration of Independence. Gérard invited the president and members of the Continental Congress to attend, and many did. Recollect Father Seraphin Bandol—once senior chaplain on the man-of-war *Le*

Languedoc in the squadron of the comte d'Estaing, now attached to the French ministry and hence frequently referred to as Abbé Bandol—preached the sermon. In his sermon, Bandol celebrated the new alliance between the United States and France; indeed, in his prayerful enthusiasm, the good abbé practically Catholicized the American Revolution or at least drenched it in ultramontane approval. "It is with this view", Abbé Bandol concluded (by "view" he meant God's approval of the alliance), "that we shall cause the canticle [the Te Deum] to be performed which is the custom of the Catholic Church both consecrated to be at once a testimonial of public joy, a thanksgiving for benefits received from Heaven, and a prayer for the continuance of its mercies."[6]

John Gilmary Shea speculates, however, that beyond such grand liturgical occasions, French chaplains also assumed an informal but welcomed ministry among ordinary Catholic Americans, even though the record of such service is sparse. "The French chaplains in both arms of the service", Shea writes, "came in contact with Catholics in all parts, and the Masses said in the French lines [regiments] were attended by many who had not for years had an opportunity of attending the holy sacrifice."[7]

Fortunately, glimpses—and at least one fully documented record—of service by French chaplains to Americans do survive, although the majority of these chaplains remain known by their names alone. Abbé Claude Robin, chaplain in chief of army chaplains, is the great exception to this rule. A friend of Benjamin Franklin, Robin assisted Franklin's efforts to secure the Franco-American alliance, and Franklin, in turn, recommended Robin to French authorities for appointment as army chaplain in chief. Abbé Robin, moreover, was not only a keen observer but also a writer of talent and industry. Upon his return to France, he produced a record of his American service, the *Nouveaux voyages dans l'Amérique septentrionale* (1782). Composed of thirteen letters Robin wrote while on duty in America, with an English translation by journalist and poet Philip Freneau published in 1783 in Philadelphia under the title *New Travels through North-America*, Robin's narrative remains a useful gloss on the military and civilian aspects of the Franco-American relationship. In addition to his military duties, Robin ministered to American civilians in Hartford and Woodbury, Connecticut, and Baltimore, Maryland. Thanks to Robin, documentation exists of Abbé de Glesnon, navy, a hospital chaplain in Newport and Providence, Rhode Island; Abbé Lacy, army, an Irishman, said by Shea to have traveled the country from Boston to Virginia; and Abbé John Rossiter, army, active in parish ministry in Philadelphia.

Nowhere was this public presence of Roman Catholic priests more dramatic than in traditionally anti-Catholic New England, where the French fleets of de Ternay and de Barras lay at anchor at Newport and Boston variously between 1780 and 1782. Thus, at Newport during these years there came ashore—and publicly ministered to one degree or another—such naval chaplains as Capuchin Father Frédéric de Bourges; Abbé La Poterie; two *prêtre Américain* secular priests, Jean Wanton and François Hobdai (most likely French Canadians); two Irish (*Irlandais*) priests, Abbé Dowd and Capuchin Father Maurice (whose real name was Charles Whelan); secular priest John Machunq (McKeon), perhaps Irish as well; and yet another possibly Irish secular, the Newport hospital chaplain Abbé Glesnon (perhaps Glennon). While stationed at the French embassy in Philadelphia, naval chaplain Seraphin

Bandol performed a number of baptisms and marriages at Saint Joseph's Church and celebrated Mass at Saint Mary's Church. That these priests and the officers and men they served made a good impression overall during the two years in which French ships were anchored in or visited Newport harbor can be inferred from the fact that in 1783, following the departure of the French squadrons from Newport, the state of Rhode Island (as noted earlier) removed its anti-Catholic prohibitions from the statute books.[8]

Even Boston is nice

Before the Revolutionary War, as John Adams pointed out, Catholics were as scarce in Boston as hen's teeth. Such was not so between 1780 and 1782 and the years immediately following; the effects of the French naval sojourns in Boston were long-lasting in terms of accommodation with Roman Catholicism. Aside from chaplains John Machunq (McKeon) of *L'Amazone* and Célestin Bureau of *La Concorde*, the names of the naval chaplains active in Boston between 1780 and 1782 are not as well documented as they are at Newport. Still, army chaplain in chief Abbé Claude Robin is documented as arriving on 6 May 1781 with letters of introduction from Benjamin Franklin, which guaranteed him a warm welcome. Better documented are the shore installations in which these chaplains served: the barracks on Governors Island, Boston, for example, and the newly founded public hospital on the western side of the city. The well-traveled army chaplain Abbé Lacy most likely spent time ministering in the latter facility. Given Boston's importance as a center of French naval activity, a French consul general was assigned there. Non-Catholic dignitaries were entertained aboard ships at various times and, out of courtesy, may have witnessed religious ceremonies. Joseph de Valnais, the French consul general in Boston, courted and became engaged to Miss Eunice Quincy; and the widow Mrs. Mary Clarke of Middletown, Connecticut, was married to the West Indies–born, immensely wealthy citizen of Boston, Louis Baury de Bellerive, who served through the war with the French fleet as a captain of shipboard grenadiers. In later years, Baury de Bellerive would join forces with Mrs. Margaret Price—whose husband had served as a provision agent for the French fleet—to bring the first permanently stationed Catholic priest to Boston.

In this era of good feeling, acknowledgment was made of Boston's earlier reaction to Roman Catholics and the corrective action that should now be taken. Governor John Hancock and Samuel Breck Senior, for example, promoted a program of pro-French friendship that included cultivating the French language in Boston circles. Breck went so far as to send his son Samuel Junior to a Catholic college in France to learn the language. Breck Junior's grandmother was so shocked that her grandson was attending a papist college in a papist country that she refused to kiss him goodbye and merely blessed and prayed over him as over one severely afflicted. Grandmother Breck's worst fears came true. While studying abroad for four years, Breck Junior converted to Catholicism and, upon his return, helped establish a Catholic parish in Boston. Even the Dudleian Lecture at Harvard for 1781, preached that year by the Reverend William Gordon, showed faint signs of tamping down the anti-Catholicism that was the founding purpose and stated theme of the annual event. After all, it made no sense to

castigate the Whore of Babylon when the French army was preparing for battle
in New England and the French fleet remained at anchor in the ports of Newport and Boston; and when the hierarchy and clergy of France, meeting in May
1780 in general assembly at the convent of the Canons Regular of Saint Augustine in Paris, were organizing a fundraising drive among the French clergy that
would provide the king with as much as thirty million livres for the prosecution
of the war against England on behalf of the rebellious American colonies. Even
the Franciscans of Alta California, responding to a request by King Carlos III of
Spain, were taking up a collection, mission by mission—infinitely smaller but
heartfelt as well—to support Spain's military efforts against Great Britain in the
war for American independence.[9]

Since the Reformation, the Roman Catholic doctrine of transubstantiation—the
Real Presence of the Risen Christ, Body and Blood, Soul and Divinity, following the Consecration of bread and wine into the Eucharist by a priest celebrating
Mass—had proven, along with the pope, the *bête noir* par excellence of Protestant
dispute. In his Dudleian Lecture, the Reverend Gordon managed an almost painful (albeit generous) admission: namely, that the doctrine of transubstantiation was
"believed by men of great abilities and knowledge in the Romish church", and
even less educated Catholics should be respected in their belief in this doctrine.
Yet the Reverend Gordon—however innovative in his refusal to unleash the full
ire of the Dudleian Lecture in the matter of this doctrine—managed to qualify his
briefly stated concession. "While we are politically allied to Popish powers", he
cautioned his Harvard audience on 5 September 1781, "and admit the right of all to
judge for themselves in matters of religion and to follow the dictates of their own
consciences, they conducting as good members of civil society, let us not through
a false complaisance decline opposing the erroneous tenets of Popery and become
indifferent to Protestant truths."[10]

The ex-Jesuit American clergy

Only a few French chaplains accepted permanent assignments in America and
thereby did little to augment the Catholic clergy of the emergent nation. (The
French Revolution would prove a different case, however.) For the most part,
decisions to remain were personal and did not come at the direction of a bishop or
the superior of a religious order; during the Revolutionary conflict, there was no
settled ecclesiastical authority for Catholic clergy serving in the United States. As
suppressed Jesuits, the twenty-five priests active in the colonies were technically
under the jurisdiction of Richard Challoner, vicar apostolic of London, who del-
egated his authority to former Jesuit John Lewis. With the outbreak of hostilities
in April 1775, however, Challoner's authority, while still in force canonically,
became a moot point (Challoner had never overused it, in any event), and Father
Lewis exercised authority as Challoner's vicar-general. While Clement XIV's brief
Dominus ac Redemptor Noster of 21 July 1773 suppressed the Society of Jesus, the
British statutes in effect at that time forbade the alienation of English property by
a foreign prince, and so the Jesuits of Maryland and Pennsylvania retained title to
their properties and slaves and continued to manage them and support themselves
in a spirit of sustained (if slightly surreptitious) corporate identity. These former

Jesuits, moreover, had personally experienced the heavy hand of the Court of Rome when their Society and its institutions were seized, and they, so recently members of the most powerful order in the Church, were left—in Latin America, the Caribbean, and New Spain especially—as little more than criminals sent under arrest into exile and poverty. Little wonder, then, that all but one of these former Jesuits—despite the fact that many came from distinguished English recusant families—took the oath of allegiance to the self-declared independent states of Maryland and Pennsylvania. In this regard, clergy and laity were on the same page, for the more Catholic the Maryland county, the more pro-independence were its citizens, starting with St. Mary's County. The Select Body of the Catholic Church, as the former Jesuits called themselves, met once a year at Newton Manor, which also served as a hospital for wounded or ill Continentals and militia, although the manor was anything but safe or peaceable when (as sometimes happened) raiding British soldiers hammered their muskets against its doors. British raiders were perhaps showing mercy on the hospital, for when they raided other manors, they often torched them.

Joseph Mosley (Jesuit alias Joseph Frambeck) of Talbot County, Maryland, on the Eastern Shore, refused to take the oath when it was originally offered on 1 March 1778, because, he claimed, he wanted first to consult with his fellow former Jesuits, all of whom were taking the oath. This feeble excuse underscores that Mosley felt conflicted about the oath, which he admitted. "I must confess", Mosley later stated, "that I thought that taking such an oath, was taking an active part in changes of government, which I conceived was acting out of character and beyond the business of a clergyman. I conceived that swearing to defend to the utmost of my power and taking up arms was much the same thing. It is true that a clergyman may advise and approve of a just war, but the greatest Justice of it will not entitle him to take up arms."[11] Even these more cogently argued scruples, however, only weakly hid the fact that Mosley had Loyalist reservations regarding independence.

Born in 1731 in Lincolnshire of a family with modest but respectable recusant antecedents, Mosley graduated from Saint Omer's before entering the Jesuit noviatiate of Watten, Flanders. He volunteered for Maryland in 1764, serving first in Bohemia Manor, Cecil County, next in Queen Anne's County, and then in the rural mission and plantation of Saint Joseph's in Talbot County—his life's work—where over the years he managed the plantation and its slaves and increased his scattered flock by converting 185 Marylanders (Shea's figure) to the Church. At the same time, Mosley kept up an observant and sensitive correspondence with his married sister Mrs. Helen Dunn of Blaydon, near Newcastle upon Tyne, Northumberland, and his older brother Michael, also a Jesuit and in later years chaplain to the Acton family at Aldenham, Shropshire. Unfortunately, only thirteen of Mosley's letters to his sister have survived. Presented to John Gilmary Shea in 1883 by Lieutenant Colonel Alexander T. Knight, a relative of Mosley, the letters are today safely deposited in the Georgetown University Library—and a good thing, too, for Mosley's letters offer intelligent and heartfelt insights into the Maryland environment and society, Jesuit life in Maryland before the suppression, and the suppression itself.

The suppression sent Mosley into an epistolary jeremiad over a catastrophic loss of identity. "To my great sorrow", Mosley wrote to his sister on 30 October 1774, the Society is abolished; with it must die all that zeal that was founded and raised on it. Labour for our neighbor is a Jesuit's pleasure; destroy the Jesuit, and labour is painful and disagreeable. I must allow with truth, that what was my pleasure is now irksome; every fatigue I underwent caused a secret and inward satisfaction; it's now unpleasant and disagreeable: every visit to the sick was done with a good will, it's now done with as bad a one. I disregarded this unhealthy climate, and all its agues and fevers, which have really paid me to my heart's content, for the sake of my rule, the night was agreeable as the day, frost and cold as a warm fire or a soft bed, the excessive heats as welcome as a cool shade or pleasant breezes—but now the scene is changed: the Jesuit is metamorphosed into I know not what; he is a monster, a scare-crow in my ideas. With joy I impaired my health and broke my constitution in the care of my flock. It was the Jesuit's call, it was his whole aim and business. The Jesuit is no more; he now endeavours to repair his little remains of health and his shattered constitution, as he has no rule calling him to expose it. In me, the Jesuit and the Missioner was always combined together; if one falls, the other must of consequence fall with it. As the Jesuit is judged unfit by His H[oli]ness for a Mission, I think that it is high time for me to retire to a private life, to spend the remains of my days in peace and quiet. I should be sorry to be quite inactive, and doing no good; but a small employ would now content my zeal. If I could hear of a vacant place in your neighborhood for a Chaplain, . . . I should accept it.[12]

Mosley eventually recovered his composure and soldiered on as a successful mis-sioner in Talbot County. Yet this letter shows a mind-set, a bitterness, a sense of loss that he shared with the other twenty-four suppressed Jesuits active in Maryland and Pennsylvania during the Revolutionary War.

Shocked at losing his right to preach because he had not taken the oath of alle-giance to Maryland, Mosley agreed to swear his loyalty but was informed that he had missed the deadline. The Maryland legislature, however, accepted a petition from Mosley and passed a special act accepting his oath and conferring on him the right to preach.

Some priestly augmentation

By this time, the twenty-five Jesuits on active duty had been joined, offshore and on land, by an estimated ninety French chaplains. These clergy, in one way or another, Shea suggests, multiplied the opportunities for Mass and other Catholic ceremonies (funerals and Te Deums especially) to be celebrated publicly and thereby presented Catholic worship to a population raised in an environment of anti-Catholicism. Even Bostonians—some of them, anyway—managed to tamp down long-standing prejudices, as the *Massachusetts Spy* on 7 November 1782 did when reporting on the military funeral attended by the Boston establishment given the chevalier de la Pine, a young ensign attached to the frigate *L'Amazone* who had died in that city six days earlier. The funeral procession, reported the paper,

began with a company of marines, their arms secured and muffled drums. A priest bearing a silver crucifix. Immediately after, *THE BODY*, carried in a sling by four marines, and the pall supported by six officers, each with a lighted taper. Two priests: one of them in his white robes reading the burial service, and both with tapers burning. Then followed his Excellency, the Marquis de Vaudreuil, his Honor the

Lieutenant-Governor, the Honorable Council, the Reverend Clergy, the Select-men, and many of the most respectable Gentlemen of the town, accompanied by the field and other officers of the Boston regiment in their uniforms. The whole escorted by a number of French officers. Upon reaching the burying grounds, the body was deposited under the Church and the marines discharged three vollies. The ceremony was very solemn and exhibited a new proof of the cordiality, sympathy and friend-ship that subsist between the citizens and subjects of the allied nations of France and America.[13]

In contrast to prior practice, the General Court of Massachusetts was no longer reluctant to send a priest to minister to the Catholic tribes of Maine and Nova Scotia (to which, incidentally, the British had long since sent a priest). Thus, when Father La Motte was recalled to the fleet in October 1779, a second naval chaplain, Father Frédéric de Bourges, a Capuchin, was sent from Admiral Ternay's fleet at Newport; and in September 1781, when Father Bourges was recalled to fleet duty, the General Court, at the recommendation of the French consul, dispatched naval chaplain Father Juniper Berthiaume, a Recollect Franciscan, to the Penobscot, with whom he remained on duty until June 1784, when he learned that the General Court would no longer be paying his salary. The war was over, the Catholic Indians of Maine were no longer strategically necessary, and—perhaps—old habits, former ways of thinking, were returning to Massachusetts.

Sea battle, siege, surrender

Now ensued in swift succession a scenario of sea, siege, and surrender that ended Great Britain's willingness to pursue its six-year military effort to thwart American independence. In each phase of this unfolding scenario—the Battle of the Chesa-peake, the siege of Yorktown, the surrender of Lieutenant General Cornwallis—French arms provided the margin of victory. A nascent nation, at its most resourceful and organized, could never have put to sea so many ships, concentrated so many trained soldiers in one place, so artfully employed the tactics and technology of siege, or borne such expenditures of funds as France did on behalf of its American ally. This final battle witnessed Catholic France, with the help of Catholic Spain (a half million silver pesos on behalf of the Yorktown campaign were raised in Havana in less than twenty-four hours) and Holland (thanks to John Adams), bring to suc-cessful conclusion a Revolutionary War that a mere year earlier seemed to have come to the end of its financial tether.

Even before the armies of Washington and Rochambeau arrived at Yorktown, a resilient Lafayette had deployed some five thousand troops in blocking arrange-ments around the Yorktown plateau. Still, the British enjoyed direct access to Chesapeake Bay and the Atlantic. Three fleets were therefore now racing toward Yorktown—a British fleet under Admiral Sir Thomas Graves and French fleets under the command of Admiral de Grasse (from the West Indies) and Admiral de Barras (from Newport)—hoping to establish naval superiority. Admiral de Grasse's twenty-four ships of the line arrived first, in late August, and when the British fleet arrived on 5 September, de Grasse sailed out of Chesapeake Bay to engage it. Thus began the Battle of the Chesapeake (or Virginia Capes), the decisive naval battle of the Revolutionary War.

Forty-three ships of the line, twenty-four French and nineteen British, deploying a total of 2,952 cannons, were engaged in the maneuvering and two-hour cannon duel that followed. No naval battle of this magnitude had ever occurred in North America. Previously, American ships had won great victories in ship-to-ship actions. Off the coast of Virginia, by contrast, the clash of two French fleets under the command of Admiral de Grasse and a combined British fleet under the command of Admiral Sir Thomas Graves represented a scale of naval warfare hitherto unknown in the Western Hemisphere. The French lost 220 killed; the English, 90. Casualties would have soared much higher if winds had not forced the two fleets to approach each other at angles that prevented maximum broadsides. In any event, the French held off the British, who returned to New York. The British were thus prevented from relieving Cornwallis by sea and facilitating his escape from Yorktown. Instead, the French fleet now controlled the York River and Chesapeake Bay. The encirclement of Cornwallis by land and sea was complete.

Admiral de Barras had brought to Yorktown eighteen transport ships carrying the latest in siege equipment. Admiral de Grasse brought some three thousand additional French troops, transported from Saint-Domingue in the West Indies. Having been in the United States for more than a year and having recently brought his army to Mount Kisco, New York, on the Hudson, for joint operations with Washington, Rochambeau admired and respected the American commander in chief. Although Rochambeau held the same rank as Washington, lieutenant general, and commanded the most troops, he placed himself under Washington's command. Thus, the besieging forces enjoyed unity of command as well as the efficient employment of Rochambeau's impressive siege skills earned across the years on the battlefields of Western Europe.

Early in the morning of 28 September 1781, the French fleet and around sixteen thousand French and American troops were in place, and a classic European-style siege commenced. Tactics included constant artillery fire, the digging of advance and defensive parallel lines and construction redoubts, sorties, and counter-sorties through abatis, sniper fire (an American specialty), trench and other forms of below-ground living (Lord Cornwallis based himself in a cave), taunting of the British (another American specialty, given the six years of misery now approaching conclusion), and the mounting British casualties. On 15 October Cornwallis attempted an escape via barges across the York River, followed by a forced march to New York. A sudden squall, however, forced him to take back the thousand troops he had managed to ferry across. The next day, the artillery fire raining down on the British was worse than ever. On 17 October Cornwallis sent an officer across the lines to offer surrender. A day and a half of discussion ensued. The British surrendered at two o'clock in the afternoon of 19 October.[14]

The ceremony of surrender

Abbé Claude Robin was on hand to witness the surrender and described the ceremony a year later in Letter 11 of his *New Travels through North-America* (1783). With its first-person observations and occasional tidbits of gossip, Robin's account adds a French perspective and liveliness to the surrender ceremony. The sheer formality of what ensued underscored the European orientation and predominance of the siege now completed. At dawn, 19 October 1781, Scots pipers announced a day of formal surrender. Although the official time for the surrender ceremony was two o'clock in the afternoon, Robin writes that it did not get underway until four. The French and American armies, the abbé tells us, were lined up on Surrender Field (as it is now called) shoulder to shoulder, single file, for nearly a mile, Americans at the right end of the line and the French at the left, with the splendidly uniformed and mounted Washington and Rochambeau facing the line. At two (or four) o'clock, the British and the Hessians—their regimental colors cased, their unloaded muskets held lowered to the ground, black cloths muffling their drums—began their march of surrender past the Franco-American line. Robin does not report, nor have historians agreed, that the British band played the popular tune "The World Turned Upside Down" as it filed past the victors of the siege. British and Hessian soldiers stacked thousands of muskets in designated places (also surrendered were 244 artillery pieces) and, having laid down their arms, assembled themselves as prisoners of war, some 7,247 now having this status.

Yet if it were played, "The World Turned Upside Down" would have perfectly expressed the feelings of Lord Charles Cornwallis, who, feigning sickness, did not attend the ceremony. In a state of depressive disorientation nearly verging on a breakdown, Cornwallis won the sympathy of the abbé. Here, after all, was the most effective British general of the war—the counterpart of Nathanael Greene among the Americans, the essential second-in-command, talented, hardworking, assured as to tactics, brave in the field, adored by his men, crucial to victory after victory throughout the past six years—disconsolately sulking like Achilles in his tent, absent from this last rite of battle, starting with the presentation of his sword to Washington, as artists of the future (the near future, in fact) would indicate. Cornwallis left that task to Guards officer Major General Charles O'Hara, who also led the British troops past the line on Surrender Field. As a calculated insult, the arrogant guardsman first offered his sword to the comte de Rochambeau, who rejected the offer and gestured toward Washington. Washington refused to accept O'Hara's sword and indicated that he would accept a sword of surrender only from Cornwallis, the ranking British officer. He designated O'Hara's equal in rank, Major General Benjamin Lincoln, to accept O'Hara's offer.

When Cornwallis recovered from his depression, he called upon Washington, and the two of them walked and talked together. On one such occasion, Abbé Robin reports, Washington advised Cornwallis to wear the hat he was carrying, lest he catch cold. "Sir," Robin reports Cornwallis as replying, slapping his head three times, "as to my head, it is no matter what becomes of it now!" To his surprise, however, Cornwallis was well received when he returned to England—in recognition, perhaps, of the gallantry with which he had served as a combat commander during six long years of a war with which the English had long since become disenchanted.[15]

In the eleventh letter of his *Travels through North-America*, Abbé Robin underscores the European dimension of the victory, defeat, and surrender by contrasting the dress and behavior of the French, Hessian, and English militia with that of American militia. Prior to the surrender ceremony, Cornwallis opened stores and supplies to his soldiers with orders that every soldier should take what he needed to bring his uniform to parade condition. When Cornwallis' troops filed out for surrender,

Robin states, their smart appearance, even in defeat, matched the equally elegant uniforms of the French lines. The French, English, Scots, and Hessian lines, moreover, contained men of soldiering age, similar height, and crisp drill. The American line, by contrast—here, one can speculate that Robin is referring to American militia soldiers from Virginia and not uniformed Continentals—suffered from "the disproportion observable among them in point of age and size, and the dissimilarity of their dress, which was also dirty and ragged", which "set off the French to great advantage, who, notwithstanding so much fatigue, maintained at all times an erect, soldierly and vigorous air". Robin also praises the dress of the British troops: "but all their finery served only to humble them the more when contrasted with the miserable appearances of the Americans; these haughty Englishmen did not even dare to look up at their conqueror."

Robin observes that the French took pity on the English as "silent and ashamed they one after another deposited their arms in the stipulated place, and that they might not sink and die under their humiliation, we kept the spectators at a considerable distance". Following the completion of the musket-stacking ceremony, moreover, "the English officers had the civility to pay a compliment to the meanest of the French, which they did not deign to do to the Americans of the highest rank."

After the surrender, an American officer complained to Robin, "the English behaved with the same overbearing insolence as if they had been conquerors." The Americans, in turn ("who seemed resolved to take ample vengeance for the robberies and murders that had been perpetrated in their habitations"), were overtly hostile to the English. Yet even here the abbé backtracks his remarks with the next detail he provides. "Among others", he notes, "I saw the lady of an English colonel come to our camp with tears in her eyes to beg the protection of a French guard to defend her and her infants from the violence of an American soldier." During the rest of his stay at Yorktown, Robin comments, the English stayed away from the Americans, "while they lived upon familiar terms with the French and sought upon all occasions to give them proofs of their esteem".[16]

The siege of Yorktown resulted in 156 British and Hessian deaths and 52 French killed, together with hundreds of casualties on either side. For eighteenth-century Europeans, victors and vanquished alike, Abbé Robin seems to be suggesting, war was, like so much else, enmeshed in code and ritual. For Americans at Yorktown, by contrast—20 dead, 56 wounded—Yorktown came at the end of six years of bloody, repressive conflict that pitted a British army seasoned by continental warfare against semiorganized local militia and an emergent Continental Army. The French and the English might meet after the surrender ceremony as military professionals, but southern American militiamen had another point of view entirely. So volatile was this situation, so bitter had become this conflict, that the British negotiated the right not to hand over but to repatriate to New York unnamed Loyalist leaders along with paroled British officers. That aggressions against the British were held to a minimum was a testimony to the control Washington and his senior officers exercised over the American militia. The only major disturbance Robin notes was when a French officer drew his sword and challenged an American officer to a duel. The American officer grabbed a halberd (a six-foot-long pike surmounted by a battle-ax and a spearpoint) and disarmed and wounded the Frenchman. "In France", opines Robin of the American officer's refusal of a challenge and his resort to a more advantageous weapon, "he would have been driven with disgrace out of the army, but General Washington contented himself with punishing the American not for having combated with unequal arms, but for raising a disturbance in the army."[17]

Philadelphia demonstrations

Celebration edged into mob action when word of the Yorktown victory reached Philadelphia on 21 October. Ostensibly, these demonstrations began as festivities but rapidly degraded into raids on homes of known or suspected Loyalists and then morphed into assaults on the homes of wealthy Philadelphians, regardless of political persuasion. Hence, the Rawle family residence became an object of attack on the night of 24–25 October, as Anna Rawle, the daughter of a mildly-Loyalist-to-neutral-Quaker household, recorded in her diary for later transmission to her absent mother. Throughout the night, Rawle writes, her neighborhood roared with men's shouts and the sounds of glass windows being shattered. "As we had not the pleasure of seeing any of the gentlemen in the house", Rawle states ironically, "nor the furniture cut up, and goods stolen, nor been beat, nor pistols pointed at our breasts, we may count our sufferings light compared to many others. Mr. Gibbs was obliged to make his escape over a fence, and while his wife was endeavouring to shield him from the rage of one of the men, she received a violent bruise in the breast, and a blow in the face which made her nose bleed."

Looting, as might be expected, was widespread. "John Drinker", Rawle itemizes, "has lost half the goods out of his shop and been beat by them; in short the sufferings of those they pleased to style Tories would fill a volume and shake the credulity of those who were not here on that memorable night, and to-day Philadelphia makes an uncommon appearance, which ought to cover the Whigs with eternal confusion. A neighbor of ours had the effrontery to tell Mrs. G. that he was sorry for her furniture, but not for her windows—a ridiculous distinction that many of them make."

Still, Rawle does record examples of Whig families coming to the aid of neutrals and, perhaps, outright Loyalists, including the Rawle family, who had been helped by their Whig neighbors. Some Whigs, moreover, advised those under attack to illuminate their home from within as a sign of Whig loyalties. "Even the firm Uncle Fisher", Rawle notes of an openly Loyalist relative, "was obliged to submit to have his windows illuminated for they had pickaxes and iron bars with which they had done considerable injury to his house, and would soon have demolished it had not some of the Hodges and other people got in back and acted as they pleased. All Uncle's sons were out but Sammy, and if they had been at home it was in vain to oppose them."[18]

Light up your house if you favor independence! That was the message. By the end of the demonstrations, most wealthy Philadelphia households had decided upon illumination as the better part of valor. The United States had a class system, true, and some class-based looting and violence took place. But Philadelphia did not suffer the full-scale rioting or semiorganized mob action soon to characterize the French Revolution. Among the three thousand Loyalists who had long since departed for New York after Sir Henry Clinton and his army left on 18 June 1778 were, presumably, the majority of Philadelphia's outspoken Loyalists. Those

Loyalists who remained behind were most likely mildly so or next to neutral. Whig Philadelphia needed to celebrate Yorktown, of course, and perhaps even break a few windows, but the men never became a French Revolution–style mob bent on wholesale retribution.

Prayers of thanksgiving

Following the victory of Yorktown, prayers of thanksgiving flowed abundantly in the devoutly Protestant nation. The morning following the surrender ceremony, Washington issued a general order congratulating the American and French armies and the French navy for the victory and directed that divine services be held in the brigades and divisions, which he urged soldiers to attend "with that seriousness of deportment and gratitude which the recognition of such reiterated and astonishing interpositions of Providence demand of us". Hearing news of the victory, Congress adjourned to "go in procession to a Dutch Lutheran Church and return thanks to Almighty God for the special favor He had manifested to their struggling country". Congress also appointed a day of National Thanksgiving and Prayer, 13 December 1781, "in acknowledgment of the signal interposition of Divine Providence".[19]

On Sunday, 4 November 1781, a Mass of Thanksgiving was celebrated at Saint Mary's Church, Philadelphia, which the French minister Anne-César, chevalier de la Luzerne, invited Congress and the leading citizens of the city to attend. Abbé Bandol preached a sermon comparing the victory at Yorktown to Joshua's victory over Jericho: a biblical reference thoroughly in tune with American Protestant sermonizing. Indeed, Protestant-Catholic and Franco-American relations were on Bandol's mind that morning as he asked, "How is it that two nations once divided, jealous, inimical, and nursed in reciprocal prejudices have now become so closely united as to form but one?" Only Divine Providence could fully explain this wonderful development, Bandol exulted. The French chaplain then launched into a hymn of praise for the American society that Providence had preserved. His rhetoric anticipated the outpouring of praiseful analysis and assertions of linked destinies by French admirers of the United States in the half century to come. "For how many favors have we not to thank Him during the course of the present year?" Bandol preached. "Your union, which was at first supported by justice alone, had been consolidated by your courage and the knot which ties you together, is become indissoluble, by the accession of all the states, and the unanimous voice of all the confederates. You present to the universe the noble sight of a society, which, founded in equality and justice, secures to the individuals who compose it, the utmost happiness which can be derived from human institutions."[20] Within the year, Abbé Robin would elaborate this French lauding of America into book length. That same year, J. Hector St. John de Crèvecoeur's *Letters from an American Farmer* (1782) was published, and in due time the magisterial *Democracy in America* (1835) by Alexis de Tocqueville brought to a triumphant conclusion French appreciation—and occasional criticism—of American society. Celebration continued with Louis XVI's royal decree issued on 26 November 1781 that Te Deums be celebrated in the cathedrals and churches of France in honor of the victory at Yorktown. The king sent the same decree to Rochambeau, informing him "that I desire it [the Te Deum] be likewise sung in the town or camp where you may be with the corps of troops, the command of which has been entrusted to you".[21]

On the American side, praise ensued from Washington himself—a letter, for example, to French corps commander the duc de Lauzun upon the departure of the duke and his soldiers for Europe, promising them lifelong friendship from state legislatures and citizen groups. The legislature of Rhode Island passed a formal vote of thanks to Rochambeau and his soldiers, who had spent a year of training and preparation in that state. ("May Heaven reward your exertions in the cause of humanity, and the particular regard you have paid to the rights of the citizens.") The merchants of Baltimore were equally admiring of Rochambeau's civility and the good behavior of his troops. In Boston on 8 January 1783, a gathering of free-holders and inhabitants of the city assembled in Faneuil Hall for a ceremony of farewell and vote of thanks to departing French troops now under the command of Baron de Vioménil. Rochambeau had already departed for France, where the king named him governor of Picardy. "May the happy alliance with France never be dissolved or impaired!" the assembled citizens voted. "And may the reciprocal fruits of it to both nations be perpetually augmented."[22]

Even the Protestant pulpit participated in this diapason of praise. "That this puissant Prince", preached the Reverend O. Hart to his congregation in Hopewell, New Jersey, on 26 November 1781, in a sermon later published as "What Hath God Wrought?" (Hart was referring to Louis XVI), "should deign to take notice of America in her infantile state when under the iron rod of oppression and declared to be in a state of actual rebellion—that he should then conclude a treaty of alliance and trade with us, upon the most honorable and generous principles, without taking the least advantage of our weakness, but rather nobly aiming to afford us relief in our time of distress, was in very deed amazing to us, alarming to Britain and surprising to the world. If this event was not indicative of the benevolence of that munificent King's heart it was no less a token of favour from the Great King of Kings."[23]

The birth of the dauphin

The culmination of these celebrations was the reception for fifteen hundred guests, including members of Congress, hosted in mid-July 1782 by the French ambassador Anne-César, chevalier de la Luzerne, in his Philadelphia townhouse in honor of the birth of a dauphin (heir to the throne) on 22 October 1781, ensuring Bourbon continuity. Taking leave of the American army to design and organize the proceedings, Pierre L'Enfant, a French army engineer serving with the Continentals, added two pavilions to Luzerne's leased townhouse, one for dancing to music provided by French army musicians and the other for the supper that began at one o'clock the next morning, prepared by thirty French army cooks. Each pavilion was decorated in ambitious symbolism: a rising sun surmounted by thirteen stars, for example, with an Indian (America) dazzled by its rays and a woman (England) emptying a sack of gold coins at the feet of another Indian but being rejected. The dance pavilion was furnished with elevated boxes for non-dancing VIPs. Fulsome toasts extolling the birth of the dauphin and Franco-American friendship lasted throughout the dinner. Outside, meanwhile, another thousand or so onlookers (kept off the property by Pennsylvania militia) enjoyed the comings and goings of the invited guests as the uninvited waited patiently for the fireworks that capped the celebration. La Luzerne subsequently submitted a bill for five thousand dollars to the French foreign office. The French army submitted its bills through military channels.

Enlightened self-interest admixed with an effort to overcome prior alienation and resentment can be seen in this outburst of mutual praise. The French—fearful that Americans would come to a separate agreement with the British—were anxious to maintain control of the alliance and the treaty process as the war entered a phase of cease-fire and negotiation. On their part, Americans continued to fear a French desire to retake Canada and therefore wished to keep as closely tied to France as possible, lest France lose sight of the alliance and indulge its continental ambitions. In regard to lingering resentments, the French were shocked at American hostility to the British and to American Loyalists now that the war was over. The French also feared lingering resentments toward them.

Age-long antagonism based on religious differences helped fuel this compensatory outpouring of praise and mutual regard. It would run counter to the structure and dynamics of human psychology and sociology to postulate that an overwhelmingly Protestant society with a strong tradition of anti-Catholicism would (like Saint Paul on the road to Damascus) experience such a dramatic and complete metanoia as, at first glance, this post-Yorktown effusive lauding of France might indicate. Even as the Enlightenment pushed toward a zenith of its influence, France remained the Eldest Daughter of the Church. Witness the more than ninety priest chaplains who accompanied the French military on land and sea. Still, Americans were capable of overlooking Roman Catholicism (for the time being) in gratitude to France for at long last entering the war in full force. A few of the more objectionable American prejudices—for example, that the French were a dwarfish race, surviving on frogs and snails, and their officers were effeminate dandies—melted away when Americans encountered French forces who were as tall as Americans and ate more or less what Americans ate, effective soldiers under the command of skilled, battle-tested officers.

Downplaying tensions

In the post-Yorktown era, Americans were willing to downplay—indeed, banish from the press entirely—reports of French soldiers' misbehavior and endlessly praise the angelic deportment of French soldiers and sailors ashore. Such a scenario strains credulity, obviously, and in *No King, No Popery* (1995), historian Francis D. Cogliano suggests a nuanced version that is more in keeping with the realities of American needs and the realities of soldiers and sailors in foreign ports. The Whig leadership of Boston, Cogliano argues, almost immediately—which is to say, upon the arrival in Boston on 20 August 1778 of the French fleet under the command of the comte d'Estaing—understood the danger of anti-Catholicism of the no-popery sort. (Indeed, Washington had come to the same conclusion three years earlier when conducting the siege of Boston.) Hence began the era of good feeling between the Whig upper class and the officers of the French fleet, as previously presented. Still, while the leadership of Boston might comprehend this quite clearly, six thousand French sailors were, as of September 1778, stationed in eleven French ships anchored in Boston Bay. Under orders from d'Estaing, moreover, this fleet had just abandoned a joint Franco-American effort to retake Newport, Rhode Island, from the British; and so French stock among rank-and-file Americans was at a low point.

New England, moreover, was suffering from a serious food shortage. And so, when, on the evening of 8 September 1778, sailors from the American privateer *Marlborough* approached a French naval bakery established on shore and asked for bread, a fight ensued. Two French officers tried to break it up, and one of them, the chevalier de Saint-Sauveur, was stabbed above his right eye and died a week later. At this point, Cogliano states, both Admiral d'Estaing and the Boston Whig leadership feared the same thing—a widespread flare-up between French and Bostonians that could destabilize the alliance. Admiral d'Estaing permitted the chevalier de Saint-Sauveur to be buried secretly on 16 September in a late-night service. The Whig elite of Boston entered into a pro-French program: a civic reception and dinner three days later for local dignitaries and four hundred French naval officers in Faneuil Hall sponsored by John Hancock, followed on 28 October by a ball at the Concert Hall for two hundred American and French guests, also sponsored by Hancock. These displays of solidarity, according to Cogliano, conveyed a clear message to lower-register Bostonians of the antipopery persuasion: the French are our honored allies; we need them to win the war; the establishment of this city is on their side. As far as the Boston elite was concerned, this program of theatrical intimidation worked. The chevalier de Saint-Sauveur's murder was attributed to British deserters attached to the crew of the *Marlborough*, but no one was indicted.

On the evening of 28 December 1780, a fight between five American and seven French sailors broke out on Long Wharf. One American died from a knife thrust into his stomach, and two other Americans were seriously wounded. Defended by Benjamin Hitchborn, a leading Boston lawyer, the seven French sailors were indicted and tried in court. At least three members of the jury were prominent Whigs. The jury acquitted one French sailor and found the others guilty of reduced charges, for which they received light sentences.

Between 1778 and 1782, the détente banning antipopery held alongside the program of lavish pro-French entertaining. Appreciative of this effort, the French foreign ministry put minister Samuel Cooper on a retainer of two hundred pounds per year to serve as its public-relations representative in Boston. In times past, Cooper, the Dudleian Lecturer for 1773, had been routinely anti-Catholic. The Quebec Act of 1774, however, convinced him that Great Britain, not France, was now the colonies' greatest enemy. Putting aside his anti-Catholicism, Cooper began to write and preach so effectively on behalf of the Franco-American alliance following the arrival of d'Estaing's fleet in 1777 that the French ambassador at the time, Conrad Alexandre Gérard, put Cooper—a member of the Harvard Corporation, the governing body of Harvard College—on the payroll as a publicist, greeter, and escort for visiting French dignitaries. The Reverend Cooper gave no further anti-Catholic sermons or Dudleian Lectures while this retainer remained in effect.

When the French ambassador Anne-César, chevalier de la Luzerne, visited Boston on 30 August 1779, the president, faculty, and robed students of Harvard College accorded him a reception in the Yard and Harvard Hall, probably arranged by the Reverend Cooper. Rochambeau was warmly and publicly received when he visited

Boston in December 1780. On 21 August 1781, Governor Hancock welcomed Admiral Louis-Philippe de Rigaud, comte de Vaudreuil, second-in-command of the French navy during the Revolutionary War, and his officers at a public dinner after the marquis' fleet had arrived earlier that month. On 4 October 1781, the leading merchants of Boston gave a dinner in Faneuil Hall for the consul general and all naval officers in the city, at which both the kings of France and Spain were toasted.

Nevertheless, the reformed 1780 constitution, affirmed by the voters of Massachusetts, prohibited Catholics from holding the office of governor, thereby demonstrating a fear of papal or Vatican interference in American political life. On this issue, Doctor Benjamin Rush proved a curmudgeonly but accurate prophet in a letter dated 16 July 1782, in which he described to a friend the recent extravaganza sponsored by the chevalier de la Luzerne in Philadelphia in honor of the birth of the dauphin. In contrast to the invitation he received and rejected two years earlier for the Requiem Mass at Saint Mary's for Don Juan de Miralles, Rush did accept an invitation to this more recent post-Yorktown fête. Still, Rush's presence at this over-the-top French reception did not represent a change of attitude. "How great the revolution in the mind of an American!" Rush observed of the evening, "to rejoice in the birth of a prince whose religion he has been taught to consider unfriendly to humanity. And above all, how new the phenomenon for republicans and freemen to rejoice in the birth of a prince who must one day be the support of a monarchy and slavery. There are no prejudices so strong, no opinions so sacred, and no contradictions so palpable, that will not yield to the love of liberty."[24] Rush seems to be struggling with himself, or perhaps, in the haste of letter writing, he is unaware of the contradiction or paradox he has stumbled into. On the one hand (firm antipapist that he is), Rush considers it ironic that American republicans should celebrate the insurance of succession for a Catholic monarchy with, from Rush's point of view, evil intentions. And yet a love of liberty, a gratitude for French assistance at Yorktown, impels Americans to do their best to put aside their long-held prejudices and opinions. For American Catholics, a mere 1 percent of the post-Yorktown United States of America, liberty was indeed welcome news.

Negotiations with Great Britain for an end to the Revolutionary War and a guarantee of American independence likewise involved two of three American commissioners who had learned to keep their anti-Catholicism under wraps while serving in Europe. Of Huguenot origins, John Jay had once held and expressed outspoken anti-Catholic views as American minister to Spain from 1780 to 1782. Jay, however, kept his opinions on hold for the time being. As a son of New England, John Adams was naturally skeptical—patronizing, even—of Catholicism. Still, as commissioner to France from 1777 to 1779 and commissioner to Holland (a partially Catholic country) from 1780 to 1782, he had not only exercised discretion, like John Jay, but also learned to respect Roman Catholicism as a sociopolitical force, like his fellow Bostonian Whigs. Benjamin Franklin, by contrast, moved in midlife from a routinized anti-Catholicism to a sophisticated appreciation of Roman Catholic organization and culture. Franklin achieved excellent relations with the French hierarchy and clerical intelligentsia as well as with the Court of Rome. These connections would prove crucial to the organization of Roman Catholicism in the postwar era.

5

Paris 1782

Veterans of the Revolutionary War resume their lives

In eighteenth-century France, the ranks of abbés included well-born freelance secular priests or at least clerics in major orders (deacons or subdeacons) who held
ecclesiastical benefices and hence enjoyed an income that allowed many of them to
pursue careers as writers, editors, scientists, diplomats, or similar occupations. Abbé
Robin was of this variety, although he was also active in the priestly ministry, as his
chaplaincy in chief suggests. Returning to France following Yorktown, Robin did
what his sort of abbé did best: write a book, in his case a task already underway in
the letters he had composed while in America. *New Travels through North-America*
is structured as a north-to-south journey from Boston to Yorktown and contains
four valuable appendices of primary documents. Thus, *New Travels* is at its most
basic a camp diary by a Catholic chaplain with a solid grasp of military matters, who
rides from Boston to New York and, from New York, marches on foot to Virginia
alongside the troops to whom he ministers and some of whom he sees through their
last hours. As a chaplain priest, Abbé Robin is attentive to his priestly duties but not
pompously pious in his approach to his military flock, mainly enlisted men, who
prefer a chaplain attuned to their psychology and hardships. In rank equivalency,
Robin is an officer but one freed from the responsibilities of command, which
confers on him a mobility that allows him to observe American society at all levels.
He is, after all, an abbé, a priest of refinement and taste, not a snob, but a gentleman of the cloth, accustomed to moving in learned and influential circles. Yet he
carries his own backpack on march alongside the troops and respects their bravery
and panache, chronicling it whenever possible. Among other descriptions, he notes
the fifteen-year-old trooper, an officer's servant, bayoneted to death by the British
in the course of a surprise sally; and the veteran artillery sergeant regretting to his
(literally) dying breath, not his shattered body, but his failure to take out the British
gunner who bested him.

Robin's synoptic vision

Abbé Robin loves the American regions he travels through. Their beauty, geology,
flora, and fauna speak to the priest and scientific savant in him of the goodness of
the Creator as well as the science and poetry of what he is experiencing: the phos-
phorescent colors of the sea beheld on the voyage across the Atlantic, dolphins
and flying fish enlivening the water; the sting of the jellyfish he ignorantly picked
up when a sailor caught one and threw it on the deck; the marine vegetation

encountered as his ship approached shore, a mass of which he personally examined, marveling at its totality of design. And once ashore: the great rivers flowing seaward and determining in partnership with coastal bays the placement of cities, the mountain ranges, the forests and trees (dozens of them, by name), the flowering plants, the birds in abundance (compared with their European counterparts), the flying squirrels—such marvels that Robin attempts an inquiry into their aerodynamics— the gigantic multicolored caterpillars and the dazzling butterflies they become. He also writes of the venomous spider that bites him in Virginia, throwing him into pain and paralysis and bringing him close to death for want of breath before his condition stabilizes and he recovers. (As of 1782, however, the aftereffects of this poisoning were still bothering him.)

Robin makes specific remarks regarding the cities he encounters: their sites and urban plans, their local economies (Long Wharf in Boston, the shipyards of Philadelphia), their homes and places of worship. Although Boston's deep quietude on Sunday slightly unnerves him, the abbé is respectful of the pervasive Protestantism and is genuinely moved by the sight of a Boston family gathered about the hearth as its patriarch reads Scripture. Although he admires their congregational hymn singing, Robin finds the Protestant churches of Boston excessively austere. "All these churches are destitute of ornaments", he notes. "No addresses are made to the heart and the imagination; there is no visible object to suggest to the mind for what purpose a man comes into these places, what he *is* and what he *will shortly be*. Neither painting nor sculpture represent those great events which ought to recall him to his duty and awaken his gratitude, nor are those *heroes* in piety brought into view, whom it is his duty to admire and endeavour to imitate. The pomp of ceremony is here wanting to shadow out the greatness of the *being* he goes to worship; there are no processions to testify the homage we owe to *him*, that great Spirit of the Universe, by whose will Nature itself exists, through whom the fields are covered with harvests, and the trees are loaded with fruits."[1]

Although he was known to be a Frenchman and a Roman Catholic priest, Robin comments, "I was continually receiving new civilities from several of the best families in this town: still", Robin lamented, concerning Roman Catholicism, "the people in general retain their old prejudices."[2] A polymathic savant, Robin visits Harvard, the College of New Jersey at Princeton, and the College of William and Mary at Williamsburg. The abbé praises their faculties, libraries, and students, noting that Harvard students write and act in plays based on recent events—the Battle of Bunker Hill, the capture of General Burgoyne, the treason of General Arnold—rather than be confined to classical or biblical subjects.

Robin displays an alert and generally approving eye for colonial architecture— the ship-like wooden homes of Boston, the stately brick domiciles of Philadelphia and manors of Maryland and Virginia—and the serviceable, well-designed furniture he finds within, all of which contrast with the urban design styles of France. He remarks on the prevalence of what he considers a somewhat careless and hasty corn-based cookery, north and south; makes suggestions regarding the further refinement of corn-based cuisine; and, while praising the wheat and rye crops of New England, New York, and New Jersey, encourages efforts to improve the art of baking bread. Americans, he complains, drink too much tea, especially in New England, and he wonders whether this excessive tea drinking is leading to tooth decay and a shortened life. Indeed, the comparative brevity of life for the men of Boston fascinates Robin, and he studies the life dates on headstones to corroborate his belief that the men of Boston died earlier than they should have—a fact he is at a loss to explain, given the suitability of Massachusetts for human habitation.

The American people observed

The people of America! The abbé never fails to note the characteristics, great or small, of all types, regions, and classes. The young women of Boston, he opines, "are of large size, well proportioned, their features generally regular, and their complexion fair, without ruddiness. They have less cheerfulness and ease of behaviour, than the ladies of France, but more of greatness and dignity; I have even imagined that I have seen something in them, that answers to the ideas of beauty we gain from those master-pieces of the artists of antiquity, which are yet extant in our days." Just as the men of Boston tend to die earlier, the women of Boston tend to lose their beauty after age twenty-five and have lost it completely by thirty-five or forty. With a French eye for fashion, Robin observes how the women of Boston— "deprived of all shows and public diversions"—employ Sunday church services as their only opportunity to show themselves as members of the beau monde, attired in their finest silks, their hair dressed in a profusion of plumes. The abbé adds a slightly critical, even catty, note: "The hair of the head is raised and supported upon cushions to an extravagant height, somewhat resembling the manner in which the French ladies wore their hair some years ago."[3]

In Newport and Providence, the abbé is impressed by the civility and good manners of the upper classes (Robin tells a touching story of how a Newport gentleman discreetly and charitably resolves his wife's affair with a French officer), the large families, the freedom afforded women in daily life and travel, the inventiveness and self-reliance of American farmers, and the more democratic concept of military rank among Americans. And yet, he discloses, American soldiers hold the Marquis (meaning Lafayette) in high regard as an astute field commander and fair-minded officer: respected virtues, to be sure, since the abbé also notes—despite American soldiers' alleged equality to their French counterparts—the frequency and severity of corporal punishment leveled against enlisted men in the American army, as well as the ability of these men, tied to wheels and being whipped, to take their punishment silently.

In New York, the abbé encounters for the first time all-black American infantry companies commanded by white officers. In New Jersey, he encounters Americans of Alsatian and Dutch descent, the women dressed in traditional attire as they deliver provisions to the French. Robin appreciates New Jersey and Pennsylvania— the soil and climate, the development of rural townships and agriculture, the diversity of peoples—and finds in the Delaware River that divides them an American version of the Loire. As capital city of the American confederation, Philadelphia (as might be expected) delights him with its stately homes, its regularity of streets and public spaces as established by William Penn, its networks of wharfs and shipyards, its Quaker heritage and elegant Protestant churches, its Roman Catholic church and chapel, its American Philosophical Society and public hospital, and Independence Hall, where independence was first declared.

Crossing into Maryland and Virginia, however, while he admires Baltimore, Annapolis, and Williamsburg, slavery has a jarring effect on him. Starting with Baltimore, the South seems so rich, the homes so spacious and well furnished, the carriages so smartly and swiftly propelled, the statehouses so assertive, the people so well dressed. "Female luxury here exceeds what is known in the provinces of France", the abbé comments. "A French hair dresser is a man of importance among them, and it is said, a certain dame here hires one of that craft at a thousand crowns a year salary." Yet slaves do the work, "unhappy blacks, whom European avarice and injustice hase taken from their native regions of Africa to cultivate possessions not their own, in a foreign soil".[4] Virginia, the abbé points out, reportedly has a population of 150,000 white residents and 500,000 African slaves. With an estimated 20,000 whites and at least 200,000 blacks, Maryland was even more disproportionately balanced between those slaves who did the work and those who were enjoying the fruits of their labor.

Meeting Washington

On the Hudson above New York, Abbé Robin meets Washington for the first time as the Americans and French reconnoiter the British fortifications defending the city. Robin's hymn of praise in Letter 3, while lavish, is still anchored in respect for the manner in which Washington made much of so little and recovered from his mistakes and defeats. Such an admission of past failures humanizes Washington and is welcomed by the twenty-first-century reader otherwise suspicious of Robin's laudatory tour de force. For the abbé, Washington is not only America's Fabius— the Roman general who defeated Hannibal by avoiding a pitched battle—but also the country's Peter the Great, the Russian tsar who prevailed over Sweden despite a string of defeats by keeping those losses to a minimum. The common people of America regard Washington as a godlike figure. "In all these extensive states", Robin writes, "the people consider him in the light of a beneficent God, dispensing peace and happiness around him—Old men, women and children, press about him when he accidentally passes along, and think themselves happy, once in their lives, to have seen him—they follow him through the towns with torches, and celebrate his arrival by public illuminations—The Americans, that cool and sedate people, who in the midst of their most trying difficulties, have attended only to the directions and impulses of plain method and common reason, are roused, animated and inflamed at the very mention of his name; and the first songs that sentiment or gratitude has dictated, have been to celebrate General Washington." Even a rational people, the abbé thus concludes, require heroes. But since Washington shares the "plain method and common reason" of the American people, his heroic stature at once expresses and reinforces the national character.[5]

Hopes for the future

Abbé Robin ends Letter 13, his last, with a capsule history of the Revolutionary War, now ending. The war, he argues, was animated in part by "the intolerant spirit of Presbyterianism, which has for so long a time been sowing the seeds of discord between them [the Americans] and the mother country". What if this same

Presbyterian spirit, the abbé asks, should reappear at a later date and, realigning itself once again with the mother country, turn against France? What if, for example, America would move against the French islands in the Caribbean because it desires a cheaper source of rum or tea? No, the abbé states, this will not happen. The sheer size and richness of the lands and resources of the United States will forestall such external aggressions. Americans will stay focused on internal development rather than on foreign wars. Besides, a new spirit is gaining strength. A universalizing of a philosophical sentiment that favors reason and tolerance offers a more productive pathway than sectarian strife. "One of the most affecting scenes, and which will do the most honour to the world," Robin concludes, "will be when all nations shall unite in erecting the same temples for the service of the Deity, and tuning the same anthems to his praise; and philosophy, which pretends to render mankind happier and better, ought to direct all her views and efforts to this great end."[6]

Molly Carroll, RIP

The year 1782 was not happy for Charles Carroll of Carrollton. That year, he lost his father, Charles Carroll of Annapolis, and his wife, Mary (Molly) Darnall Carroll, the mother of his three surviving children. Regarding women, Charles Carroll of Carrollton had a difficult history. He adored his mother but was separated from her by being sent to Europe for his education at the age of eleven and never saw her again. Nor did he actually meet seventeen-year-old Louisa Baker, with whom he fell madly in love when his Jesuit tutor pointed her out as a prospective wife as she walked on a Paris street with other students from a convent boarding school. Returning to Maryland at the age of twenty-seven after sixteen years of study at Jesuit colleges on the Continent and law in London, Carroll became engaged to a cousin, Rachel Cooke, despite his obsession with Louisa Baker. Unfortunately, Miss Cooke died shortly before their intended wedding. Charles Carroll thereupon married even closer within his family; the young woman he did marry, Molly Darnall, was the daughter of his father's cousin and housekeeper Rachel Brooke Darnall, who was permanently separated from her scapegrace husband, executed in 1772 by the colony. Following Charles Carroll's marriage to Molly Darnall on 5 June 1768, a complicated set of emotional relationships developed. At the apex of these relationships was Charles (Charley) Carroll's father, Charles Carroll of Annapolis (Papa), who held the primary affection and allegiance of everyone: Charley, his son; Cousin Rachel, actually the niece of Papa's late wife (Papa's niece by marriage) and his housekeeper; and her daughter Molly, Charley's wife, raised by Papa since she was twelve. Charley, meanwhile, revered Cousin Rachel, who had seen Charley's late mother through her final illness.

That tangle left the husband-wife relationship between Charley and Molly for consideration. As Charley's letters at the time of his engagement indicate—and as Molly's portrait painted by Charles Wilson Peale in 1771 corroborates—Molly Darnall Carroll was a beautiful red-headed woman of kindly temperament to whom Charles Carroll was genuinely attracted. Carroll's lingering obsession with Louisa Baker and his feelings of bereavement regarding his late fiancée, Rachel Cooke, however, affected him (he kept Rachel's portrait and a lock of her hair in his desk). Charles Carroll had every chance of happiness married to his cousin Molly.

True, Molly's father, whom she barely knew (if she knew him at all), was executed in 1772, but the Carroll fortune was far beyond any vulnerability to social disgrace. Charley and Molly leased Papa's fine four-story brick mansion in Annapolis, while Papa himself and housekeeper Cousin Rachel moved to Doughoregan Manor, Papa's country estate.

Molly Carroll loved fashion, entertaining, romance novels, and the social scene. Charles Carroll preferred work, privacy, the company of a serious book by the fireplace. He was frequently away from Annapolis on private business and, after 1777, on congressional business in Philadelphia. During these absences, Papa and Rachel came to live with Molly at Annapolis, or Molly took her children and lived at Doughoregan Manor under the affectionate care of her children's doting grandparents, Papa and her mother, Cousin Rachel.

Molly Carroll endured many closely spaced pregnancies early in her marriage. She bore seven children, but only three survived, two girls and a boy. Multiple pregnancies, childbirth, the death of children: being a wife and a mother was a dangerous and frequently sorrowful calling in late-eighteenth-century Maryland. Molly experienced pain, followed by grief, followed by anxiety and insomnia; she became increasingly addicted to laudanum, an opiate derivative. Charles Carroll—often away on business, in any event—coped with the loss of four of his children by accepting their deaths quietly if they died at birth or by keeping his distance from them if they survived but were sickly. In time, he maintained emotional distance from his wife and all his children, to his later remorse. Papa and Cousin Rachel became Molly's primary support as her health—a bilious disorder was diagnosed—deteriorated and her use of opium continued. It was Papa who emerged as the center of the three-generational family: Papa who encouraged Charley to be more supportive of Molly; Papa (and Rachel) who welcomed Molly back to her girlhood home and doted on her children, thus compensating for their father's distance; Papa who encouraged Molly to stay away from laudanum ("I earnestly beg it for the sake of Her family and Children, and as I love her", Papa wrote to Charley in May 1781); Papa who urged Charley to take his wife for a six-week stay in the summer of 1779 at Bath (Berkeley Springs, present-day West Virginia), named in honor of the Roman and English spa.[7] At Bath, Molly welcomed the social life more than the waters, and she especially appreciated the companionship of Baroness Frederika von Riedesel, wife of General Friedrich von Riedesel of the Convention Army—the officers and men of Burgoyne's forces defeated at Saratoga and placed on parole on the promise that they would never again take up arms against the United States. Molly Carroll loved drinking tea with the baroness and her distinguished husband or enjoying the impromptu musicales the baroness organized, at which the paroled general's wife sang Italian arias as her husband's aide-de-camp accompanied her on the violin. Invited to visit Doughoregan Manor, the von Riedesels were charmed by Papa, Cousin Rachel, the loving and affectionate Molly, her darling children, the plantation itself, and the manor—but no mention is made of Molly's husband in the baroness' later memoir of her American sojourn. While she praised the European-style landscaping Charles Carroll had developed for Doughoregan Manor, the baroness wrote, "In other respects he was not such a lovable man, but rather brusque and stingy, and not at all a suitable mate for his wife, who, although she would not let any of this be noticed, did not seem to be very happy."[8]

Charles Carroll of Carrollton was away from home on business when Molly gave birth in 1780 to her last child, Elizabeth, named in honor of Charles' mother. Nor was he present when Papa, age eighty, staying at Annapolis with Molly and the children, stood on the porch of his house—spyglass to his eye, focusing it on a sailboat in Spa Creek, Molly looking on with him—stepped off the porch, fell heavily to the ground, and died immediately. The horror of it all! The sudden death right before her eyes of the man who had raised her from the age of twelve, who was the beloved grandfather of her children and her own best friend, sent Molly into shock and prompted a return of those pains, physical and emotional, that had afflicted her for so long.

Taking to her bed, Molly died on 10 June 1782, two weeks after Papa's unexpected death. She was only thirty-three; but as Henrietta Hill Ogle's eyewitness account of her death indicates, Molly Darnall Carroll seemed almost eager to die. "I am afraid this cold Weather will make us all sick", writes her good friend Ogle. "I am now very unwell & quite low Spirited, was much shock'd at Poor Mrs. Carroll's death, but think she was almost to be envied, she died so happy, & and was sensible till a little time before she breathed her last, & frequently said to her Women, who were crying about her not to grieve but pray for her. That her God call'd & and she must go & wish'd to be with him & did not desire to live, & was as perfectly resign'd & compos'd as a person could be. She ask'd Doctor Scott several times the day she died how long he thought she could live, or if she was dying. We attended the Funeral. Mr. Ogle was a Pall Bearer. She was buried 4 miles out of Town.... Mr. Carroll has not been ill tho' in great grief[.] Thy favorite Betsy Carroll & her Brother the Priest is now with Mr. C."[9]

A year after Molly's death, her seventh and youngest child, Elizabeth (Betsy), a comfort to the still-grieving Charles Carroll, died, as had three of the other children Molly Carroll had brought into the world. Charles Carroll never remarried. In the years to come, he regretted the neglect of his family wrought by his earlier political fervor and did his best to remain close to his surviving daughters and their female offspring. In time, Carroll's three granddaughters took their Grandmother Molly's love of gaiety and social life to the pinnacle of beau monde London, to the benefit of Roman Catholicism in Great Britain.

Passages

And so the war was won, a treaty signed, and a republic loomed on the horizon. Time and history swept forward with a new, independent nation occupying the Atlantic seaboard of North America. Roman Catholics—Anglo-American, Irish American, French, Spanish, Polish, Hungarian—in various numbers and to various degrees had contributed to this victory. In doing so, they won a measure of religious freedom, and even acceptance, from Protestant states once committed to the anti-Catholic values of the Glorious Revolution of 1688 and the anti-Catholic restrictions of the prewar colonies. The war had cost Catholics fatalities proportionate to their numbers. Those who fought and survived or who otherwise participated in the war as elected officials or civilian participants of one sort or another now went on with their lives on stages grand and small. For some, the war ended before Yorktown and its aftermath, and so it is best to move forward as chronologically as possible in chronicling their passages from the Revolutionary or post-Revolutionary scene.

The behavior of Thomas Conway, the Gallicized Irish French army officer turned American major general, whose anti-Washington attitudes prompted the attachment of his name to the so-called Conway Cabal, which sought to replace Washington with Horatio Gates, so infuriated Brigadier General John Cadwalader that Cadwalader challenged Conway to a duel, which they fought on 4 July 1778. Cadwalader sent a bullet through Conway's mouth and neck, and at first the wound seemed fatal. It was not, however, and while Conway hovered between life and death, he dictated a letter of apology to Washington. Returning to France, Conway resumed his career in the French army, with distinction, and married the daughter of Maréchal, Baron de Copley, in the process. Serving in India as a regimental commander, a maréchal de camp (senior colonel), and governor-general of French possessions, Conway was awarded commander's rank in the Order of Saint Louis, France's highest military honor. An outspoken Royalist (Conway had a habit of being outspoken), he and his noble wife fled France in 1793 during the Reign of Terror.

Charles-Hector, comte d'Estaing, commander of the first French fleet to arrive in America, was not as fortunate. Although he supported the French Revolution and the National Assembly named him commanding general of the Versailles National Guard and later promoted him to admiral, d'Estaing remained faithful to Marie Antoinette and in 1793 testified on her behalf in the queen's trial. Charged with being a reactionary, d'Estaing was sent to the guillotine on 28 April 1794.

Jean-Baptiste Donatien de Vimeur, comte de Rochambeau, narrowly escaped the same fate. Returning to France, he was granted a pension of thirty thousand livres and appointed governor of the province of Picardy by Louis XVI, who awarded him the distinction of Marshal of France on 28 December 1791. The following year, Rochambeau took command of the Armée du Nord against the Austrians but suffered several reversals and resigned. During the Reign of Terror, he was arrested and spent time in prison awaiting the guillotine but was subsequently released. Once in power, Napoleon put Rochambeau on a pension, and the Marshal of France died of old age (at eighty-five) during the empire.

Rochambeau's naval counterpart, Admiral François Joseph Paul de Grasse, did not share Rochambeau's fate. Having played a coequal role with Rochambeau in the success of the Yorktown siege, de Grasse had not yet finished his war with Great Britain. Sailing to the West Indies, de Grasse deployed his fleet in a rematch of the Battle of the Chesapeake against the very same fleets commanded by Admiral Sir Samuel Hood and Admiral George Brydges Rodney overwhich he had recently prevailed. As in the Chesapeake encounter, de Grasse had under his control a second, smaller fleet commanded by Admiral Jacques-Melchior Saint-Laurent, comte de Barras. The same four fleets and the same admirals met as at Chesapeake, but this time the outcome was different. On 26 January 1782, Hood defeated de Grasse and de Barras at the Battle of Saint Kitts. Two and a half months later, Admiral Rodney captured de Grasse at the Battle of the Saintes, and de Grasse was ignominiously taken to London. Released with the signing of the Treaty of Paris, de Grasse returned to France, where, resentful of the criticisms being leveled against him, he demanded and received a court-martial inquiry into his conduct in the Caribbean. Although de Grasse was acquitted of any negligence or malfeasance, all this—the defeats, the captivity, the court-martial—constituted an unexpected acts 2, 3, and 4 for a Knight of Malta whose act 1 had been the victories of Chesapeake and Yorktown. De Grasse wrote and had published a *Mémoire justificatif* (1784), which served to underscore how misused he considered himself. He died four years after its printing and, now past all criticism, was laid to rest in a tomb in the Church of Saint-Roch in Paris.

Before Yorktown, the war in the South claimed the lives of two prominent European Catholic cavalrymen as well as Lafayette's mentor. Fighting with Pulaski's Legion as colonel commandant (deputy commander) during the siege of Charleston, Hungarian hussar Michael Kovats de Fabriczy fell in battle on 11 May 1779 leading the European-style hussar force he had personally recruited and trained. Polish count Casimir Pulaski, brigadier general and Commander of the Horse by Act of Congress, commanded the legion named in his honor and a number of French cavalry units in an effort to retake Savannah from the British. On 9 October 1779, while rallying fleeing French forces, Pulaski fell from his horse, mortally wounded by grapeshot. Taken aboard a South Carolina privateer brigantine patrolling offshore, he died two days later. Tradition holds that Pulaski's last words consisted of the cry "Jesus, Mary, and Joseph!" in his native Polish.[10]

The Americans' disastrous defeat at the Battle of Camden on 16 August 1780 cost Major General Johann de Kalb his life and Major General Horatio Gates his reputation. Through the influence of Lafayette, Johann von Robais, Baron de Kalb (a nobility he either granted himself or obtained from a minor German prince), had received an American generalship, gained the respect of Washington and other American officers in the course of his service—Valley Forge, brigade command, command at the division level of Maryland and Delaware regulars—and very soon abandoned delusions of putting de Broglie on an American throne. Lafayette's bravery in battle and sincere commitment to Revolutionary ideals no doubt changed de Kalb's mind (de Kalb had sought to use Lafayette as a trophy marquis in pursuit of the de Broglie plot). As major general, de Kalb had hoped to command at Camden, South Carolina, but he accepted the appointment of Horatio Gates, allegedly responsible for the victory of Saratoga, and served as Gates' second-in-command. Shot at repeatedly but remaining on horseback, the fifty-nine-year-old de Kalb—who might otherwise have been peacefully picnicking in the sun with his family under the fruit trees of his château outside Paris—fell to the ground when his horse was shot from beneath him. Charging British soldiers thereupon shot the prostrate de Kalb thrice and bayoneted him numerous times as they passed his fallen figure. Shielding de Kalb, his friend and aide the chevalier du Buysson most likely prevented de Kalb's instantaneous dispatch by absorbing bayonet thrusts into his own body. Cornwallis' personal surgeon tried to treat de Kalb's wounds, but the general passed three days later, remarking—so it was reported in 1855—to a British officer that he was dying the kind of death he had always prayed for: that of a soldier fighting for the rights of man.[11]

In the aftermath of the defeat at Camden, Congress replaced Horatio Gates with Nathanael Greene as commanding general in the South. Reluctant to investigate or charge the hero of Saratoga, Congress allowed Gates to remain on active duty, and he served in a lesser capacity until the end of the war.

Earlier that year, however, on 10 January 1780, Congress dismissed from the army Washington's fiercest critic, Major General Charles Lee. Refusing to follow orders during Washington's retreat across the Hudson at the beginning of the war, guilty of treasonous behavior while a prisoner of war (although evidence came to light only in 1858), and failing miserably as field commander in the Battle of Monmouth Courthouse, Lee nevertheless remained such an outspoken critic of Washington that at one point he faced challenges from two fellow officers. The first, Colonel John Laurens, wounded him, thereby preventing Lee from meeting his second challenger, Brigadier General Anthony Wayne. Court-martialed in the wake of Monmouth and suspended from the army for a year, Lee continued his habit of writing insulting letters, including several to Congress, which thereupon dismissed Lee from the service.

On 2 October 1780, following the verdict delivered by a board of general officers convened on 28 September by General Washington, Major John André, adjutant general of British forces in New York—having been apprehended within American lines in civilian clothes on Saturday, 23 September, outside Tarrytown with documents on his person relating to the surrender of West Point and its garrison by its commanding general, Benedict Arnold, who had fled to British lines—was hanged as a spy in the town of Tappan. His death distressed the general officers who convicted him, the officers and soldiers who guarded him in captivity, Lieutenant Colonel Alexander Hamilton (who befriended him in his last days), and many sobbing women and girls who lined the pathway that led to the gallows. One of them handed the twenty-nine-year-old André a peach as he passed by, from which, legend has it, a peach tree took root over the major's grave, adjacent to the gallows where André died so bravely.

Two years and four and a half months earlier, in Philadelphia, when the British occupied that city, then Captain André had organized the Meschianza festival celebrating the change of command from Sir William Howe to Sir Henry Clinton. While in Philadelphia, André had become friends with Miss Peggy Shippen, a Loyalist. On 8 April 1779, Miss Shippen married Major General Benedict Arnold, military commander of Philadelphia following its reoccupation. For the seventeen months prior to his capture and execution, André—now a major and the adjutant general (aide for special projects and executive secretary) to Sir Henry Clinton in New York—was secretly and intermittently helping Peggy Shippen Arnold and her husband organize something more serious than the Meschianza: Arnold's surrender to the British of a major American command (for a fee to Arnold and his incorporation into the British army) that would, for all practical purposes, end the war. With this scheme in mind, Arnold had secured from Washington the command of West Point. Holding this strategic fortification, the British might advance up the Hudson and cut the American states into fatally weakened sectors. The following year, Arnold, now a British brigadier, was commanding troops in Virginia in the countdown to Yorktown, perhaps knowing that an order existed among American forces that he should be summarily hanged if captured.

Stephen Moylan in good company

The siege of Yorktown brought together two French officers important to this narrative: the marquis de Lafayette in a major command and Louis Lebègue Duportail, in charge of American engineers, commended by Washington and promoted to major general by Congress following the surrender. A Calvinist with an expertise in

Roman Catholic theology and the former *Hofmarschall* (court chamberlain and chief administrator) of the German Catholic principality of Hohenzollern-Hechingen, Baron von Steuben was in command of one of the three American divisions. (Von Steuben's Italian greyhound, Azor, was most likely present, since the baron never went anywhere without him.)

Colonel Stephen Moylan was serving as a commander of the American Light Dragoons at Yorktown, although it is not certain whether his fellow former secretary and aide-de-camp to Washington, Lieutenant Colonel John Fitzgerald, was present as well. Moylan had served throughout the war, from Bunker Hill to Yorktown, and would soon receive promotion to brigadier general.

In July 1778 the forty-one-year-old Moylan (an Irish bachelor marrying late) found time, while wintering in Middlebrook, New Jersey, to court a much younger Mary Ricketts Van Horne, daughter of a colonel of New Jersey militia. Miss Van Horne was quite taken with Moylan's geniality, robust presence, polished manners, and dragoon's uniform of bright green coat, red vest, brown buckskin breeches, shiny black boots, and bearskin hat. All five daughters of Colonel Philip Van Horne found American husbands that winter, according to local lore. A wealthy eccentric in his early sixties, Colonel Van Horne held his militia title from the Royalist era. As far as the Revolution was concerned, Van Horne took no side in the matter and entertained ranking officers of whatever troops happened to be passing through the neighborhood. Somehow, he was allowed to exercise this neutrality, which others of his advanced age must have shared, although Washington thoroughly distrusted this colorful survivor from another era who entertained American and British officers indiscriminately.[12] Of the four children born to the Moylans, two daughters, Maria and Elizabeth Catharine, survived into adulthood. Moylan's wife was an Anglican, and none of Moylan's daughters, grandchildren, or descendants carried on Moylan's Roman Catholic identity.

For reasons unknown, Moylan was not present at the dinner of the Friendly Sons of Saint Patrick given at the City Tavern in Philadelphia on 1 January 1782, honoring George Washington, who was in attendance along with eight general officers, including Benjamin Lincoln, Baron von Steuben, and Henry Knox. Also attending were the French ambassador Anne-César, chevalier de la Luzerne, and thirty-five members of the Friendly Sons, among them congressman and Revolutionary War financier Robert Morris. Stephen Moylan, however, now promoted to brigadier general, was among the guests at the anniversary dinner (it "exceeded in brilliancy even the preceding dinner on the first of January", the club's official history, published in 1892, tells us) held at George Evans' tavern on 18 March 1782. Once again present, Washington signed the Rule Book that evening, signifying his full membership. John Barry was listed as "absent beyond sea" and Anthony Wayne as "absent at camp". When on 3 March 1790 the Friendly Sons of Saint Patrick spun off a service organization, the Hibernian Society for the Relief of Emigrants, Moylan's son-in-law Edward Fox joined and was later elected secretary, suggesting that Moylan had good relations with his Episcopalian in-laws.[13]

Promotion and subsequent career

When on 4 December 1783 Washington bade farewell to his officers at a gathering in the Long Room of Fraunces Tavern in New York City, only three foreign officers were present: Lafayette, von Steuben, and Tadeusz (Thaddeus) Kościuszko. On 14 November 1782, leading a small cavalry patrol of some sixty troopers, Kościuszko had attacked a British foraging party, three hundred strong, on James Island, South Carolina, in the last documented hostility of a very long war. Promoted to brevet brigadier general in October 1783, Kościuszko was highly respected by Washington and was a founding member of the Society of the Cincinnati (Washington was president), an association of select Continental Army officers. Membership in the aristocratic and politically conservative society was passed on through heredity, leading critics to castigate the group as a protonobility emerging from the upper strata of the officer class.

Returning to Poland on 15 July 1784, Kościuszko, who had served throughout the Revolutionary War as a colonel—setting a record, in fact, for years spent at that rank—lived for four years in modest rural retirement (Congress still owed him $12,286 in back pay) before being recruited to serve as second-in-command of the Polish army as major general. During the next six years—as major general, lieutenant general, freedom fighter, insurrectionist, and chief of state (*Naczelnik*, or leader) of a partitioned nation with an empty throne, fighting and winning major battles against Russia and Prussia on behalf of a nation that would soon be partitioned out of existence for 123 years—Kościuszko became one of the best-known figures in Europe. Freed from a Russian prison, where he served two years, but forbidden to return to Poland (which technically no longer existed), Kościuszko set off again for the United States. Stopping in London, he was surprised to find himself so famous. Putting aside the minor matter of Kościuszko's seven years of service in the American Revolution, King George III dispatched his personal physician to tend to the Polish patriot's unhealed wounds. A young medical student and aspiring poet by the name of John Keats composed a sonnet praising Kościuszko as a man of religion and aligning him with King Alfred the Great as a refounder and defender of nationhood.

When Kościuszko arrived in Philadelphia in August 1797, Congress voted him his back pay and granted him five hundred acres in Ohio. Returning to Europe in May 1798, where he would live out his life in France and Switzerland, Kościuszko asked his close friend Thomas Jefferson to liquidate his assets and use the money to purchase freedom for slaves and pay for their education. In 1800, at the request of the American government, then in the process of rebuilding its army, Kościuszko—an artillery officer as well as an engineer—wrote a manual for horse-drawn artillery. Published in New York in 1808, *Manoeuvres of Horse Artillery*, the first military manual adopted by the United States Army, remained in use through the Mexican-American War and was taught for decades at West Point, whose Revolutionary War fortifications Kościuszko had designed and built. After Kościuszko's death in 1817, his body was returned to Kraków and interred in Saint Leonard's Crypt beneath Wawel Cathedral, alongside the kings and national heroes of Poland.

Escape from New York

When the war was over and independence assured, the American states began a process of punishment for those Americans who, out of continuing loyalty to the

Crown or through guerrilla warfare or actual fighting on the battlefield, had given aid and comfort to the enemy. Even as the Treaty of Paris was being negotiated—a treaty, Loyalists hoped, that would mandate fair treatment of Loyalists who wished to remain in the United States or fair compensation for seized properties—several states embarked upon programs of confiscation. Loyalists thus were forced to leave for England, if they could manage to, or flee to New York City and its environs, which were still in British hands.

On 2 March 1782, meanwhile, Sir Guy Carleton—nominated by King George III as "the Man who would in general by the Army be looked on as the best officer"—was named to replace Sir Henry Clinton as British commander in chief in North America. Initially, Carleton was reluctant to take up a post that, as he put it, now consisted "only to be employed as a mere inspector of embarkations". Carleton was persuaded nevertheless to accept a job that was as he described it: the evacuation from New York to the Maritime Provinces and mainland Canada of some 30,000 troops and up to 27,000 refugees, including as many as 3,300 escaped slaves as well as numerous free black Americans with Loyalist sentiments. Southern states—ignoring the irony that many of them had repudiated prewar debt owed to British merchants—demanded the return of these slaves or some form of compensation for their loss, but Carleton held that any slave reaching British lines automatically achieved freedom.

The refugee total began to soar as an increasing number of states authorized confiscations and when the Treaty of Paris failed to protect Loyalists beyond Great Britain's offer to help them go into exile. Included among the military evacuees were not only British and Hessian troops but also a roll call of Loyalist units—the King's American Dragoons, the Prince of Wales' American Regiment, the Queen's Rangers, the Forty-Second Regiment (a fragment of the famed Black Watch)—whose fusion of Royalist and American identities recalled crushed Loyalist hopes. Evacuations began with the soldiers and dependents of many of these units to Nova Scotia, where land grants of varying size (according to rank) awaited them. Settlements on St. John's (present-day Prince Edward) Island and in Upper Canada (present-day Ontario) followed. Disembarking their passengers, crews returned their ships to New York as quickly as possible for another consignment.

And so the evacuation continued through 1783. Sir Guy Carleton—the general who had helped form British North America as the second governor-general of Quebec, befriended its influential Roman Catholic bishop (indeed, fostered his promotion to the See of Quebec), aided in preserving the biculturalism of British North America through his advocacy of the Quebec Act of 1774, and defeated its American invaders at Quebec on the last day of 1775—was now supervising the repeopling of the North American regions under British control with United Empire Loyalists, as they would ultimately be designated. In years to come, Carleton (named first Baron Dorchester on 21 August 1786) would return to British North America as governor-general and commander of forces and continue to play his destined role in the long-term process of creating Canada. For the time being, however, seated at his cabin desk in HMS *Ceres*, anchored in New York harbor, following a plea for support of pensions for Loyalist widows, Carleton finished his final dispatch from the United States of America: "His Majesty's troops and such remaining loyalists as chose to emigrate were successfully withdrawn on the 25th inst. from the City of New York in good order, and embarked without the smallest circumstances of irregularity or misbehaviour of any kind."[14]

Hessian repatriation and resettlement

Sir Guy Carleton was taking with him some 2,000 German soldiers in British service requesting discharge in Canada along with numerous civilian Loyalists of German descent who preferred not to return to Germany. Altogether, 30,000 or so German soldiers—fully one-quarter of all troops deployed against the rebellion—fought for Britain during the Revolutionary War. They were recruited from a number of provinces but were referred to as Hessians, since the largest number came from the Landgraviate of Hesse-Kassel. In America, these soldiers encountered a society 10 percent German in its total population, with Pennsylvania proving the most welcoming to Germans, Protestants and Catholics alike. The mid-Atlantic states, in other words, offered German soldiers in British service suggestions of a German-friendly society. Examples of such receptiveness were the marriages of German soldiers with German soldiers' widows or American-born German girls performed by Father Farmer during the British occupation of Philadelphia. Or consider the fact that the Marechaussee provost corps (military police) of the Continental Army was predominantly German American and was commanded by Captain Bartholomew von Heer, a Prussian officer who had immigrated to Pennsylvania before the war. On 25 May 1776, moreover, Congress authorized an all-German regiment as part of the Continental Army. German soldiers in British service must have eventually known of the German American units as well as the 2,500 German soldiers in various regiments of Rochambeau's army; they also must have been aware of the prominence of such American generals as the barons von Steuben and de Kalb.

Even more relevant to German mercenaries was the congressionally authorized campaign to offer fifty acres to any German soldier who deserted British service. Equally positive, overall, was the experience of German soldiers who became prisoners of war, whether as a result of the Battle of Trenton, Burgoyne's surrender at Saratoga, or Yorktown. They were, by and large, treated fairly and well (certainly well in comparison with American prisoners of war, packed into British prison ships). Indeed, the Germans taken into custody after Burgoyne's surrender were treated more like parolees than prisoners, living in barracks rather than in prison camps. Hessian prisoners in custody in Lancaster, Pennsylvania, could volunteer for work furloughs on local farms. After the Treaty of Paris—even before—many Germans with agricultural experience accepted American offers of land and early release.

An estimated 1,200 Hessians were killed in combat. A high number, 6,354, died of illness, and a smaller number from accidents. Some 15,300 returned to their German homelands. That left approximately 5,000 in the United States or Canada. The generally accepted total of those who remained in the United States is 3,000. Around 10 percent, or 300, of these can—very tentatively—be counted as Roman Catholics. German Catholic settlements in southern Pennsylvania welcomed the recruits, particularly parents of marriageable daughters in communities to which young German American men who lost their lives in service to the Revolution would not be returning.

Squaring accounts

Slightly to the north or east of these German Catholic Pennsylvania villages, the city of Philadelphia was consolidating as the capital of the new nation, governed under the Articles of Confederation and Perpetual Union, formally adopted by Congress and the states on 1 March 1781. The resumption of Friendly Sons of Saint Patrick dinners in early 1782 signaled the regathering of the city's Hibernian elite in a festive mood of homecoming. Pennsylvanian Oliver Pollock, yet another Irish-born Catholic merchant from Philadelphia, would not be returning home for a while, however, for he remained in custody in Havana. As American agent in New Orleans during the war, Pollock had contracted debts on behalf of Congress and Virginia to finance George Rogers Clark's campaign in the upper Mississippi Valley. When those funds failed to be repaid promptly, Pollock began to borrow money in his own name to help keep Clark's militiamen on campaign. By the time of Yorktown, Pollock's Spanish creditors were taking him to court, and, traveling to Havana to negotiate, Pollock found himself in custody, along with several American merchant ships and their crews being held as leverage against unpaid debts.

It took Pollock—now bankrupt, with his New Orleans assets either sold or seized in an effort to satisfy his creditors—nearly eighteen months to negotiate his freedom and return to Philadelphia; and when he did, Congress investigated him for malfeasance in contracting so much debt on its behalf. Pollock survived this investigation and returned to Havana from 1783 to 1785 as (once again) American commercial agent, before returning to the United States and resuming his business career. Not until a full thirty years after Yorktown did Congress and Virginia make good on the debts Pollock had legitimately contracted in an effort to drive the British from the West and keep the Mississippi open to American traffic.

Despite the inconveniences, Oliver Pollock did not grow bitter and fade away. The same cannot be said, sadly, of Colonel George Rogers Clark and the Catholic priest Pierre Gibault, who had aided him in the seizure of Kaskaskia and Vincennes. Clark became a resentful alcoholic when the United States failed to recognize the validity of his title to western lands in which he had invested. While Pierre Gibault continued his ministry as a priest on the Spanish side of the Mississippi, he did so as a man without a country or, at the least, as a diocesan priest without a bishop; Bishop Briand of Quebec refused to accept Gibault back into his home diocese, and Gibault, now in his late fifties, desperately wanted to go home. "As for opposition to me because of the fear that I may have been or was active for the American Republic", Gibault argued in a letter dated 22 May 1788, in his third and final appeal to be recalled to Quebec, "you have only to reread my first letter in which I gave you an account of our capture, and my last letter in which I sent you a certificate of my conduct at Fort Vincennes, in the capture of which they said I had taken a hand, and you will see that not only did I not meddle with anything, but on the contrary I always regretted and do regret every day the loss of the mildness of British Rule."[15]

Bishop John Carroll also avoided formally accepting Gibault into his jurisdiction, despite Gibault's American reputation as Patriot Priest of the West. Carroll did not want to distress further Briand or his successor, Jean-François Hubert, already upset at Carroll for assuming authority over French-established missions in the West. Even worse: when Gibault, once the Northwest Territory passed to American jurisdiction in 1787, successfully petitioned the United States to recognize his title to the land at Cahokia, on which stood the church and rectory Gibault had built at his own expense (President Washington himself approved the request), Bishop Carroll objected on the basis that the property belonged not to Gibault but to the Diocese of Baltimore. Rather than face yet another rejection from Carroll, Gibault moved to the recently founded village of New Madrid in Spanish Louisiana (present-day Missouri), became a Spanish citizen, and served for the next nine years until his passing as pastor of the parish of St. Isidore in New Madrid.

Friendly Sons of Saint Patrick

Two other Irish Catholic Philadelphian merchants, brothers-in-law George Meade and Thomas FitzSimons, plus naval captain John Barry—Friendly Sons of Saint Patrick, one and all—fared far better post-Yorktown than did Oliver Pollock, George Rogers Clark, or Pierre Gibault. George Meade began his career as captain of a merchant vessel, trading between Philadelphia and Barbados, where in 1768 he met and married his wife, the daughter of a British official. Making the transition from merchant ship captain to merchant investor, Meade entered into a partnership with his brother-in-law Thomas FitzSimons to form George Meade and Company, which specialized in the West Indies trade. Both men belonged to Saint Mary's parish, although FitzSimons later supported the construction of Saint Augustine's (1796), Philadelphia's third church. Meade and FitzSimons were ardent Whigs, as were all their Irish Catholic counterparts in the Friendly Sons of Saint Patrick. During the war, Meade and FitzSimons were active financial supporters of the Revolution. In 1780 George Meade and Company helped found the Pennsylvania Bank, which, in turn, financed purchases of food and clothing for Washington's army.

While George Meade remained in the private and voluntary sector, Thomas FitzSimons entered politics in 1782 as a member of the Congress newly organized under the Articles of Confederation. In 1787 he was a member of the Constitutional Convention, in whose debates he argued on behalf of a strong national government, and was one of the two Roman Catholics to vote for and sign the Constitution, along with Daniel Carroll of Maryland. Between 1789 and 1795 FitzSimons served in the newly established House of Representatives while continuing to be active as a trustee of the federally authorized Bank of North America and the University of Pennsylvania.

The final Friendly Son of Saint Patrick to be accounted for, John Barry, as captain of the frigate USS *Alliance*, fought and won the last naval battle of the war on 10 March 1783 off the coast of Cape Canaveral and remained on active duty in the post-Yorktown period. In 1785, however, Congress sold a decommissioned USS *Alliance* to private interests, and the ship was employed in the India trade until it ran aground in the Delaware River in the spring of 1790 and was sold as a wreck. In

1788 Barry reentered the merchant marine as captain of the *Asia*, sailing to Canton in the China trade. Barry alternated voyages with long periods of residence with his wife, Sarah, at the couple's country estate, Strawberry Hill, just outside Philadelphia. When his sister Eleanor and brother-in-law Thomas Hayes passed on, the Barrys took on the upbringing of their sons, Patrick and Michael. Aggressions from the Dey of Algiers and Barbary pirates as well as other considerations led Congress and the executive branch to reestablish the American Navy with the commissioning and construction of six frigates in 1794. On 5 June of that year, Secretary of War Henry Knox notified Barry that the president of the United States, with the advice and consent of the Senate, had appointed Barry senior captain and commander of the resuscitated American Navy.

So, too, was Thomas Sim Lee of Maryland called back to public life following his service as a two-term wartime governor of his state and delegate to the Continental Congress. In 1792 Lee was once again elected governor of Maryland but in 1794 turned down an ensuing offer by the Maryland legislature to send him to the United States Senate. Having served one more term as governor and first lady of Maryland (their fourth), Thomas and Mary Digges Lee retired to their country estate, Needwood, in Frederick County, and wintered in their second home in Georgetown, where they ran a salon for Federalist politicians. Had he learned of the two hundred slaves required to keep the Lees in comfort, Abbé Claude Robin would have once again voiced his opposition to slavery in the United States, but that worthy cleric—so fascinated with the brevity of life in New England—died in 1794 at the early age of forty-four.

Chesapeake connections

As evident thus far, the post-Yorktown era saw the Roman Catholic population of the new nation still largely confined to the shores and the immediate hinterlands of the Chesapeake. In terms of the Catholic population, moreover, the Revolution and independence created no new leaders. The same elites were in charge before, during, and after the Revolution. Not surprisingly, this leadership was politically conservative (Federalist), slaveholding or connected to the trade in indentured servants and their contracts, business oriented (especially but not exclusively in Philadelphia), and lay dominated concerning Church affairs. Prominent Catholics also enjoyed a continuing connection to George Washington, a resident of the Chesapeake both before the war and through his return to agriculture, his presidency, and his brief retirement.

Daniel Carroll, for example, was a member of Congress under the Articles of Confederation, a delegate to the Constitutional Convention, a firm supporter of a strong central government—and hence of the proposed Constitution—a United States senator after 1789, and one of three federal commissioners named by Washington (at whose Mount Vernon home Carroll had dined) to survey ten square miles on the Potomac between Virginia and Maryland for a new federal capital. At Washington's request, Major Pierre Charles L'Enfant drew up a grand design in the baroque style—intersected boulevards radiating outward from a central space, imposed over a grid of public squares linked to each other by avenues— inaugurated by Pope Sixtus V between 1585 and 1590 in the refashioning of Rome as Counter-Reformational capital. As usual, Congress ran out of money, and Washington abandoned the project; L'Enfant joined George Rogers Clark in the ranks of the disappointed and embittered.

The postwar career of Colonel John Fitzgerald brings together the people, places, and pursuits of this Catholic Chesapeake circle. As already narrated, the Irish-born Fitzgerald was a friendly acquaintance of Washington before the war and married Jane Digges, the daughter of Washington's close friend Doctor William Digges of Warburton Manor, across the Potomac in Maryland. Following his service as one of Washington's secretaries and aides-de-camp, Fitzgerald threw himself into the promotion of the ultraconservative, aristocratic Society of Cincinnati and the import-export trade in which he had been involved before the war. A frequent guest of Washington at Mount Vernon, or the general's host when Washington was detained in Alexandria (where Fitzgerald lived and was elected mayor in 1787), Colonel Fitzgerald served as an investor in and director of the Potomac Navigation Company, whose president was George Washington (other Catholic investors included Charles Carroll of Carrollton and Governor Thomas Sim Lee). The company intended to develop the upper Potomac via canals and locks into a direct water route to the Shenandoah and Ohio valleys. Not noticeably a slaveholder, Fitzgerald, like many shippers during this era, did, however, purchase the contracts of white indentured servants at auction for resale. (For service at Mount Vernon, Washington purchased the contracts of Irishmen Thomas Ryan, shoemaker, and Caven Bowers, tailor, at twelve pounds sterling each.) Defenders of this system point out that convicts transported to America preferred it to shipment to Australia, and nonconvict craftsmen such as Ryan the shoemaker and Bowers the tailor, having finished their three to five years of indentured service at Mount Vernon or wherever else they were sent, could carry on in their present employment for wages or seek employment elsewhere as free agents.

Needless to say, Fitzgerald, like all these Chesapeake Catholics under discussion, belonged to the Federalist Right, a persuasion hardening its hostile attitude—the French Revolution was in full sway—toward the propertyless mob (as they saw it) consolidating itself behind the Democratic-Republican Party and Thomas Jefferson, whom Fitzgerald and his circle loathed. In 1798 Federalist president John Adams appointed Fitzgerald to the lucrative post of collector of customs for the port of Alexandria, which was losing out to other coastal cities as a seaport. Fitzgerald needed the job at the time. The Potomac Navigation Company was foundering. In 1799 he was forced into bankruptcy. Still, thanks to his connections, he had the port collectorship and a seat on the board of directors of the Alexandria Bank.

Regarding service to the Church, Fitzgerald maintained his home in Alexandria as a Mass House, now that Roman Catholic worship (since 1776) was no longer illegal; and in 1787, Fitzgerald joined Charles Carroll of Carrollton, George Meade, Thomas FitzSimons, and others in assisting John Carroll, now prefect apostolic of the Church in the United States, in the founding of Georgetown Academy. Fitzgerald was also instrumental in acquiring land for a small chapel at Washington and Church Streets in Alexandria. A Requiem Mass was said there following Fitzgerald's death on 2 December 1799, less than a fortnight before the death of Washington. Fitzgerald was buried with full military honors. Infantry, artillery, and cavalry companies accompanied his casket, borne by Potomac Navigation investors and

Alexandrian merchants. Casket and clergy were followed by Fitzgerald's widow, his grown children, and their spouses as the procession moved to the long wharf for shipment of the casket across the Potomac to Warburton Manor (present-day Fort Washington) for burial. An artillery salute—thirty-six rounds fired at the rate of one round per minute—accompanied the procession. Colonel John Fitzgerald was the first wartime veteran of the Chesapeake circle to make this Charon crossing of a Potomac he had crossed so many times previously, coming to or leaving Mount Vernon.

A triptych of reconciliation

As the fiftieth anniversary of the Revolution approached, three events—the recovery in 1821 of Major John André's remains from a gravesite in Tappan, New York, for burial in Westminster Abbey; Lafayette's triumphal visit to the United States in 1824–1825; and the crowning of Charles Carroll of Carrollton's granddaughter as vicereine of Ireland—provided Americans and Britons with a sense of reconciliation. Such a sentiment helped bridge animosities lingering from the American Revolution, which Britain had lost, and the War of 1812, which the British had almost won. In the latter war, Americans had again failed in their effort to invade Canada; suffered defeat after defeat on land; found the Atlantic coast once more under blockade, including a reprise of coastal landings against the Chesapeake; and, with the exception of hard-fought naval victories at sea and on the Great Lakes and a climactic land battle in New Orleans (fought two weeks after a peace treaty had been signed), had thereby come close to being reduced to a client state of Great Britain. Signed in Belgium on 24 December 1814, the Treaty of Ghent solved none of the issues for which the United States had entered the war, and only the skilled negotiations of the American commissioners prevented a tie (at most) from becoming a formalized defeat.

The repatriation of Major John André

With Americans put in their place, the Battle of Waterloo won, and a defeated Napoleon languishing on Saint Helena (dying there of cancer on 5 May 1821)—his imprisonment signifying the final victory of Britain over France after more than a century of warfare—it was time, Frederick, Duke of York, decided, to bring Major André's remains home. A monument in André's honor had been erected in Westminster Abbey in 1783. Below the sarcophagus, an inscription reads: "Sacred to the memory of Major John André who, raised by his merit at an early period of life to the rank of Adjutant General of the British forces in America and, employed in an important but hazardous enterprise, fell a sacrifice to his zeal for his King and Country, on the 2nd of October, 1780, aged 29, universally beloved and esteemed by the army in which he served, and lamented even by his foes. His gracious Sovereign, King George III, has caused this monument to be erected."[16]

Reviewing the sentimentalization of André as a romantic figure, a skeptic might point out that André was an ambitious officer playing for big stakes. For seventeen or so months, he had been corresponding in shifting codes with Arnold and Arnold's Loyalist wife, Peggy Shippen Arnold of Philadelphia, André's friend from

Meschianza days, regarding Arnold's facilitating the surrender of troops and fortifications to the British in exchange for money and a high-ranking appointment in the
British army. Arnold, in fact, had requested the command of West Point with such
a betrayal in mind. Having arranged this surrender, André wished to see it through
personally and gain his share of the glory, and he wrangled permission to do so
from a reluctant Sir Henry Clinton. He would return to a knighthood, remarked
Clinton, as André, a cloak covering his regimentals, a wide-brimmed hat pulled
down over his features, embarked up the Hudson upon his mission under the name
of John Anderson.

Coordinating the betrayal of such a key fortress and its troops constituted
advanced espionage, however, and André had no background whatsoever in this
field. Nor did he possess the instincts or the cunning of a good spy prepared for the
unexpected, knowing best what next to do or not to do, depending. André carried
a pass signed by Benedict Arnold himself to come and go behind American lines.
The pass, plus regimentals worn under his cloak, would have rendered him traveling under a flag of truce. No matter how nefarious Arnold's intent might be, Major
André, apprehended in such a situation, would be guilty only of getting caught
in the line of duty and hence taken into custody as a prisoner of war. Perhaps the
playwright in his nature got the best of him. Heading up the Hudson, André was
acting in a script of multiple playwrights, actors, and contingencies. Removing his
regimentals in favor of civilian attire, he began to play out the role of John Anderson, spy.

Why, then, did the André narrative play out so emotionally on both sides, American as well as British? In probing this paradox, we begin with the obvious. Handsome,
charming, well-mannered, good-humored, and forthright, André possessed the cha-
risma of the perfect adjutant—that is, he was the perfect British gentleman as the British preferred to see themselves and as the American officer corps, so recently British,
aspired to see itself as well. André had partially absorbed and partially taught himself
to become the perfect English gentleman. Born in London to a wealthy Swiss merchant and his Parisian wife, both of whom had immigrated to England and most likely
spoke with accents, André had grown up alongside his émigré parents, learning to be
ultra-English. Made financially independent by his father's death, André decided on
a military career and purchased a commission. His suavity and uber-English manner
exactly suited him for an adjutant's role.

André's charm, moreover, was androgynous: men and women found him equally
attractive. He sketched flattering portraits of Loyalist ladies of Philadelphia and New
York (including Miss Peggy Shippen, when he was serving in British-occupied
Philadelphia); the village women and girls of Tappan tearfully witnessed his brave
walk to the gallows and covered his shallow grave with flowers. Peggy Shippen
Arnold was a fully equal coconspirator with her husband and André through the
long, drawn-out months of plotting and negotiations. (In their correspondence,
André posed as a New York hairdresser advising Mrs. Arnold on the latest fashions
and hairstyles.) Despite her father's professed neutrality and her marriage to an
American general (however aggrieved), Peggy Shippen was, for the time being, the
most effective British secret agent in America.

André's amiable suavity as an American captive concealed the fact that, like Benedict Arnold, he was in search of revenge. Captured in Canada in 1775 by American

forces, André spent a harrowing year as a prisoner of war in Lancaster and Carlisle, Pennsylvania, before being exchanged. During that time, as he later noted in
a letter to relatives, André and other captive officers were constantly harassed by
the decidedly ungentlemanly members of the Pennsylvania militia. "We were every
day pelted and reviled in the streets", André wrote regarding his time in the frontier
town of Carlisle, "and have been oftentimes invited to smell a brandished hatchet
and reminded of its agreeable effects on the skull, receiving at the same time promises that we should be murdered the next day. Several of us have been fired at and we
have more than once been waylaid by men determined to assassinate us, and
escaped by being warned to take different roads. Such is the brotherly love they
in our capitulation promised us."[17] In short, André experienced not only danger
but also an anti-British animosity, compounded by class hostility, which no doubt
helped motivate his rise to prominence as adjutant and aide-de-camp to Major
General Charles Grey, commanding general of the British Light Infantry's take-
no-prisoners bayonet massacre of Anthony Wayne's militia forces at Paoli, Pennsylvania. André coolly noted this slaughter in his *Journal*: two hundred rebels killed,
André succinctly writes, "put to the bayonet all they [the British] came up with
and, overtaking the main herd of the fugitives, stabbed great numbers and pressed
on their rear till it was thought prudent to order them to desist".[18] No right to
surrender. British officers slashing the faces of Americans with their swords before
having their infantrymen bayonet them to death. This butchery was followed by a
repeat performance a year later—bayonets, crushing blows with musket stocks for
those lying on the ground, and no chance for surrender—by Grey's Light Infantry
when the British, informed by a local Loyalist, descended upon American dragoons
under the command of Colonel George Baylor sleeping in barns outside Tappan
(yes, the very same Dutch village outside New York where André was hanged),
with British officers shouting, according to surviving witnesses, "No quarter! No
quarter to the damned rebels! No prisoners are to be taken!"[19] As horrible as war
was, General Grey made it even more horrifying.

And so, André's participation in organizing the Baylor attack is uncertain. Paoli, however, was a full-scale assault, which André chronicled in his *Journal* in laconically
approving tones. However he might like to play the poet, the playwright, the
sketch artist, the charmer of men and women alike, André could also play the hard-
boiled soldier in the Major General Charles Grey model. André knew Americans
as rebels and threatening captors and had come of age as adjutant to a general who
believed that the only way to suppress the rebellion was to kill as many American
soldiers as possible. This element, too, had to be added to the mix of André's complex character. Still, he touched a vein of residual Britishness in the American generals who heard his case, in Alexander Hamilton, who escorted him to the gallows,
and perhaps even in Washington himself, who had the doors and windows of his
headquarters closed against the sounds of André's execution.

And so, on 10 August 1821, upon instructions from his government, James
Buchanan, British consul in New York, arrived in the village of Tappan and, after
some investigation, ascertained André's gravesite. A large crowd gathered and
grew silent as Buchanan's diggers reached the coffin. Opening it, the consul espied
André's skeleton in perfect order, with one exception. The roots of the peach tree
spreading its branches above André's grave had formed a protective mask twined

around his skull. Returned to London, Major André's remains were entombed in his until-then empty sarcophagus in Westminster Abbey on 28 November 1821.

The return of Lafayette

Following Yorktown, the twenty-three-year-old Gilbert du Motier, marquis de Lafayette, departed for France on 18 December 1781 as a major general in the Continental Army and a beloved American hero. Promoted to maréchal de camp and made a Knight of Saint Louis by the king, Lafayette threw himself into planning the next stage of the war, a Franco-Spanish campaign against British-held islands in the West Indies. The Treaty of Paris ended that possibility, and in 1784 Lafayette returned to the United States for his first triumphal tour of the country. He also had another campaign in mind—ending slavery—as being advocated by the Paris-based Society of the Friends of the Blacks, of which he was a member. As of 1783, Lafayette was urging George Washington by letter to set an example in this regard: free his slaves and reestablish them as tenant farmers at Mount Vernon. (Lafayette had purchased land in French Guiana to be developed as such a model colony.) Addressing the Virginia House of Delegates in mid-August 1784, Lafayette made the same recommendation and, during his stay at Mount Vernon, most likely brought it up with Washington again.

Fast-forward to 7 October 1824. A gathering of notables, including Charles Carroll of Carrollton, one of the three surviving Signers of the Declaration of Independence (now that only three Signers remained, "Signer" was capitalized and used as an honorific), was on hand to greet the marquis de Lafayette as he arrived by ship at Fort McHenry in the Baltimore harbor. The marquis was on his second triumphal tour of the United States, invited there by President James Monroe and Congress as part of the upcoming fiftieth anniversary of national independence. Lafayette was traveling in the company of his son Georges Washington and one aide-de-camp and a secretary. The arriving celebrity party acknowledged the cheers of welcome and then proceeded into George Washington's headquarters tent for a reception with Revolutionary War veterans who had fought under Lafayette's command four decades earlier.

As they chatted away (perhaps in French, in which Carroll was fluent), Lafayette must have known that the Signer with whom he was so amiably conversing was most likely the largest slaveholder in the nation, owning four to five hundred slaves, by various estimates. Lafayette loathed slavery. Charles Carroll, by contrast, was like most Roman Catholics in Southern slaveholding states, including members of the restored Society of Jesus. While they might have sustained doubts regarding America's "peculiar institution", as it was called, they never allowed such doubts to percolate into theological questioning, much less abolitionist sentiment. Still, at some level they must have experienced a burden of guilt. Carroll, in fact, refused to use the word *slave* when referring to his human property. They were his "people", which implied for Carroll (one supposes) a higher degree of acknowledged humanity, thus lessening his guilt. As a legislator, moreover, Carroll had tried to join the Lafayette camp of total emancipation. When in 1789 Nicholas Hammond introduced a bill in the Maryland legislature to abolish slavery gradually, Carroll supported it in the Maryland Senate and proposed the creation of a joint committee with the House of Delegates to discuss the matter. The bill and Carroll's motion went nowhere. Eight years later, Carroll made his own proposal: Let the state purchase all female slave children, provide them with an education, and free them at age twenty-eight. Over time, male slaves would come under the influence of an increasing number of educated free women, which would eventually raise the entire race to self-sufficiency. Carroll's proposal went nowhere as well.

In the final years of his life, Carroll served as president of the Maryland chapter of the American Colonization Society, founded in 1816 to assist free black Americans to emigrate to Africa. Although it did help some twelve thousand free blacks and former slaves move to Africa before it went out of business in 1865, the American Colonization Society did not offer a viable, practical program and was critically flawed in its basic assumption—namely, that the solution to slavery was a form of freely chosen (for the time being) expatriation of black elites (free blacks), leaving only enslaved African Americans behind. Whatever his thoughts or intentions toward slavery might have been, Charles Carroll was the largest and wealthiest slaveholder in Maryland. By buying and selling human beings, breaking up families, resorting to the lash if one of them was guilty of a serious offense (and advising his son to do so when necessary), growing richer and richer by slave labor, Carroll was personally at the core of the loathsome system of slavery.

For the time being, the Missouri Compromise, which established a balance of power between slave and free states, was the only action the nation was politically willing to take to limit slavery. As a slaveholder, Charles Carroll of Carrollton lived within the Missouri Compromise to his own advantage. Of the 334 slaves he owned at his death, Carroll freed only one, Bill, a personal servant, whose humanity and shared Roman Catholic faith were almost impossible to ignore.

Religious freedom

During the founding of the republic, Roman Catholics advocated for religious liberty. As Charles Carroll grew older, he increasingly tended to take comfort in the role he had played in helping to ensure religious freedom in the United States. Throughout his life, Charles Carroll remained a practicing Roman Catholic with an Enlightenment orientation. Thus, he continued to read and appreciate Montesquieu and Voltaire, despite their placement on the Index of Forbidden Books, and his favorite philosopher remained John Locke. Carroll's Catholicism in these years was far from Augustinian or evangelical—animated, that is, by a sense of sin and redemption, error, failure, and forgiveness. Carroll's Catholicism represented, rather, a highly reasoned refraction of rationalism that offered a corroborating coda to Enlightenment thought. As advanced by Montesquieu, the Catholic doyen of Enlightenment Catholicism now at rest in the Church of Saint-Sulpice, or the Jesuit-trained Voltaire, who kept a Jesuit chaplain on his staff at Ferney, his estate outside Geneva, Carroll valued the role played by a rationalized religion in stabilizing society through an economy of rewards and punishments.

Carroll did, however, experience disappointments over his own failures and those of others: his neglect of Molly, most dramatically; the alcohol-fueled extravagance and brutality of his only son, whom he repeatedly tried to bring around to a better way of living; his competitive and quarreling daughters; the end of conservative Federalism and his political career, the French Revolution, and the ascendancy of what he considered radicalism in the United States and in France. All this led to a renewed interest in his Catholic Christianity (which he had never forsaken) as a source of solace coming not only from rationalized stability but also from a personalized experience of Catholic teachings and the sacraments, touched now and then by an element of evangelical fervor.

At some point in the late 1810s or early 1820s, Carroll, guided by a reading list from John Carroll, spent three or so years in private study, comparing and contrasting Catholic Christianity with Protestantism and the world's other great religions. From this self-conducted seminar, Carroll emerged more convinced than ever of the truth of Catholicism in its general outline and—herein a new note—his dependence on Jesus Christ. Thus, when discussing religion following this enquiry, Carroll evinced a certain warmth and power of personal conviction.

In the case of Carroll's English contemporary William Wilberforce, such a metanoia led to a lifelong commitment to ending the slave trade. While not a Catholic, Wilberforce also became an advocate of Catholic emancipation. Unfortunately, neither Charles Carroll nor any other Roman Catholic American slaveholder, prominent or otherwise, followed the devout Anglican Wilberforce down both these paths. But following his evangelization, Charles Carroll did begin to speak and write more energetically about his role during the Revolutionary era in helping his fellow Catholics achieve religious emancipation; he also advocated such a development on behalf of the Roman Catholics of Great Britain. In 1829 George Washington Parke Custis, the adopted son of the Father of His Country, was serving as president of the Society of the Friends of Civil and Religious Liberty in Ireland. Charles Carroll had always maintained a lively interest in Irish affairs. It took a revolution to emancipate the Roman Catholics of the United States. Looking back at the grand drama in which he had played such a conspicuous part, Carroll, on 20 February 1829, wrote to Custis, "When I signed the Declaration of Independence I had in view not only our independence from England but the toleration of all sects professing the Christian religion and communicating to them all great rights. Happily this wise and salutary measure has taken place for eradicating religious feuds and persecution and become a useful lesson to all governments." When he noted "all governments", Carroll had Great Britain in mind especially. By emancipating the Roman Catholics of the United Kingdom, Carroll was suggesting, Parliament and the Crown might avoid Irish Roman Catholics' continuing alienation and resistance, which could, in time, reprise the American scenario of armed rebellion.[20] Charles Carroll made these remarks, moreover, in the full knowledge that one of his granddaughters was in an overwhelmingly advantageous position to help effect such change. Carroll's granddaughter Marianne Patterson Caton, Lady Wellesley, was married to Lord Richard Colley Wellesley, second Earl of Mornington and elder brother to the Duke of Wellington. Carroll urged his granddaughter to use her influence to convince the prime minister, the Duke of Wellington, to end the disenfranchisement of Catholics in England, Scotland, and Ireland. In 1829 the Duke of Wellington, partly due to his beloved sister-in-law's persuasion, sponsored a bill emancipating Roman Catholics in Great Britain. Once again, a Carroll had played a role in ensuring religious liberty for Roman Catholics of Irish descent with whom the Carrolls of Maryland shared the faith.

PART TWO

Diocesan Formation in the Republic

6

White Marsh Plantation 1783

Ex-Jesuit clergy reorganize their plantations

On 27 June 1783, six ex-Jesuit secular priests met at Saint Francis Borgia mission church at White Marsh Plantation, Maryland, to discern the best way to reorganize the American clergy now that the United States had gained its independence and they no longer reported to the vicar apostolic of the London District. The very choice of Saint Francis Borgia mission on the 3,500-acre White Marsh Plantation resonated with meaning. In the years before the suppression of the Society of Jesus in 1773, Saint Francis Borgia had been the headquarters of John Lewis, Jesuit superior in Maryland and Pennsylvania, and his assistant. White Marsh Plantation yielded 180 pounds sterling per year for their support. Following the suppression, Lewis continued on as American superior, this time as prefect apostolic to Bishop Richard Challoner, vicar apostolic of the London District; but that relationship, while remaining technically in force, became moot between 1775 and 1783 (Challoner died in 1781), and Challoner's successor, Bishop James Talbot, quite understandably refused to take charge of the Roman Catholic Church in a recently belligerent and now foreign country.

Among the priests attending the three meetings at White Marsh held between 27 June 1783 and 11 October 1784 was John Carroll of Rock Creek and Saint John's Chapel. In 1782 Carroll had prepared a first draft for the new Form of Government under discussion and parts of the plan for plantation management. Turning fifty at the time the Treaty of Paris was approaching closure, Carroll had by then earned his place among these priestly veterans, as he served a large congregation scattered around Rock Creek Manor near Georgetown, where he lived with his mother, Eleanor Darnall Carroll, and based his ministry out of the Chapel of Saint John that his brother Daniel had built for him. Upon his return to the colonies in 1774, Carroll refused to take orders from Lewis because he did not believe that the American Jesuits had the right to conduct a shadow society as if the suppression had never happened. Denied support from the ex-Jesuit slave plantations because he would not report to Lewis, Carroll commenced conducting a privately supported ministry in an autocephalous American church whose ex-Jesuit clergy were reporting to no one save the ex-Jesuit superior Lewis, who, while technically still holding the office of prefect apostolic, was no longer reporting to the vicar apostolic of London. Carroll, in short, disapproved of a shadow society driven by drift.

At this point, John Carroll, previously a party of one in opposition to a shadow society, emerges as a constitutional theoretician for the reorganization of an American Roman Catholic Church. Carroll's motivation: something had to be done, given the tendency of former Jesuit clergy, some now rapidly aging, to let the drift continue. What was called for, Carroll believed, was a future-oriented plan appropriate to American circumstances drawn up by the clergy themselves, not as former Jesuits, but as the founding clergy of the Church in a new nation. "But", Carroll complained to his English friend John Plowden in a letter dated 20 February 1782, "ignorance, indolence, delusion (you remember certain prophecies of reestablishment) and above all the irresolution of Mr. Lewis puts a stop to every proceeding in this matter."[1]

Carroll's plan

The theoretical basis of Carroll's ecclesiology was simple and straightforward, albeit ahead of its time. As of 1781, European Catholic churches tended to be seminational in organization, with monarchs having a say in the nomination of bishops, the distribution of benefices and livings, and the awarding of ecclesiastical honors, such as promotion to the College of Cardinals. Mission territories came under the jurisdiction of the Sacred Congregation for the Propagation of the Faith (Propaganda Fide); and the papacy, in addition to constituting the government of the Papal States, exercised a unifying Petrine ministry of spiritual authority over the universal Church.

The United States, by contrast, was an independent republic in which freedom of religion was guaranteed but no one religion was established by the federal government. This republic did not accept any foreign power's authority over it, nor could its citizens accept titles or appointments to office offered by foreign powers. As loyal citizens, the Catholic people of this republic accepted the nature of its government and its restrictions regarding foreign involvements. These Catholic people, moreover, while equal in terms of their citizenship, came in three categories in terms of their Church identities: laity, nonordained religious, and ordained clergy. Carroll was a Marylander who had come of age in a colony founded by people who had refused to participate in Anglican religious services, who were termed "recusants" in English law. As a former member of the Jesuit English Province and an Anglophile in terms of his English recusant connections and his Federalist party orientation, Carroll considered the laity—especially Catholic laity of birth, means, and accomplishment—as participants in the life of the Church; they, along with vowed religious and ordained clergy, constituted the Body of Christ as outlined by Saint Paul. Thus, Carroll had no problem, theoretically, with a lay trustee system of oversight for parish churches—reflecting as it did the English recusant, Maryland, and (perhaps even) American Protestant system—provided that such lay oversight remain orthodox and concerned mainly with temporal administration and support. And yet, Carroll argued, the United States was not missionary territory—that is, it was not *in partibus infidelium* (in the lands of the nonbelievers), although American Catholics did bear responsibility to defend the faith when that became necessary and to evangelize whenever and wherever possible. The American Catholic Church was, rather, an emergent and localized instance of the universal Church, with 150 years of development behind its present status. Thus, the American Catholic Church constituted a body of the already extant faithful, joined in an ongoing mission of service and evangelization.

As an ecclesial community, the American church enjoyed the presence of ordained priests to sustain its sacramental life. It was now time to bring this clergy to a new state of organization, pending Rome's authorization of a diocesan structure headed by a bishop. Carroll saw the proper development of American church organization in two phases: regularize the clergy, and obtain a diocesan bishop with full authority. Carroll used the term *regular clergy* to refer not only to priests belonging to religious orders (regulars) but to all priests, secular and regular, serving in the new nation, who were regularly (Latin *regula*, "law")—that is, formally and legally—appointed by the pope or a bishop.

As an orthodox Roman Catholic, Carroll believed that the appointment of a diocesan bishop was required to bring the American church to full maturity. *Ubi episcopus, ibi ecclesia* (Where the bishop is, there is the Church) had been Catholic doctrine since the apostolic era. But that statement did not hold for the United States, should that bishop be vicar apostolic, a missionary bishop, or titular of some defunct diocese *in partibus infidelium*, reporting to the Propagation of the Faith in Rome. Such a model was necessary for missionary territories in the first stages of church development, but not for the American Republic. Carroll maintained that, although the Holy Father had the power to create such a diocese and authorize such a bishop, nominations for such an American appointment should come to Rome via a vote of the regular clergy of the United States, who held the priestly franchise, as it were, analogous to the franchise held by the cathedral canons of Europe, who recommended candidates for appointment as diocesan bishops. The regular clergy of the United States, in turn—although Carroll said nothing explicit about this matter—would be foolish not to consult the laity, as well as their own consciences, on so vital a matter as the best candidate for bishop. The selection of candidates for episcopal jurisdiction, in any event, must never be seen by the American people as coming unilaterally from a foreign power, whether Propaganda Fide or the pope himself, lest it meet with damaging resistance from the American public at large.

Sharing Carroll's plan

In 1782 Carroll drafted and circulated a plan for clerical organization in the United States. Throughout 1783 and 1784, clerical delegates debated Carroll's plan at three meetings at White Marsh Plantation. First for consideration: the protection of ex-Jesuit properties from seizure by Propaganda Fide. In an earlier letter, Plowden told Carroll that ex-Jesuit John Thorpe, the English agent in Rome, had alerted him that Propaganda Fide had its eyes on ex-Jesuit properties in the United States. Carroll's outspoken response to this possibility, as outlined in a letter to Plowden dated 26 September 1783, revealed his suspicion of Vatican-based clerical apparatchiks, which dated back a decade to his time in Rome during the final phases of the suppression. "Your information of the intentions", writes Carroll, "gives me concern no farther than to hear that men, whose institution was for the service of Religion, should bend their thoughts so much more to the grasping of power, & the commanding of wealth: For they may be assured, that they never will get possession of a sixpence of our property here, & if any of our friends could be weak enough to deliver any real estate into their hands, or attempt to subject it to their authority, our civil government would be called upon to wrest it again out of their dominion.

A foreign temporal jurisdiction will never be tolerated here; & even the Spiritual supremacy of the Pope is the only reason why in some of the United States, the full participation of all civil rights is not granted to the R. C."[2] Here, then, in no uncertain (albeit private) terms, Carroll outspokenly stakes out a claim for Roman authorities to observe American protocols regarding the ecclesial development of the United States. While Carroll the priest has no trouble in asserting the spiritual supremacy of the pope in spiritual matters, Carroll the citizen understands the hostility with which some American states regard that spiritual supremacy, because they mistakenly believe it involves a capacity for political intervention by the Court of Rome, the term Carroll favored when referring to the papacy as a temporal power.

In 1783 Carroll and four other priests wrote (in excellent Latin) to Pope Pius VI, requesting John Lewis' renewed appointment as prefect apostolic in the United States, but they asked that he report directly to Rome rather than to the vicar apostolic in London. The letter requested that Lewis link the American church in unity with the Holy Father, exercise spiritual authority over clergy and laity, authorize priests to exercise sacramental functions, and administer the sacrament of confirmation as well as bless holy oils, chalices, and altar stones, ministries usually performed by bishops. This request constituted a dress rehearsal for a diocese. It also underscored the American clergy's loyalty to the papacy, despite challenges arising from American independence, diversity of Christian denominations, religious liberty, and a republican distrust of foreign powers. The sixty-two-year-old John Lewis—like Carroll, a graduate of Saint Omer's College and the Watten novitiate who studied philosophy and theology at Liège and was also a twenty-five-year veteran of the Maryland mission professed of the four vows—represented a safe and tested nominee to lead the American church as it formally separated from the London District.

A constitution for clergy

Behind Lewis would be the sustaining and clarifying presence of the Constitution of the Clergy, hammered out by six priest delegates at White Marsh Plantation between 27 June 1783 and 11 October 1784. Constitutions were in the air, for one thing. In the course of the Revolutionary War, thirteen former colonies had written state constitutions. In addition, major colleges, hospitals, and related institutions redrafted their constitutions following the war to conform to independence and republican governance. The clerical delegates to White Marsh had little trouble drawing up the Constitution of the Clergy (which now covers six closely printed pages of *The John Carroll Papers* from the University of Notre Dame Press). In summary, the document stated that one procurator-general and three regional chapters—Pennsylvania and the Eastern Shore of Maryland; the Western Shore of Maryland as far south as Charles County; and Charles and St. Mary's County—will govern the clergy. The procurator-general will be elected by the chapters, with a minimum of two-thirds of eligible clergy present and voting in each chapter. A procurator-general will serve a three-year term and will be eligible for reelection to an unspecified number of terms. A general chapter will be held every three years to review conditions and make recommendations. This general chapter will have final authority in the administration of estates. District chapters will have the authority to examine new candidates for admission to the Select Body of the Clergy and to reject or recommend them to the superior *in spiritualibus* (the prefect apostolic) for faculties. No clergy shall be arbitrarily removed from assignment except for cause after a thorough investigation by district and general chapters and the superior *in spiritualibus*. Any member of the body of the clergy may apply for a vacant position. Items seventeen through nineteen, finally, dealt with the sensitive issue of properties:

> 17. Neither Procurator Genl. nor any other Person shall have power to sell, dispose of, remove or anywise alienate the property of any plantation, without the consent of the General Chapter for real property, or of the District for personal Property.
> 18. In extraordinary emergencies the Procurator Genl. or a Majority of Members of Chapter in any two Districts, may convene the General Chapter.
> 19. The Person invested with Spiritual Jurisdiction in this Country, shall not in that quality have any power over or in the temporal property of the Clergy.[3]

Six highly specific administrative rules, separately numbered and covering a variety of contingencies, followed these nineteen general principles. If two clergy share the same house, for example, neither shall be considered superior to the other. Aged clergy shall retire at full salary if they remain in the United States or at thirty pounds annually if they retire to Europe and are partially supported there by friends or family. Should any two clergy have a falling-out, they shall submit their differences to a panel of three priests for arbitration.

A separate set of lengthy rules regarding plantation management completed the Constitution of the Clergy. Aimed at estate managers, these rules deal with hospitality to guests (keep it simple), disposal of real properties (a checklist of required permissions), allocation of profits (including the creation of funds for reserve and repair), crop failures or accidents (a controlled resort to reserve funds), debt (each district carries its own, with no mixing of debts), legitimately distressed estates (district chapter surplus funds can be allocated), and procurator-generals serving as estate managers (no favors allowed—they are accountable to district chapters, like anyone else). In each of these three sets of rules, moreover, members of review panels are specified by name. Here, then, was the best governance, so John Carroll and his colleagues believed, for the clergy of a newly formed, independent nation governing itself without the benefit of a bishop or diocesan supervision.

Prefect apostolic

Like most priests in the rebellious colonies, John Carroll spent the war years in near anonymity. Between 1782 and 1784, however, he would become the best-known Roman Catholic priest in the United States and the designated founder of the American Catholic hierarchy. All this happened suddenly (in the eighteenth-century understanding of that word) and involved church and state at their highest levels. Carroll's mission to Canada on behalf of Congress in the spring of 1776 set the stage for this transformation, as did his status as distant cousin to Charles Carroll of Carrollton, who recruited him for the Canadian mission, as well as the growing political prominence of his older brother Daniel in the war effort, the Maryland legislature, and the Continental Congress.

John Carroll was not ambitious in any secular sense of that term, nor was he overly concerned with wealth, although he had a well-honed sense of the empowering dimensions of properly secured property. He had, after all, renounced his inheritance when taking vows as a Jesuit. Yet he was highly socialized, which is to say, he was interested in the drama of life, whether sacred or profane or combinations thereof. Thus, Carroll was loyal to his family, the Carrolls and the Darnalls, and his friends in the Society of Jesus, pre- and postsuppression. He appreciated items of news or inside information (as his letters to Charles Plowden bear witness) and showed a lively interest in power, church or state or combinations thereof on a grand stage. In short, Carroll possessed the requirements of an ecclesiastical leader in the Federalist era: patriotism, political moderation, administrative ability, a superb education and lifetime love of learning, physical grace, good manners, friendliness but not familiarity, and the value of the right word at the right time, with these attributes enhanced by faith, hope, and charity, and a love of the priesthood as a vocation and profession.

The years 1782, 1783, and 1784 constituted a flurry of overlapping events, publications, and correspondence back and forth among Rome, Paris, Annapolis, Philadelphia, and New York that brought John Carroll into prominence and left him prefect apostolic of the Roman Catholic Church in the United States. In 1782, most likely on his own initiative, Carroll wrote the first draft of the "Form of Government" section for the Constitution of the Clergy. A month after this constitution was finalized, on 10 November 1783, Carroll wrote to Cardinal Vitaliano Borromeo, a Roman cardinal influential at Propaganda Fide, explaining the context, secular and ecclesiastical, in which the Constitution of the Clergy had been drawn up and lobbying for the cardinal to urge the Holy Father and Propaganda Fide to appoint a prefect apostolic for the United States: a superior in spiritual matters, as the constitution put it, who would also serve as a sign of spiritual unity between American Catholicism and Rome. Carroll also asked Cardinal Borromeo to lobby the American minister in France, the French foreign minister, and the Russian minister to Rome in this matter and requested that the Rome-based ex-Jesuit John Thorpe facilitate these contacts on the cardinal's behalf and advise the cardinal on how best to deliver to His Holiness the enclosed petition for the appointment of a prefect apostolic. Thus, John Carroll of Rock Creek Manor, Maryland, an ex-Jesuit secular priest of uncertain status in a new nation, acting with the knowledge and approval of his priestly peers, entered in an attitude of polite but full confidence into discussions with a Roman cardinal regarding the establishment of a lobbying effort at the highest level (three foreign ministers) and offered the services of John Thorpe, formerly the English Jesuit procurator in Rome and now a freelance art consultant and agent for English Catholic nobility building chapels and a guide to the Court of Rome, in matters of great delicacy: how best to get the enclosed petition from the American clergy to His Holiness under the most favorable circumstances.

A phantom conspiracy

Carroll thus became part of a high-level correspondence, then in its eleventh month, that involved Cardinal Leonard Antonelli, prefect of Propaganda Fide; Prince Archbishop Doria Pamphili, papal nuncio in Paris; Benjamin Franklin,

American plenipotentiary to the French court; the comte de Vergennes, French foreign minister; Jérôme Marie Champion, archbishop of Bordeaux; and Charles Maurice de Talleyrand, bishop of Autun. The subject: How should the United States be organized ecclesiastically, and should France play a role in this organization? Briefly, across the proscenium arch of these conversations, flitted notions of a French bishop resident in Paris with authority over the American church, the attachment of the American church to an existing French archdiocese, or a French priest to be appointed prefect apostolic. These momentary notions, however, played themselves out for the obvious reason—American resistance to any form of authority exercised in the United States by a foreign power—and, most importantly, because they never rose to the level of a deliberate French plot to take over the American church, as so vociferously propounded by John Gilmary Shea. Indeed, Shea's Francophobia in his discussion of this matter is difficult to explain. (French officers were mainly Masonic deists, Shea argues, as was the tired sentimentalist Abbé Robin. French army and navy chaplains did next to nothing to help the Church in America.) Perhaps Shea, a former Jesuit seminarian, was getting even for the Third Republic's anti-Jesuit attitudes. Yet the Shea scenario dominated the American Catholic narrative down to Peter Guilday's *The Life and Times of John Carroll* (1922) until Sulpician historian Jules Albert Baisnée challenged it in 1934 through analysis based on an exhaustive presentation of relevant correspondence.

Even Benjamin Franklin comes in for Shea's ire because of Franklin's early offhanded ruminations that (1) it was better to have a vicar apostolic for the United States stationed in France rather than in England and (2) certain English-speaking Benedictine monasteries in France could be used to educate young Americans for the Catholic clergy. Still, despite these ruminations, Franklin initially did approve of the proposal to have a vicar apostolic in bishop's orders to govern the American church in spiritual matters from France because (1) it would bring honor to an ally and (2) Congress would not prevent it, since Congress would have no regulatory opinion on what was a purely religious matter.

According to Shea, however (and here Shea is on more solid ground), three former Jesuits of the English Province—Charles Plowden and the Maryland-born Charles Sewall and John Mattingly, then in England—provided the tipping point in this discussion. Writing to Franklin separately, the three updated the minister plenipotentiary as to American Catholic affairs and, apparently, put a word in for John Carroll's appointment as prefect apostolic over the official recommendation of John Lewis. Chagrined that he had backed a scheme contrary to the wishes of American Catholic laity and clergy alike, Franklin began to press the prefect of Propaganda Fide, Cardinal Leonardo Antonelli, on behalf of his longtime friend, the highly respected and well-placed Reverend Mr. John Carroll. In separate letters to Antonelli, Anne-César, chevalier de la Luzerne, French minister to the United States, and Prince Archbishop Doria Pamphili, Vatican nuncio to France, chimed in with praise of John Carroll, about whom Antonelli had already received enthusiastic reports from Benjamin Franklin. Whether the cardinal prefect had already made up his mind upon hearing earlier from Franklin or whether Luzerne's and Pamphili's letters proved further tipping points, Antonelli wrote John Carroll from Rome on 9 June 1784 and said that he, not the aged John Lewis—who, Antonelli opined, deserved repose rather than more arduous labor after his long service in the vineyard—had received from His Holiness appointment as prefect apostolic for the United States. In time, moreover, this appointment would be upgraded to vicar apostolic with the rank of bishop, thereby enabling Carroll to ordain clergy for the American states. "Reverend Sir," Antonelli lauded Carroll, "you have given conspicuous proofs of piety and zeal, and it is known that your appointment will please and gratify many members of that republic, and especially Mr. Franklin, the eminent individual who represents the same republic at the court of the Most Christian King."[4]

Negotiation and delay

Still, closure on the matter of Carroll's appointment—or, rather, his acceptance of the appointment—remained a half year into the future. The official document appointing Carroll did not reach him until 26 November 1789 via François Barbé-Marbois, French chargé d'affaires of New York. Carroll read the document carefully and—as he informed Ferdinand Farmer by letter in December, asking Farmer to share Carroll's thoughts with the other priests in Farmer's district—was dissatisfied on two major points: the impending appointment of a vicar-general by the pope (meaning by Propaganda Fide) and the failure to include the American clergy in the deliberative process leading to the selection of a bishop.

In a rare display of lingering bitterness, moreover, Carroll briefly speculated that this ignoring of the American clergy arose from the fact that the regular clergy of the United States were all former Jesuits and hence could not be trusted. Propaganda Fide was treating the American church as missionary territory, Carroll complained, and not as a national church, and the regular clergy of the United States as missionaries to a foreign non-Christian nation. By unilaterally appointing a vicar apostolic, Propaganda Fide, representing a foreign power, would be offending the American people. Carroll differed from Franklin on this matter, for a resident vicar apostolic with the rank of bishop would govern in both spiritual and temporal matters. The correct solution for the next stage of Catholicism in America should be, rather, the raising of the United States to the dignity of a diocese and the election of a diocesan bishop by the regular clergy of the nation. In opposing a measure that had taken so long to make its way through the deliberative process, Carroll knew that he was taking a risk. "I am well aware", he wrote to Roman agent John Thorpe on 17 February 1785, "that these suggestions will sound ungrateful at Rome; and that the mention of them from us will be perhaps imputed by some of the officers of the Propaganda to a remaining spirit of Jesuitism: but I own to you, that tho' I wish to treat them upon terms of sincere unanimity & cordial concurrence in all matters tending to the service of God; yet I do not feel myself disposed to sacrifice, to the fear of giving offence, the permanent interests of Religion."[5]

On 27 February 1785, Carroll wrote a long and very diplomatic letter (in Latin) setting forth his objections to aspects of his appointment, followed on 1 March 1785 by an equally long memorandum (in Latin) presenting statistics and describing conditions in the nascent American church. Carroll was in the process of compiling new documents for Propaganda Fide and back-channeling his preferences via Thorpe when a modified but final version of Carroll's appointment, dated 23 July 1785, reached the United States. *Roma locuta est. Causa finita est.* (Rome has spoken. The case is decided.) There would be an American church.

The regular clergy of the nation would exercise a onetime responsibility for the election of a diocesan bishop. For the time being, however, the appointment of such a bishop would be postponed to a later date. The Sacred Congregation for the Propagation of the Faith, however, would continue to support, monitor, and encourage the expansion and development of this American church and its attached missionary territories.

Visitation 1785

Having received a supply of the holy oil required for confirmation and extreme unction (last rites), Prefect Carroll in the summer of 1785 set forth on a formal visitation of the stations, congregations, residences, and houses of his prefecture, beginning with Maryland, administering confirmation wherever he stopped and giving judgment in a few matrimonial cases. He then went on to Virginia, where by now some two hundred Catholics were living in the northern counties along the Potomac. Carroll broke off traveling in August to avoid the heat and took up his journey again in September, visiting Pennsylvania, New Jersey, and New York. In each district, Carroll—having learned to respect Propaganda Fide's hunger for information, which was needed for current decisions before being deposited in an archive of global Catholicism—would compile statistics and commission reports for a Relatio to Rome as well as celebrate Mass, preach, and confirm.

Carroll was especially attentive to the growth of the laity, the aging of the formerly Jesuit clergy, and the recruitment of younger priests to the prefecture. Maryland had nineteen priests. The good news: each of them was permanently assigned and enjoyed a fixed residence. The bad news: they were aging rapidly. Joseph Mosley, for example, who came under temporary suspicion as a Loyalist during the war, wrote his sister in England on 4 October 1784 that the farm he had bought twenty years earlier now fully supported his ministry. (Mosley had started the farm with the labor of eight slaves.) Without asking for money from "our Gentlemen" (ex-Jesuits) or his growing congregation (English, Irish, Scots, French, Dutch, and American-born), Mosley had built a chapel in honor of Saint Joseph that was capable of seating up to three hundred congregants. On the previous Easter Sunday, the chapel was full to overflowing. Mosley had also built a small (sixteen by twenty-four feet) two-story rectory with a fireplace in each room. Still, when he considered his confreres, Mosley wrote his sister, "we are all growing old, we are very weak handed, few come from England to help us. I suppose they are much wanted with you; I understand that few enter into Orders of late years, since the destruction of the Society. Here, I can assure you, the harvest is great: but the laborers are too few. Where I am situated, I attend ten Counties, by myself; to have it done as it ought, it would take ten able men." Mosley died at St. Joseph's Station three years later at age fifty-six and was buried in the chapel he had built.[6]

As of the fall of 1785, Pennsylvania enjoyed the services of nine priests: five ex-Jesuits with definite parishes to attend to and four recent arrivals in specialized ministries. Reverend Mr. Pierre Huet de La Valinière, a French Canadian, ministered to the French community; Reverend Mr. Thomas Hassett served the Spaniards. Lancaster was under the care of Recollect Father John Causse (Father Fidentianus was his religious name). A Dominican, William O'Brien, awaiting assignment, was serving as needed in Philadelphia. Ex-Jesuits Robert Molyneux and Ferdinand Farmer held co-pastorates at Saint Mary's Church and Saint Joseph's Church. A tireless circuit rider into New Jersey and New York, the German-born Ferdinand Farmer (whose real name was Steinmeyer) was highly respected in diverse Philadelphia circles. (In an era of uncertain clerical dress, Farmer dressed as a Quaker elder, as a compliment to the founders of the colony.) An accomplished astronomer, he was elected to the Philosophical Society and to the board of trustees of the University of Pennsylvania, the first Roman Catholic to hold the latter position. Passing away in Philadelphia on 17 August 1786 at the age of sixty-six, following an arduous circuit ride through New Jersey, Farmer received the honor of a municipal funeral at Saint Mary's. City elders, Protestant clergy, members of the Philosophical Society, and professors and trustees of the University of Pennsylvania attended the Requiem Mass and accompanied the casket to interment in the nearby Saint Joseph's cemetery.

Corporate identity

All but two of the twenty-six clergy John Carroll encountered in his 1785 visitation were ex-Jesuits and hence were shaped by similar experiences and hopes for the future. Indeed, twelve of these priests, including Carroll, were born in Maryland and shared with their English-born colleagues in the English Province such communalities as a Saint Omer's education, novitiate training at nearby Watten, and study of philosophy and theology at Liège—all in French Flanders (present-day Belgium)—followed by short assignments in England before being posted to Maryland. Together, they had signed the Act of Submission (1774), demanded by Bishop Challoner, testifying by their signature their acknowledgment of the suppression of the Society of Jesus and their new status as secular priests under the authority of the vicar apostolic of the London District. The war years, 1775 to 1781, had most likely proved a challenge to the four priests of English birth. Yet most of the ex-Jesuits—especially the Marylanders as well as priests born in Germany (five), Ireland, Belgium, and Luxembourg (one each)—were either Anglo-American colonials or foreign-born men who had received English Jesuit educations or had become partly Anglicized (the Germans) through mastery of English, incorporation into the English Province, and bilingual ministries. With the exception of John Carroll's diplomatic mission to Canada, Joseph Mosley's failure to observe the proper deadline for taking Maryland's oath of allegiance, and the Irish Catholic Loyalists of Philadelphia unilaterally electing Ferdinand Farmer as chaplain of the regiment they were forming, the ex-Jesuits maintained a low profile during the war, although it does perhaps testify to their sentiments that none of them abandoned their American assignments for political reasons. Instead—and this disquieted Carroll when he returned from England in 1774—they were content to live in the old manner, with John Lewis, their superior before the suppression, continuing to supervise their efforts as a de facto corporate entity of secular priests sustaining a once and future dream of restoration.

The independence of their Jesuit ministry, which was self-supporting through slave-worked plantations, continued into their postsuppression ministries as secular priests. This economic self-sufficiency supported a priestly self-sufficiency as well. As English Jesuit Charles Plowden would soon write—in a history of the suppression never published in the author's lifetime, lest it ruffle the feathers of a number of anti-Jesuit Court of Rome officials—the suppression had a catastrophic effect on the spiritual, physical, professional, and psychological lives of those twenty thousand Jesuits being suppressed. They were, Plowden wrote, "stripped of their property, driven from their peaceable habitations, deprived of a state which they had embraced under the protection of the law, and which they preferred to every other employment; many thousand pious, religious men are reduced to an impossibility of observing their vows, the obligation of which is of Right Divine; and many thousand Priests and Clerks are interdicted from the sacred ministry, and forbid to exercise the duties of education, and instruction of youth; they are annihilated by the Holy See."[7] Yet while their colleagues in France, Spain, Portugal, Italy, Austria, Latin America, Mexico, and Canada were arrested, exiled, imprisoned, or otherwise destroyed, the Jesuits of Great Britain, Maryland, and Pennsylvania were left undisturbed in the ownership of their properties by an English government not accustomed to taking orders from the pope, which meant that their ministries survived.

In the aftermath of the Revolutionary War, the experiences of English and American ex-Jesuits ran parallel in a number of ways, with the exception—a major exception!—that Roman Catholics in the United States enjoyed emancipation and freedom of religion a half century before comparable privileges were accorded British Catholics. Yet the process of emancipation was underway in Great Britain, as the progressively liberating Catholic Relief Acts of 1778 and 1791 and the Roman Catholic Relief Act of 1829 took effect. A British Catholic community possessed of a strong cisalpine movement emphasized to the realm at large the acceptably Britishness of British Catholicism on behalf of English Catholics weary of being perceived as strangers in their own land.

By cisalpine (this side of the Alps), English Catholics meant to suggest, if not outright Gallicanism (a national French church), at least a high degree of local identity, loyalty to the Crown, and nondependence on the Court of Rome for close supervision. Since its founding, Catholic Maryland had been Jesuit in its governance structure, and the Maryland mission remained somewhat semiautonomous within this Jesuit framework. A dozen years as minimally supervised secular priests following the suppression localized the Maryland and Pennsylvania clergy even further. There were signs of such localization, of course: a respect for republicanism, for example (the equivalent of the Realm in Great Britain as an imaginative ideal), a non-Romanized clerical lifestyle, a country-squire way of living that favored lay attire over cassocks and birettas and other signs of *romanità*, a regard for the lay gentry (from which so many of them had their origins), and—in Carroll's case, at least—an initial toleration of lay trusteeism and a willingness to consider a vernacular liturgy. Then there was the matter of their ambivalence to the Court of Rome, which, for purely political and financial reasons, ex-Jesuits believed, had forced Clement XIV to agree to the suppression. This resentment, above all else, kept *romanità* to a minimum in the American church of 1785.

At the same time, however, neither the ex-Jesuit clergy nor their prefect apostolic were overly cisalpine (or Americanist) in their ecclesial orientation. One and all accepted the papacy as a sign, symbol, and reality of spiritual unity in the Church; they also acknowledged Rome's primacy to exercise the authority of

Peter over local churches in a range of administrative prerogatives. Such an adherence to the ultramontane (beyond the Alps, Rome-centered) values might have turned out differently had the American clergy from the beginning been secular priests, as the leading clerical intellectuals of the cisalpine party in Britain tended to be. Diocesan clergy were by definition localized: belonging to one diocese, one parish, governed by one bishop, from whom they received their ordination and their faculties. The American clergy, however, had acquired their clerical culture from a Society centered on Rome and expressly loyal to the papacy. At the end of the sixteenth century, the Jesuits had supported Rome's appointment of an "archpriest" to supervise the church in England, an appointment that was resisted by the English secular clergy. It placed the Jesuits in direct opposition to the localizing tendencies of the secular clergy in favor of a panoptic ultramontanism centered on Rome but global in reach. Indeed, in little more than a hundred years since its founding, the Society of Jesus had spread Catholic Christianity over vast portions of the planet and had mastered dozens of local cultures while remaining Rome-centered in its deepest loyalties. Rome, these American ex-Jesuits knew so painfully, had taken away the Society of Jesus, but Rome could one day—soon, many hoped—bring it back again. That was their dream: the full and open restoration of the identities so many of them continued to nurture within themselves, for which the Form of Government and its careful management of the plantations formed a bridge between past and future.

A troublesome debate

One ex-Jesuit, two secular priests, and an Irish Capuchin caused Carroll grave concern during his time as prefect. Born in Maryland in 1748, Charles Wharton experienced a *cursus honorum* typical of Maryland-born Jesuits: Saint Omer's, the novitiate at Watten, and philosophical and theological studies at Bruges and Liège, where he was posted as professor of mathematics following ordination in 1772 and tertianship (a further nine months of spiritual training). When the Society was suppressed in 1773, Wharton—like a number of other Maryland-born Jesuits—fled to England, where he remained on mission for nine years. By the early 1780s, however, Wharton was having a crisis of doubt regarding Roman Catholicism in general and his membership in the Society of Jesus in particular. By the summer of 1782 he was defending the validity of his doubts in a treatise anchored in Scripture, patristics, and Church history and aimed at such recurring points of argument in polemics of this kind as transubstantiation, papal authority, denial of salvation outside the Catholic Church, and mandatory celibacy for clergy and religious. Wharton's treatise evenhandedly avoided the usual pyrotechnics of polemical games in favor of a tone of meditation, scholarship, memoir, and regretful leave-taking. The ordeal of composing the treatise and upending a lifetime of beliefs and allegiance brought Wharton to the edge of nervous and physical collapse. Resigning his chaplaincy in England, he returned to Maryland in June 1783 and lived quietly with his brother on the family plantation about sixty miles from Carroll's home at Rock Creek. Wharton had no faculties at the time (Bishop James Talbot of the London District was refusing to grant faculties to Americans now that the United States had become an independent nation), and Wharton made no effort to practice as a priest. As Carroll informed Charles Plowden in a letter dated 26 September 1783, he had visited Wharton once and enjoyed his company. Carroll's slightly defensive remarks underscored that rumors of theological instability had grown up around Wharton in England and had followed him to the United States.

Imagine, then, Carroll's disappointment when Wharton left the Church and announced his decision in a pamphlet titled *Letter to the Roman Catholics of the City of Worcester*, which was published in Philadelphia in June 1784. The *Letter* was well received in Protestant circles, and Wharton became a minister of the Episcopal Church. Carroll was stung by the pamphlet. He thought that pamphlet wars were a thing of the past. Certainly no Catholic pamphlets of this type had appeared of late. Far from it: the Catholic clergy of the United States had done everything in its power to avoid such public polemics against Protestantism, the Christianity of preference for a believing American nation. But to have pamphlet wars revived by a former Jesuit, a Marylander—how embarrassing!

Still, Carroll decided, Wharton's *Letter* had to be answered, but not with an attack on the Protestant community that would reignite the old animosities. Carroll would write his rebuttal as the pastorally oriented *An Address to the Roman Catholics of the United States of America by a Catholic Clergyman*, as it appeared in print in the fall of 1784. Running 115 pages in its original pamphlet version, Carroll's *Address* represents a breakthrough document from a number of perspectives. It addresses the American Catholic community as a whole, for one thing, and, in doing so, offers a level of instruction keyed to intelligent Catholics, lay and clerical. By keeping Wharton in the third person, moreover—referring to him as "the Chaplain", with a capital *C*—Carroll avoids the emotionalism of direct and hostile confrontation in favor of corrective scholarly, but not pedantic, commentary. More than a touch of schoolmasterly reproof is evident, however, as Carroll connects Wharton's use or misuse of an erroneous or incomplete text from Scripture, Church Fathers (Irenaeus, Tertullian, Cyril of Alexandria, Athanasius, Gregory the Great, Jerome, Augustine, and the ubiquitous John Chrysostom), conciliar decrees, a frequently cited Cardinal Robert Bellarmine, and more contemporary commentators. Indeed, Carroll's discovery of such sources in the Annapolis library in and of itself offered a testimony to the Catholic (and Anglican) legacy of Maryland in times past.

Carroll's tone is not harsh. It matches the civility of Wharton's *Letter*. Two American gentlemen were engaged in debate, with Wharton the more emotional and confessional of the two and Carroll remaining evenhanded, albeit given to restrained irony and rebuke on more than one occasion. Only in the conclusion of Carroll's *Address*—which deals with the most sensitive issue under discussion, mandatory celibacy—does Carroll approach the subject from heightened emotion and a personal point of view by gently taking Wharton to task for walking away from this particular obligation. Having touched on the topic, however, Carroll knew that he was in a danger zone as far as the Protestant clergy of the United States was concerned. It ill behooved a Roman Catholic prefect apostolic with a Vatican appointment to be castigating an Episcopalian cleric on such a delicate issue in an overwhelmingly Protestant nation served by a married clergy with no tradition of mandatory celibacy since that requirement had been left behind during the Reformation. On what basis was this prefect Carroll standing in judgment of the married Protestant clergy of the United States? this clergy might very well ask. When Carroll chided Wharton for marrying, were they and their Christian wives being judged as well?

When Charles Wharton published *A Reply to an Address to the Roman Catholics of the United States* (1785) in response to Carroll, Carroll made no reply. The last thing the Catholic Church in America needed at this time of emergent organization, Carroll realized, was a pamphlet war and a resurgence of hard feelings in the Republic in which Catholics were seeking integration and acceptance.

The saga of Charles Whelan

It is difficult to ascertain—beyond simple pique—why the normally evenhanded John Gilmary Shea criticized French army and navy chaplains for doing so little to assist the Roman Catholic Church in the United States during the Revolutionary War. Chaplains were by definition under military discipline and could not leave their assignments at will. A few, however, sought and received reassignments—Recollect Seraphin Bandol to the French embassy in Philadelphia, Capuchin Sebastian De Rosey to Maryland, Carmelite Paul de Saint Pierre to the Illinois Country—but French chaplains generally remained in their assignments during the war.

This discussion brings us to the case of French naval chaplain Charles Maurice Whelan of Ballycommon, Ireland. Because of anti-Catholic penal laws in Ireland, Whelan immigrated to France and in 1770 entered the Irish Capuchin Franciscan novitiate at Bar-sur-Aube. Following the novitiate, profession (in which he added the name Maurice), philosophical and theological studies, and ordination, Whelan held responsible positions in his order—prior, provincial secretary, novice master— before answering Louis XVI's call for volunteer chaplains to accompany the French fleet to America. As a chaplain on the man-of-war *Jason*, Whelan served nearly two years at sea as part of Admiral de Grasse's fleet, which relocated to the West Indies in 1781 following the Battles of Chesapeake and Yorktown. After the defeat of de Grasse's fleet at the Battle of Saint Kitts in 1782, Whelan spent thirteen months as a prisoner of war in Jamaica, one of seven thousand French captives. During this time, the Irish-born Capuchin continued to serve his flock—mostly dying prisoners of war—as a chaplain with no need of local faculties. Nor did Whelan believe that he required faculties when, following his release from confinement, he relocated to New York City in October 1784 and began serving as a private chaplain to Portuguese merchant José Ruiz Silva. Silva's home, however, was also a center of worship for many of the two hundred Catholics then living in the city; and so, being a devoted priest, Whelan drifted into an informal ministry while still devoid of proper licensing from local church authorities.

Hearing of Whelan's ministry, the district dean, Ferdinand Farmer—who had served the New York Catholic community on a part-time basis before the British army occupied the city early in the war—informed Carroll of the new arrival. Farmer wrote approvingly of Whelan, with the exception of his rushing into ministry with no faculties. Whelan had replied to Farmer that, as he had understood it, Carroll himself had not yet received his faculties from Rome as prefect apostolic, so to whom was he to apply? Whelan's observation was somewhat cheeky, yet nevertheless true. "A lame excuse", Farmer harrumphed in his letter to Carroll, while at the same time asking Whelan to provide an estimation of the number of Catholics in New York City for Prefect-elect Carroll to include in the Relatio he was preparing for Rome. Two hundred, Whelan replied, suggesting his growing involvement in a New York City ministry. Carroll used this total in his Relatio to

Rome. Farmer advised Whelan that, given the fact that Prefect-elect Carroll had not yet received notice of his appointment and powers from Rome, Whelan should write the papal nuncio to France, Prince Archbishop Doria Pamphili, and request faculties. Whelan did so forthwith, enclosing a letter of recommendation from Hector St. John de Crèvecoeur, consul general of France in New York.

Dated 8 January 1785, Whelan's letter to Pamphili, written in French (he could have written in Latin, Whelan noted, "had I not been persuaded you were acquainted with all the languages of Europe"), is interesting in what it tells us about Whelan as well as New York. In the first quarter of the letter, Whelan chronicles the responsible positions he has held in the Irish Capuchins. The second quarter gives vivid details of his one-man prisoner-of-war ministry in Jamaica, caring for the sick and the dying (flux, yellow fever, war wounds) when other chaplains, fearing infection, refused this dangerous duty. In the second half of the letter, Whelan describes how his New York ministry developed out of his chaplaincy in the house of José Ruiz Silva, a Mass House for churchless New York. In the course of this ministry, Whelan recounts, he learned firsthand how colonial New York's severe penal laws (a priest could receive a death sentence for saying Mass or administering the sacraments) had erased any serviceable knowledge of the faith even in those—most of them poor Irish—who continued to identify themselves as Catholics.

While Señor Silva continued to lend his home as a Mass House, New York needed a chapel, and Whelan was raising money for this purpose, encouraged in this pursuit (here some judicious name dropping) by no less than the marquis de Lafayette, to whom outgoing French consul general Hector St. John Crèvecoeur had kindly introduced him. (Incoming French consul general François Barbé-Marbois was proving equally supportive, Whelan notes.) Lafayette had intervened on Whelan's behalf with the governor of New York, George Clinton, and a number of city officials. To work effectively in New York, Whelan comments, a Catholic clergyman must know at least Irish, English, French, Dutch, Spanish, and Portuguese—the languages in use by members of the Silva congregation—which Whelan implies that he does understand, given his polyglot career. Finally, Whelan requests faculties, as suggested by the Reverend Mr. Farmer, whose letter Whelan includes, advising him to seek faculties from the French papal nuncio: "which is the cause I trouble your Eminence hoping you will be kind enough to spare me the pains of writing to Rome as work presses and Easter is coming on which is the harvest of the Lord to assemble the stray-sheep lost from the flock these many years past. I have brought over to our Faith (Deo adiuvante) a great many of every denomination since I am here. I was surprised to find how easy it is to convince them of their error in this country."[8] Archbishop Pamphili sent Whelan's request on to Rome for a decision by Propaganda Fide. Having now officially heard from Rome that he would be named prefect apostolic, however, Carroll granted Whelan faculties on 16 April 1785. On 4 June 1785, Carroll received a letter from Cardinal Antonelli granting faculties to Whelan as well. Father Whelan was doubly credentialed.

Lay trustees

And a good thing, too, for the intrepid Capuchin friar was busy raising money for the construction of a Catholic chapel, Saint Peter's, on a five-lot site on Barclay Street previously leased by Whelan from the nearby Episcopal parish of

Trinity Church, on the advice of Silva. In the manner of the time, the site (on which stood a carpenter's shop being used as a temporary chapel) and the church, whose cornerstone was laid on 5 October 1785, were purchased from Trinity in August by a group of lay trustees incorporated on 10 June as "The Trustees of the Roman Catholic Church in the City of New York". The trustees constituted such luminaries as Spain's minister to the United States, Don Diego de Gardoqui y Arriquibar, who donated a thousand dollars toward the purchase in the name of King Carlos III; Hector St. John de Crèvecoeur; Portuguese merchant José Ruiz Silva; and Irish-American merchants Dominick Lynch, Thomas Stoughton, James Stewart, and Henry Duffin. On 4 November 1786, an unfinished Saint Peter's Church was dedicated for use. New York City now had a parish church, where Mass was being said for the public on a regular basis, and two legations, French and Spanish.

Prefect Carroll had no trouble with New York's trustee system, which reprised the Maryland experience in terms of the Jesuit plantations registered under the names of lay trustees prior to suppression and now by outright ownership by ex-Jesuit secular priests no longer under a vow of poverty. Indeed, Carroll's own Saint John's Chapel at Rock Creek belonged to his brother Daniel, who had financed and built it for him on Carroll's return from England. Besides, this system of lay trusteeship was congruent with Protestant America's ownership of parishes and hence, offered a point of acceptable consilience, provided that ownership did not confer on lay trustees autonomous power to hire or fire clergy at will.

Schism, deception, disobedience

That power was soon being claimed at Saint Peter's. Shortly after Carroll conferred temporary faculties on Whelan, a second Irish Capuchin by the name of Andrew Nugent arrived in New York. In contrast to Whelan, Nugent was an accomplished preacher. Whelan had expressly written to his Capuchin superiors requesting such a preacher for the growing Catholic community. Whelan, meanwhile, had begun to run afoul of some of the Irish congregants of the future Saint Peter's. When Nugent arrived, he volunteered for New York, and Carroll, reviewing Nugent's testimonials (which he later believed to have been forged), gave Nugent temporary faculties to function as a priest in that city.

Charles Whelan could be prickly on occasion. Andrew Nugent had the kind of inflated ego that frequently accompanies flamboyant preaching. In both men, moreover, an Irish love of a quarrel overcame their shared Franciscanism, and the spirit of Saint Francis of Assisi definitely did not prevail between them. In short order, Whelan and Nugent were fighting with each other; Nugent was quarreling with Whelan's supporters among trustees and congregants; and Whelan's detractors among trustees and congregants were gaining strength. Soon, Prefect Carroll had on his desk three letters: one from Ferdinand Farmer, reporting that Whelan had alienated a growing number of Catholic New Yorkers; the second from the Reverend Mr. Pierre Huet de La Valinière, a French Canadian priest loyal to the American cause during the Revolution whom Carroll had sent to New York at the request of the French and French Canadian community developing there, chronicling the Capuchins' quarrels; and the third from Whelan himself, filled with complaints against Nugent. From Farmer, Carroll also learned that more and more trustees wanted Whelan dismissed. Some were talking of political action, having New York State pass a law prohibiting any church congregation from having a clergyman forced upon them by church authorities. On 25 January 1786, Carroll wrote a long letter to the trustees of Saint Peter's that was in effect a brief treatise on Church unity, Church authority in spiritual matters, the absence of canonical reasons for dismissing Whelan, and, indeed, Saint Peter's lack of canonical status as a parish, due to the lack of a diocese and a diocesan ordinary (a bishop) in the United States. Shortly after sending this missive to New York, Carroll learned from yet another letter from Ferdinand Farmer that he had heard from Dennis McReady, the trustee leading the Nugent faction, that Nugent supporters were on the verge of ending the Saint Peter's project altogether.

At this point, a thoroughly defeated and demoralized Charles Whelan left the city to spend time with his brother, a physician and farmer in upstate New York. Whelan was not on hand for the dedication of Saint Peter's on 7 November 1786. Assisted by the chaplains to the French and Spanish embassies, Nugent celebrated the Solemn High Mass of dedication. The chargé d'affaires for Spain, Don Diego de Gardoqui y Arriquibar, who had arranged the thousand-dollar gift from King Carlos III, was accorded a seat of honor in the sanctuary. A ceremonial banquet, at which thirteen formal toasts were offered, followed the Mass.

Andrew Nugent, meanwhile, having distanced himself from his Capuchin vow of poverty, was quarreling with the trustees regarding his salary; and the trustees, in turn, so recently Nugent's supporters against Whelan, were telling Nugent to accept the offered salary or forfeit his assignment. With his claque of supporters solidly behind him, Nugent continued his complaints and refused to resign. By the summer of 1787, the trustees were begging the prefect apostolic to rid Saint Peter's of this troublesome priest. Carroll, meanwhile, had heard from Dublin sources that Nugent had been suspended in Ireland. And so, in the course of his visitation that year, Carroll journeyed to New York to hear the trustees' complaints against Nugent and to replace him with the Irish Dominican William O'Brien, who had previously served in Philadelphia and New Jersey.

Thereupon ensued a scene at once disgraceful and embarrassing. At Sunday morning Mass, Carroll announced Nugent's dismissal and O'Brien's appointment to the congregation of Saint Peter's and cautioned the congregation against attending any Mass Nugent might celebrate. Nugent at once entered the sanctuary and began to berate Carroll to his face. Carroll then withdrew from the sanctuary and invited the congregation to accompany him to de Gardoqui's home for Mass. Nugent celebrated Mass for those who remained.

Nothing like this had ever happened in the recorded history of Catholicism in the British colonies. How disruptive, how embarrassing, for John Carroll, prefect apostolic of the Catholic Church in the United States, to be shouted out of the sanctuary by an emotionally disturbed presbyter of the first Roman Catholic church to be built in the city that was now the temporary capital of the nation! And to have numerous congregants remain behind for an unauthorized Mass, defiantly celebrated.

Shortly thereafter, Carroll published an open address to the Catholics of New York denouncing this dagger of dissension and disobedience being plunged into the heart of religion in their city. Dramatically, Carroll framed this crisis in an

American as well as a scriptural and apostolic context. In times past, Carroll chided, American Catholics had respected "the maxims of church government, by an adhesion to which nations have been brought out of the darkness of paganism into the light of the Gospel". Despite their being a people living under "the false coloring of prejudice and misrepresentation", Carroll went on, American Catholics had respected the sacredness of the sanctuary and proper ecclesial governance and hence "preserved in their own country, and to the present day, the purity of the faith delivered down to them from the first apostles of Christianity" and accomplished this preservation "under every temporal discouragement, and against the influence of every worldly interest". And how did these earlier American Catholics do this? Carroll answered this question with a series of questions that constituted a stunning rebuke of what had happened at Saint Peter's. "Was it by intruding themselves into the sanctuary?" he asked.

> Did they, did you before you crossed over into this country, assumed to yourselves the rights of your first pastors? Did you name those clergymen who were charged with the immediate care of your souls? Did you invest them with their authority? Did you confer on them those powers, without which their ministry must be of no avail? No, dear Christians; neither your forefathers nor you assume to yourselves those prerogatives; you never plunged that fatal dagger into the vitals of true religion. Too deeply was it impressed on your minds, that the ministry of the word, and the administration of the sacraments, cannot be given in charge but by His divine authority whose doctrine is to be preached, and who has enriched his sacraments with the treasures of grace and salvation.[9]

With these queries Carroll was particularly rebuking the trustees; in backing the self-assigning Nugent, a priest who had already blotted his copybook in the old country, they had plunged the dagger—schism, heresy, riots in the sanctuary—into the heart of the Catholic Church in this new American nation. Carroll concluded this address by once again naming Dominican William O'Brien as priest in charge of Saint Peter's. The trustees accepted Carroll's rebuke and had new locks put into the doors of the church against any attempt of a return by Nugent and his followers. Carroll also conferred new faculties on Whelan for a ministry in Kentucky, but Whelan's spirit had been broken by these New York events and the ingratitude of the people he had done his best to serve. Unable to perform in the demanding frontier assignment, Whelan returned to more established ministries in Pennsylvania and Delaware before retiring in 1805 to Bohemia Manor, where the ex-Jesuits gave him sanctuary. He died there the following year, at age sixty-five.

Ex-Jesuit backlash

The year 1788 witnessed a brief eruption of anti-ex-Jesuit sentiment on the part of two disgruntled secular priests. Advanced as pamphlet attacks, these polemics—one coming from unexpected treachery and the other from (most likely) mental instability—were aimed at Prefect John Carroll via Rome, where anti-Jesuit feelings lingered in some Court of Rome circles. (Unfortunately for Carroll, Cardinal Antonelli of Propaganda Fide was one of these high-placed prelates who feared a restoration.) Although these attacks failed to gain traction, they did cause Carroll stress and embarrassment, given the predominance of ex-Jesuits, including himself, in the American clergy. Could these attacks, Carroll feared, revive in the United States the Jesuit-secular antagonisms of the early seventeenth century?

The first source of Carroll's anxiety was the Reverend Mr. Patrick Smyth, a diocesan priest of the Diocese of Meath in Ireland, who arrived in the United States in 1787 on family business, applied to Carroll for faculties, which were granted, and was stationed at Frederick, Maryland. On 15 March 1788—his family obligations attended to—Smyth wrote Carroll that he was coming to Baltimore to resign his faculties personally to him before returning to Ireland. Smyth complained in this letter about how discourteous the English Catholics had been while he was serving in Maryland, making him feel unwelcome as an Irish priest educated in Ireland. Especially guilty in this regard was one Henry Darnall, who happened to be a cousin of the prefect.

Carroll wrote Smyth a soothing letter in return and lodged him for a month at his prefect's residence in Baltimore. Following Smyth's departure, a letter from Smyth to a Robert Welsh of Fells Point was brought to Carroll's attention. Reading the letter, Carroll was shocked to discover that Smyth was writing to him under the guise of writing to Welsh, for in it Smyth returned to his prior theme: the disrespect shown Irish secular priests—this time, however, not only by Anglo-American Roman Catholic laity but by the ex-Jesuit clergy as well. Hostility to Irish secular priests by ex-Jesuits, Smyth continued, had already dissuaded six or seven secular priests of his acquaintance from volunteering for the United States. Ex-Jesuits, Smyth implied, were behind reports "industriously circulated in America that the Irish secular clergy would crowd to this country to make their fortunes". What an insult to the secular clergy of Ireland—Smyth complained—the very priests who had sacrificed so much to keep Ireland Catholic![10]

Going on the offense as the best defense, Carroll enlisted the Dominican William O'Brien, the most prominent Irish priest in America, whom Carroll had appointed to Saint Peter's in New York, to defend the fair-mindedness of clerical assignments in the United States. Likewise attacked in Smyth's pamphlet, O'Brien agreed and wrote a letter to this effect to John Thomas Troy, the archbishop of Dublin, to whom Carroll also wrote. Smyth's pamphlet, *The Present State of the Catholic Missions Conducted by the Ex-Jesuits in North America*, appeared in Dublin in late 1788, and Carroll received a copy from a Philadelphia publisher in January 1789.

He was writing a reply to Smyth's attack, Carroll wrote to Archbishop Troy. Leave it be, Troy counseled. The pamphlet was a mere diatribe. Carroll's unpublished first draft of a refutation eventually found its way into the archives of the Baltimore cathedral. Comprising six and a half closely printed pages in Peter Guilday's comprehensive and pioneering biography, Carroll's response—like his reply to Charles Wharton—was a textbook instance of refutation via an inventory of errors. Still, Archbishop Troy had given Carroll good advice. Why create a pamphlet war that would confer equality and further publicity on Smyth's charges?

Smyth's pamphlet, however, had already reached its maximum level of damage. Cardinal Antonelli read it and called in for questioning Felix Dougherty and Ralph Smith, two young American men whom Carroll had sent to Rome for an ecclesiastical education before their ordination as diocesan priests. The cardinal's interrogation of the young men lasted several hours, Roman agent John Thorpe later reported to Carroll. Among other criticism, Smyth had charged that Carroll's newly founded academy at Georgetown was a cover for a Jesuit novitiate prior to a restoration of the Society of Jesus in the United States. Seminarians Dougherty and Smith managed to convince Antonelli that they had never met a Jesuit novice or even heard rumors of a Jesuit novitiate. Intrepidly, Thorpe subsequently criticized the cardinal to his face for holding the hearing. Had not the archbishop of Dublin and the eminent Rome-based Irish Dominican Richard Concanen (later first bishop of New York) dismissed this pamphlet as scandalous, ill-written, and worthless? Antonelli's willingness to take Smyth's pamphlet seriously enough to look into the matter must have disquieted Carroll, bringing back memories of his Roman sojourn of 1773, when the suppression movement was gaining its final force.

Another troublesome priest

Neither disquieting times nor bad memories were over for Carroll, however, for in December 1789 a second anti-Jesuit pamphlet surfaced. Entitled *The Resurrection of Laurent Ricci; or a True and Exact History of the Jesuits*, the pamphlet bore a Philadelphia imprint and was written by Abbé Claudius Florent Bouchard de la Poterie. In 1773 the eighteenth general of the Jesuits, seventy-year-old Laurent Ricci and his assistants were placed in solitary confinement in Castel Sant'Angelo by order of Clement XIV (whom Ricci had personally sponsored for the cardinalate ten years earlier) and subjected to interrogation regarding alleged Jesuit conspiracies and secret wealth. Ricci was never released and, two years later, died in prison. For Abbé Poterie to equate Carroll with Ricci was to suggest comparable treatment for Carroll, which was beyond anything called for by either Andrew Nugent or Patrick Smyth.

Like Nugent, Poterie, a priest of the Diocese of Angers, had his faculties suspended back in France. He immigrated to Guadeloupe in the West Indies, where he had relatives, and then wrangled an appointment as a naval chaplain. When his squadron visited Boston in the fall of 1788, Poterie jumped ship, which French naval authorities let happen, given the fact that Poterie had already caused more trouble than he was worth. Failing to obtain an assignment from the bishop of Quebec, Poterie—who spoke limited and highly accented English—cast his lot with Boston's small French Catholic community centered on the home of French merchant Louis Baury de Bellerive. In late October, Poterie began to celebrate Sunday Mass for this group at Baury's home. The French were thrilled to have a French-speaking priest in their midst and launched plans to acquire and reconfigure for Catholic worship an unused former Huguenot church on School Street.

Carroll had planned to assign the Reverend Mr. John Thayer, a Boston-born convert from Congregationalism, to Boston; but Thayer was delayed in London, where he had been on mission for two years following study at Saint-Sulpice and ordination by the archbishop of Paris, and would not arrive in Boston until January 1790. And so, to fill the gap, the ever busy Carroll (hastily, as he later admitted) approved Poterie's request for faculties without what is today called a background check. In any event, by January 1789, Abbé Poterie was fully licensed. The congregation also procured a house at 223 Union Street for the abbé to use as his rectory and placed him on salary.

Meanwhile, Poterie was busy redecorating the School Street church, acquiring debt in his own name, despite the French community's ownership of the church.

In the matter of ecclesiastical furnishings, Abbé Poterie had excellent taste, as the newly renovated Church of the Holy Cross clearly demonstrated. Liturgically, the abbé was equally exacting in his celebration of Mass and related ceremonies. Although his liturgical style included a few controversial Gallicisms (praying for the king of France, for instance), Poterie also introduced a prayer, which he read aloud in the vernacular before the Scripture readings, that was fully and loyally American: a prayer for the pope, for Prefect Carroll, for Congress, in gratitude for the founding of the Republic, for the state of Massachusetts, for the governor and magistrates, for (here the Gallicism) "the King of France and the other friends and allies of America [and] for all those who represent the interest of His Most Christian majesty in foreign countries". Poterie had this prayer printed and distributed, and it most likely inspired Carroll to compose a similar prayer—minus the king of France!—a few years later.

In five short months, the thirty-five-year-old Abbé Poterie—suspended *a divinis* in Paris, deserted from the French navy, not really entitled to use the title "de Poterie" (it belonged to another branch of his family)—had acquired a church, a rectory, a salary, and faculties in one of the capital cities of New England. Who was this priest who had so much presented to him in so short a time, who claimed long residence in Rome and Roman degrees and honors? Who was this cleric praying so grandly for pope, king, and American authorities, who presented to the Catholic trustees of his church the most sacred relic of Christendom: an enshrined sliver of the True Cross, recovered in the early fourth century (so Catholic tradition taught) by Helena, mother of Constantine! In refurbishing the Huguenot church, Poterie described himself as a Knight of the Holy Sepulchre, and it was through this chivalric order that he claimed to have acquired this precious relic. Pompously, from the pulpit of the Church of the Holy Cross, the abbé proclaimed himself a doctor of divinity and a protonotary (administrative clerk) of the Holy See in Rome. In the manner of a French bishop, he issued grandly signed pastoral letters ("Given in Boston in North America, under our hand, and the seal of our arms, the 22nd of February, Quinquagesima Sunday, anno salutis 1789. La Poterie, Vice-Prefect and Apostolick Missionary, Curate of the Holy Cross at Boston"), having promoted himself to vice prefect of New England at the least, if not the entire nation![11]

How long could all this go on? Not too long is the answer. Briefed by the French consul general in New York on Poterie's troubles in France, the French consul general in Boston, Étienne L'Etombe—no friend, in any event, of Baury de Bellerive—never attended any of the abbé's services and forbade his staff to do so. L'Etombe also refused to accept from Poterie statistics of marriages, baptisms, and funerals for transfer to France. He was not a chaplain to the French consulate or embassy, Poterie was informed from New York. He was serving in Massachusetts under the authority of Prefect Carroll. France respected the recently achieved separation of church and state in Massachusetts, where in prior times the mere practice of Roman Catholicism was a crime. Dated 20 January 1789, the letter from the New York embassy hinted darkly that the embassy was aware of Poterie's European background. Even more ominously, some of Poterie's congregation—in the course of soliciting vestments and sacred vessels from the archbishop of Paris—learned of Poterie's background as well, but, desperate to secure the services of a priest, kept the matter to themselves.

At this point, Poterie began to pile indiscretion upon indiscretion. He quarreled openly with L'Etombe. Even worse, he embarrassed the French government by using the French king's name to solicit money from Protestant and Catholic Bostonians alike to pay off the five-hundred-dollar debt he had incurred in refurbishing the Church of the Holy Cross. The abbé even had a circular printed up to advance his unauthorized fund drive, associating the Catholic Church in Boston with a foreign power. The Congregationalist minister historian Jeremy Belknap was one of a number of prominent Protestant clerics to be offended by the campaign being waged by Poterie, who attended one of Belknap's lectures in his cassock ("dressed in his toga", as Belknap put it). By 21 April Belknap was sharing the news that Poterie had managed to raise sixty dollars, but "his clerk has decamped with the money", leaving Poterie naked to his creditors. Ten days later, Belknap reported that a writ for nonpayment of debt had been issued against Poterie on behalf of his creditors, and the abbé had fled to Maryland to confer with Carroll.[12]

Carroll, meanwhile, having grown concerned after receiving and reviewing one of Poterie's pastoral letters, sent William O'Brien up from New York to investigate. While O'Brien interviewed parishioners in Boston, Carroll personally interviewed Poterie for the first time in Baltimore and found him presentable and expressed appreciation for the abbé's knowledge of liturgy and Church culture, which perhaps gave credence to Poterie's claim to a doctorate of divinity and service as a Roman protonotary. In any event, Carroll directed, the abbé was not to pray openly for the king of France alongside American officials, and he was not to use the title protonotary, which would make him an agent of the Court of Rome—that is, a foreign government. And, no! Carroll would not assume Poterie's debt for the renovation of Holy Cross. He had no funds for such a subvention. Holding the lease on the Church of the Holy Cross, Poterie and his congregation were responsible for debts incurred in Poterie's name.

Following this interview, a chastened abbé agreed to Carroll's terms and returned to Boston. Carroll then learned of the abbé's loss of faculties for malfeasance in the Archdiocese of Paris. At this point, four parties—Carroll, two French diplomats, and a group of Holy Cross congregants—knew of Poterie's checkered past. The number of parties may have even been five, depending on what Father O'Brien had discovered in Boston, if any of the informed but silent Holy Cross congregants had communicated to him privately. O'Brien, in any event, had persuaded the congregation to pay off the debt, as might be expected from any responsible board of lay trustees. Returning to New York, O'Brien—Carroll's vicar for New York and New England—received instructions from Carroll to suspend Poterie's faculties. Given the nascent lay-trustee culture of the era, O'Brien sent the letter of dismissal to layman Louis Baury de Bellerive as president of the congregation to deliver to Poterie. O'Brien also directed Baury to inform the Holy Cross congregation of the suspension and to encourage them not to attend any services the abbé might continue to offer.

O'Brien's letter was dated 29 May 1789. Poterie's last recorded baptism was dated 7 June. In the months that followed, the abbé tried, with next to no success, to establish a schismatic congregation. Like Andrew Nugent, but less successfully, Poterie attempted to enter the sanctuary for Christmas Eve 1789 services, as several backers yelled support. He was repelled by his successor, Louis de Rousselet, a

French priest who, like Poterie, had relatives in the New World (Dutch Guiana), where (again like Poterie) he had taken refuge when suspended *a divinis* back in France. The ejected Poterie then took his case to the press, attacking Rousselet as an ex-Jesuit (which was untrue) in a tour de force of diatribe: "this wordy and tedious Rousselet, this very poor orator and bad preacher, not able to persuade a single proselyte, but made to scare everyone by his rough speech and insupportable accent, and by his eyes dark and hollow, this discordant and melancholy singer, in a word this *jesuit*, by mission, by conduct, by manners, by rule and principle".[13] Poterie's attack on Rousselet as a Jesuit indicated the second prong of his counter-offensive: to inaugurate a public relations campaign centered on a theme he had introduced in a prior letter to the bishop of Quebec, that the ex-Jesuits of America were using their control of the prefecture apostolic to revive the Society of Jesus under the cover of an American clergy. Patrick Smyth's pamphlet might very well have prompted Poterie to seize upon this strategy. Hence appeared (most likely from a Boston printer using a Philadelphia imprint) *The Resurrection of Laurent Ricci; or a True and Exact History of the Jesuits*, dedicated "to the new Laurent Ricci in America, the Reverend Father John Carroll; Superior of the Jesuits in the united States; also to the Friar-Monk-Inquisitor William O'Brien (one of his [Carroll's] many contrivers to set his Engines at Work without interfering visibly himself)". In June 1789, moreover, a month before he left Boston forever, Poterie outlined his case to Cardinal Antonelli at Propaganda Fide, who had already been more than slightly spooked by the Patrick Smyth pamphlet.

Writing to Charles Plowden on 12 July 1789, Carroll openly acknowledged his distress at Poterie's letter campaign to Rome. In an earlier conversation with Carroll, Poterie had subtly suggested his personal relationship to Henry Benedict, Cardinal Duke of York, the second son of the Old Pretender and, since the death of his older brother, the Jacobite Pretender in his own right as Henry IX, and—of more importance to Carroll—the leader of the victorious anti-Jesuit faction behind the 1773 suppression of the Jesuits and still very much a cardinal of top-tier influence. Fortunately, Carroll remarked in the same letter, Archbishop John Troy of Dublin had written to inform him that the archbishops and bishops of Ireland, meeting recently in Dublin, had censured Patrick Smyth for his pamphlet of false charges against the restoration ambitions of the ex-Jesuits of America. This was a plus. Still, Carroll urged Plowden to get John Thorpe busy countering Abbé Poterie's pamphlet in Roman circles. The abbé's advertised history of Jesuit crimes in America might very well be a mere four pages of false charges and another twenty or so pages of equally false indictments of Carroll's and Father O'Brien's management. Yet Thorpe could help the cause by launching a counternarrative in the right circles, building on the Irish bishops' censure of the similar smear by Patrick Smyth.

John Carroll, bishop-elect of the United States, sailed for England on 9 June 1790 to receive episcopal consecration. Smyth's and Poterie's embarrassing attacks had been safely neutralized, yet they signified future challenges Carroll would have to face in the matter of recalcitrant trustees and priests. Abbé Poterie returned to his home parish of Saint Clement in Craon, where he took the oath prescribed by the 1790 Constitution of the Clergy and thus regained—civilly, at least—his right to practice. Poterie served as a chaplain for French Revolutionary troops, winning a reputation for his exhortatory addresses, and spent time as an English prisoner of war. With the Concordat of 1801 between Pius VII and Napoleon, the abbé once again became a priest in good standing in his native France. He served two years in the Diocese of Versailles, but by his seventies, having long since repented of his earlier attempt at schism, he was serving as curé in a small village near the Poterie family's ancestral home.

7

Dorset, England 1790

John Carroll is consecrated bishop of Baltimore

In 1788 Thomas Weld, the influential Catholic squire of Lulworth Castle in Dorset, England, wrote to the Reverend Mr. John Carroll of Baltimore, then serving as prefect apostolic for the United States, to invite Carroll, should he ever be appointed bishop, to return to England and be consecrated in the new freestanding chapel he had just completed at Lulworth Castle. Mr. Weld's invitation took on special significance when Carroll received from Rome the brief *Ex hac apostolicae,* issued 6 November 1789, naming him the first bishop of Baltimore, with authority over Church affairs in the United States, and was thus forced to consider where he would go for consecration. The brief specified that Carroll was free to choose which bishop in good standing would consecrate him and that, contrary to the usual format requiring two or three bishops on the altar for this ceremony, only one bishop would be necessary in Carroll's case.

Being the closest to Baltimore, Quebec would be the most convenient city for Carroll to choose. Yet consecration in Quebec could give the impression that the newly established See of Baltimore was in some sense subordinate to the See of Quebec. Such a choice would also overlook the American invasion of French Canada in 1775–1776 and the decidedly pro-British attitude of the Quebecois, clergy and laity, during the American Revolution. Carroll's close association with Archbishop John Thomas Troy of Dublin, with whom Carroll had been in correspondence regarding the recruitment of Irish priests to the United States, suggested another possibility: consecration in the land of his ancestors, as Carroll phrased it. Still, his ancestor Charles Carroll the Settler had immigrated to Maryland one hundred years earlier, and John Carroll, in his long sojourn in Europe, had never even paid a visit to that long-held English colony, where, for so long, the Roman Catholicism of its Celtic population had been held in disfavor and repressed.

Rome offered an option, although, the option was not suggested by Rome itself, perhaps for the same reason Carroll would not choose it. The suppression of the Society of Jesus had resulted from Roman intrigue, and Carroll, like all ex-Jesuits, while remaining loyal to the universal Church, could not brush aside the violent disruption to their lives that Roman anti-Jesuit intrigue had wrought. Like nearly all of his former Jesuit brethren, Carroll would not designate Clement XIV, the pope responsible for the suppression, by his papal name. Rather, Clement XIV was Ganganelli, pure and simple. No, indeed, John Carroll would not go to Rome for his consecration.

As a native of Maryland, however, even one of Irish descent, educated from boyhood in the English Jesuit schools of the Continent, Carroll had followed up this formative experience with twenty years of English Jesuit life. The English Province, moreover, had not returned Carroll to Maryland following his ordination but had kept him in the English Jesuit continental school system, where—had there been no suppression—Carroll would have most likely remained the rest of his life. After so many years in such circumstances, Carroll must have spoken with more than a trace of Englishness in his accent and use of the language. Following the suppression, Carroll spent a few months at Wardour Castle as chaplain to his Saint Omer's College classmate Lord Henry Arundell of Wardour, who offered Carroll the position on a permanent basis, which Carroll turned down to return to Maryland. John Carroll, in short, was an English Jesuit from Maryland of Irish descent. His closest friend from Society of Jesus days, Charles Plowden, an Englishman, was now chaplain and tutor to the Weld family at Lulworth Castle and had most likely introduced Carroll to the Welds when Carroll was serving as chaplain at Wardour Castle.

During the Revolutionary War, Carroll had favored independence and had served the Revolution as a member of the congressional commissions to Canada; but following the Treaty of Paris, he was aligned with the Federalist Party, which preferred closer ties to the mother country. John Carroll's distant cousin Charles Carroll of Carrollton, along with most of the Anglo-American Catholic gentry of Maryland and the Irish-American Roman Catholic mercantile and shipping elite of Philadelphia, Federalists all, shared the same inclination to forgive and forget. England was not, for them or for John Carroll, a foreign country. It was, rather, a stabilizing presence in trade and politics now that a much different kind of revolution had broken out in France.

And so, John Carroll accepted Thomas Weld's offer of the chapel of Lulworth Castle in Dorset as the site for his consecration as bishop. Dorset was familiar territory to Carroll, and he was comfortable with the Weld family. Of equal importance: the consecration ceremony could be kept private in such circumstances. Plus, as a former member of the English Province of the Society of Jesus as well as a chaplain at Wardour Castle, Carroll might enjoy a form of homecoming to a life he might have had.

A letter to the president

John Carroll's Englishness—to whatever degree it had resulted from his twenty-six years of English Catholic life on the Continent—existed within a Federalist matrix of American values enlivened by an Anglo-American point of view. The American Revolution, one must remember, had been initiated by Anglo-American colonials and their affiliates and allies on a basis of traditional English rights being denied by the mother country. Indeed, a number of leading American generals had only recently been members of the British army; and, prior to the Revolution, there could be no more London-oriented Virginia gentleman than George Washington. Thus, when Washington was inaugurated as the first president of the United States, elected under its newly adopted Constitution, John Carroll and his fellow Roman Catholics of the Federalist persuasion experienced at once a new beginning and a continuity; for the leading Anglo-American gentleman in the nation was now president of the United States.

In late 1789 John Carroll, on behalf of the Roman Catholic clergy, joined lay-men Charles Carroll of Carrollton, Daniel Carroll, Thomas FitzSimons of Phila-delphia, and Dominick Lynch of New York in sending a letter of congratulations to George Washington upon his election to the presidency. Of the five signers of this letter, only John Carroll could have written it. In its range of sentiments, its republican dignity and classical cadences, its heartfelt patriotism and self-confidence as to citizenship earned on the field of battle, the letter ranks as one of the finest tributes to Washington written then or since. Washington's reply, dated 12 March 1790, moreover, has, down through the decades, served as a writ of acceptance—an Emancipation Proclamation, even—extended to a religious group that was still under restriction in many states' constitutions, as were members of the Hebrew Congregation of Newport, Rhode Island, who had likewise written their con-gratulations to the president and received a reply. In his letter of 18 August 1790, Washington, quoting from the Hebrew Bible and echoing its cadence and imagery, wrote, "May the Children of the Stock of Abraham, who dwell in this land, con-tinue to merit and enjoy the good will of the other inhabitants; while every one shall sit in safety under his own vine and figtree, and there shall be none to make him afraid. May the father of all mercies scatter light and not darkness in our paths, and make us all in our several vocations useful here, and in his own due time and way everlastingly happy."[1]

Whatever restrictions continued in the various states, President Washington, the chief spokesman for national identity and value, was saying something far, far different in long-term implications. Jews and Roman Catholics were part of the founding pact, the originating covenant of the Republic, and they would always be treated fairly and with respect for what they had contributed to the founding of this new nation. So Washington promised as he envisioned the American future.

"The prospect of National prosperity now before us", Washington noted to Catholics,

> is truly animating; and ought to excite the exertions of all good men, to establish and secure the happiness of their Country, in the permanent duration of its freedom and independence. America, under the smiles of Divine Providence—the protection of a good Government—and the cultivation of Manners, Morals, and Piety—cannot fail of attaining, an uncommon degree of Eminence, in Literature, Commerce, Agricul-ture, Improvements at home, and Respectability abroad. As Mankind become more liberal, they will be more apt to allow, that all those who conduct themselves worthy members of the Community, are equally entitled to the protection of civil Govern-ment. I hope ever to see America among the foremost Nations in examples of Justice and Liberality. And I presume that your fellow-citizens will not forget the patriotic part, which you took in the accomplishment of their Revolution, and the establish-ment of their Government—or the important assistance, which they received from a Nation, in which the Roman Catholic Faith is professed.[2]

Electing a bishop

Constitutionalism and contracts were sweeping the United States in the late 1780s; and so, for the Roman Catholic clergy of the nation, it was time to petition Rome for an upgrade to diocesan status. Without a bishop, the Catholic community remained only partially fulfilled ecclesially and difficult to manage. Prefect Carroll was finding the truth of this with the German Catholics of Philadelphia, who were demanding a German national parish, which they unilaterally incorporated in October 1788 as Holy Trinity Church. They then appointed their own priest, John Charles Heilbron, a German Capuchin, rejecting Carroll's nominee, the Reverend Mr. Laurence Graessl. Once again, as in New York, it was an instance of an unlicensed, self-assigning Capuchin. Two German Capuchin blood brothers, John Charles and Peter Heilbron, having read a letter by layman Peter Millar of Conewago published in the German magazine *Mainzer Monatschrift* appealing for German priests for the Pennsylvania missions, answered the call, showed up together in Philadelphia, and delighted the German community with their preaching; one of them, John Charles, received a pastoral appointment from the lay trustees.

Even more delicately, given the ex-Jesuit issue, Carroll's candidate, the fully licensed Laurence Graessl, had been a novice in Munich at the time of the suppression before going on to be ordained a secular priest for the Archdiocese of Munich. No one less than the famed and beloved Ferdinand Farmer had invited Graessl to America, where the deeply religious and self-sacrificing priest immediately distinguished himself on the Pennsylvania and New Jersey circuits, hearing confessions in German, English, French, Italian, Dutch, and Spanish, as he told his parents in a letter of 9 December 1788. So respected did Graessl soon become that his fellow clergy elected him to serve as John Carroll's coadjutor bishop in 1793. But for the time being, Carroll could not get this charismatic Bavarian priest assigned to a German national parish, whose trustees had entered a zone of resistance that constituted a de facto state of schism from Carroll's authority as prefect apostolic.[3]

What was obviously needed was a diocese authorized by the pope and governed by a bishop in full authority. Already the autonomous Anglican parishes had come to a similar decision and in 1783 elected Samuel Seabury—a graduate in theology from Yale and in medicine from Edinburgh, a Loyalist during the War of Independence— and sent him to Aberdeen, Scotland, to be consecrated on 14 November 1784 by nonjuring Scottish bishops (hence not requiring an oath of loyalty to the king) as the first bishop of the newly organized Protestant Episcopal Church of the United States (later simply referred to as the Episcopal Church). Carroll's support of the notion of a papal appointment—a purely spiritual appointment authorizing an autonomously conducted diocese and thus not disturbing to Congress or Protestant America— might make Carroll seem ambitious, since Rome had already linked the prefecture apostolic to an eventual upgrade to a vicar apostolic in bishop's orders. Yet Carroll had to do what was best for what he always designated as the cause of Religion, meaning good order in every sense of the term. Having been in authority for nearly five years, Carroll had firsthand knowledge of the difficulties involved in national leadership and, as he confessed in a letter to Charles Plowden, was more than a little tempted to plead *nolo episcopare* (I wish not to become a bishop)—as Plowden himself, offered a miter, had already done—so as to be able to continue his writing and lobbying on behalf of Catholic emancipation.

And so, in the late winter and early spring of 1788, the Select Body of the Clergy of the United States, meeting in general chapter, authorized a committee of three— John Carroll, Robert Molyneux, and John Ashton—to prepare a *Memorial* for Pope Pius VI, requesting a full-fledged diocese and a bishop, and not a vicar apostolic reporting to Propaganda Fide. Carroll performed the bulk of the work researching and writing the *Memorial*, which observed all protocols and proper terms of address in the stylized Latin of curial communication. The *Memorial* asked for a bishop appointed directly by the Holy See, not Propaganda Fide, to be elected for the first time only by the clergy of the United States and, after that, in a manner commensurate with the character of the American Constitution.

As a skilled diplomat, Carroll also wrote a frank and detailed letter on 18 March 1788 to Cardinal Antonelli that, though in Latin as well, used a more direct and urgent tone, as Carroll chronicled the difficulties he was experiencing as prefect. Carroll then cut to the chase.

> While we ponder these and other things, my priestly brothers, whose labors and experience in America are of long duration, believe that the time has come, provided it seems so to the Holy See and the Sacred Congregation, for the appointing of a bishop over the Church of America, because his very title and dignity may be effective in coercing those of intractable disposition. I am not unaware, Most Eminent Cardinal, that there may be some who will suspect me of sinful ambition, but I would rather risk this and even greater suspicion than by silence pretend that religion is not menaced. In addition to the fact that the authority of a bishop will be more weighty in church government, the sect which professes the Anglican religion gained no little glory and esteem with the public by introducing bishops, whereas formerly the very name was abhorred in the states of America. Another result was greater observance and attention to morals on the part of their so-called ministers. For these and other reasons we thought it well to offer a petition to His Holiness which he undoubtedly will send to the Sacred Congregation. In it our reasons for the suggestion are explained more fully. In this connection my only comment is that you, Most Eminent Cardinal, and the other fathers who watch over the propagation of the faith so carefully and with much success, seriously weigh the spirit and the prejudices which prevail in these States, and that you so arrange the naming of a bishop and give him such authority that, while union and due obedience to the Apostolic See is maintained, in so far as is possible, he be fixed from the suspicion of any kind of subjection which is not absolutely necessary.[4]

Carroll also dispatched a copy of the *Memorial* that would arrive through diplomatic channels courtesy of the Spanish embassy.

The *Memorial* was sent to Rome in April 1788 via the diplomatic mail of the Spanish consul Diego de Gardoqui y Arriquibar, who sent it along with his recommendation that Carroll be appointed bishop, which Gardoqui believed to be essential to any further progress for the Church in the United States. Gardoqui also dispatched a copy of the *Memorial* and his letter of recommendation of Carroll to Prince Florida-Blanca, prime minister of Spain and its empire. The *Memorial* reached the Spanish ambassador to the Court of Pius VI, Don José Nicolás de Azara, who presented it to Cardinal Antonelli on 29 November 1788.

While this ceremonial progress, with its growing list of endorsements, added gravitas to the American cause, Antonelli had already taken action upon receiving Carroll's letter of 18 March. After submitting Carroll's request to a general meeting of Propaganda Fide on 23 June, which voted to grant the petition of the American clergy, Antonelli took the request to Pius VI himself, who concurred in an audience on 6 July. On 12 July Antonelli wrote to the three memorialists, informing them of the pope's favorable decision, and authorized them to hold an election and designate an episcopal see.

After receiving Antonelli's letter, Carroll, Molyneux, and Ashton sent out a circular letter dated 25 March 1789, calling for an election. There seem to have been two options for voting, either at a convocation at White Marsh, Maryland, by direct ballot, or by letter submitted through the three regional chapters for those unable to attend the White Marsh meeting. Carroll received twenty-four out of twenty-six votes cast; Carroll and one other priest had voted for other candidates. The clergy also chose Baltimore as the episcopal see, being as of 1790 the fifth-largest city in the United States (the third-largest by 1800), in the most populous Catholic state in the nation. Carroll approved of the selection of Baltimore, he wrote to Plowden on 8 May 1789, but as for the other part of the election, "it deprives me of all expectation of rest or pleasure henceforward, and fills me with terror, with respect to eternity. I am so stunned with the issue of this business, that I truly hate the hearing or the mention of it, and therefore will say only, that since my brethren, whom in this case I consider as the Interpreters of the divine will say I must obey, I will e'en do it; but by obeying, shall sacrifice henceforth every moment of peace & satisfaction. I most earnestly commend myself to your prayers & those of my other friends."[5]

Pius VI issued the brief *Ex hac apostolicae* on 6 November 1789 from the basilica of Saint Mary Major, signing and stamping its waxen seal under the Fisherman's Ring. The short but comprehensive document established the See of Baltimore, with jurisdiction over Catholics, lay and clerical, throughout the United States and named as bishop of the see John Carroll, priest, elected by the Catholic clergy of America on a onetime privilege. Any and all previous lines of ecclesiastical authority were now voided. The newly created diocese, moreover, would not be subject to any metropolitan (archbishop) but would report directly to the Holy See, with instructions given to keep Propaganda Fide informed on a regular basis. As bishop, Carroll should begin the development of a cathedral in Baltimore as well as a seminary for the education of young men for the priesthood, to be established in Baltimore or another city. He should oversee clerical incomes and assignments. The cathedral should have assigned to it a chapter of clergy responsible for divine worship. (Rome would later remove the privilege establishing chapters of canons in American Catholic cathedrals.)[6]

The brief *Ex hac apostolicae* most likely reached Carroll sometime in April 1790. With it arrived a fulsome letter of congratulations from Cardinal Antonelli, who had been crucial to this process of founding the Church in America. Antonelli's office had obviously written the first draft of the papal brief appointing Carroll—making sure that the requirement of the freestanding Diocese of Baltimore to report regularly to Propaganda Fide was fully spelled out—and the sincerity of his high regard for Carroll shines through his letter of congratulations. Thus, a onetime member of the anti-Jesuit faction prior to suppression—a prelate only recently willing to cross-examine two American seminarians as to the possibility of a plot by the ex-Jesuit clergy of the United States to revive the Society of Jesus in America—promised his warm and continuing support to ex-Jesuit Bishop-elect Carroll.

This promise of support was no idle matter, for Leonard Antonelli was among the most powerful cardinals in Rome at the time. Like Carroll, Antonelli came from a well-established background. His uncle was the famed canonist, historian, and Orientalist Nicolò Maria Cardinal Antonelli. Entering the diplomatic service of the Court of Rome (Papal States), Leonardo Antonelli (born in 1730 and, hence, Carroll's contemporary) had, again like Carroll, distinguished himself among his peers and been suitably recognized for his talent and achievement (canon of Saint Peter's, prefect of archives, secretary of the Sacred College of Cardinals, assessor of the Holy Office) and had been created cardinal priest in 1775 by Pius VI, who personally appreciated Antonelli's diplomatic and curial service. Like Carroll, moreover, Antonelli maintained a notable private library; befriended scholars, writers, and artists; and earned some fame himself as an archaeologist. This polished and powerful prelate would now, in effect, serve as the de facto cardinal protector of John Carroll personally and the American church in general through its challenging early years of organization and development.

Lulworth Castle

The original Lulworth Castle dated to the first half of the twelfth century. A branch of the Howard family, headed by the Duke of Norfolk, acquired the castle and property near the Dorset coast in the mid-sixteenth century, and in 1588 Henry Howard began work on the existing castle, designed in a fantasy-driven Elizabethan style that featured a circular tower at each corner. The western county of Dorset, however, was far from the Howard estates to the east, and in 1640 the then heir, James Howard, sold the estate and the unfinished castle to the extremely wealthy Humphrey Weld and his wife, Clara, youngest daughter of Lord Arundell of Wardour. Their marriage linked the Arundells and the Welds from that time forward and transformed Lulworth Castle into a center of Catholicism in the West Country.

In 1740 Edward Weld married Mary Teresa Vaughan, thus linking a third prominent recusant family to the existing Wardour-Weld consanguinity. The couple's oldest son, Edward, married Maria Anne Smyth. In 1785 George, Prince of Wales, secretly married the now-twice-widowed Mrs. Maria Anne Fitzherbert, thus linking the Wardours, Welds, and Vaughans with royalty itself, although the marriage was soon set aside on the grounds that the prince was underage and Mrs. Fitzherbert was a Roman Catholic. Coming to the throne in 1830, however, William IV, the younger brother of George IV, offered to raise Mrs. Fitzherbert to the rank of duchess, which she refused. King William IV, however, insisted that she use royal insignia in her household and personally introduced her to each member of his family as his brother's widow.

Journeying to Lulworth Castle, then, for his consecration, John Carroll was reassociating himself with the heart of the English recusant establishment. His host, Thomas Weld, was a discreet but effective activist on behalf of the emancipation of Roman Catholics in Great Britain and on friendly terms with none other than King George III, so roundly denounced a few short years before in the American Declaration of Independence. Three times between 1785 and 1789 (or after), King George and Queen Charlotte were entertained at Lulworth Castle during their Majesties' progress through the western counties. The king also enjoyed visiting with the Weld daughters and their tutor, John Carroll's good friend Charles

Plowden, himself a scion of minor recusant gentry and a well-known writer and controversialist in English Catholic circles. During one visit by the monarch, Weld escorted the king on a tour of his new chapel.

Lulworth Chapel was an anomaly. Most recusant chapels were discreetly located within the main building of the estate. Lulworth Chapel, by contrast, was a free-standing structure outside the castle. Circular in shape, it reflected the towers of the castle, and its dome suggested a mausoleum rather than a Catholic chapel, an impression Weld accentuated by reinterring his Catholic ancestors within. Eleven or twelve years earlier, the Rome-based former Jesuit Father John Thorpe had assisted Lord Henry Arundell of Wardour in the design and furnishing of his chapel. Thorpe was also on hand to secure the services of the noted Italian architect Giacomo Quarenghi to design the altar and the oversize candlesticks for Lulworth Chapel and to secure its statuary and art.

Weld envisioned his chapel as a regional facility as well as a place for family worship; indeed, John Carroll was one of three bishops to be consecrated at Lulworth during this period. (The other two—William Gibson and John Douglass—would be consecrated in the forthcoming Advent of 1790 as vicars apostolic for British districts.) In a letter dated 28 June 1790, Weld personally recruited the learned Benedictine bishop Charles Walmesley, vicar apostolic of the Western District, to consecrate Carroll. The ceremony should be as private as possible, Weld urged: "The less it is spoken of the better, the more privately it can be done the better."[7]

Why the secrecy? Weld does not say, nor does Carroll. Part of the answer, one suspects, was English-related: the need to maintain discretion in the matter of Roman Catholic bishops being consecrated in an England still uneasy in such matters. Another part of the answer involved the United States, where—unlike in Great Britain—Roman Catholics had enjoyed emancipation since the Revolution, which was itself a painful subject, especially for Thomas Weld, Catholic host to King George III, who opposed emancipation. Nor would John Carroll be taking the customary oath of loyalty to the king in the course of the ceremony, oaths taken by the Roman Catholic vicars apostolic of England, Wales, and Scotland when they were consecrated and installed in office as missionary bishops loyal to the sovereign of the realm in which they served.

John Carroll was to arrive at Lulworth in mid-July, Weld wrote to Bishop Walmesley. Perhaps Bishop Walmesley might arrive a week or more before the ceremony of consecration—scheduled for Sunday, 15 August 1790, the feast of the Assumption of Mary into Heaven—and enjoy Bishop-elect Carroll's company. When exactly Carroll arrived at Lulworth is not recorded. His last surviving letter from Number 28 King Street, Bloomsbury, London (to Archbishop Troy of Dublin, discussing, among other topics, Irish priests at work in the United States), suggests that Carroll might have arrived at Lulworth in early August: enough time before the event to have a happy reunion with his longtime friend and correspondent Charles Plowden and his patron Lord Arundell of Wardour after years of separation and perhaps to get reacquainted with his host, Thomas Weld, whom he might have met during that same time.

And so, here was John Carroll, returned to the environment of recusant worship, piety, community, and hospitality that had welcomed him sixteen-plus years ago when, at the invitation of Charles Plowden and Lord Arundell, he had shown up on the doorstep of Arundell Castle depressed by the dissolution of the Society, which had been his home for twenty years, and not knowing what his future might be. Through friendships at Arundell and priestly service to the surrounding community, the Jesuit professor of philosophy learned to function as a parish priest and took that identity and skill set back to Rock Creek, Maryland. There, he was still a scholar, yes, but a pastor and a circuit rider as well, ministering to the people of Maryland as his Jesuit predecessors had been ministering since 1634.

From the second floor of Lulworth Castle, just above its well-stocked library, Carroll could look out over well-designed and meticulously tended green-carpeted parkland lined with hedges and flowering shrubs. Cultivated acreage extended concentrically from this parkland; in the mid-distance lay gently rolling hills covered in elm, beech, and cedar, beneath which grazed herds of tawny and white-breasted deer. In the far distance, two or more miles away, the great headland of Arish Mell and adjacent cliffs framed a triangle of blue sea. Three miles to the southwest were the villages of East and West Lulworth: whitewashed, thick-thatched houses with small leaded windows set in irregular groups and surrounded by flowering gardens, clustered around a green in one village and an ancient country church in the other. Woods, streams, and sown fields bordered each settlement.

Here was the landscape of rural recusant England that the Roman Catholic founders of Maryland remembered and would in time reprise in American circumstances and materials whenever possible. From this perspective, recusant England was home country for tidewater Marylanders: a memory—a dream, if you will—running parallel to the realities of a colonial frontier, not as an alternative or a refuge (although a few did go back), but as a guide to what they had been trying to create in Maryland, especially in St. Mary's County, before the Glorious Revolution disemancipated them.

Carroll's consecration

The big day, at once splendid and secret, arrived: Sunday, 15 August 1790, the feast of the Assumption, in Lulworth Chapel, dedicated to Mary. For the Solemn Pontifical High Mass—during which the consecration would occur via ancient prayers, anointing with holy oil, and laying on of hands—the bishop, bishop-elect, and attendant priests wore gold vestments appropriate for a major feast day. A well-trained choir, backed by the chapel's excellent organ and organist, provided hymns and music. Thomas Weld's son and heir, the recently married seventeen-year-old Thomas Junior, served as Carroll's Gospel bearer and acolyte. (In 1821 the now-widowed Weld would be ordained a priest and, in 1830, following Catholic emancipation, would be the first English cardinal to be created since the seventeenth century.) Charles Plowden preached the sermon. That John Carroll selected his closest friend, a former member of the same suppressed Society and an Englishman of recusant descent, to deliver this sermon in this recusant setting on behalf of the consecration of America's first bishop offered further testimony to Carroll's deep attachment to his years in the English Province of the Society of Jesus.

Plowden opened his sermon with a reference to the recent dismemberment of the British Empire that "has called forth into existence a new empire in the

Western world". Such dismemberment—in America, at least, if not yet in Great Britain—has resulted in, Plowden noted, "the extension of the kingdom of Christ, the propagation of Catholic religion, which heretofore fettered by restraining laws is now enlarged from bondage and is left at liberty to exert the full energy of divine truth". Following his consecration, Plowden intoned, Bishop Carroll will return to a nation of religious liberty, set in an immense continent, whose Roman Catholic population is "earnestly demanding Catholic instructors" in the context of its newly acquired religious freedom.

At this point—in recognition of the Anglo-American context of Carroll's consecration—Plowden compared Carroll to the patron saint of Catholic England. Bishop Carroll, Plowden continued, will go forth to his nation as Saint Augustine of Canterbury, dispatched in 596 by Pope Saint Gregory the Great, went forth to Kent, England, which he evangelized and where he later established the episcopal See of Canterbury. So, too, will Bishop Walmesley, a prelate in full communion with Rome, now consecrate another Augustine of Canterbury, dispatched, in Carroll's case, to an offspring of English Catholicism, the Roman Catholic Church in the United States, and the site of this commissioning, Lulworth Chapel, "shall be revered through succeeding ages, even by churches yet un-named, as the privileged, the happy spot, from whence their episcopacy and hierarchy took their immediate rise".[8] Thus, Plowden historicized his friend Carroll's consecration at the deepest possible level, while celebrating a continuing relationship between Catholic England and Catholic America that even a long, bloody Revolutionary War could not destroy.

Educational ambitions

While on the high seas, Carroll had written Cardinal Antonelli (in Latin) to thank him for his past support and to pledge his enduring loyalty to the See of Peter. Precisely because of this loyalty, Carroll continued, he was "consumed with the desire to complete as soon as possible the school for the education of Catholic youth. From this school those who are called by God to the sanctuary may pass to the seminary to be built. With God's help I shall take pains that they be schooled in the belief that unity of faith cannot endure apart from the authority of the Holy See."[9] Like the founders of Harvard in 1636, Carroll was suggesting a continuity of higher education for young men, including those going on to clerical careers, as preparations for life and faculties of divinity that would provide clerical candidates with theological and spiritual formation as a form of concurrent or postgraduate instruction. The Council of Trent had encouraged each bishop, if possible, to establish such a program in his diocese for the education of parish clergy. Bishop Laval successfully established such a program in Quebec in the late seventeenth century. In 1782 Carroll had already set forth a comparable program—academy, college, seminary—in his *Plan of Organization*, leading up to the self-organization of the ex-Jesuit clergy.

But Laval, himself educated by the Jesuits, enjoyed the propinquity of the Jesuit College at Quebec, an impressive institution staffed by French Jesuits and qualified lay educators who offered instruction in humanities and philosophy to pretheology students in residence at Laval's seminary, developed in association with the Paris

Foreign Missions Society. Carroll, by contrast, did not as of yet have such a college. Given the suppression, moreover, he lacked experienced Jesuit instructors in the humanities, science, and philosophy. Indeed, even before the suppression, the Jesuit academy at Bohemia Manor had gone into decline, and during the Revolution, Catholic Marylanders could not send their sons or daughters past British blockades to French Flanders for an education. Thus, as of the mid-1780s, Catholic education, as a whole, had been in a state of eclipse for more than a decade.

Then there was the question of educating young Americans for the priesthood. A few Marylanders had managed to send sons interested in the priesthood to the academy at Liège—which Pius VI had raised to the level of a pontifical seminary in 1774—staffed by ex-Jesuits of the former English Province. These priests wanted more American seminarians, as their academy was coming on hard times. Regrettably, as the Reverend Mr. John Ashton, procurator for the Select Body of the Clergy, was pointing out by 1786, it would take an estimated two hundred pounds sterling for the two transatlantic voyages and six years of boarding expenses to send an American seeking ordination through the Liège program, and few (if any) American Catholic parents could afford such a sum.

Nor was the Roman option a viable alternative. In 1784 Cardinal Antonelli offered Prefect Apostolic Carroll two scholarships to the Collegio Urbano, Propaganda Fide's seminary in Rome. For various reasons—available funds and a shortage of candidates, mainly—Carroll took nearly three years to act on this gift. As usual, moreover, Carroll had difficulties with the Mission Oath required of each Collegio Urbano seminarian—namely, to accept ordination, to return to his home province and function as a diocesan priest, and to report to Propaganda Fide regularly (every two years) as to his health and progress in ministry. Informed by Carroll of his reservations regarding Americans being put under oath to the Court of Rome, Antonelli promised to reconfigure the oath to fit American circumstances if necessary, and so Carroll went along with the Propaganda Fide program and sent fourteen-year-old Ralph Smith of Maryland and thirteen-year-old Felix Dougherty of Pennsylvania to Rome, where they arrived with their escort on 10 January 1788.

For the next ten years, the two young men pursued their studies, although, upon finishing their humanities program and beginning the study of philosophy, both wrestled with the promise to accept ordination according to the Mission Oath. After some grumbling, however, each did take the oath. Yet neither of them persevered to the priesthood, although Felix Dougherty was chosen to preach in Latin on Pentecost Sunday before Pius VI in 1796. The next year, though, Smith and Dougherty returned to the United States: Smith because he openly and honestly said he had no vocation to the priesthood, Dougherty because of ill health. Smith most likely studied medicine (or so someone named Ralph Smith informed Carroll in 1803); and Dougherty made a brief effort in later life to resume his clerical studies before disappearing from the record.

One can only salute these two young Americans for braving the complexities and restrictions of seminary life in Rome—including the acquisition of Latin and Italian—at such a young age and with no prior preparation. For the time being, the Roman Catholic culture of the early American Republic and the seminary culture of Rome in the continuing era of the Papal States did not constitute a good fit. The European tradition of priestly formation would have to play a part in his seminary plans, Carroll knew, but some adjustments to American culture and conditions would have to be made.

A Georgetown solution

In 1786 the Second General Chapter of the Clergy, meeting from 13 to 22 November at White Marsh, was dealing with this very issue as it drew up a plan for the founding of a school "for the education of youth and the perpetuity of a body of the clergy in this country"; the plan also called for a fund drive in the United States, the islands of the West Indies, and Europe on behalf of this fledgling institution. Five directors were appointed: the Reverend Messrs. John Carroll, James Pellentz, Robert Molyneux, John Ashton, and Leonard Neale. Laymen Dominick Lynch of New York and George Meade and Thomas FitzSimons of Philadelphia were authorized to raise and receive funds in their districts. By the end of January 1787, Carroll had acquired a one-acre plot in Georgetown, Maryland, atop a rise overlooking the Potomac River. Founded in 1751, the settlement of Georgetown had been rapidly developing as a port city since the peace that followed the Treaty of Paris (1783) had revived the tobacco trade, and Georgetown—250 houses and approximately 1,500 residents—replaced Annapolis on the Chesapeake as a shipping center and city of choice for southern Maryland gentry. A few years later, with the establishment of the proposed City of Washington in the District of Columbia as the national capital, the adjacent Georgetown would acquire an even greater level of urban panache. John Carroll, meanwhile, was doing all that he could to persuade his friend Charles Plowden to emigrate to the United States and accept the presidency of the proposed academy. But if Plowden turned down the episcopal role of vicar apostolic, as would soon prove the case, in order to continue his efforts on behalf of Catholic emancipation in Great Britain, even his longtime friendship with Carroll could not persuade him to change his plans.

Resistance to the proposed academy began to develop under the leadership of the brothers Leonard and Francis Neale in the Southern District, epicenter of ex-Jesuits hoping for the revival of the Society. Who was going to pay for this academy, they asked, or pay for a diocese, for that matter, except for the ex-Jesuit plantations and other properties? Were a diocese to be established with Carroll as bishop, could he not transfer these properties to the diocese and use the income as he pleased? And where would that leave the Society of Jesus once it was restored? How would it then be able to support its ministries? Was such an appropriation of funds, should it occur, fair to those generations of Maryland Jesuits in times past who, under penal conditions, had acquired and developed these properties for the support of the Society?

Summoning his best diplomacy and persuasiveness, Carroll reminded the Southern District's ex-Jesuits of the grand reputation of the Society of Jesus as educators and personally promised that, when the glorious day of restoration arrived, jurisdiction over the academy would be transferred to the American Jesuits. Carroll also wrote a formal letter of promise to that effect. The Southern District's opposition to the school temporarily subsided. Carroll would later submit in writing a similar promise that, as bishop of Baltimore, he would not seize ex-Jesuit properties or revenues for support of diocesan projects.

Fundraising went slowly. The Catholic gentry might be willing to pay tuition for their own sons but not for someone else's. An annual subsidy of one hundred *scudi* for three years from Propaganda Fide, however, voted through on 18 February 1788 at the urging of Cardinal Antonelli, gave Carroll and the directors the confidence to begin by mid-April construction of a three-story, eleven-room structure (Old South, it would eventually be called), with the third-story attic to serve as a dormitory. Finances were tight. Building could not begin until Carroll had made the final payment on the seventy-five pounds required to secure the deed for the property. It took three full years to complete Old South, since construction stopped every time money ran out.

Carroll, meanwhile, was still—and rather desperately—searching for a president. What, after all, was he offering? Not the directorship of a college comparable to those already in existence in Protestant America and certainly not a seminary such as the seminary in Quebec, which had been flourishing for more than a century. Besides, Carroll was keeping close to his vest plans for a seminary program to be developed as part of his academy program. If the proposed institution seemed overly clerical in its orientation, that would limit its scope—and fundraising as well. American Catholics had become used to receiving the ministries of Jesuits and ex-Jesuits for free; they had no experience in, and gave little thought to, contributing to the education of secular priests who would one day serve them in diocesan-authorized parishes. Another reason, moreover, that Carroll delayed securing a civil charter for the Georgetown Academy was to preclude possible state interference with the seminary aspects of its program.

The prospectus for the Georgetown Academy issued in 1787 promised a solid preparation for collegiate and university-level studies for students of every religious persuasion. So, for the time being, the Georgetown Academy remained a middle and secondary school en route to collegiate instruction, a common condition for start-ups of this sort for the next hundred years in American education. Indeed, St. Omer's and the other Jesuit colleges of Europe had been educational institutions of this type. But aside from the one or two priests serving the briefly existing academy at Bohemia Manor, the Jesuits of Maryland had lost their taste for and touch for schoolmastering. They had instead become planter-missioners, riding the circuits on mission and running plantations as part of their ministries: gentry in lay attire who bore the prestigious family names of Maryland and were received in the best houses. These men were devout and good Jesuit priests, but in their own Maryland way; they did not resemble their cassocked counterparts in the Jesuit colleges of Europe, living in large communities, tied to the exacting day-by-day drill of schoolmastering, trained to this calling by required stints of teaching in their years of seminary preparation. Even the one local ex-Jesuit to whom Carroll offered the presidency of the academy—the erudite and well-meaning yet somewhat indolent and intermittently indecisive Robert Molyneux—turned down the assignment.

The Sulpician factor

Thus Bishop-elect John Carroll left for England with the Georgetown Academy construction undone and its presidency unfilled. In the month he spent at 28 King Street, Bloomsbury, London, following his consecration, however, Bishop Carroll

significantly advanced the seminary half of his educational agenda through conversations with the French Sulpician François-Charles Nagot, vice rector of the Seminary of Saint-Sulpice in Paris, on behalf of Jacques-André Emery, superior general
of the Society of Saint-Sulpice, a congregation of secular priests dedicated to the
education of diocesan clergy.

Founded in 1642 by Jean-Jacques Olier, pastor of the megaparish of Saint-
Sulpice in Paris, the Sulpicians arose out of a nationwide effort in seventeenth-
century France to develop a theology and ascesis for the secular priesthood and
to reform and regularize clerical education. Out of this movement emerged the
French School of spirituality, which stressed mental prayer and an intensified personal relationship to Christ, and such clerical congregations as the Oratory, the
Mission, the Congregation, the Congregation of Jesus and Mary, and the Sulpicians, each dedicated to the French School of spirituality and to seminary education.
While other congregations pursued other missions as well, the Sulpicians remained
focused exclusively on seminary education. By the late eighteenth century, France
had 140 diocesan seminaries. Oriented toward service to the poor, the Congregation of the Mission (also known as the Lazarists or Vincentians) conducted fifty-six
of them; thirty were conducted by diocesan clergy; thirty-nine by other clerical
congregations; and a mere fifteen by Sulpicians. The latter, however, including the
Seminary of Saint-Sulpice in Paris, were among the most powerful and prestigious
of the French seminaries.

In contrast to his spiritual mentor, Saint Vincent de Paul, a shrewd peasant with
a taste for evangelical ministry to the poor, Abbé Jean-Jacques Olier was a wealthy
nobleman with Jesuit training and a doctorate in theology from the Sorbonne,
who had turned down (to his family's distress) promotion to a bishopric in order to
devote himself to his Paris parish (the largest in the nation) and seminary education.
An alternative name for Olier's society was the Gentlemen of Saint-Sulpice; the
group tended to recruit its members from candidates who came from the gentry and
professional classes. Sulpicians maintained their private wealth, took no vows, but
lived simply in community with their students and tended to use whatever wealth
they personally possessed to support the Sulpician mission. While not overly pronounced, a note of pro–French Gallicanism was evident in the Sulpician ethos, as
it was in the French church in general following the Four Gallican Articles issued
by the bishops and clergy representatives in Paris on 19 March 1682, which stressed
the rights and privileges of the French church. In any event, the Sulpicians did not
venture beyond France or French Canada until they arrived in the United States,
and American Sulpicians maintained a strong connection to France into the twentieth century.

The French Revolution upended the ecclesiastical culture of France. The Civil
Constitution of the Clergy (1790) made bishops and priests agents of the state and
subject to civil election. Bishops left the country en masse, and thousands of priests did
likewise rather than take the civilly required but papally condemned oath of loyalty
to the government. (Pope Pius VI excommunicated Charles Maurice de Talleyrand,
bishop of Autun, for consecrating two constitutional bishops.) Thus, the Very Reverend Jacques-André Emery, superior general of the Society of Saint-Sulpice, was
concerned about the future of his institute if religion remained under state control
in a bishopless France in which all the seminaries, including Saint-Sulpice, had been
closed by order of the government. A respected administrator as well as seminary

professor, Emery had earlier served a term as vicar-general of the Diocese of Angers, where he was superior of the seminary, and when the archbishop of Paris went into exile, he named Emery administrator of the archdiocese, which landed Emery in prison on at least two occasions. Facing the guillotine himself, Emery solicitously and effectively ministered to the condemned.

With seminaries closed in France, Bishop John Carroll hoped to persuade Emery to authorize the creation of a Sulpician seminary in the United States as part of Carroll's overall plan for Catholic higher education—not now, of course, given the absence of a college to prepare seminarians for graduate-level work in theology, but eventually, once the Georgetown Academy had advanced into collegiate-level instruction in philosophy and humanities. Returning from Lulworth Castle to London in late August 1790, Carroll found a letter (in French) from Emery, dated 25 August, in which Emery offered to establish and staff a seminary in Baltimore at Sulpician expense. In his reply to Emery, dated 3 September 1790, Carroll, while grateful, was somewhat hesitant. He had been busy the past three or four years putting together a "literary establishment", Georgetown Academy, whose primary purpose would be to provide students for a seminary such as the one Emery was proposing, but at the moment, supplying students in sufficient numbers would not be possible. Still, he would be happy to talk with Emery's representative regarding long-term prospects.

Between 14 and 18 September Carroll found himself in discussions with another formidable Sulpician, François-Charles Nagot. Like Emery, Nagot had petitioned for entry into the Sulpicians following a Jesuit education in humanities and philosophy. Following his service as a theology professor at the Sulpician-staffed seminary at Nantes (Nagot held a doctorate in theology from the University of Nantes), Nagot had recently been appointed vice rector of the Seminary of Saint-Sulpice in Paris. He brought with him a list of seventeen questions relating to two Sulpician proposals: the seminary at Baltimore and, as an alternative, a Sulpician mission to some of the formerly French western territories now under Carroll's jurisdiction until an American seminary was sustainable. The sheer practicality of Nagot's questions demonstrated how thoroughly the Sulpicians had thought through the Baltimore proposal. What was the cost of rent in Baltimore? Should the Sulpicians bring their own household furniture and linens? What was the climate like? How much would it cost to purchase a revenue-producing farm? Was the consent of Congress required for them to immigrate? Could they wear their cassocks in public? Nagot also informed Carroll that the Sulpicians were willing to pay their own way to the United States. In the weeks that followed Nagot's visit, Carroll wrote approvingly of the venture to Archbishop Antonio Dugnani, apostolic delegate to France, Charles Plowden, and Cardinal Antonelli. In his letter to Antonelli, dated 27 September 1790, Carroll stated that the arrival of Sulpicians would further diversify the American clergy and hence counter Smyth's and Poterie's charges that Carroll favored ex-Jesuits when it came to clerical appointments.

Baltimore

On 7 December 1790, Carroll arrived in the city of Baltimore, chosen by the American clergy as the location of his episcopal see, and moved into the small house adjacent to Saint Peter's Church, his procathedral. That Sunday, 12 December,

Carroll preached his first sermon. Rather than present his program at length—he does touch briefly on his responsibility to enforce proper ecclesiastical discipline—Carroll returned a number of times to the magnitude of the challenges and duties facing him and the terror that came upon him when he imagined himself failing. "In God alone can I find any consolation", he confessed. "He knows by what steps I have been conducted to this important station; and how much I have always dreaded it. He will not abandon me, unless I first draw down his malediction by my unfaithfulness to my charge. Pray, dear brethren, pray incessantly, that I may not incur so dreadful a punishment!"[10] So much for the claim that John Carroll was somewhat of a cold fish reinforced by Enlightenment equipoise. Patient, reserved, upper-class—fair enough! But few evangelical divines, or even few Calvinists, could equal the Augustinian intensity of fearing to be alone before God and found wanting that Carroll was sharing with his congregants. Hence his need for lay and clerical support as, together, they went about the business of establishing an American church under diocesan discipline.

Baltimore, Carroll knew—for he had already been living there as prefect—was part of the solution. Baltimore was the dominant city of Maryland, home state of the majority of ex-Jesuit clergy who had voted for its designation as episcopal see and the epicenter of the American Catholic experience. By contrast, Philadelphia—despite the fact that it supported an influential Catholic population, had three Catholic churches in operation, and was the most developed English-speaking city on the planet after London and Edinburgh—was Quaker in its founding ethos and Protestant in its present establishment. New York and Boston had only recently supported Catholic churches, and New England continued to be the most anti-Catholic region in the nation. While big enough to support a bishop, a seminary, and (eventually) a cathedral, Baltimore was neither too small nor too large. Nor was it too Southern, as was Charleston, or too overwhelming, as Philadelphia might have proven during the founding years of a diocese.

Centrally located between north and south, Baltimore was then in the process of doubling its size and its Roman Catholic population, thanks to an influx of French Creole refugees from Saint-Domingue. In 1782 Baltimore had 13,503 inhabitants and was the fifth-largest city in the United States. Due to its emergence as the shipping center for exported grain and for flour milling for the Chesapeake region, as well as its sugar refineries, rum distilleries, and tobacco factories, Baltimore (incorporated as a city in 1792) enjoyed a growing population: 15,000 as of 1795; 26,500 as of 1800; and 46,500 by 1810.

It was a handsome city, moreover, as Médéric Louis Élie Moreau de Saint-Méry—a native of Martinique trained as a lawyer in Paris—noted when he first saw Baltimore in May 1794. Its three thousand brick buildings, most of them two stories, fronted broad, paved, straight streets with sidewalks. Public buildings—the courthouse, two banks (the Bank of Maryland and the Bank of the United States), the exchange, the theater, the three markets, the prison, the poorhouse—were likewise well-designed brick structures. Men in carts patrolled the streets, gathering refuse. Lamps of English design lit the city by night. Baltimore advanced up two slopes from its well-equipped port on the Chesapeake, whose shipped or received tonnage had more than doubled between 1790 to 1794, with exports reaching $5.3 million. The Patapsco River served the city from the interior.

Yellow fever, Moreau lamented, presented the major disadvantage for the city, which it shared with other large cities on the Atlantic seaboard, especially Philadelphia. The 1790s saw a rash of yellow fever outbreaks. Between August and November 1793, Philadelphia lost approximately 5,000 citizens. Between July and October 1795, New York City lost 739. In the summer of 1798, concurrent outbreaks in Boston, New York, and Philadelphia resulted in more than 5,000 dead. In the summer of 1800, Baltimore lost 1,200. It is difficult to imagine the scale and scope of these devastations, given the relatively modest-sized populations of these cities at that time. As the nineteenth century wore on, however, yellow fever outbreaks would increasingly be confined to the southern United States, with New Orleans proving to be particularly vulnerable.

An influx of refugees

On 10 July 1793, a fleet of twenty-two vessels arrived in Baltimore, bringing the first wave of French Creole refugees—including household slaves and free people of color—who had fled Cap-François, the urban center of the French colony of Saint-Domingue, when that city was sacked by rebels. By 13 July, thirty-six vessels from Cap-François were at anchor in the harbor. By 22 July, a total of fifty-three ships had brought in a thousand whites and five hundred people of color, slave and free. A local relief committee went into action, raising funds ($12,000, which was soon augmented by $15,000 in federal funds personally allocated by President Washington) and temporarily placing some four hundred refugees in Baltimore households. "O worthy and generous inhabitants of Baltimore!" intoned Abbé Adrien Cibot, superior of clergy in Saint-Domingue. "O, all you who dwell on this Continent! O, our brethren and benefactors! May this heroical act of benevolence be told and proclaimed amidst all nations of both hemispheres!"[11]

In time, these Saint-Domingue refugees fanned out across Maryland (all the way to the state's western frontier), Delaware, southern Pennsylvania, and Philadelphia, where they joined refugees from the revolution in France and where some settled in Acadian neighborhoods. Others migrated as far north as New York. Baltimore absorbed the largest share of Saint-Domingue refugees—white, black, and mulatto—thus increasing its Catholic population and upgrading its general culture, economy, and range of professional services. Medical services, for example, were enhanced by the arrival of several formally trained French physicians. Pierre Chatard, a graduate of Toulouse in humanities and medicine from Montpellier, rose to prominence as a general practitioner and published authority on diseases of the eye; his sons and grandsons followed him into the medical profession (although one grandson left medicine for the priesthood and became the first bishop of Indianapolis). Refugee Edmé Ducatel brought university-based pharmacology to Baltimore. Trained locally and abroad, Ducatel's son Jules-Timoleon Ducatel taught chemistry and geology (as state geologist, Ducatel spent three years exploring the upper Mississippi and Lake Superior), wrote a popular manual on toxicology, and founded the Maryland Academy of Science and Literature.

Teaching attracted numerous refugees. Madame Marie Lacombe, a widow, opened a boarding school for girls. Several émigrés, including priests Louis William DuBourg and John Francis Moranvillé, found temporary employment on her staff.

Other émigrés offered private instruction in painting, music, fencing, and short-hand. Advertising herself as "singer to the Queen of France", before she fled the French Revolution to yet another revolution in Saint-Domingue, Mademoiselle Buron gave voice lessons and popular public recitals. Performances such as the one on 31 July 1793 in Grant's Assembly Room helped Mademoiselle Buron support her elderly parents, win a favorable review in the *Baltimore Daily Advertiser* of 2 August, and recruit students. Various émigrés went into agriculture. Paul-Aimé Fleury, for example, tried schoolteaching for a while before meeting and marrying Miss Clare Young and thereafter devoting himself to the care and development of Woodbine, his wife's farm in Baltimore County.

A number of refugees established small businesses. Monsieur and Madame Marex operated a coffee shop and a boarding house à *la française*. Peter Vandenbussche reopened his snuff and tobacco manufactory (formerly of the rue du Bac in Paris) and made plans to distribute his products throughout the nation. Sieur Pontier (Gentleman Pontier) opened a wig-making shop on Gay Street. On the other end of private enterprise, Jean-Charles-Marie-Louis Pascault, marquis de Poléon, established what eventually became one of the largest mercantile houses in the country. Born in Saint-Domingue, Pascault left his native island for Baltimore several years before the revolt and the destruction of Cap-François. In 1789 he married Mary Magdalen Slye of St. Mary's County, and the couple eventually raised a large family.

Like more developed Philadelphia, Baltimore acquired éclat-producing after-effects of not only the Saint-Domingue rebellion but also the French Revolution. In short order, Baltimore became a city in which French was spoken (which John Carroll must have enjoyed) and French books widely read. In 1793 Louis Pascault established a subscription lending library, making available to interested Baltimoreans "the best French authors". In 1796 the library was reorganized as the Library Company of Baltimore, of which John Carroll later served as president. Its first salaried librarian, Jean Edouard de Mondésir, served for only two months and was replaced by Abbé Georges de Pérrigny, a Saint-Domingue refugee who had been living at Doughoregan Manor as the chaplain and houseguest of Charles Carroll of Carrollton. De Pérrigny served the Library Company of Baltimore for fifteen years at an annual salary, as of 1797, of $350, which steadily increased, before the abbé returned to the West Indies.

Sulpicians arrive

The French quotient of Baltimore also increased with the arrival on 10 July 1791 of four Sulpician priests. Accompanying François-Charles Nagot, superior, were three young priests: Anthony Garnier, a linguist and theologian from the seminary in Lyon; Michael Levadoux, former superior of the seminary at Bourges; and John Tessier, recently professor of theology at the seminary of Viviers. With these priests came five volunteer seminarians—two Englishmen, one English-speaking Canadian, an American (a recent convert from Elizabethtown, New Jersey), and a Frenchman. Having recently studied in Sulpician seminaries in France, these seminarians constituted a start-up student body for the proposed Baltimore seminary. A non-Sulpician, Louis Delavau, a cathedral canon of the Archdiocese of Tours, had attached himself to the Sulpician party for the Atlantic crossing from Saint-Malo but was not scheduled for seminary work. A priest of independent income, Delavau donated funds to the Baltimore seminary and spent the remaining four years of his life ministering to the French community in Baltimore, much to the satisfaction of Bishop Carroll. (Also on board the vessel was a young nobleman by the name of François-René, vicomte de Chateaubriand, fleeing the French Revolution and destined to win fame in later years as a poet, diplomat, and Christian apologist.) With these Sulpicians came a letter from Sulpician superior general Emery notifying Carroll of two gifts for the new institution: 30,300 livres from personal friends of Emery and 100,000 livres from the Society of Saint-Sulpice.

Taking lodgings at 94 Market Street, the Sulpicians went searching for a purchasable structure suitable for a seminary. After eight days of hunting, they found what they were looking for: the former One Mile Tavern on Paca Street, a four-story structure on four acres, which they purchased for £850 Maryland currency ($2,266) and formally opened as the Seminary of Saint Sulpice on 3 October 1791. Containing residential rooms on its upper floors and large public rooms on its first floor, the former tavern converted easily to a residential seminary that included a chapel on the second floor and a refectory and classrooms on the first floor; adjoining grounds offered space for recreation and future growth. By the December retreat, a number of the volunteer seminarians had left, thereby reducing the student body. But on 29 March 1792, a second group of five Sulpicians arrived, three priests and two seminarians. As in the case of the first cohort of Sulpicians, two of the priests were experienced professors or seminary directors, or both: Jean-Baptiste Chicoisneau at Orleans and John Baptist Mary David at Angers. (The recently ordained Benedict Flaget was scheduled for missionary service in the West.) On 24 June 1792, yet another group of Sulpicians made their appearance: Ambrose Maréchal, Gabriel Richard, and François Ciguard, later followed by Sulpician candidate Louis William DuBourg (admitted in 1795) and Sulpician Jean Dilhet.

In 1790, there had been no Sulpicians in the United States. Now there were a dozen, half the number of ex-Jesuits in service: priests of education, resources, and entrepreneurial spirit. In one short year, Carroll had been able to address the imbalance between ex-Jesuits and non-ex-Jesuit clergy in the United States, with the added benefit that Sulpicians were diocesan clergy (secular priests), a seriously underrepresented group of clergy. Among these arrivals, moreover (although not known at the time), were two future archbishops (Maréchal and DuBourg), two future bishops (Flaget and David), a founder of the University of Michigan and the first of two priests to be elected to Congress (Richard), a future seminary rector (Tessier), and, with Stephen Badin, the first seminarian to be ordained a priest in the United States.

As Sulpicians, furthermore, these priests were devoted to an exacting presentation of the liturgy and had arrived in the United States with a full selection of vestments and sacred vessels. Because of their regard for the liturgy, Carroll informed Cardinal Antonelli, he intended to make them his cathedral clergy for the procathedral now in use and for the cathedral that Pius VI, in his letter of appointment, had urged him to build.

For the time being (it was hoped) the seminary had few students, and hence few ordinations—Stephen Badin in 1793; Demetrius Gallitzin, a Russian Orthodox convert, and English émigré John Floyd in 1795; French Sulpician Jean de Mondésir in 1798; and William Matthews, the first American-born candidate, ordained in 1800. For this reason, Carroll sought and received Superior General Emery's permission to assign a number of Sulpicians temporarily to nonteaching posts. Levadoux, Flaget, and Dilhet went to the Illinois Country, Richard to Michigan, Ciguard to the Mi'kmaq Indians of Maine, David to the missions of lower Maryland, Garnier to establish Saint Patrick's parish in Baltimore, and DuBourg to organize a parish for the free colored people of the city, now a significant population following the flight from Saint-Domingue. Emery did not take these temporary reassignments lightly. The priests of Saint Sulpice were few in number, and although they took no vows and remained secular priests, they followed a highly regulated way of life that emphasized community life with seminary students and was marked by a fixed schedule of worship, study, prayer, teaching, and spiritual direction. Emery feared a drift away from the Rule, as it was called, but at the time the Sulpicians of France were relocating to England, Italy, and the United States, so the entire Society of Saint-Sulpice was facing the challenges of exile and reestablishment. It would take the rest of the 1790s for positive relations to be restored between Emperor Napoleon and the Church, which would lead Emery to reassess the long-term viability of the Baltimore project.

Synod, incorporation, Georgetown

The influx of Sulpicians and other worthy priests from France had multiple effects on the ex-Jesuit clergy. First of all, they could see the possible end of their 150-year monopoly on clerical life. A bishop, a diocese, and a non-ex-Jesuit clergy was now a reality, one made clearer with each French priest who arrived in the United States and applied for and received faculties and assignments. On 23 December 1792, however, the Maryland legislature recognized the Select Body of the Clergy as a legal corporation, which meant that it legally owned all ex-Jesuit properties, including Georgetown Academy. For dedicated restorationists such as the three Neale brothers, state-authorized incorporation put ex-Jesuit properties safely in the hands of the once and future Jesuits of a restored Society and would thus be available to support its ministries. Although Carroll helped the ex-Jesuits draw up the bylaws for the corporation, the term *bishop* was not even mentioned in the act of incorporation. The bylaws, however, permitted the bishop of Baltimore to nominate worthy priests without Jesuit background to the Select Body of the Clergy and for said bishop to continue to draw from the corporation a salary of £210 (Maryland pounds) per annum. Carroll's successor, moreover, would also receive a salary, provided that, like Carroll, he be freely elected by the clergy or its representatives.

Carroll, meanwhile, was leading an effort to regularize local church law and clerical practice in a manner congruent with Church teachings and canon law as well as with the overall culture of the United States. From 7 to 10 November, Carroll convened at procathedral Saint Peter's the first and only diocesan synod (meeting of the clergy as a whole) he would ever call. Twenty-four priests attended, debated, and passed twenty-four decrees, among them: sacraments should be administered uniformly according to the laws and practices of the Roman rite; hymns or prayers in English could be recited by the congregation during Mass or administration of the sacraments; priests should ordinarily dress in black and wear a cassock and vestments when saying Mass. Carroll had his own recommendations, which were adopted. The era of the gentry-supported home chapel (Mass House) was ending. Lay trustees or other benefactors might still build churches, but parishioners were now responsible for their support. A collection should be taken up at every Mass: one-third to support the pastor, one-third for the relief of the poor, one-third for the upkeep of the church. In short, Carroll wanted all active priests (not only ex-Jesuits) to be provided with a church and to be given personal support so as to achieve stability and develop a localized congregation. The era of the circuit rider would yield to a culture of parishes.[12]

Georgetown in the 1790s

As the Baltimore seminary languished for lack of candidates for the priesthood, Carroll's Georgetown project was slowly, painfully taking shape, although not as a feeder school to the Baltimore seminary, as Carroll had initially planned. Carroll secured the services of Robert Plunkett, an English émigré priest who had graduated from the English College at Douai and joined the Society of Jesus four years before the suppression, to act as first president. Faculty turnover averaged two years during the school's first decade, and Plunkett himself—who never really wanted the job—lasted a mere eighteen months at the helm before resigning to join the ex-Jesuit planter-missioners of southern Maryland. He was replaced by Robert Molyneux, the English-born, portly, and erudite ex-Jesuit pastor of Saint Mary's Church in Philadelphia, to whom Carroll had initially offered the presidency when he had failed to persuade Charles Plowden and a number of other English ex-Jesuits he contacted to accept the position. Molyneux lasted three years as president, and in 1796 he was replaced by Sulpician Louis William DuBourg.

Herein lay a prophetic changing of the guard, for Sulpician faculty dominated Georgetown during its first fifteen years. Georgetown's first full-time faculty member, Sulpician seminarian Jean Edouard de Mondésir, served as a resident housemaster and taught French and Latin while at the same time taking English lessons from President Plunkett and privately studying Greek. Mondésir astonished ex-Jesuits on the faculty by wearing a cassock, in contrast to the conservative civilian dress favored by the Jesuits and ex-Jesuits of Maryland since the penal era. The other Sulpician senior seminarians teaching at Georgetown in these early years wore cassocks as well. This choice of garb underscored the contrast between the exactingly clericalized Frenchmen, living and teaching in seminaries, and the ex-Jesuits who had come of age as self-supporting planters, missioners, and circuit riders, living and dressing like laymen—indeed, increasingly developing into a species of Maryland country gentry, as the English Province returned a growing number of Maryland-born Jesuits to their homeland.

Surprisingly, given the importance of French Sulpicians to the Georgetown teaching faculty, a majority of the student body remained Anglo-American and Catholic. Not that this helped fundraising. For more than 150 years, Catholics in the colonies had been served by self-supporting Jesuits at no charge and hence did not have a tradition or sense of obligation in the matter of giving. Pay tuition and boarding costs for their sons' educations? That was a clear-cut business deal. Answer Bishop Carroll's appeal for funds to support and develop the academy? That was another matter entirely. Nevertheless, to serve the growing Catholic population of the city, the laity of Georgetown did manage to organize, finance, and build Holy Trinity Catholic Church in 1787 and, after 1791, Georgetown Academy.

Despite this absence of financial support, the Select Body of the Clergy, now responsible for Georgetown, begged from Propaganda Fide and borrowed from a Baltimore bank and from former president Plunkett ($2,000 to be paid off in an annual annuity of $180) or otherwise secured between groundbreaking (1794) and completion (1797) sufficient funds to complete an impressive four-story, tripartite, brick building with a 154-foot front. Designed by Baltimore engineer Leonard Harbaugh, Old North—as it was eventually named, because of its position vis-à-vis Old South—reprised Nassau Hall at the College of New Jersey (Princeton) and was at the time the most ambitious building in the city. Encompassing classrooms, a study hall, dormitories, and an infirmary, Old North signaled the residential destiny of the fledgling institution. A raised stone platform porch extended from the center-pedimented section of the building, and from this porch former president George Washington addressed the student body on a hot August day in 1797. While president, Washington had wanted to build a federally sponsored national university in the District of Columbia, but funds were lacking, and so the appearance of the Father of His Country at Georgetown showed his appreciation for the first college established in the district.

Between 1791 and 1805, sixteen Georgetown students opted for the priesthood. Thirteen of them signaled their intention to become Jesuits once the Society of Jesus was restored. Between 1805 and 1817, twenty-four Georgetown students either signaled their intent to enter or entered the Society of Jesus, universally restored by Pope Pius VII in December 1814. Georgetown had become a feeder school for the clergy—not for diocesan clergy, as Carroll had originally planned, but for the Society of Jesus, now in full control of the college. Yet by 1814 a quarter of the Georgetown student body was Protestant. Georgetown College was developing a predominantly lay and ecumenical profile in terms of its students; this reprised the profile of Jesuit colleges in Central and Eastern Europe and Asia before the suppression.

As impressive as the Jesuit vocations to come out of Georgetown during these years were, the school's destiny was not, as Carroll had hoped, to serve as a stage-one preparation for diocesan clergy. Rather, the college educated socioeconomically secure or upwardly mobile laity as well as a nearly equal number of young men entering clerical careers. This Georgetown laity, moreover, while steadily Catholic in composition—and hence predominantly Southern, as was the majority of the Catholic population in the Early Republic—at any one point included a minority of non-Catholics largely from the same class, which is how Carroll originally envisioned the school.

The very first student to register at Georgetown in early November 1791, William Gaston of New Bern, North Carolina, was a devout young man of thirteen who prepared for Georgetown under the tutelage of Francis Fleming, an Irish Dominican working in Philadelphia. The Gastons were upper-middle-class, a narrow sector of society at the time, and also Catholic, an even narrower sector in that state. William's late father, a surgeon retired from the British navy, was killed during the Revolution by North Carolina Loyalists for his support of independence. William Gaston loved the variety of students he met at George-town Academy—from New York, Philadelphia, Virginia, Maryland, and the West Indies, so he wrote to his widowed mother—and he, in turn, impressed President Plunkett "as the best scholar and most exemplary youth in Georgetown". Gaston was fascinated by Sulpician teacher Jean Edouard de Mondésir, whose talk of the Almighty, Gaston wrote to his mother, made his heart "almost burst with crying". Mondésir informed Gaston's mother that her son had the makings of a bishop and arranged for the youngster to spend the summer months with the Sulpicians in Bal-timore. What she interpreted as signs of incipient tuberculosis led Gaston's mother to withdraw her son from Georgetown with a promise to return. William Gaston, however, finished his education at the College of New Jersey (Princeton), to the great distress of his spiritual director, Francis Neale, who perhaps saw in the brilliant lad a future Jesuit. Neale warned Gaston of Princeton's Presbyterianism and sent him a copy of his *Pious Guide to Prayer and Devotion* (1792) to take to Princeton as a usable reminder of his Catholicism. Princeton prepared Gaston for a distinguished career as a politician, judge, and jurist in the resistantly anti-Catholic state of North Carolina. But Gaston sent his son and grandson to Georgetown, not Princeton, and facilitated the passage through Congress of a charter for Georgetown College in 1815.[13]

End of an era

No matter what the temporary situation might be, a Georgetown institution con-trolled by the Select Body of the Clergy, and increasingly oriented toward instruc-tion of laity and the restoration of the Society of Jesus, was not Sulpician territory. Still, Sulpician Louis William DuBourg, the third president, who served from 1796 to 1798, brought the Sulpician era to a brilliant conclusion with the assistance of Sulpician faculty members John Baptist Mary David, Benedict Joseph Flaget, and Ambrose Maréchal. These four Sulpician future bishops saw Georgetown through three crucial years, as under DuBourg's guidance it made the transition from acad-emy to college. Among other things, DuBourg upped the number of lay faculty from three to twelve and paid them a living wage. This increase in faculty allowed for an expansion of curriculum in the school's move to collegiate status. Out-going and congenial, DuBourg formed alliances with the Georgetown lay establish-ment and members of the federal government, including former president George Washington. Impulsive, however, and ever hopeful for the future, DuBourg ran up a debt and hence ran afoul of the Select Body of the Clergy, whose Jesuit principles included a commitment to financial prudence. In October 1797 college directors appointed by the Select Body of the Clergy reappointed DuBourg to a second term but removed Sulpician Flaget as vice president. Replacing him was ex-Jesuit Francis Neale, already a director, to serve as vice president and financial watchdog to the ever-optimistic, ever-spending DuBourg.

Meanwhile, in January 1798 the General Assembly of Maryland passed a law incorporating Georgetown College into the general property owned by an already incorporated Roman Catholic Clergymen. Ex-Jesuits now owned the college out-right. When the directors of this corporation passed an ordinance at their Decem-ber 1798 meeting stipulating that only members of the ex-Jesuit corporation were eligible to spend corporation funds, DuBourg found himself all but fired—a president in name only—and resigned. The Maryland-born ex-Jesuit Leonard Neale became the fourth president of Georgetown, and his brother Francis remained vice president and treasurer. The ex-Jesuits of Maryland had regained Georgetown. In time, they would regain an even more impressive prize, a reestablished Society of Jesus.

8

Baltimore 1808

Rome raises the See of Baltimore to metropolitan status

On 8 April 1808, Pope Pius VII signed the briefs *Ex debito pastoralis officii* and *Pontificii muneris*, raising Baltimore to a metropolitan see; creating the Dioceses of Boston, New York, Philadelphia, and Bardstown, Kentucky; and appointing bishops for these newly established suffragan sees. The pope appointed Jean-Louis Lefebvre de Cheverus, a French émigré who had fled France to avoid taking the oath required of clergy by the revolutionary government, to serve as first bishop of Boston. For New York, the pope—at the request of Dublin archbishop John Troy—nominated the Irish Dominican Richard Luke Concanen, longtime agent in Rome for the Irish hierarchy as well as prior of Saint Clement's Dominican convent there and librarian for the Minerva, the Dominican university. To Philadelphia was assigned Irish Franciscan Michael Egan, then serving as pastor of Saint Mary's Church in that city. For Bardstown, Pius VII chose French Sulpician Benedict Joseph Flaget, a veteran of frontier service as missionary and pastor of Fort Vincennes (in present-day Indiana) and teaching assignments at Georgetown and Baltimore. John Carroll was to remain at Baltimore as archbishop of this new province, with the Maryland ex-Jesuit Leonard Neale, president of Georgetown, staying on as he had been since his consecration in 1800 as Carroll's coadjutor bishop with right of succession.

For nearly two decades, Carroll had been lobbying the cardinals who governed the Sacred Congregation for the Propagation of the Faith (Propaganda Fide) for such a division. It made no sense, Carroll argued, to have a single diocese for the entire United States, the Ohio Territory, and, after 1803, the Louisiana Purchase. On the contrary, Propaganda Fide argued in return, it well served the Church in the United States to have one face, his, and to speak with one voice, his as well, during these formative years. As early as 1792, however, Carroll had successfully made his case for a coadjutor bishop with a right of succession, lest there be too long an interval between Carroll's death (when that happened) and a new bishop's taking office. Carroll even gained permission to consult his clergy as to who should be nominated.

Something like a de facto election must have been held by the ex-Jesuits of the Select Body of the Clergy—in civil law, the Clerical Corporation of Maryland—who selected former Jesuit novice Laurence Graessl, now a secular priest. Graessl, a Bavarian of commitment and piety, was capable of hearing confessions in six languages. Alas, he succumbed to yellow fever in the Philadelphia epidemic of 1793. In 1795—after once again consulting the Select Body of the Clergy—Carroll obtained from the ex-Jesuit community a recommendation for the appointment of Leonard Neale, then serving as pastor of Saint Mary's in Philadelphia. It took another five years for Propaganda Fide to respond favorably and to obtain the necessary papal brief before Neale could be consecrated bishop by Carroll at Saint Peter's pro-cathedral in Baltimore.

Had he lived, Laurence Graessl most likely would have proven an active coad-jutor bishop for Carroll, who was increasingly kept in Baltimore due to his age and reluctance to travel. Leonard Neale, by contrast—a laconic, introspective fig-ure, more contemplative than dynamic by nature—remained equally centered on Georgetown, where he served as president from 1799 to 1806, when a partially restored Society of Jesus took over the institution. Aside from his duties as presi-dent, Neale devoted any spare energy to the spiritual direction and development of a community of younger Catholic laywomen en route to organizing themselves as a Visitation sisterhood. Still, if Carroll unexpectedly died or was incapacitated, North America would continue to have a bishop—that is, if Neale, younger by a decade, survived Carroll. As far as lightening Carroll's administrative burden, however, Leonard Neale added little, beyond his presidency at Georgetown and the long-delayed role he played in founding a Visitation sisterhood. A full-time secretary to help Carroll handle his voluminous correspondence would have proven more useful.

The sad case of Bishop Concanen

Because of distance, war, Bishop-elect Graessl's death, and Leonard Neale's disen-gagement, Carroll received no relief in his workload as bishop of the United States and its affiliated territories for two years. Since Richard Luke Concanen was already in Rome, Pope Pius VII directed that the Irish Dominican bishop-elect of New York be consecrated there immediately and, following his consecration, sail for the United States. Concanen would carry the official copies of the two papal briefs that divided the United States into five dioceses, appointed four new diocesan bishops, and conferred on Carroll the pallium, a narrow band of white wool worn around the neck and shoulders to signify the authority of an archbishop. Despite the fact that he was sixty-one years old and barely recovered from a long, serious illness, Concanen agreed to a Roman consecration and, on 24 April 1808, was consecrated bishop with great pomp in the Dominican Church of Saint Catherine by Cardinal Michele di Pietro, the new prefect of Propaganda Fide, and two archbishops. Pro-ceeding to Leghorn on 3 June with his extensive luggage (clothes, vestments, sacred vessels, books, papal briefs and pallium, and even filing cases), Concanen hoped to secure passage to the United States as soon as possible.

The resurgent Napoleonic War, however, was blocking maritime traffic to the United States, and Concanen remained in Leghorn and Locanda for months, des-perately trying to secure passage. Running out of funds, he returned to Rome, leaving his official documents and pallium with the import-export firm of Filicchi Brothers, Leghorn, to forward to Archbishop Carroll when an opportunity pre-sented itself. Back in Rome, Concanen survived for two years on a small papal pension and added to his resumed role as agent of the Irish bishops the routine diocesan duties of an assistant bishop for the Diocese of Rome. Unable to arrange passage to the United States, and fearing advancing age, Concanen grew depressed and seriously considered resigning his appointment as bishop of New York.

In the summer of 1809—at the request of Bishop-elect Flaget, who was in France to recruit priests for his future diocese of Bardstown—Cardinal Joseph Fesch, the uncle of Emperor Napoleon, facilitated the issuance of a French passport to Concanen for a voyage to the United States, but Concanen turned down the offer because of diplomatic complications and declining health. Then, at long last— thanks to the intervention of Antonio Filicchi and Alexander Hammett, an American consul general in Naples—Concanen received a passport from the military governor of Rome as well as tacit permission from the Naples police granting him permission to embark from Naples to the United States on Sunday, 7 June 1810, on the ship *Francis*, whose home port was Salem, Massachusetts. Concanen's passport, however, required that he sail alone, which meant that he could not be accompanied by the small number of priests he had recruited for New York. Nevertheless, after a delay of two years, Concanen accepted the offer and left Rome for Naples.

The night before the *Francis* set sail, however, a Naples police officer showed up at Concanen's lodgings and informed him that his papers were not in order. This might have been the case, or it might have been the beginning of a Neapolitan-style shakedown, to be followed by a seizure of the *Francis*. In any event, the failure of this second effort threw Concanen into a death spiral. "Well now I may bid a farewell to America forever", Concanen remarked to a local priest. "I pray you, my dear Abbé Lombardi, to see that whatever regards my funeral and burial be done in a decent manner, so as not to disgrace my rank and character." Taking to his bed, Concanen died of fever and disappointment on Tuesday morning after receiving the last sacraments and leaving his property to the Dominicans of Kentucky.[1]

Bishop-elect Flaget delivers papal briefs

Fortunately, in the autumn of 1809 Concanen had been prevailed upon to create notarized copies of the official documents he was trying to deliver to Carroll, and a file of these copies was sent to Sulpician superior general Jacques-André Emery in Paris, where Sulpician Bishop-elect Flaget was soon to call upon Emery in hopes of having his Sulpician superior general use his influence to have Flaget's nomination voided in favor of another candidate. "My Lord Bishop", Emery greeted Flaget upon his arrival, "you should be in your diocese!" He wished to remain a Sulpician, Flaget replied. To this Emery answered, "You will not cease to be a member of the Society, for you accept the bishop's mitre in obedience to my mandate." When Flaget passed, Emery continued, every Sulpician shall, according to custom, say three Masses for him as a departed member of Saint Sulpice.

At this, Flaget acquiesced and devoted his remaining time in Europe to raising funds and interviewing prospective clergy. When Flaget was about to return to the United States in August 1810, Emery informed Flaget that he was reassigning Sulpician John Baptist Mary David from seminary teaching in Baltimore to assist Flaget for three years in Bardstown. (Before Flaget's departure, David had already volunteered to do so. The sturdy and affectionate Breton stayed in Kentucky to become Flaget's coadjutor and successor.) Upon Flaget's departure for the United States, Emery presented him with (in ascending levels of importance) a box of needles, a

French cookbook, a chalice and vestments used by Jean-Jacques Olier—founder of the Society—and the official documents sent to Emery by Bishop Concanen.[2]

Episcopal consecration and an American code

Receiving these papal briefs, Carroll proceeded in good order to fulfill their intent. Episcopal consecrations were organized and carried out for Bishop-elect Egan at Saint Peter's procathedral on 28 October 1810; for Bishop-elect Cheverus at Saint Peter's on All Saints' Day (1 November), with Bishop Cheverus assisting Carroll; and for Bishop-elect Flaget at Saint Patrick's Church, Fells Point, Baltimore, on Saint Charles Day (4 November), with Bishops Cheverus and Egan assisting the archbishop. To commemorate the consecrations, at the request of the newly consecrated bishops, Bernard Dornin, Baltimore's Catholic publisher, printed Irish Dominican William Vincent Harold's eloquent sermon for the consecration of Bishop Cheverus, followed by a second pamphlet explaining the rites and ceremonies associated with episcopal consecration.[3]

The three newly consecrated bishops remained in Baltimore for several weeks and got to work drawing up an agreement regarding church governance, building upon the decrees of the Synod of 1791. As such, the agreement constituted a second installment of a code of canon law for the United States. The majority of the decrees of the agreement, issued on 15 November 1810, seem reasonable codifications of traditional Catholic practice. The encouragement of the use of vernacular prayers and hymns at prayer intervals along with the required Latin might seem innovative. (Carroll himself briefly favored a vernacular liturgy but in time grew silent on the subject.) The prohibition of Freemasonry (no Communion for those attending Masonic lodges) and the active discouragement of dancing, theatergoing, novel reading, and similar distractions, however, bespeak a reaction to the devastations of the French Revolution in the matter of Freemasonry and the assimilation of an evangelical Protestant ethos regarding the dangers of various entertainments. After all, Shakespeare—and the Jesuits—had excelled in theater, and Cervantes had written a formidable Catholic novel. Certainly, slaveholding posed more danger to morals than a reading of *Tom Jones* or *Clarissa* or an evening of dancing or theater. Horse racing and card playing, though, two pursuits beloved by the Maryland elite, escaped condemnation. In any event, it would be some time before American Catholic artists would be writing novels or plays for a nationwide audience.

Nonpuritanical Maryland

Whatever reservations John Carroll and his fellow bishops held regarding dancing, theatergoing, and novel reading, Baltimore—the most populously Catholic city in the Early Republic as well as an ascendantly Episcopalian town—could not be described as remotely Puritan, with the possible exception of its municipal ambition and work ethic. Initially, as long as the tobacco trade lasted, Baltimore had been an active but relatively restricted product-driven pass-through port. Even at that, it was not overly favored, given the competition by the locally maintained ports of coastal Virginia and Maryland as well as the shallowness of the Baltimore harbor and its location on the upper Chesapeake, some 150 miles from the open Atlantic. During the Revolutionary War, with Charleston and Savannah under siege or occupation, or both, Baltimore became the major entrepôt for supply shipments for the Southern campaign, culminating in the siege and surrender at Yorktown. From this involvement emerged a wheat trade, which forced development of the harbor and ship-loading techniques. Wheat processing led to flour milling, the start of another important local industry. Baltimore already supported foundries that melted iron ore into pig iron. The shipbuilding industry on Fells Point at the entrance to the harbor grew and diversified, resulting in the city's shared hegemony with Boston in the design and construction of clipper ships.

Prior to the achievement of that sailing miracle, the Baltimore clipper found itself challenged by the opening of the Erie Canal (1825), which connected New York City to the Great Lakes, and by Pennsylvania's plans to construct a canal from Philadelphia to Pittsburgh. For Baltimore to continue to flourish, its leading citizens determined, it must connect itself to its northern, southern, and (most importantly) western hinterlands via road construction and the recently invented steam-driven railroad train. Baltimoreans Philip E. Thomas, a transportation entrepreneur, and George Brown, an investment banker, spent the year 1826 in England studying that nation's experience with and costs of this new technology. Arriving in Baltimore from Ireland in 1800, Brown's father, Alexander, a linen merchant, had created in partnership with his four sons the first investment bank in the United States, with branches in Liverpool, Philadelphia, and New York. Thus, some twenty-five Baltimore investors heard with confidence Thomas and Brown's report following their return from England and subscribed $3 million out of $5 million authorized toward the construction of the Baltimore and Ohio Rail Road Company, formally incorporated on 24 April 1827.

Ninety-one-year-old Charles Carroll of Carrollton, the last surviving Signer of the Declaration of Independence and an investor in the railroad, was on hand on 4 July 1828 on the site of the future Mount Clare Station to turn the first shovelful of earth for construction. A great stone block put in place by Freemasons in official regalia before a cheering crowd of five thousand (so much for the war of the Catholic Church on Freemasonry!) constituted the starting point for some 380 miles of track and superb arched viaducts of stone—in position by 1854—that linked Baltimore with Ohio to the west and with the District of Columbia via a thiry-eight-mile spur line. In 1843 this Baltimore and Ohio spur line provided the cleared pathway for a congressionally financed experimental telegraph line connecting the District of Columbia and Baltimore. "What hath God wrought?" telegraph inventor Samuel F. B. Morse tapped in this first communication for yet another Baltimore-sponsored technological breakthrough. Baltimore, in short, was a self-actualizing city that reflected a strong Protestant work ethic as well as cooperation between Protestants and Catholics in its development.

Whatever the bishops' case against novel reading might have been, moreover, their condemnation of this diversion had little impact as time went on, if one is to judge by the experience of the young lawyer Henry D. Gilpin of Philadelphia, Charles Carroll's guest at Doughoregan Manor, where the elderly Signer spent half the year. At Doughoregan, Carroll entertained in an English style of guest autonomy, as Gilpin described in a letter to his father dated 22 September 1827. Carroll would greet his guests warmly but leave them largely to their own devices during the day. Evenings were festive. Guests gathered in one of two brightly decorated parlors, where one encountered "a singular medley of old and modern fashions—there are here fine new curtains of the gayest colours; there sofas & chairs, covered with glorious old cushions, and so deep that you cannot sit, but must really lie back in them—there is perhaps a large fire in one room, & none in another—a card table in full operation in one—a harp, guitar, and songs sounding in another—in one people eating away, in another chattering or whispering in corners. Everybody seems to catch in ten minutes all the freedom & ease of the place."

Each morning, the chapel bell rang at seven for prayers and, on Sundays, Mass. Following services, Carroll would greet his guests at the breakfast table. No one sat down until the old gentleman was seated. An amply stocked breakfast table remained available in the hall until midday for those who missed the first seating. "You can eat when you choose", Gilpin informs his father. There were punch toddies on the table, "lemonade, wine cakes, & all that sort of thing, with heaps of newspapers, new novels & You may loll on the sofa & read them, & nobody expects you to rise, even ladies, unless inclined—you meet little parties in the garden, but you need not join them unless you like—there are guns, & you may go to shoot, there are horses and you may ride—a bath & you can bathe. You stay a day or a week, welcomed when you come, & going away at any hour you choose. You meet the pleasantest people of Baltimore and the neighbourhood & many strangers—the family itself, which embraces, children, grandchildren, & great grandchildren is large & contains several characters."[4]

A sure sign of Baltimore's resistance to the puritanical was its undisputed status as cuisine capital of the Early Republic. The cuisine was assembled from common usage: corn and rice-based colonial pudding; ham and available game, which included pigeon, duck, and turkey; an abundance of seafood from the Chesapeake; vegetables and fruit prospering in good soil, a moderate climate, and convenient sources of water; Franco-African spices and flavoring preferences from the West Indies as well as classic and regional French cuisine; molasses; a plenitude of wheat for bread and for cake and confectionery, German specialties. Baltimoreans also enjoyed a locally produced rye whiskey, plus the sherries, ports, Madeiras, and wines derived from commercial trade with Spain and Portugal.

African American Baltimore

No, indeed, Baltimore was not a puritanical city, or even a Jansenist city, despite its Irish population. It had become, in fact, something of a French city, and the arrival of so many French refugees and émigrés, lay and clerical, had given it a balanced Catholic-Protestant flavor. Like all Maryland, however, it was slave-supported, including in its clerical culture. John Carroll had two African servants, for example, one free and the other enslaved. A twenty-first-century observer cannot help but feel the shadow of slavery cast its ominous noir over one's desire to praise the architecture, gardens, cuisine, gracious lifestyle, civic entrepreneurism, and Catholic culture of Baltimore. Yet the Baltimore of the Early Republic, historian Christopher Phillips notes, showed signs of an impending inefficiency in the matter of lifetime slavery. As of 1810, Baltimore had a slave population of 4,672 and a free black population of 5,671. By 1830, these numbers had shifted to 4,120 slave and

14,790 free. By 1860, Baltimore had become a city of free blacks, 25,680 of them, in comparison with 2,218 enslaved. The driving dynamic behind this imbalance, Phillips argues, was the fact that slavery was growing out of date in Baltimore. Not oriented to an urban economy, slavery was getting to be an expensive luxury. Slave labor, moreover, could not compete with the labor market created by free people of color. In 1790 Baltimore had 1,255 slaves to 323 free blacks. That figure evened out in 1800—2,843 slave to 2,771 free. In 1810, free blacks outnumbered slaves by nearly a thousand, as white Baltimoreans increasingly were maintaining slaves as household servants as opposed to utilizing them for more arduous work. These enslaved household servants constituted an indication of status and maintenance of tradition for whites. Such household slaves, moreover—many of them descendants of racially mixed unions—tended to be of lighter coloration, as were the hundreds of free people of color who had immigrated to Baltimore in 1798 following the sacking of Cap-François in Saint-Domingue. This mixed-race population was at once free and competitive in terms of the skills required by an urban economy. The more complex the Baltimore economy became, the more the labor of skilled free people of color became integrated into daily life.

As the nineteenth century wore on, Phillips maintains, more and more Maryland field slaves were being advertised for sale "for want of employment". Such slaves cost more than they could earn. Slaves not needed on plantations—carpenters and bricklayers, for example—were furloughed to Baltimore as quasi-manumitted workers, who returned a percentage of their wages to their legal owners. Like household servants, skilled craftsmen were frequently of mixed ancestry and hence fit into the communities created by mixed-race artisans, many of them from Saint-Domingue and their descendants. Phillips cites one instance of a white Catholic male West Indian living in Baltimore who demanded and received a Catholic wedding for his marriage to a free woman of color, something technically against the civil law.

Originally, the majority of slaves manumitted "for want of employment" were on time-dated assignment: so many years of work in Baltimore and payments back to owners, followed by legal manumission. As field or plantation slavery became less and less economically sustainable, moreover, a growing number of plantation-based slaves were verbally manumitted by their owners, with no paperwork required. Thus, Baltimore increasingly featured an expanding free black population that was not of the mulatto class. Almost a half century before Washington, D.C., similarly developed, this free population was showing signs of heightened urbanization in terms of its employment patterns and internal social organization, including status stratification and social structure that mirrored white society. An all-black sisterhood, for example, the Oblate Sisters of Providence, was founded in 1829 to minister to the free black Catholic community.[5]

Priority one: priests

All things considered, then—people, economy, identity, ethos, and lifestyle— Baltimore offered John Carroll the best possible American city in which to develop a primatial metropolitan see. From the very beginning of his appointment as diocesan bishop in 1790, a stated assumption existed in documents and discussions of what was established by Rome in 1808: an archdiocese and suffragan sees. From 1790 to 1808, Carroll developed the essential components of a national Church. Since a laity—Anglo, Irish, German, Spanish, French, African, and Native American—was already in place and would continue to grow steadily through immigration and natural increase, one of Carroll's first priorities had always been (and would go on being) the training and recruitment of diocesan priests. Hence Carroll's negotiations with the French Sulpicians in London in the first weeks of his episcopacy and the subsequent foundation of Georgetown Academy as a feeder school to the seminary they established.

Hence also Carroll's near despair in September 1801 when Sulpician superior Jacques-André Emery—having patiently waited for ten years for the Baltimore seminary to gain momentum—informed Carroll by letter that he was seriously thinking of recalling the Baltimore Sulpicians back to France by 1804. Carroll was upset to the point of shedding tears when he received Emery's letter, and he instantly replied to Emery to beg him to reconsider his program of Sulpician repatriation, beginning with the immediate recall of seminary professors Anthony Garnier and Ambrose Maréchal. Carroll's letter teems with anguish as he implores Emery with a near oath to reconsider. France, Carroll argues, has talented priests aplenty to do its work. Each Sulpician at work in America, by contrast, represents a guide into the future of the American church. "Sir", Carroll entreats, drawing upon a medieval English oath, "by the bowels of Our Lord not to take them all away; and if it is necessary that I submit to the terrible trial of seeing the greatest number depart, I beseech you to leave at least a germ which can fructify in the season decreed by the Lord.... These gentlemen know our language and our customs and desire ardently to remain here provided that they can work according to their vocation and always remain members of your Society. I should esteem the success of my petition far beyond my powers of thanksgiving for it. This is the greatest good that you could ever do for us after that of preserving all the members here, where sooner or later they will produce all the good which you expected from their zeal."[6]

Garnier and Maréchal departed for France, but Carroll found an unexpected ally. Meeting Pope Pius VII in Paris for the coronation of Napoleon on 2 December 1804, Emery related to the pontiff his plans to abandon the American mission. "My son", the pope replied, "let it stand—yes, let that Seminary stand; for it will bear fruit in its own time. To recall its directors in order to employ them here in other seminaries would be to rob Peter to pay Paul." Receiving the pope's advice as an oracle, Father Emery canceled his plans to withdraw the Gentlemen of Saint Sulpice from America.[7]

John Thayer, convert and priest

Even before the Baltimore seminary thus saved began to produce its first few diocesan priests, Carroll as prefect apostolic acquired the services of his first secular priest, John Thayer, then finishing his studies with the Sulpicians in Paris prior to his ordination on 2 June 1787 by the archbishop of Paris. A convert clergyman from Boston, Thayer was already a minor celebrity in ecclesiastical circles; he represented the first of a genre that, as the nineteenth century progressed, would play an increasing role in English and American Catholicism and, indeed, would in time produce two archbishops of Baltimore. If a New England minister from the most assertively anti-Catholic region in the United States could convert to Catholicism and qualify for holy orders, did this not suggest that Roman Catholicism might win acceptance—and, even more than acceptance, converts—in this overwhelmingly Protestant nation?

In the very year of his ordination, Thayer—a Yale-educated former Congregationalist minister and Protestant chaplain during the Revolutionary War—wrote and published *An Account of the Conversion of the Reverend Mr. John Thayer: Lately a Protestant Minister at Boston, in North-America, Who Embraced the Roman Catholic Religion at Rome, on the 25th of May, 1783.* Thayer's autobiographical statement abounded in an intensified *romanità* that was itself prophetic of a direction the American church would take in later years as the semi-Gallicism of the Early Republic yielded to the *romanità* of an immigrant generation. Traveling to Europe in 1781 in an effort to expand his horizons, Thayer spent ten months in France, where he mastered the language and came grudgingly to respect Catholicism. His interest piqued, Thayer went on to Rome, where he acquired Italian and marveled at Romans' friendliness, including their warm and lively acceptance of him, a Protestant.

Rome, in short, converted Thayer to Catholicism. Visiting surviving monuments from the classical world, now Christianized—the Pantheon, for example, a Roman shrine to all the gods, first built in 27 B.C., rebuilt in the second century A.D., and converted to a Christian church consecrated to Mary and the Christian martyrs in 609—proved especially effective in prompting Thayer to meditate on the history of Christianity from the perspective of the unity lost when Eastern Orthodoxy and the Protestant North departed the fold. A born preacher, Thayer began to compose in his head a sermon extolling the continuities so evident in the Roman churches and monuments he was studying.

The art of these Roman churches, moreover, spoke to Thayer's Protestant sense of Scripture while introducing him both to an appreciation of Mary, Mother of Christ, in the scheme of salvation and to the reverence paid to saints and martyrs. Thayer began to discuss these matters with local priests, who may or may not have been former Jesuits. The life of the recently deceased Benedict Labre—a lay contemplative who spent his life as a wandering pilgrim and with whom reports of miracles were associated—represented a final Rubicon for Thayer to cross; the paradox of Labre's life (refused admission by the Trappists because of his youth, he became a homeless holy man) and the reports of miracles connected to Labre's intervention (miracles that Thayer came to accept as true) presented to this Yankee preacher a decidedly non-Protestant case study in holiness and a worthwhile life.

In any event, after more reading in theology and history, further struggling to understand and accept the reverence paid Mary in the Catholic tradition and the role played by guardian angels and canonized saints in the grand and daily drama of Catholicism, Thayer was ready to make an emotional assent to the religion he had been exploring in Rome. "Yes," Thayer exulted, "this religion is adapted to the heart: however powerful and solid the proofs are which convince me that it is the True Religion of Jesus Christ, the satisfaction, the pure joy which accompanies it, is for me another kind of proof, not less persuasive. The truths, which I had most difficulty in believing, are those in which I now find the greatest consolation. The mystery of the Eucharist, which appeared to me so incredible, is become an ever flowing source of spiritual delight: Confession, which I had considered as an insupportable yoke, seems infinitely sweet, by the tranquility which it produces in the soul."[8] Following his conversion (officially dated 25 May 1783), Thayer proceeded on to the College of Navarre and Saint-Sulpice in preparation for ordination. After his ordination on 2 June 1787, he spent two years on mission in England before returning to the United States, where Carroll assigned him to Boston to relieve Abbé Louis de Rousselet, temporarily in charge of the largely French congregation of some 120 Catholics. Having learned of Rousselet's prior suspension in his home diocese of Constance, Carroll had decided to appoint Thayer as sole pastor.

While Carroll might have approved of Thayer's piety and was grateful for Thayer's subsidized education at the College of Navarre and Saint-Sulpice, neither conversion, Romanization, ordination, nor two years in England could take the rough edges off Thayer's personality and pastoral practices. Visiting Boston for three weeks from late May to mid-June 1791—the first Catholic bishop to visit that city—Carroll was well received by the Protestant establishment but was deeply disappointed to learn that Thayer had failed to reconcile the French community to his leadership. Indeed, Thayer was so openly quarreling with the French community that members were boycotting Roman Catholic services. Carroll skillfully reconciled the French and Irish communities to Thayer's leadership.

Rather than take Carroll's irenic approach to the Protestant community, moreover, Thayer was engaging in printed disputes with the leading Protestant divines of New England, which prompted local newspapers to call him "John Turncoat". Carroll, to whom Governor John Hancock and Vice President John Adams had been so gracious during his visit, was deeply embarrassed. When Thayer announced an open debate with one opponent, to be held at Holy Cross Church, his challenger— the Harvard-educated Reverend George Leslie of Washington, New Hampshire— refused to show up at the sparsely attended event. Thus began what turned into a refined New England boycott of silence leveled against the troublesome Catholic priest. The situation further embarrassed and offended Carroll, who prized good relations with the Protestant establishment.

Carroll also disapproved of Thayer's freelance preaching in Hartford, Connecticut, where he stayed at the same lodging house as his Yale classmate Noah Webster, whom he invited to Mass, celebrated by Thayer in his room the next morning. In New Haven, calling on Ezra Stiles, the president of Yale, Thayer showed the arch-Congregationalist a medal he had received from Pius VI and earned a startling invective in Stiles' *Literary Diary*: "The Romish Priest, born at Boston, commenced his Life in Impudence, Ingratitude, Lying and Hypocrisy, irregularly took up preach'g among the Congregationalists, went to France and Italy, became a Proselyte to the Romish church & is returned to convert America to that club. He showed me a medal of Pius VI ... of haughty insolent & insidious Talents."[9] Thankfully, Bishop Carroll did not have an opportunity to read this private expression of the further breakdown of his program of friendly outreach to Protestant America, but he had already decided to reassign Thayer to Kentucky to work under the supervision of French-born Stephen Badin, Carroll's vicar-general for the West.

Fortunately for Carroll, few, if any, of the convert priests Carroll accepted for assignment shared Thayer's farouche belligerence. Ordained by Carroll on 18 March 1795, for example, Demetrius Augustine Gallitzin, the first priest to receive his entire training at Saint Mary's, was the son of a Russian prince and his Roman Catholic wife, Princess (and Countess in her own right) Amalia Gallitzin, daughter of a Russian field marshal. Raised in the Orthodox faith, Demetrius Gallitzin converted to his mother's religion in 1781 following her return to her ancestral Catholic faith. Entering the Austrian army in his late teens, he served as a general's aide-de-camp before taking temporary leave of the service to make a grand tour not of Europe but—at his mother's insistence—of the United States. If Rome brought John Thayer to Catholicism, Demetrius Gallitzin arrived there via Orthodoxy and his mother's influence, which likewise sent him to the United States, where he discovered his vocation as a diocesan priest, assigned initially to the German Catholic communities of Baltimore and Conewago, Pennsylvania. As the son of a Russian prince, moreover, who himself became a prince after his father's death, Gallitzin found an even larger dream: the creation of an ideal Roman Catholic community fusing land and faith as only a Russian with an Orthodox sense of the holiness of people and place might imagine.

The French Revolution

Following the passage in July 1792 of a Civil Constitution of the Clergy, which demanded that clerics take an oath of allegiance to the Republic, mobs of French revolutionaries had massacred 223 priests in Paris in the first week of September alone and by the end of the year had driven thousands of others into exile across Western Europe, Spain, and England. Nearly 5,500 French émigré priests sought refuge in England alone, the majority of them (perhaps as many as 5,000) surviving on small parliamentary pensions, the rest supporting themselves as teachers, if they could find such positions, or—as Abbé Augustin Sicard itemizes in his *L'ancien clergé de France* (1903)—as tailors, embroiderers, watchmakers, shoemakers, hatters, jewelry makers, or, in one case, a highly successful real estate agent.[10] Those few who could—meaning the well-born and educated—might find a place in the active ministry. In England, that was so, where Catholics were few but there was a high degree of upper-class lay control. In the Catholic kingdom of Spain, by contrast, émigré priests posed a threat to the employment of a large and already established diocesan clergy.

With the Sulpicians' arrival in Baltimore in 1791 and 1792, John Carroll—who had previously been getting by with a mere thirty-five priests, ex-Jesuits in the main—soon had the services of nearly a dozen diocesan secular priests who belonged to an elite teaching community (and a number of whom were future American bishops). These men he assigned to his seminary, to parish work, or—rather dramatically—to the trans-Allegheny frontier. The Sulpicians formed the advance guard for the nearly one hundred French émigré diocesan priests who would soon be arriving. Like the Sulpicians, moreover (indeed, many were Sulpician-trained), these secular priests were, by and large, educated clerics. Several came from privileged backgrounds, some even with their own funds, and hence—and Carroll cared deeply about this—were socially acceptable to upper-strata Protestant America.

To replace John Thayer in Boston, Carroll assigned Francis A. Matignon, the scion of a wealthy and cultivated Parisian family. Educated at Saint-Sulpice and having earned a doctorate in theology at the Sorbonne, Matignon was teaching at the College of Navarre when the French Revolution broke out. Fleeing to New England, the erudite and polished priest came to the attention of ex-Jesuits, one of whom, Thomas Talbot, enthusiastically recommended him to Bishop Carroll, who received Matignon into his diocese and assigned him to Boston. Shortly after his arrival in Boston, Matignon wrote his priest friend Jean-Louis Lefebvre de Cheverus, then employed in England as a private tutor in a noble household, a teacher of mathematics and French in a nearby boarding school, and chaplain to Catholics living in the neighborhood. A native of Mayenne in the Diocese of Mans, Cheverus came from the same background as Matignon and was a graduate of the Collège Louis-le-Grand and the Seminary of Saint-Magloire in Paris and the last priest to be ordained publicly in Paris prior to the Revolution. Having returned to his home diocese, Cheverus was serving as a youthful vicar-general before being forced to flee to England, where he organized a community of émigré French priests living in common.

In his letter to Cheverus, Matignon evoked the size, scale, and scope of the United States and the opportunities there for priestly ministry. Rather than remain marginally employed as a priest in England, Cheverus volunteered for the United States. Adept in French, English, Latin, Greek, and Hebrew, Cheverus could have been assigned to teaching, but Carroll assigned him to join Matignon in Boston and establish a visiting ministry to the Catholic Indians of Maine. Extending his ministry into greater New England, Cheverus recruited John Romagné, a fellow diocesan priest of Mayenne then living in England, to volunteer as a full-time chaplain to the Catholic Indians now receiving only part-time attention. Romagné served twenty years in this capacity, delighting the Indians with his mastery of their languages.

Thus, in a few short years Carroll was able to replace two French priests in bad standing in their home diocese and a sincere but unmanageable convert Congregationalist with three learned recent French émigrés capable of befriending and winning the respect of one and all, including the Yankee mandarins of Boston. At a civic banquet, Cheverus found himself sitting next to President John Adams, who had been so patronizing to things Catholic just a short time earlier. When the Commonwealth of Massachusetts drew up a revised oath of allegiance to be required of voters, legislators asked Cheverus to review a first draft so it would be acceptable to Catholics. Cheverus rewrote the draft, and his version became state law.

A generation of émigré priests

The fall of Cap-François, Saint-Domingue, brought even more French émigré priests into service. By the early 1800s, French priests constituted the majority of clerics active in the United States. Abbé Ambrose Songé, for example, a canon of the Diocese of Dol, arrived in the United States after mastering English in the course of five years of pastoral service in England. Following a stint in Hartford, Connecticut, as private chaplain to the émigré vicomte de Sibert-Cornillon and his family, Songé requested and received faculties from Carroll to expand his ministry into lower New England and was joined in this effort by J. S. Tisserant, a refugee priest from Saint-Domingue, who later ministered to Saint-Domingue refugees in Elizabeth, New Jersey. Another refugee priest, Louis Sibourd, originally ordained for the Diocese of Embrun, France, took care of the Saint-Domingue refugee community in New York City. The register of Saint Peter's Church on Barclay Street, the first parish in New York, bears the signatures of many French émigré or Saint-Domingue refugee priests who served there for differing periods of time, as do the registers of Saint Joseph's, Saint Mary's, and Saint Augustine's churches in Philadelphia.

The majority of these priests were seculars, yet a French Carmelite, a Holy Ghost Father, a Father of the Faith (a French congregation of ex-Jesuits), and émigré Trappists were at various times active in the ministry. Only three men's religious orders, however—the Augustinians of Philadelphia, the Dominicans of Kentucky, and the partially restored (1806) Jesuits of Maryland—were capable in these years of organizing canonically established communities. Three separate groups of French Cistercians from La Trappe (Trappists) made valiant efforts but eventually returned to France. Before the Trappists were recalled to France, however, monks in their peregrinations ministered in Boston, New York, Philadelphia, Maryland, Kentucky, and Missouri, while maintaining their monastic identities as much as possible. Even when they later returned to Kentucky, moreover, French Trappists—from necessity—partially remained in the active ministry for the rest of the nineteenth century.

Many of the French seculars in service during these years had impressive backgrounds. They were educated at leading seminaries. A number of them were serving as cathedral canons when the Revolution broke out and were experienced administrators. Carroll appointed one of them—Matthew Héard, a Holy Ghost Father—vice prefect apostolic of the Danish West Indies when the islands of Saint Croix, Saint Thomas, and Saint John came under Carroll's jurisdiction. Before entering the Sulpicians in France, Ambrose Maréchal qualified as a lawyer and Simon Gabriel Bruté de Rémur earned a medical degree. Sulpician James Hector Nicholas Joubert de la Muraille attended military school at Rebois-en-Brie and entered the civil service before being posted to Saint-Domingue. Upon the fall of that colony, Joubert entered the seminary at Baltimore and, following his ordination in 1810, joined Saint Sulpice.

In some cases, ancillary talents were useful in priestly service. In other cases, they served as a means for temporary financial survival; in a few cases, they morphed into new identities. In 1794 some thirty French families of rank established an émigré colony in Luzerne (present-day Bradford) County, Pennsylvania. Significantly named Asylum, the colony included a spacious log chalet prepared for Marie Antoinette, should that unfortunate queen ever escape to the United States. Four priests moved to Asylum as self-supporting participants, but only one, Anthony Carles, remained active in the ministry. A former cathedral canon in the Diocese of Quercy and a missionary to Saint-Domingue, Carles pursued a dual career as a priest-farmer. Abbé Colin de Sévigny, formerly the archdeacon of Toul, concentrated on his role as a partner in a successful men's clothing store. Another Asylum priest, Abbé John de Bec-de-Lièvre, formerly a canon in Brittany, entered into a business partnership with two émigré army officers. Despite these entrepreneurial interludes, the Abbés Carles, Sévigny, and Bec-de-Lièvre remained priests in good standing and later, receiving faculties from Carroll, rejoined the active ministry in Savannah, Charleston, and Asylum, respectively.

The fourth priest, Abbé Eligius Fromentin, studied law upon leaving Asylum. At some point in the early 1800s, following the Louisiana Purchase (1803), he moved to New Orleans, established a legal practice there, and entered politics. Serving from 1807 to 1811 in the territorial House of Representatives, Fromentin played a major role in the state constitutional convention of 1812 and the next year rose to secretary of the newly established Louisiana State Senate. In 1813 the Louisiana State Senate elected Fromentin to the United States Senate, where he served one term, 1813–1819. Did United States Senator Fromentin request and receive laicization before this extraordinary rise? The matter might have been as simple as a letter of resignation to his home diocese in France. Or did he merely put his priestly identity aside while remaining a Catholic—this, after all, was New Orleans, a Catholic city—whether nominal or sincerely so? In any event, there he was: a onetime émigré priest from France turned Democratic United States senator and, after 1819, a criminal court judge in New Orleans and after that a federal judge in Florida, where he crossed swords over jurisdiction with military governor Andrew Jackson.

Because so many French émigré and Saint-Domingue refugee priests arrived in the United States, Carroll was able to staff all existing parishes as well as serve Saint-Domingue refugee settlements in New York, Philadelphia, Baltimore, Savannah, and Wilmington. He was also able to authorize the creation of new parishes from Maine to Georgia and staff the trans-Allegheny frontier with talented and experienced priests. Thus, places such as Salem, Plymouth, Newburyport, and New Bedford in Massachusetts as well as Maine, New Hampshire, and Vermont; Hartford, Connecticut; Norfolk and Richmond, Virginia; Raleigh, North Carolina; Charleston, South Carolina; and Savannah and Locust Grove, Georgia, enjoyed either a resident or a regularly visiting priest. As for Maryland, thanks to the seventeen French priests who arrived between 1791 and 1798, Carroll extended coverage to St. Mary's County and the Eastern Shore (ex-Jesuit Joseph Mosley had died in 1787, leaving only one priest on active duty there), and staffed new parishes and stations in Baltimore (including Saint Patrick's at Fells Point), Emmitsburg, and Frederick. French priests also enabled Carroll to begin staffing the trans-Allegheny frontier. The majority of these French priests were émigrés, not immigrants, which is to say, they had no intention of remaining permanently in the United States and returned to France as soon as the political situation allowed. Yet when Carroll laid the cornerstone of his new cathedral in an elaborate ceremony held on 7 July 1806, twenty vested priests in cassocks and surplices as well as seminarians in cassocks accompanied him in procession. Their numbers underscored the development of diocesan clergy in Baltimore and its hinterlands, thanks to a politically volatile France.

Trustees

As was the case in all parishes in the United States, the cathedral whose cornerstone Carroll was laying was being financed by donations from the lay community and was legally owned by a corporation of lay trustees responsible for the maintenance of the building once it was developed. In the twentieth and twenty-first centuries, historians have chronicled the trustee system long after the Roman Catholic Church in the United States in the mid-nineteenth century had transferred over to a system of corporation sole ownership, which is to say, either the diocesan bishop or a religious order owned a specific parish church. The trustee system of the Early

Republic has been thus recorded historically in terms of its abuses and failures and hence, to put the matter mildly, roundly condemned as an aberrancy requiring correction—which, in some cases, it did become.

The trustee system began, however, from necessity and initially had Carroll's approval. First of all, lay involvement in church construction and temporal management was as old as the Church itself. Yet from earliest times various synods and councils had restricted such participation to construction and furnishing, not spiritual authority. The Council of Trent recognized and further defined a trustee system, authorizing it but retaining the bishop's ultimate authority. French Canada developed a system (which it exported to Upper and Lower Louisiana) of *marguilliers* (church wardens) responsible for maintaining church property, collecting its state-authorized taxes, and serving as the trustees, under the ex officio leadership of an ordained pastor appointed by the bishop, of the incorporation of the parish as a legal entity.

In the United States, the trustee system was also influenced by Catholic adaptations to Protestant practice, especially in Congregational and Presbyterian communities. First of all, the Jesuits maintained a self-supporting ministry from their slave-served plantations up to and beyond the suppression via the ownership of these plantations by the Select Body of the Clergy, which in 1792 received state recognition as a corporation of clergy. The churches the Jesuits did build, moreover, were registered as the properties of individual laymen or, later, individual Jesuits or ex-Jesuits. In 1806 the Maryland Assembly enhanced the powers of the Corporation of Roman Catholic Clergymen to receive and hold title to properties, including Georgetown College. A form of clerical trusteeism was therefore finalized. Even John Carroll, given the absence of support from parishes or other sources, had to negotiate with this corporation to receive personal support (a salary) in his early years as prefect apostolic and diocesan bishop. Only with the partial restoration of the Society in 1806 was he able to settle for a buyout, now that support from parishes had become available. Even then, however, Carroll had no diocesan funds to build parish churches. So, beginning with procathedral Saint Peter's, he permitted Catholic laymen to finance and build churches and manage temporalities as an incorporated body of trustees.

This, of course, mirrored the Presbyterian and Congregational system and was likewise present in Lutheran and Protestant Episcopal church ownership and management. The very Americanness of this pattern, moreover, allowed Carroll not only to find sources of support for parish churches but also to align Roman Catholicism with an American practice and hence serve the public relations profile of an emergent, socially acceptable Roman Catholic Church. As such, lay trusteeism enabled a rapid development of parish life in these early years. The trustee system also urged and empowered Catholic laity accustomed to receiving church services supported by slave labor or Jesuit or ex-Jesuit plantations to man up and pay their own bills to support clergy and the physical fabric of parish life.

Traditional Catholic practice, however, had long drawn a distinction between lay management of temporalities and episcopal authority over clerical assignment. Yet in kingdoms in which Catholicism was the established religion, the Crown and nobility woefully blurred this distinction, although it remained technically on the books. In turning to the trustee system for parish organization and construction,

John Carroll was administering the emergence of a church in a republic that insisted upon separation of church and state as well as freedom of religion. As such, Carroll felt that ancient distractions had once again come into focus. Laity incorporated themselves and built the parish church. The bishop, who would also sit as an ex officio member of the parish corporation, appointed its pastor; and the pastor, granted his faculties by the bishop, would teach, preach, conduct liturgies, and administer the sacraments.

Three factors, however—unruly priests, arrogant laymen, and the notable cities in which one or another or both trustees and priests misbehaved—cast such discredit on the system that before his passing in 1815 Carroll confessed that he regretted having given trusteeism his initial support. Troubles began in Saint Peter's Church in New York in 1784, when Carroll had to go to court to regain control of the parish. Then, in 1786 German trustees and congregants of Saint Mary's in Philadelphia—dissatisfied with Carroll's appointment of ex-Jesuit Laurence Graessl, recruited from Germany by Ferdinand Farmer—left Saint Mary's, organized and built their own church (Holy Trinity), and unilaterally appointed to the church two German Capuchins, the brothers John Charles and Peter Heilbron, neither of whom possessed faculties from Carroll, with John Charles serving as pastor. Carroll eventually ceded on the Holy Trinity issue, given the touchiness of German Catholics fearing Irish domination. But trouble returned to Holy Trinity ten years later, when its trustees expelled Father Heilbron in favor of another unauthorized candidate and went into schism when Carroll resisted. In Charleston, South Carolina, trustees in 1803 defended their Irish-born pastor, Simon Felix Gallagher, whom Carroll (for various reasons, including intemperance) was seeking to replace with a French émigré priest. Gallagher went to Rome to defend himself, and the trustees of the Charleston parish, rejecting yet another French émigré priest candidate from Carroll, unilaterally reappointed Gallagher and remained in schism into the 1820s. In New Orleans, meanwhile, Spanish Capuchin Antonio de Sedella, backed by the marguilliers of Saint Louis Church, defied efforts by Carroll to replace him and his vicars following the American acquisition of Louisiana in 1803. Wildly popular with the people of the city as well as with the marguilliers, Sedella remained in office until his death in 1829 and was accorded a civic funeral.

A tale of one president and two colleges

A former instructor himself in the Jesuit schools and colleges of French Flanders, Carroll played defining roles in the foundation of Georgetown and the Sulpician seminary in Baltimore because he wanted to create models for American Catholic educational development, lay and clerical alike, but especially clerical. As he moved through his seventies, Carroll had the satisfaction of witnessing the two educational models he established survive, however tenuously. He was surprised, however—as were most Sulpicians—by the rapid and continuing success of the largely lay-oriented Saint Mary's College attached to the Baltimore Seminary of Saint Sulpice and the rise of a second successful Sulpician lay-clerical college and clerical seminary in Emmitsburg, Maryland. By the time of his death in 1815, Carroll had under his jurisdiction two seminaries and three colleges, although one of them, Georgetown, remained dangerously close to failure.

The success of Saint Mary's College in Baltimore was due to its founding president, Louis William DuBourg, a larger-than-life, highly unconventional Sulpician educator. Born in 1766 to a wealthy coffee-growing Saint-Domingue family; sent to France at the age of two to be raised by his grandparents following the death of his mother; educated in philosophy, humanities, mathematics, and science at the Collège Royal de Guyenne, DuBourg decided on the diocesan priesthood as his vocation and was sent by his archbishop to Saint-Sulpice in Paris, where he was enrolled among the Robertins, the house for gifted students. Along with his formation at Saint-Sulpice, DuBourg took courses at the Sorbonne and the College of Navarre and grew attracted to the Sulpicians. At the time, Jacques-André Emery, superior general of the Gentlemen of Saint-Sulpice, made a candid and prescient analysis of this brilliant young seminarian. "Your fault," noted Emery, "which is a relative one rather than absolute, consists in an ardent enormous imagination which carries you to notions and enterprises—all worthy in themselves, but whose inconveniences and very basic obstacles you do not always weigh carefully."[11]

DuBourg, in short, was an enthusiast with a capacity for quick recovery when things went wrong—and a good thing too, one might add. Following his ordination and acceptance as a candidate for Saint-Sulpice, DuBourg, then only twenty-five, was assigned to supervise a Sulpician boarding school, retreat, and vocation center at Ville-Issey, outside Paris, for younger pupils under the care of DuBourg and five seminarians. DuBourg thus began his priestly career schoolmastering and was highly successful in the role. By then, however, the revolution was raging throughout France, and on 16 August 1792, while DuBourg was in Paris on business, a mob broke into the Issy establishment and kidnapped and slaughtered four of the seminarians. (Hidden in the kitchen by a cook, the fifth seminarian survived.) The next month, on 2 September, similar mobs killed hundreds of priests and seminarians as part of an anticlerical frenzy that arose in the aftermath of the expiration of the deadline for priests to sign the required Civil Constitution of the Clergy or be gone from France.

Since DuBourg refused to swear an oath of allegiance to the state under the provisions of the 1790 Civil Constitution of the Clergy, he bade his father, now retired to France, a fond farewell (Pierre DuBourg died a year later) and fled to Spain. There, while not yet a Sulpician, he associated with other Sulpicians, mastered Spanish during his two-year stay (adding that language to his native French and prior study of English), and served briefly in the city of El Toboso in Castilla–La Mancha, made famous by Cervantes in *Don Quixote* (1614). "Now that you have breathed the air of Toboso known to Don Quixote de la Mancha", Emery would later tease DuBourg, "you have something of that knight's spirit." Quite true! Rather than languish in Spain, where opportunities for French émigré priests were next to nonexistent, DuBourg thought to join François-Charles Nagot, his former director at Saint-Sulpice, at the seminary in Baltimore that Nagot was now directing. Meeting an American sea captain in Cádiz who knew his family in Saint-Domingue, DuBourg booked passage (the ship was leaving the next day!) for the United States.

Arriving in Baltimore on 14 December 1794, DuBourg threw himself into the life of that highly Gallicized city. He tutored (in Spanish) the family of the Spanish consul. He taught (in English) at the school for young ladies recently established by the refugee widow Madame Marie Lacombe. When another émigré priest teacher at the academy, John Francis Moranvillé, was named pastor at Saint Patrick's Church, Fells Point, DuBourg, who held faculties from Carroll, became Moranvillé's assistant and developed a large following among Saint-Domingue exiles, including its large population of people of color, for whom DuBourg conducted Sunday vespers and catechism lessons in the chapel of the Sulpician seminary.

At some point after arriving in Baltimore, DuBourg was formally admitted into the Society of Saint Sulpice, although he had not yet fulfilled the requirement of a full year of solitude, formation, and prayer at the Sulpician novitiate at Issy. In the three short years since his arrival in Baltimore, Abbé DuBourg had become a celebrity priest, famous for his devotion to his pastoral duties; his sermons and teaching in French, English, and Spanish; his rapport with all classes and colors; his teaching abilities (the young ladies at Madame Lacombe's academy gathered around him and wept when they learned he would be leaving); his priestly bearing and manly manners; his wit and humor. John Carroll had taken approving notice of this accomplished gentleman of the cloth, and, on 14 September 1796, DuBourg learned that he had been elected president of Georgetown Academy.

The thirty-year-old DuBourg and his fellow Sulpicians transformed Georgetown from an academy (or, worse, a failed minor seminary) into a college with panache. It featured an augmented lay faculty retained on a living wage, an expanded curriculum (mathematics, natural sciences, philosophy) and such added amenities as drawing and dancing classes, a college Great Seal, and a college uniform (blue coats with red waistcoats) for Sundays and special occasions, such as dinners in honor of prominent guests. Cultivating Georgetown as he had previously cultivated Baltimore, DuBourg made friends and supporters of such prominent citizens as real estate speculators James and Joanna Barry (close friends of John Carroll), Thomas Law (brother of Lord Ellenborough, chief justice of England), and Law's wife, Elizabeth Parke Custis Law, Martha Washington's eldest granddaughter. Through the Laws and the Barrys, DuBourg received an invitation to meet the Washingtons at Mount Vernon. A month later, in August 1797, George Washington paid a visit to Georgetown and addressed the student body. Law sent his son to Georgetown; Barry sent a nephew. DuBourg, in other words, was a companionable priest and, with his bonhomie and flair for socializing and development, a natural-born college president.

In his memoirs, Jean Edouard de Mondésir, DuBourg's Sulpician colleague at Georgetown, explained DuBourg's character in terms of *tertium quid*, or third pathway. DuBourg, de Mondésir noted, was obviously not an ex-Jesuit shaped by long training in the former Society, with its quasi-military ethos that emphasized personal discipline, obedience, and group action. Nor was DuBourg a fully formed Sulpician, prizing a simple lifestyle and a quasi-hidden ministry of seminary teaching, prayerfulness, spiritual guidance, and an exacting conduct of liturgy. DuBourg was, rather, something else, a third entity: a modern categorizer, looking back to this era, might describe him as an entrepreneurial abbé, happy and effective as a priest, and orthodox, but loving big challenges and the limelight, and fundamentally festive and accepting by temperament.

He was not afraid of debt, either, when run up in the service of big projects, such as Georgetown. The trouble was, even as DuBourg was developing Georgetown, the ex-Jesuit directors of the Select Body of the Clergy were growing restive. Even in flush times, the Jesuit ethos was to avoid debt beyond reasonable levels in favor of an every-tub-on-its-own-bottom approach to institutional development. Now these ex-Jesuits were watching DuBourg accumulate a debt they feared would seriously cut into the assets put aside for their survival and, it was hoped, to be of service to a revived Society of Jesus in the United States. Even worse: here were French Sulpicians—at a time of growing hostility between France and the United States over impressment of maritime crews and related issues—reaping the rewards of more than a century of labor by English, German, and Maryland Jesuits to support and develop the Catholic cause in America.

And so, in January 1798 the General Assembly of Maryland was encouraged to include Georgetown College as part of the holdings of the Corporation of Roman Catholic Clergymen, which allowed the ex-Jesuit directors of the Select Body to install one of their own, Francis Neale, as vice president for finance. At their December 1798 meeting, the directors passed a resolution that only members of the Select Body of the Clergy could administer its property. DuBourg, who was not a member of the Select Body, resigned within the week.

A college established in Baltimore

After a stint in Havana—working unsuccessfully with Sulpicians Pierre Babade and Benedict Flaget to establish a preparatory school for Cuban students who would finish their studies for the priesthood in Baltimore—DuBourg and his colleagues returned to Baltimore, where, in August 1799, they established Saint Mary's College, a preparatory or minor seminary for French and Cuban students on the grounds of the Sulpician major seminary. At this time, the seminary had only one student pre-enrolled, and so Carroll and Sulpician superior François-Charles Nagot, anxious to keep the failing seminary alive, allowed the creation of an associate lay college for young men, with DuBourg serving as president and Flaget as vice president, in hopes that some vocations to the priesthood might develop from this lay college. Once again, DuBourg and his fellow Sulpicians and a gradually recruited lay faculty went into action, the Sulpicians being especially glad to be busy in the classroom until a true seminary culture developed. Indeed, in 1802 the Sulpicians gave the One Mile Tavern building to Saint Mary's College and moved to a large double house on the corner of Franklin and Howard Streets, so as to distinguish more clearly the two institutions. In 1803 DuBourg opened the college to Protestants as well as Catholics, and in April he began construction of a second college building, which was ready by July. In 1805 the Maryland legislature incorporated Saint Mary's as an institution of advanced education authorized to grant college and university degrees. By August 1806 four students qualified for bachelor's degrees and one for a master of arts, granted to the future writer, editor, and diplomat Robert Walsh, a previous year's graduate.

DuBourg, meanwhile, was developing the culture and student life of an increasingly residential college. Amenities included student-faculty jaunts into the countryside to the Sulpician farm, the college dogs Sultan and Süleyman loping alongside the students; college-wide seated dinners on major feasts and saints' days or visits by notables; and public disputations (which audiences of up to five hundred attended) on Prize Day at the end of term. Admission standards were high, but enrollments steadily increased, including the sons of French diplomats (who called Saint Mary's "the French college"). Emperor Napoleon's minister plenipotentiary to the United States sent two sons. The son of James Madison, President Jefferson's secretary of state, and the son of architect Benjamin Henry Latrobe, then busy designing the nation's Capitol, were enrolled, along with young men from Boston and other coastal cities as well as New Orleans. DuBourg maintained a lively correspondence with parents when issues arose and, to add a feminine touch, added to the staff one boy's mother, Madame Benjamin du Parc—in charge of linens and the infirmary—when she accompanied her son from Jamaica to attend the school.

For fundraising, DuBourg in 1807 secured from the legislature a state-authorized lottery yielding thirty thousand dollars (a New York supporter bought ten thousand tickets), along with the normal support of tuition and solicited gifts. Carroll, Sulpician superior general Emery, and Baltimore seminary superior Nagot, fully aware of the president's tendencies regarding financial matters, kept DuBourg under close scrutiny and required him to vet all expenses through the seminary's économe (treasurer).

DuBourg and his fellow Sulpicians, meanwhile, established the Catholic focus of the college through mandating Sunday Mass (Protestants exempted), classroom catechism lessons (with a specially edited catechism in use for Protestants), opportunities for confession and counseling, confirmation preparation and conferral, Christmas and Holy Week liturgies, a Corpus Christi procession, morning and evening prayers, and other services and observances. Midnight Mass on Christmas Eve ended with a festive candlelit supper and the singing of carols. DuBourg himself assisted at Saint Peter's on Sundays, and Bishop Carroll considered him the semiofficial diocesan preacher for special occasions.

An American debut for Gothic Revival

For the college chapel at Saint Mary's, DuBourg and his fellow Sulpicians commissioned, fundraised for, and saw to completion in 1808 nothing less than the most beautiful Catholic church in the United States to that date: a still-standing, still-in-use, and still-extolled Gothic-style structure (the first Gothic Revival church in the nation) designed by the French émigré architect Maximilian Godefroy. Born in 1765 and trained as a civil and military engineer, Godefroy came of age as an architect during a period of romantic eclecticism in French design that nevertheless remained in dialogue with a recent period of Classical Revival hegemony. A Royalist in politics and a romantic who tended to be enamored of the past, Godefroy combined this eclecticism with the solidity and sense of purpose of classicism and military engineering—which is to say, buildings should do what they are supposed to do and to be clear about what they are doing—enlivened by a sense of the Romantic Sublime, as advanced by Edmund Burke in his *A Philosophical Enquiry into the Origins of Our Ideas of the Sublime and Beautiful* (1757). The Romantic Sublime demanded of architecture that even solid and purposeful buildings must inspire and set moods and tones of transcendence.

Running afoul of Joseph Fouché's secret police for suspected anti-Napoleonic activities, Godefroy spent eighteen months in confinement in the fortress of the town of Bellegarde and Château d'If (put to good use in 1845 by Alexandre Dumas in *The Count of Monte Cristo*) before being paroled to American exile, thanks to the sponsorship of two influential friends. Arriving in Baltimore in December 1805, Godefroy—elegant, well mannered, well tailored, and charismatic, as an 1814 portrait by Rembrandt Peale reveals—found employment as a professor of painting, architecture, and drawing at Saint Mary's College. He entered Baltimore society, married wealthy bluestocking Eliza Crawford Anderson, the editor of her own periodical, and combined architecture with teaching at Saint Mary's, where he made his private library of art, architecture, and engineering books (1,400 volumes by 1819) available to his students. Saint Mary's Chapel (1808) was Godefroy's first important Baltimore commission, followed over time by the Commercial and Farmers Bank (1812–1813), augmentations to Fort McHenry during the War of 1812 (completed in 1814, when the British besieged the city), the Didier House (1814), the Battle Monument (1815–1822) commemorating the defense of Baltimore in 1814, the Baltimore Exchange (1816–1820, with Benjamin Latrobe), and the Unitarian Church (1817–1818), as well as a number of funereal vaults in Baltimore. Godefroy also designed Saint Thomas Church in Bardstown, Kentucky (1812–1816), and the Courthouse (1816–1817) and the Virginia and Farmers Banks (1816–1817) in Richmond, Virginia.

Whether Egyptian, Greek, Roman, Gothic, or English Classical Revival, or combinations thereof, each of these buildings (and one monument) showed solidity and purpose as well as an element of the Romantic Sublime. Sulpicians matured in an era of Classical Revival and tended to continue favoring that style. Two generations and earlier, for example, architect J. N. Servandoni employed Neoclassical for the façade of the new Church of Saint-Sulpice (1739) in Paris; the basic proportions and spatial volumes of the Chapel of the Presentation of the Blessed Virgin Mary serving Saint Mary's College were vaguely Neoclassical. Godefroy's façade also recalled Notre Dame Cathedral; and Gothic elements—sometimes scholarly, now and then fanciful—predominated fenestration and interior treatments. Even as architect Benjamin Latrobe was beginning work on Baltimore's Cathedral of the Assumption in the Federalist Classical style of the Early American Republic, Godefroy was providing the Sulpicians of Baltimore with an ensemble of medieval references and spaces—fenestration, a circular rose window, columns (albeit Americanized, with acorns and oak leaves, or Egyptianized, with palm branches), gargoyles, choir stalls, vaulted ceilings—designed to evoke the European Catholic past.

And everywhere within, as congregants immediately noted, there prevailed a stillness, a quietude that created a mood of recollection resistant of distraction. As a practitioner of the Romantic Sublime, Godefroy had studied carefully François Blondel's discussion of Gothic and Gothic Revival in his twelve-volume *Cours d'architecture enseigné dans l'Académie Royal d'Architecture* (1771–1777), tomes that most likely resided on the shelves of his Baltimore library. In this authoritative guide of text and plates that dominated Godefroy's practice as a source of theory and illustration, Blondel writes of Gothic Revival:

> The Sublime style of which we speak should be, for example, the very style of our temples; every part, in fact, should seem designed by a divine hand; their disposition should have a sacred character that summons man to God, to religion, to himself.

Note carefully, certain modern Gothic churches convey this impression: a great vaulted height in which there is nothing ungraceful, spacious naves and side aisles, subdued lighting in accord with the spiritual mystery, lofty and peaked facades, internal symmetry between the respective sides; finally, measurements which show that rules were followed, even though they are for the most part unknown to us—these are the beauties that are observed in some works of this style, and that should at the least serve us as examples in the construction of the monuments of which we speak.[12]

Complying with these guidelines, Maximilian Godefroy brought a version of Gothic Sublime to the United States and hence introduced a high European Catholic form of sacred space, forecasting the Gothic Revival engendered by the Oxford Movement in England and America and the long-range and long-term use of Gothic Revival for American Protestant academic buildings.

A recent convert, the widow Mrs. William Seton, and her three daughters were on hand for the dedication of the Chapel of the Presentation of the Blessed Virgin Mary on the feast of Corpus Christi, 16 June 1808. Indeed, they had arrived in Baltimore from New York that very day. Mrs. Seton was especially overwhelmed by the ceremony. "My dear, dear, dear, dear, dear," she entered in the journal she was keeping for her sister-in-law Cecilia, "all I can tell you is a Carriage conveyed us to the Seminary—the organ's solemn pause first—then the bursting of the Quire—this was the moment of the consecration of Mr. Dubourg's chapel—we entered without a word—prostrate in an instant—St. M's voice resounded the *Kyrie Eleison*— human nature could scarcely bear it—your imagination can never conceive the Splendor—the Glory of the Scene all I have told you of Florence is a Shadow."[13]

9

Emmitsburg, Maryland 1812

The first American sisterhood is granted canonical status

Located in St. Joseph's Valley near the village of Emmitsburg, fifty-two miles north-west of Baltimore, close to the Pennsylvania border in the remote Catoctin spur of the Blue Ridge Mountains, the Mountain, as this interconnected community came to be known—a parish, a college, a seminary, a convent, and a school for girls conducted by the first sisterhood to be founded in the United States—emerged as one of the most important centers of Catholic culture in the Early Republic. At the heart of this community was the founder of the Sisters of Charity of Saint Joseph, Mother Elizabeth Bayley Seton, who was guided and supported in her efforts by Sulpicians Louis William DuBourg, John Dubois, and Simon Bruté, as well as Archbishop John Carroll.

On 11 May 1811, Sulpician Benedict Joseph Flaget returned from France, where he had been consecrated bishop of Bardstown, Kentucky. When Flaget left Baltimore to assume the direction of his diocese, he took with him Sulpician John Baptist Mary David, who had taught under Flaget's supervision at the seminary at Angers before the French Revolution. David immigrated with Flaget in 1791 to the United States, where he served as a missioner in southern Maryland, a professor at Georgetown (where Flaget also taught), superior of the Baltimore seminary, and chaplain to Archbishop Carroll. A pious priest, scholar, teacher, and accomplished organist and composer, the loyal David was a perfect second-in-command for Flaget, whom he served across three decades of ministry as seminary rector, cathedral pastor, confessor and advisor, and coadjutor bishop.

The problem was, David's departure left the Sisters of Charity of Saint Joseph without the father superior canonically required of sisterhoods in that era—not that this represented a great loss to each and every sister. David resided in faraway Baltimore, and although not a quarrelsome man, he was in the process of trying to replace the founder and superior of the Emmitsburg sisters, the widowed convert Elizabeth Bayley Seton, mother of five, with Rose Landry White, likewise a widow and a mother. At age fourteen, cradle Catholic Rose Landry had married a prominent ship's captain (Bishop Carroll performed the ceremony) who was subsequently lost at sea, leaving her with two children. The Reverend Mr. David had helped Rose Landry White through bereavement and her subsequent decision to join Mrs. Seton's fledgling sisterhood.

David and Seton, unfortunately, were not compatible, to say the least. First of all, David had been imposed upon the sisters by the Sulpicians of Baltimore, who shared with Archbishop Carroll sponsorship of this sisterhood in formation. Carroll had already received a simple, temporary, one-year renewable vow from Mrs.

Seton in the newly opened seminary chapel designed by Maximilian Godefroy and had formally conferred on her the designation "Mother Seton", in tribute not only to her status as a consecrated widow and mother but also to her role as a mother superior of a future sisterhood that was already attracting recruits, including Seton's sister-in-law Harriet, on the verge of conversion. As Seton's bishop, advisor, and friend, John Carroll bore the ultimate responsibility for assisting the young widow in defining her vocation and in assembling her first recruits. The Sulpicians, however, saw themselves as coequals in this process, given the fact that canon law required a father superior for religious orders of women, and one of theirs—none other than the Reverend Mr. Louis William DuBourg—had recruited Mrs. Seton to Baltimore from New York City, backed the relocation of the sisters to Emmitsburg a year later, and was currently functioning as Mrs. Seton's director of development and de facto father superior.

Mrs. Seton appreciated DuBourg's optimism, savoir faire, and laissez-faire style of guidance. She also revered the poetic spirituality of her trusted confessor, DuBourg's Sulpician colleague the Reverend Mr. Pierre Babade, cofounder of Saint Mary's College as a school for Cuban and French students. Complex, emotional, high-strung, and, like DuBourg, at ease in female company, the cleric and amateur poet Babade enjoyed a psychological affinity with Mrs. Seton, who had her own complex, emotional personality, and he was equally revered by the other sisters for his sympathy and intuitive regard for them as individuals. Because of his white hair and his importance to them as confessor and spiritual director during the year they ran a school for girls on Paca Street adjacent to the new seminary chapel, the sisters nicknamed Babade "the Patriarch". He dubbed Mrs. Seton *Mon Unique* (My Own) and her sisters-in-law Cecilia *Colombe* (Dove) and Harriet, not yet a Catholic, *Magdalene* or the more complimentary "dear new child in Jesus Christ, and soon of hope in his holy church our common mother".[1] When Mrs. Seton's sisters-in-law arrived from New York, Babade wrote a poem ("Romance pour l'arrivée") in their honor. Whatever his virtues might have been—his sympathetic counseling in the confessional, his encouraging homilies, his skills in preaching and teaching, his candid but nonthreatening delight in female company—such cooing familiarity and posing as beloved patriarch among adoring women, however pleasing to the Paca Street and, later, Emmitsburg communities, represented a crossing of boundaries that DuBourg himself, a master of bonhomie within borders, most likely recognized and felt uneasy about.

In any event, the Patriarch served the sisters as confessor, as the priest they asked to prepare their student charges for First Holy Communion, as their correspondent when he was away on other assignments, as a sender of chatty little notes when he was in town. More important, Babade brought the first two candidates to Paca Street, the O'Conway sisters from Philadelphia, one of whom eventually joined the sisterhood. Pierre Babade was definitely not a by-the-book chaplain to a sisterhood. Had the sisters been members of a more developed community, they would have easily recognized that boundaries were being crossed. As it was, however, they were not formed religious, not even Mrs. Seton at the time, albeit John Carroll already considered her a saint and called her so in his correspondence. True, the women religious wore habits—a black gown with a rosary attached to its belt, and a white widow's cap—and they lived communally and adhered to a daily schedule of work and prayer that extended from early morning Mass to vespers in the

adjacent Chapel of the Presentation. But they had not been formed as young novices and postulants in their self-adapted calling, nor had they any previous experience of a chaplaincy beyond DuBourg's approval, distracted by busyness, and
Babade's flamboyant patriarchy, the latter of which constituted a form of deceptive
power masquerading behind his playacting as the white-haired father among his
adoring daughters and granddaughters.

DuBourg might have recognized—how could he not?—Babade's growing resentment of DuBourg's success as president of the college they had founded together
such a short time earlier. As early as 1804–1805, the meticulous liturgist Babade was
writing Carroll, Sulpician superior general Emery in Paris, and officials of Propaganda
Fide in Rome querulous, nitpicking letters criticizing what Babade considered slip-
shod liturgical practices among his fellow Sulpicians, which, in the case of liturgical
transgressions at Saint Mary's College, Babade seemed ever anxious to trace back to
DuBourg. Babade had preceded DuBourg into the Society of Saint Sulpice, moreover, and was now obviously overshadowed by his younger colleague. Furthermore,
Babade was earning a reputation among his Sulpician colleagues of being overreli-
ant on alcohol. John Carroll, meanwhile, was openly suggesting that the Sulpicians
return Babade to France, something that Superior General Emery refused to do.

As of 30 July 1809, ten sisters were living in the Stone House at St. Joseph's Valley,
Emmitsburg, built for them by the Reverend Mr. John Dubois as work continued
on an even more commodious dwelling, called the White House, which Dubois
was also constructing for them. Already the ten sisters, on their own initiative, had
regularized their community life according to a rule and assigned roles. The sisters
arose at five o'clock, dressed, made up their rooms, and prayed and meditated until
six-thirty, at which time they recited the Rosary as they filed into their chapel as
Dubois arrived to say Mass. Another period of prayer followed Mass, and then came
manual work or teaching, examination of conscience and readings from the New
Testament at eleven forty-five, dinner at noon (further reading aloud from Scripture by one sister during the meal), a brief period of recreation at two, more work
or teaching for the rest of the afternoon, supper at five (reading aloud from spiritual
literature), a second brief period of recreation at eight-thirty, and finally evening
prayers and retirement. Mother Seton served as superior and Sister Rose Landry
White as assistant superior. Other assignments included Sister Catherine Mullen,
housekeeper; Sister Cecilia Seton, secretary and teacher; Sister Sarah Thompson,
business agent; Sisters Maria (Burke) Murphy, Mary Anne Butler, Veronica Cecilia
O'Conway, Susan Clossy, and the postulant from Emmitsburg, Ellen Thompson—
duties as assigned (teaching, baking, washing clothes in the nearby creek).

Starting on 10 August 1809, the sisters made a week's retreat under Dubois, an
experienced chaplain from his four years of service to the Sisters of Charity in Paris.
Accepted as of the previous year into the Society of Saint-Sulpice, Dubois was
respected but not ecstatically received by Mrs. Seton and the sisters, as were DuBourg
and Babade; but the sisters contented themselves with writing to these gentlemen, the
Patriarch in particular.

Difficulties ensue

Just as the Emmitsburg community was making such a brave, effective beginning, a
crisis in governance occurred. First, Louis William DuBourg was appointed father

superior to the sisters when the rector of the seminary, François-Charles Nagot, grew too ill to accept the added responsibility. That change should have been thoroughly acceptable to Mother Seton and the sisters—except for one dramatic development soon to come to light. When DuBourg heard of the continuing correspondence between Babade and the sisters, he was shocked by Babade's persistent influence on the community now that it had (at DuBourg's suggestion) relocated to Emmitsburg, begun its formal development as a sisterhood, and drawn in new recruits. Although DuBourg's speech or writing on this matter is not documented, he had previously had ample opportunity to observe disapprovingly Babade's boundary-negligent and personalized relationships with the community when it was in Baltimore. Should those connections continue, they would prevent the growth of a mature community devoid of emotional attachments that could be manipulated and thus obscure or otherwise damage the true purposes of religious life.

Rather than approach the problem delicately, however, the ever-busy DuBourg merely sent a hasty note to Mother Seton that she should do as much as possible to discourage "an inordinate attachment to Babade". DuBourg put this suggestion somewhat elliptically, but Mother Seton understood what he meant. Arriving a few days later at Emmitsburg—where he received a chilly reception during a sweltering August—DuBourg circulated a memo clarifying his position. Any sister could write a director of her choice once every two months, provided the letter be concerned with spiritual matters. This was the standard procedure in France.[2] "None of us desire more", Mother Seton replied.

She was doing her best to be obedient. Her daughters Anna Maria and Rebecca wanted more, and so did her sisters-in-law, Cecilia and Harriet—as did Mother Seton herself. Sisters Cecilia O'Conway, Mary Anne Butler, Susan Clossy, and Maria (Burke) Murphy were disconcerted to be told to sever their relations to the Patriarch. "The truth is", Mother Seton wrote Sulpician superior Nagot, "I did not relish the nomination of Mr. DuBourg."[3] Nagot was shocked by this statement, since he had no record of Mother Seton's previously speaking or writing to this effect. DuBourg, after all, had persuaded Mother Seton to relocate from New York and had helped arrange Paca Street and Emmitsburg for her. Plus, he had gotten her sons, Richard and William, admitted to Saint Mary's College in Baltimore and then to Mount Saint Mary's at Emmitsburg, free of charge. Could this be true? Nagot must have asked himself. Had the Baltimore Sulpicians forced an unwanted father superior on the sisters? Defensively, Nagot asked Mother Seton in a later letter for a confirmation of this reluctance regarding DuBourg. To one degree or another, Babade, the white-haired Sulpician with his pet names for one and all, was a compelling father figure for these women who had not yet come to terms with the calling they had embraced—professed religious under vows of poverty, chastity, and obedience—and the loneliness that now and then would come with rules and traditions associated with such a calling.

Pierre Babade had parallel needs. Who was he without his family? "My children", he called the sisters, "given to me by the Father, the mother, and the Son", edging into irreverence, if not blasphemy, by inserting Mother Seton into the Trinity. Or by "mother" did Babade mean the Holy Mother Church? In any event, he was wrong on both counts. Mother Church was taking him in the exact opposite direction: leave these women alone; afford them an opportunity to grow on their own into maturity as vowed religious outside any possible cult of the Patriarch. Yet Babade began to fight back, and he was a skilled skirmisher. He continued to write his children, but he put all his letters in one bundle for Harriet Seton, who was not a sister, not even yet a First Communicant formally received into the Church. So, no harm done, right? When the day for Harriet's First Communion arrived, Babade—who had previously promised to "fly to the mountain on wings of love" to administer the sacrament and had recently received letters from Mother Seton requesting him "to go to the sacred place which encircles what is dearest to my heart"—was not in Emmitsburg but in Baltimore, defending himself to Carroll and John Marie Tessier, the new seminary rector and regional superior of the Sulpicians. Babade was at Emmitsburg on 24 September 1809, however, to receive Harriet Seton into the Church and to present her with a neck cross engraved with the date of her reception to commemorate their "precious and great day".[4] Sadly, Harriet Seton suffered from the family complaint, tuberculosis. Babade was not on hand when, on 22 December 1809, Harriet lay on her deathbed and in her final delirium sang hymns and called out for him by name.[5]

A change in father superiors

At some point following Babade's visit to the sisters to receive Harriet Seton into the Church, DuBourg—weary of it all, perhaps, or hurt by Mother Seton's reception— resigned as father superior of the sisters; and on 6 October, Mother Seton received from Dubois a letter from Babade and another from Sulpician superior John Marie Tessier announcing DuBourg's resignation and the appointment of Bishop Flaget's assistant, John Baptist Mary David, as the new father superior of the Emmitsburg community. Elizabeth Seton was instantly plunged into remorse over the role she had played in motivating DuBourg's resignation. She begged him not to leave. "My father", she implored, "the pleadings of so weak a creature does not merit your attention I know, yet once more be patient with one you have borne with so long. It seems but a dream that things are as they are—that you have given your children to a Father-in-law while their real father still lives and loves them with a parent's tenderness—and why—The Mother is worthless. Pity them, pity her and if she ever vexes you again, quit her forever."[6] As a vowed religious, Mother Seton realized, she should have accepted DuBourg's efforts to lessen the influence of Babade on the sisters as God's holy will. Instead, she had protested the decision of the Church (like a good Protestant, one might say), and now a stranger would assume direction of the sisterhood. And Babade, the prize she had fought for—who was offered a position as pastor of Emmitsburg two years later by John Dubois, so pained was he by Mother Seton's distress—was now saying with bland assurance that he preferred to keep his distance from the entire contretemps. DuBourg, moreover, replied non-committally to her pleas. He already had so much to do.

"Conform with all the simplicity of a humble servant of God", the elderly Sulpi-cian Nagot advised Mother Seton, "docile to His commands, like a child. Inspire the same sentiments in all your Sisters; it is the true way to have peace and to find that the yoke of the Lord is as sweet as self-will is disquieting and discontenting, so long as one does not know how to conceal it, and sacrifice it, and obey in silence."[7] She would try to take Nagot's advice, Mother Seton decided, and in a letter dated

14 December 1809 she shared this effort with Bishop Carroll, who had likewise counseled her when he visited Emmitsburg the previous month to administer confirmation. "I have had a great many very hard trials, my Father," she wrote, "since you were here, but you will of course congratulate me on them as this fire of tribulation is no doubt meant to consume the many imperfections and bad dispositions our Lord finds in me. Indeed it has at times burnt so deep that the anguish could not be concealed, but by degrees custom reconciles pain itself, and I determine, dry and hard as my daily bread is, to take it with as good grace as possible."[8] Mother Seton would need to recall this moment of understanding in the months to come, when she would be even more sorely tested.

A European-based sisterhood

A distinction is now in order. The women gathering together first in Baltimore and then later in Emmitsburg formed the beginnings of the first canonically recognized sisterhood to develop in the United States. Prior to this, English and American-born Carmelites had permanently established themselves in Maryland; and French Second Order Franciscans (Poor Clares) had managed to gain refugee status before returning to France.

In colonial times, American women who wished to become nuns would enter one or another of the Continental convents favored by English candidates. Thus, Ann Matthews of Charles County, Maryland, at the age of twenty-three had received the veil at the Carmelite convent at Hoogstraet, Belgium, on 3 December 1755, and at the end of the Revolutionary War was serving as superior there under the name of Mother Bernardine of Saint Joseph. Meanwhile, two of her nieces, Ann Theresa Matthews (Sister Mary Aloysia) and Susanna Matthews (Sister Mary Eleanor), joined the Hoogstraet Carmelite convent as well, along with two other Americans, John Carroll's cousin Ann Louisa Hill (Mother Ann of Our Blessed Lady) and Ann Mills (Sister Mary Florentine).

When Emperor Joseph II of Austria closed the Carmelite convents of Belgium in 1789, three of these Americans—Mother Bernardine and her nieces Sister Mary Eleanor and Sister Mary Aloysia—at the urging of Mother Bernardine's brother, the ex-Jesuit Ignatius Matthews, commenced plans to return to Maryland and establish a Carmelite convent devoted to praying for the American church. The chaplain at Hoogstraet—Charles Neale, also a Marylander and a Jesuit novice at Ghent at the time of the suppression—offered the three Carmelites the income from a family-owned farm at Port Tobacco, Maryland, for their support. Following a long, harrowing sea voyage (southern latitudes, intense heat, poor food), the three Carmelites, now joined by a fourth, the Englishwoman Miss Dickinson (Sister Mary Clare Joseph), and their escorts, chaplain Charles Neale and the Reverend Mr. Robert Plunkett, the first president of Georgetown College, reached New York on 2 July 1790. From there they sailed to Norfolk, Virginia, arriving the next day at Bobby Brent's Landing near Port Tobacco, where the Sisters took up residence in a house on the Brooke estate, exchanging their secular clothes worn on the voyage for the brown and black habit of a cloistered Carmelite contemplative.

They insisted upon remaining exactly that over the next three years as Bishop Carroll did his best—including gaining permission from Propaganda Fide in Rome for cloistered Carmelites to do such work—to persuade them to open a school for girls. No, Mother Bernardine of Saint Joseph politely responded on a number of occasions, the Rule for Discalced Carmelites called for cloister, prayer, and contemplation; and that is what they would be doing here in the United States, praying for the success of the American mission, the clergy in particular and the American church in general.

And so, the Carmelites—having put on their habits and organized their convent, formally dedicated on 15 October 1790, the feast of Saint Teresa of Ávila, foundress of their branch of the Carmelite family—adhered to their Rule and, in doing so, prospered (twenty-three nuns as of the early 1820s). They only briefly resorted to teaching for a few years to keep financially afloat following their expensive move to Baltimore in 1830.

Aside from adhering to their Rule and not becoming a teaching convent, as Bishop Carroll proposed, the Carmelites at Port Tobacco enjoyed the distinction of admitting the first American-born woman to be professed as a nun in the United States: Elizabeth Carberry, the daughter of a prosperous farming family in St. Mary's County, southern Maryland. Ever since she was twenty, Carberry had been attracted to the Discalced Carmelite way of life, but her father refused to allow her to enter a Carmelite convent in Belgium because he believed (correctly, had she gone) that he would never see his daughter again. During the Revolutionary War—while her three brothers were serving in the military—Carberry managed the family farm following the death of her father and turned down at least one offer of marriage.

Not until she was in her mid-forties could Carberry leave the farm to other management, pack up her belongings, and arrive at the Carmel of Port Tobacco in a horse-drawn wagon filled with her bedstead, kitchen utensils, and farm implements. She brought along as well the marriage dowry of 150 British pounds left to her by her father. On 1 May 1791, at the age of forty-seven, Elizabeth Carberry was admitted to Carmel as Sister Teresa of the Heart of Mary and Joseph. In addition to pursuing the contemplative life, Sister Teresa exercised her skills in farm management. On 18 January 1814 she died in her sleep at the age of sixty-nine, having spent a quarter of a century in the order.

The arrival of Poor Clares

Founded in 1212 by Saint Clare in cooperation with Saint Francis, the Second Order of Franciscans, more popularly known as the Poor Clares, was equally contemplative and in France noticeably aristocratic—a doubly dangerous identity during the French Revolution, when so many aristocrats and contemplative religious went to the guillotine. Thus, when the Monastery of Saint Clare in Tours was forcibly emptied on 1 October 1792, the expelled nuns' lives were at risk. Fleeing to the seaport of Havre-de-Grace in secular clothes under the protective escort of an equally disguised Franciscan lay brother, Mary de la Marche, the nobly born abbess of the Poor Clare convent, and two colleagues, Mother Céleste de la Rochefoucault, another noblewoman, and Mother Saint Luc, managed to gain passage on a ship sailing for Charleston, South Carolina, on 4 November 1792.

The trio arrived in Charleston on 11 January 1793. Being Catholic nuns and speaking next to no English, they were poorly treated. Moving north to the more

Catholic-friendly city of Baltimore, the sisters were well received by Bishop Carroll and encouraged to open a school for girls, which failed to attract a sufficient number of tuition-paying students. Carroll advised the sisters to try to establish themselves in the French-speaking portions of the Louisiana Territory, then under Spanish governance. Reaching the settlement of Sainte Genevieve in present-day Missouri after heroic travel, the Poor Clares were welcomed by French Catholics and (again) encouraged to open a school. The governor of Louisiana, however, hearing of their arrival, ordered them to report to New Orleans and provided a boat and crew for the journey. The three Poor Clares spent two years as guests of the French Ursulines of that city.

Hearing that France was once again safe, the Poor Clares sailed for Havana as the first phase of a journey homeward. In Havana, the sisters came under the influence of Pierre Babade, who helped them raise funds and directed them back to Baltimore. There the Sulpicians informed the nuns that, contrary to what they had heard, France remained dangerous for priests and religious. Then serving as president of Georgetown College, Sulpician Louis William DuBourg in the spring of 1797 recruited the Poor Clares to open a school in Georgetown, which they did, first renting—and later purchasing with a three-hundred-dollar loan from the Sulpicians of Baltimore—a commodious house and grounds on the corner of Third and Fayette Streets. The property featured a small stream, an orchard of 150 young fruit trees, and a well-stocked fish pond, perfectly suited to the Poor Clares' meatless diet.

In 1799 the fourth president of Georgetown, Leonard Neale, recruited from Philadelphia three young Irish women desiring to become nuns—Alice Lalor, Maria McDermott, and Maria Sharpe—to assist the Poor Clares in running their school, housing them nearby as a separate community of Pious Ladies (so they were named) en route (by 1817) to receiving recognition from Rome as a highly successful Visitation sisterhood. Isolated as aristocratic, French-speaking refugees who planned to return to France eventually, the Poor Clares of Georgetown attracted no American recruits. The Pious Ladies, by contrast, attracted recruits and opened their own school following the two surviving Poor Clares' return to France. Mary de la Marche died in the convent on Fayette Street on 20 November 1804. The following year, Mother Céleste de la Rochefoucault sold the property to Leonard Neale for four thousand dollars, due in five installments, and returned to France with Mother Saint Luc in July 1806. Not until 1875 would Poor Clares establish themselves permanently in the United States.

An Anglican convert

Who was this Elizabeth Bayley Seton? How had she become in such quick succession a Catholic convert and a mother superior by the special designation of Bishop Carroll? And—despite the accretion of identities—how had she managed to preserve harmoniously so many traces of her former evangelical identity? Born in 1774 in New York City to socially prominent parents (Anglican and Loyalist during the Revolutionary War), Elizabeth Bayley grew up as the second and favored daughter in a family headed by a well-known English-educated physician father, professor of anatomy at King's College, who successfully negotiated a postwar transition to an American and Protestant Episcopal identity and a continuing appointment as health officer for the port of New York and professor at the renamed Columbia College.

An attractive young woman who loved family and social life (her dancing slippers from these years remain on display at Emmitsburg), Elizabeth Bayley at the age of nineteen years and five months on 25 January 1794 married the English-educated merchant banker William Magee Seton. Deeply in love, the couple established a home at 27 Wall Street, where the first of five children was born. The unexpected death of her twice-married father-in-law in 1798 left behind a total of thirteen children for the young couple to help raise and educate: the beginnings of Elizabeth's lifelong vocation as a motherly educator. Elizabeth loved children, her own three daughters and two sons as well as her bevy of younger half sisters-in-law. She showed a genius for motherhood, vibrant with emotion and spiritual feeling that signaled a future direction. She also did volunteer social work with a group of other young matrons, Episcopalians and Quakers, organized as a guild (and in 1803 chartered as a registered charity of the state of New York) to help destitute mothers and their children with food, gifts, house calls, and other forms of support. As a member of Trinity Church on Wall Street, young Mrs. Seton especially appreciated the preaching and spiritual direction of its brilliant rector, the High Church clergyman John Henry Hobart, who later became Protestant Episcopal bishop of New York.

Family, husband, children, faith: Elizabeth Bayley Seton had all that she could wish for and was grateful to God for these gifts. However Roman Catholic she later became, Elizabeth was by this point already a profoundly religious woman formed by an evangelical Christianity instilled in her through the King James Bible, by Anglican worship from the Book of Common Prayer—including a reverence for the Eucharist that drove her to receive the sacrament with belief in the Real Presence—by devotional reading, by her father's love and guidance, and by love, marriage, and motherhood. Shaping her also was the preaching and spiritual direction of Hobart, who in later years would win praise from John Henry Newman as one of the early initiators of the Oxford Movement. Elizabeth's prayer life, as recorded in her letters and journals, abounded in the fused fervor of Anglo-Catholicity and the evangelical emotion characteristic of the Oxford Movement, whose religious ethos and temperament she was anticipating in her highly personalized emotive and unsystematic manner.

Elizabeth Bayley Seton came from a New York Loyalist background. Both her father and her husband were English-educated; indeed, her husband sailed with her on his final voyage with his papers signed by the British consul general defining him as a British subject, and her brother-in-law bore the name Guy Carleton Seton in honor of the British general responsible for the repatriation of American Loyalists to Canada. Elizabeth never fully surrendered a vestigially English sense of caste typical of New York during this era, an attitude shared by her soon-to-be mentor John Carroll and other Federalist Catholics. It explains why she paid so much in terms of social capital when she converted to Roman Catholicism, to the astonishment of many of her New York contemporaries—or even, if the truth be told, why it took her so agonizingly long to enter Saint Peter's Church on Barclay Street and request admittance long after she had become a convinced convert.

An Italian conversion

As of 1803, William Seton was so fully showing the ill effects of the Seton family complaint, tuberculosis, that his business was in decline and heading toward outright bankruptcy. Thus, in October 1803 William, Elizabeth, and eight-year-old Anna Maria—the older children and baby Rebecca remained safely with relatives and close friends—sailed on the *Shepherdess* for Leghorn, Italy, in a desperate search for recovery of health and perhaps business fortunes through William's connections with the firm Filicchi Brothers in that city. Upon arrival in Leghorn, however, the *Shepherdess* was kept in quarantine because of the yellow fever epidemic in New York, and the Setons were assigned to Room 6 of the public lazaretto (isolation hospital) several miles outside the city. There, in a condition of medical imprisonment, Elizabeth tended to her frightened child and dying husband for the ensuing month. And yet she did not despair. "With God for your portion", she wrote in her journal for 1 December 1803, "there is no prison in high walls and bolts—no sorrow in the Soul that waits on him, though beset with present cares and gloomy prospects. For this freedom I can never be sufficiently thankful, as in my William's case it keeps alive what in his weak state of body would naturally fail—and often, when he hears me repeat the psalms of triumph in God, and read St. Paul's faith in Christ, with my whole soul, it so enlivens his spirit that he makes them also his own, and all our sorrows are turned to joy. Oh well may I love God, well may my whole soul strive to please him, for what but the pen of an angel can ever express what he has done and is constantly doing for me. While I live, while I have my being in time and through eternity, let me sing praises to my God."[9]

Four days later, however, it was evident that William Seton was nearing the end. On 19 December, the Setons secured release from the lazaretto, and William Seton was moved to comfortable quarters in a Leghorn lodging house provided by the Filicchis. Attended in his final days by Elizabeth, praying with her but refusing all nourishment, William Seton, age thirty-two, died on the morning of 27 December 1803 after raising his emaciated arms to his wife and crying out, "You promised you would go. Come, come, fly!" Elizabeth and Anna Maria prayed briefly over his body. Since the mistress of the lodging house feared yellow fever and tuberculosis and refused to enter the room, Elizabeth and the lodging's washerwoman washed and prepared William's body for burial.

As in the case of John Thayer, Italy helped Catholicize Elizabeth Bayley Seton. Yet, unlike with Thayer—a once rigid Congregationalist who became an even more rigid Catholic—Italy fostered in Mrs. Seton the maturation of a Catholicity that was already part of her religious formation without damaging her Anglican-inspired evangelicalism or significantly altering her basic personality and religious beliefs. Like a later evangelical, John Henry Newman, wrestling with the Catholic question as a member of an Anglican community at Littlemore outside of Oxford, Mrs. Seton required a crisis to move her even futher in the direction of a Christianity she already possessed. From this perspective, she—like Newman—became a reluctantly given gift of Anglicanism to its Roman Catholic counterpart.

Elizabeth and her daughter remained in Italy as guests of the Filicchis—Philip and his wife, Mary (an American, the former Mary Cowper of Boston), and Antonio and his wife, Amabilia—for three months before sailing home to New York under the escort of Antonio, who had business in the United States. During these months Mrs. Seton was in a state of crisis, which for her meant a state of religious crisis born of great personal loss. William and her children had been her life, the very basis of her happiness and religiosity. Now she was a mother of five facing life with uncertain means of support. Still, she and Anna Maria managed to visit the museums and art galleries of Florence, where they spent more than a month in the company of Mary and Amabilia Filicchi. Elizabeth enjoyed the Boboli Gardens and even attended the opera (heavily veiled), as William had planned to take her (she left at intermission). Yet it was the churches of Florence—especially Santissima Annunziata and San Lorenzo, where she beheld the simple and attentive piety of people at Mass and noted their added reverence at the Consecration of the Eucharist—as well as the city's religious art that most impressed her. In Leghorn, an Irish priest, Abbé Peter Plunkett, had politely evangelized her, to which she responded amicably but unconvinced. But the people of Florence and Leghorn—male and female of all ages and classes—attending Mass so devotedly, made a deep impression. At night in her room, after Anna Maria had fallen asleep, she read—*The Imitation of Christ* by Thomas à Kempis, *The Introduction to the Devout Life* by Francis de Sales—and reflected in letters or her journal regarding what she was experiencing via such exposure to Christian faith in a Roman Catholic idiom.

When Anna Maria contracted scarlet fever and lay seriously ill for three weeks, it seemed as if vengeful death were stalking Elizabeth once again. Then, as Anna Maria recovered, Elizabeth herself came down with the dreaded disease, and their voyage back to America was postponed. The delay gave her the opportunity to experience all over again the kindness of the Filicchis, their attendance at daily Mass, Amabilia's Lenten fasting, and processions in the Leghorn streets behind the Blessed Sacrament, held high in a monstrance by a priest. Antonio Filicchi taught her how to make the sign of the cross. Indeed, during her Italian sojourn, Antonio Filicchi became Elizabeth Seton's primary instructor and guide in Roman Catholic matters.

Between Elizabeth Seton and Antonio Filicchi, Seton's biographer Annabelle Melville tells us, "there began in Italy a friendship which was to last for the rest of her life." As young men, Antonio Filicchi and William Seton had been friends to the point of brotherhood. Following William's death, Antonio adopted Elizabeth as his Dearest Sister, as he called her, and was not embarrassed to address her in loving and personal terms. Nor did he consider it improper for him as a married man to do so. "Your dear William was the early friend of my youth", Filicchi wrote Seton from Leghorn on 9 January 1804, when Seton was away in Florence. "You are now come to his room. Your soul is even dearer to Antonio, and will be so forever." On 6 April 1804, Seton wrote Filicchi, her "Most dear A", that she had been contemplating their relationship from the perspective of its propriety and religious significance. "We often receive blessings from the hand of God", Seton wrote, "and convert them into evils. This has hitherto been my fault in respect to a very sincere and uncommon affection I have for you, and I am determined with God's help no more to abuse the very great favor he bestows on me in giving me your friendship and in the future will endeavor to show you how much I value it by doing all I can to contribute to your happiness—on your part I intreat [*sic*] you will behave to me with confidence and affection—the more you confide in me the more careful I shall be—trust me and the angel." Filicchi was relieved by her response, as he wrote back to her; he apparently had been experiencing second thoughts regarding his extravagant language. "Afraid", he confessed, "of some reproaches, or of a like thing that I might have deserved for my too crazy manners, I have been most agreeably surprised in perusing all over ten times your favorite lines, addressed to me in so delicate, so easy, so witty a style, and I hasten to give them my poor reply of acknowledgement and admiration. Believe me, my beloved Sister, that for the purpose of obtaining one of your letters in the week I would cheerfully scribble all the 24 hours of the day."[10]

Thus, Filicchi and Seton both realized the intensity of the terms with which they were addressing each other and, after some hesitation, agreed that this language was religiously acceptable. Widow Elizabeth Seton was in a highly emotional state, which Antonio Filicchi seems to have shared. Seton appeared to struggle with this delicate balance, this necessary sublimation, in the journal she kept on the fifty-six-day voyage to the United States on the *Pyomingo* that she, her daughter Anna Maria, and their escort, Antonio Filicchi, made in the spring of 1804. Throughout her life, including the Catholic years, Seton employed the emotionally fervent discourse of Protestant evangelical reflection. Mrs. Seton was now heading Romeward, but even crossing the Tiber would not eliminate her hunger for close friendship as well as the expressiveness of evangelical language. For the rest of her life, she would open her letters to Antonio Filicchi with such salutations as "Dear", "My ever dear", or "My ever dearest Antonio"—introductions to missives that abounded in loving language, intense emotion, scriptural quotations, humor, narrative vignettes, and exclamations of joy or laments anchored in deepest sorrow. Run-on or half-finished sentences carried the narrative, with exclamation points and dashes strewn everywhere (the dash seems to have been her favorite form of punctuation). This lifetime of correspondence and journalizing showed a breathless femininity that remained consistent from her days as a New York Episcopalian matron to her last years as the mother superior of sixty-one Sisters of Charity.

Directors of one sort or another

Throughout this life, although she spent the bulk of her time teaching girls and living in a community of nuns, Mother Seton sustained dynamic relationships with the men, mainly clerics, who came into her life as guides and directors. Three of these mentors—her father, her husband, and Antonio Filicchi—were laymen. One, John Henry Hobart, was an Episcopal priest who later became a bishop. Biographers record some twenty-two Roman Catholic priests or bishops as Mrs. Seton's advisors at one point or another: testimony, indeed, to her capacity for outreach as well as her recognized status in the Catholic circles of the Early Republic.

What did Elizabeth Bayley Seton learn from these men, Protestant and Catholic, laymen and clerics? From her twice-married father, Doctor Richard Bayley, she acquired three sisters, three half sisters, and three half brothers, along with sustained personal support and tutelage. From her husband, William Seton, import merchant and banker, she received the gifts of a loving marriage and five adored children who first defined her enduring identity as Mother Seton. From the Reverend John Henry Hobart, American pioneer in the High Church movement, predecessor of the Anglo-Catholic Oxford Movement, she absorbed her first impressions of Catholicity in an Episcopalian context. In Leghorn, Abbé Peter Plunkett was the first to counter Hobart's Anglican arguments with an exposition of arguments for another scenario regarding the unity and continuity of Catholic Christianity. Her late husband's friends and business associates Philip and Antonio Filicchi and their wives,

Mary Cowper Filicchi and Amabilia Filicchi, provided her and her daughter Anna Maria with a home, kindly support, and financial backing when she found herself stranded and impoverished (William Seton died bankrupt) in the country in which she first encountered Roman Catholicism. Antonio Filicchi supplemented Abbé Plunkett's instruction, taught her to make the sign of the cross as the badge of her newly emergent religious identity, financed her return to the United States, escorted her and Anna Maria on this long voyage home, and remained her correspondent and perhaps her closest friend for life: her brother in Christ, as he described himself. Augustinian friar Father Michael Hurley OSA, pastor of Saint Peter's Church, New York, received her into the Catholic Church and offered her continuing counsel. Jean-Louis Lefebvre de Cheverus, the first bishop of Boston, and the Reverend Mr. Francis A. Matignon of that diocese advised her from a distance via correspondence regarding her developing vocation to the religious life. Louis William DuBourg brought her to Baltimore, capital city of American Catholicism, where she established her first school and assembled her first community. DuBourg also pointed this community and its foundress toward St. Joseph's Valley, Emmitsburg. Bishop Carroll received her first vows as a religious and gave her the title "Mother", suggesting her crucial role of service to the American church.

Now, as of 1810, it was time for even more clergymen to play roles in her life. Indeed, it sometimes seemed that, by the thoroughly Anglican American evangelical nature of her piety, by her distinctive saintliness, by her eagerness for direction, by her demanding ways that were so mitigated by her commitment to motherhood and motherly care of others, Mother Seton offered the American Catholic clergy of her time a short course in directing other converts of productivity and achievement who would heighten the religious and intellectual profile of American Catholicism in the decades to come.

Founder of the Mountain

Because he played such a crucial, continuing role in the founding and development of Mount Saint Mary's College and the sisters' convent and school at St. Joseph's Valley nearby, the Reverend Mr. John Dubois requires a somewhat detailed introduction. He was, after all, the founder of the Mountain, this interconnected Emmitsburg community that consisted of a parish, a college, a seminary, a convent, and a school for girls. Initially, Mother Seton respected but maintained her distance from this direct, understated builder-priest (ironically, the only priest she came in contact with who had prior experience as a chaplain to sisters), so busy with the realities of administration. Little Napoleon, he was called, in reference to his assertive attention to detail as well as his barrel chest and short height. Yet no priest did more for the sisters—housed them, clothed them, fed them, wrote the first draft of their Rule, saw Mother Seton's sister-in-law and daughter Anna Maria through their last hours on earth—and received so little credit. A native-born (1764) Parisian of the middle class, Dubois graduated from the Paris-based Collège Louis-le-Grand, secularized since the expulsion of the Jesuits, and Seminary of Saint Magloire, conducted by Oratorians. Following ordination, Dubois joined the sixty-priest staff of the parish of Saint-Sulpice without joining the Society itself and was attached as well as chaplain to a community of Daughters of Charity, who were doing their best for the hospitalized insane and nonhospitalized orphans under their care at the Petites Maisons (hostels) on the rue de Sèvres. Dubois had done well academically at college and seminary and in the future would show the instincts of a born teacher, but for the next four years, this was his life as a diocesan priest of middle-class origins: parochial service in a vast urban parish; a chaplaincy with the sisterhood founded by Vincent de Paul and Louise de Marillac in 1633 (the first congregation of nuns to be exempted from enclosure); and a ministry to the insane and to orphans.

Fortunately, as things turned out, as a student at Louis-le-Grand Dubois had made friends with an older student by the name of Maximilien Robespierre, with whom Dubois had studied Latin, and at Saint-Sulpice he came to the friendly attention of the deeply religious Adrienne Noailles de Lafayette, wife of the marquis and a devoted member of the parish. By June 1791, the French Revolution was in full swing, the marquis de Lafayette was in command of the National Guard, and Dubois—along with nearly all the parish priests of Saint-Sulpice—was refusing to take an oath of loyalty to the Civil Constitution of the Clergy and hence was making plans to flee France in fear for his life. Instead of a temporary sojourn in England or Spain, however, the twenty-seven-year-old Dubois was considering a more ambitious, permanent move to the United States. Thanks to Adrienne de Lafayette, the marquis was prevailed upon to write letters of introduction on Dubois' behalf to United States Senator James Monroe, who had served with the marquis at the Battle of Brandywine (during which the young French major general was wounded), and to Patrick Henry, governor of Virginia during the war years. A chance meeting on the street with Robespierre, now a rising member of the National Constituent Assembly, followed by Robespierre's invitation to breakfast, resulted in Dubois' receiving from his former school friend falsified papers that allowed Dubois to leave the country.

Having assured himself that his widowed mother was financially secure and politically low-profile—and hence safe—Dubois sailed for the United States on his falsified papers and arrived in Norfolk, Virginia, in late August 1791. Thanks to his letters of introduction from Lafayette, Dubois made excellent contacts in Richmond, the state capital. Senator James Monroe, who spoke French, put him up as a houseguest. Former Virginia governor Patrick Henry taught Dubois English and secured permission for him to celebrate Mass in the Richmond capitol as part of a state program underscoring religious equality and freedom. Dubois likewise found himself befriended by two leading Protestant clergymen, John Buchanan and John Blair, who supported the school Dubois soon opened in an effort to support himself. As soon as it was feasible, Dubois applied for American citizenship.

Short in stature but mesomorphic, Dubois rapidly cultivated a more assertive personality as he grew increasingly accustomed to—and favorable toward—the United States as he was encountering it in Virginia. Soon gone was the shyness of a very young priest, ordained at twenty-three (one year below the canonical age), which had perhaps attracted the kindhearted Madame de Lafayette. Dubois lacked DuBourg's flair for languages; he mastered English in terms of comprehension but never lost his heavy French accent. And in place of DuBourg's suavity, persiflage, and impulsiveness, the ever-busy Dubois gradually developed a leonine directness and get-the-job-done approach to life. When Dubois applied to Carroll for an assignment in 1794, Carroll correctly judged him as a missionary type with a gift for making friends in high places and assigned him to circuit duty: not on the frontier, but closer to home, in Virginia, Pennsylvania, and Maryland, based out of Frederick, Maryland, where Dubois' diplomatic entrepreneurialism might prove to be of use.

As it certainly did. Like Stephen Badin, Demetrius Gallitzin, Gabriel Richard, Benedict Joseph Flaget, and Louis William DuBourg, John Dubois was an entrepreneurial builder of institutions. In Dubois' case, moreover, he was literally a builder—an architect, landscapist, and on-site contractor and construction boss, with roughened hands and broken fingernails to show for it. But that was in the future. For nearly fifteen years, John Dubois rode circuit, based out of Frederick. In the course of these years, the hard-riding Dubois served and befriended all classes: Signer Charles Carroll of Carrollton; former Maryland governor Thomas Sim Lee and his wife, Mary Digges Lee; an up-and-coming lawyer by the name of Roger Brooke Taney, en route to becoming chief justice of the United States; while continuing his contacts with Patrick Henry and James Monroe, the future president of the United States. But these Anglo-American worthies, while appreciated, were not Dubois' main focus, although he did have recourse to Monroe (unsuccessfully, most likely) to intervene for the life of a slave condemned to death for murdering his master, who had separated him forever from his wife and children and was in the course of shipping him in chains to the Ohio Territory for sale.

More directly related to Dubois' ministry were Irish settlers who basically preferred an Irish priest, Anglo-American and Irish settlers hostile to France as its revolutionary government and the United States came closer and closer to open war (Dubois kept a low profile in political matters), and Catholics of Anglo-American, Irish-American, and German-American background who, on a priestless frontier, had drifted away from the Church or, craving religion, had turned to Protestant clergy for marriages, baptisms, and funerals. Bishop Carroll had taken a hard-nosed approach to those who had married in a civil ceremony or before a Protestant minister: no Communion until the couple had been remarried in the Church and publicly apologized and begged pardon before a Catholic congregation. Dubois approved of the Catholic ceremony but openly opposed Carroll as to the need for a public apology. Furthermore, when performing the wedding of Catholic Roger Taney and Episcopalian Anne Key (sister of Francis Scott Key), Dubois let stand the prior Maryland solution to mixed marriages—boys raised Catholic, girls raised Protestant—and did not require the couple to promise that all children be raised Catholic. One detects tension on such matters between Carroll and Dubois in Dubois' sometimes sly referral to Carroll for adjudication of matters that hardly required the judgment of an upper-class prelate based in Baltimore, such as the woman Dubois described as refusing to sleep with her husband because he was a heavy drinker and she could not abide his breath. She was willing to render her husband the marital debt, Dubois informed the somewhat fastidious Carroll, anywhere else in the house but not in bed. The husband, in turn, required his wife to be in bed when paying the marital debt; he claimed it was for warmth and was charging her with abandonment. "Which of the two ought to be compelled to give up? Must not the sacraments be refused to the one who refuses and [so in this case] to which of the two?" Was Dubois innocently asking such a Rabelaisian question? Or was Dubois craftily suggesting to his bishop the limits of cut-and-dried solutions to pastoral problems encountered in circuit-riding practice?[11]

In Frederick in 1804, Dubois began construction on a new church, Saint John's, with the assistance of a state-authorized lottery organized by Roger Taney and a generous donation from merchant John McElroy, who later entered the seminary, was ordained, and served some twenty-three years there as pastor. A few years earlier, the Irish residents of adjacent Emmitsburg had also built a church, which Dubois served. The Anglo-American Catholic residents of Emmitsburg, however, still hoped to build at least a chapel on the Elder Family Farm, where their ancestors had worshipped in a Mass House during the penal era. In the course of exploring the Mass House site at the base of a picturesque mountain, Dubois and several companions rambled up the mountain and came upon a stretch of level ground that commanded a panoramic view of the valley. When Arnold Elder, the current owner of the Elder Family Farm, was brought to the site, he told Dubois that thirty years earlier his father had said that it would be a fine place to build a church. A resurvey of the area confirmed Arnold Elder's ownership, and he donated it to the Diocese of Baltimore for Saint Mary's Church. Dubois was delighted to discover that the original owner of the locality, a Protestant, had named it St. Mary's Valley.

In November 1805, in honor of the property's previous Protestant ownership, both Catholics and Protestants gathered for a construction party, which Dubois kicked off by burying an axe in a tree. In 1807, using his own money, Dubois purchased a second seventeen-acre site just below the now-finished church. This site he kept in his own name. Then forty-three, Dubois planned to build on it one day a home for retired priests, including himself. Carroll suggested that the land be registered in the name of the diocese, meaning himself. Dubois refused. Had not the ex-Jesuits, he pointedly asserted, kept their property in the name of their corporation without infringing on Carroll's prerogatives as bishop? Like the ex-Jesuits, he had experienced (because of the French Revolution) the loss of everything. If he knew that he would die before Carroll, he would certainly cede the acres to him, but for the time being, "I give you my word that I will give them for the use of the Church there although I wish to keep them in my hands as a refuge in my old age."[12]

Pigeon Hill

In the post–Council of Trent seminary system as it operated in France, Spain, Italy, and other Catholic countries, young men of nonaristocratic, nonwealthy backgrounds who showed evidence of being inclined to the diocesan priesthood were accepted into minor seminaries, where they received a secondary education prior to enrolling in major seminaries for studies in philosophy and theology prior to ordination. Aristocratic or upper-middle-class young men, by contrast—many of them already tonsured as clerics—from whom the Church hierarchy was recruited did not require the remedial education minor seminaries offered, and many of them enrolled in Jesuit colleges prior to seminary and advanced university study. Minor seminaries, then, enabled young men of less advantaged, even peasant, backgrounds to qualify for the higher studies that the Council of Trent demanded and, once ordained, to join the ranks of the diocesan clergy.

The Sulpicians of Baltimore faced the same challenges as the seminary educators of Catholic Europe: finding qualified candidates for major seminary training for diocesan clergy in a population for which an education beyond a few years of grammar school was not the norm. Neither Georgetown nor Saint Mary's College in Baltimore could fully meet this need for the early education of future clerics, given the cost and lay-dominated cultures of these institutions, although offering a pre-seminary education remained a stated goal of both schools. Thus, when French émigré Joseph Harent, planning to visit France, offered the Sulpicians the use of his farm, Pigeon Hill, in Adams County, Pennsylvania, near the German Catholic settlement of Conewago, they readily accepted and sent Sulpician Jean Dilhet and two seminarians there in August 1806 to open a minor seminary for twelve German American farm boys from the region who had expressed interest in becoming priests.

John Dubois, meanwhile, developed a habit of making his annual retreat with the Sulpicians in Baltimore. Attracted to their way of life, Dubois applied for admission to the society but was refused on a number of occasions on the basis that he was not needed in their educational endeavors. Dubois contented himself with establishing a school at Emmitsburg for local children, making an annual retreat with the Sulpicians, and entertaining Sulpicians traveling to and from Baltimore. When Joseph Harent wrote to announce his return to Pigeon Hill from France, however, the Sulpicians—at the urging of Louis William DuBourg, now serving as president of Saint Mary's—began to take a second or third look at Dubois and his seventeen-acre mountain site at Emmitsburg. As usual, DuBourg began the development of a plan that others would have to bring to completion: the transfer of the minor seminary at Pigeon Hill to Emmitsburg.

First of all, DuBourg persuaded Dubois to promise to donate the seventeen-acre plot to the Sulpicians and to build a seminary building on it. Dubois agreed and was admitted to the Society of Saint Sulpice without needing a novitiate period. Second—again, the promoter at work—DuBourg persuaded Arnold Elder and his wife to donate their farm and its slaves to the seminary in exchange for an annuity of eight hundred dollars a year. Impossible! Dubois protested. No fledgling school could carry such a debt! The Sulpicians voted in favor of the measure anyway. The Elders, moreover, also agreed to feed and house eighteen seminarians for a fee of eighty dollars, plus five dollars for washing, until the minor seminary buildings— financed by DuBourg, so he promised, but built by Dubois—could be completed. By November 1809, however, even as not-yet-paid carpenters and masons were at work, DuBourg was writing Dubois that he had run out of money. *Nemo dat quod non habet,* DuBourg pointed out with regret. No one gives what he does not have. It was now up to Dubois to finish what DuBourg had initiated. In DuBourg's defense, his health was declining—from overwork, most likely—and in November 1810 he left for a ten-month sojourn in Martinique to regain his health.

Difficulties at Georgetown

Georgetown College, meanwhile, was languishing under the administration of its fourth president, Leonard Neale, Carroll's auxiliary bishop after December 1800, and his brother, vice president and treasurer Francis Neale. There could be no greater contrast than that between the exuberant, outgoing Frenchman DuBourg and the ascetic, retiring Anglo-American Neale (foisted on Carroll by the Select Body of the Clergy following the death of Bishop-elect Laurence Graessl); and while Sulpician économe John Marie Tessier kept a close watch on DuBourg's expenditures, Francis Neale underspent what was necessary. The combination of Leonard's reclusive piety and Francis' closefistedness—so starkly different from Abbé DuBourg's non-Sulpician *tertium quid*, larger-than-life style of leadership—conferred on Georgetown the ambience of a strict, repressive seminary, compared with the stylish, pleasurable Saint Mary's. Beyond Bohemia Manor and a few other brief experiments, the student-centered panache of the Jesuit colleges of Europe—with their sports, games, holiday treks, oratorical contests, and lavish production of plays—had not reached Catholic Maryland or Pennsylvania during the colonial era. It would require the worldwide revival of the Society of Jesus, so recently the Schoolmaster of Europe, to bring this tradition to the United States.

Meanwhile, the students at Saint Mary's seemed to be having all the joy of life, and contrasting enrollments, campuses, and general morale underscored an obvious scenario. By 1806—with twenty-six students enrolled in spaces designed to accommodate two hundred, its campus plant deteriorating (windows boarded up for lack of glass), its president, Bishop Neale, sleeping on a folding cot in the library—Georgetown was on the verge of closing its doors. In retaliation for the Sulpicians' granting DuBourg permission to expand Saint Mary's into a full-service lay and clerical college, Bishop Neale authorized pretheology philosophy classes designed to keep seven prospective priests (a number of them attracted to Ignatian ideals) at Georgetown. John Carroll now had two major seminaries, one minor seminary, and three colleges under his jurisdiction.

An unexpected patron

Georgetown also played a role in bringing Mother Seton and her community to Emmitsburg. Prior to her removal to Baltimore, Mrs. Seton's two sons had been attending Georgetown on scholarship. Once she moved, DuBourg suggested that it would perhaps be more convenient if they transferred to Saint Mary's College in Baltimore while Mrs. Seton began her teaching ministry on Paca Street. And so, in mid-June 1808, a few days after her arrival in Baltimore for the dedication of the Chapel of the Presentation, Mrs. Seton traveled by coach to Georgetown. Accompanying her were Father Michael Hurley, the respected pastor of Saint Augustine's in Philadelphia, and Samuel Sutherland Cooper of that same city, a wealthy thirty-nine-year-old convert, originally from Virginia, who planned to enter the Baltimore seminary and study for the priesthood. Cooper became attracted to maritime life through the example of his older half brother Richard Dale, a lieutenant under John Paul Jones on the *Bon Homme Richard* during the Revolutionary War and a squadron commander with the rank of commodore during the war with Tripoli. Investing in a Philadelphia-based merchant ship, Samuel Cooper personally commanded it on successful trading voyages to South America, Europe, and India and, when ashore in Philadelphia, acquired a minor reputation as a man-about-town recognized for his skills at billiards and dancing. Struck ill in Paris, the Episcopalian Cooper experienced an intensification of his religiosity that, after much study, debate, and prayer, led to his reception into the Church by Father Hurley in the autumn of 1807, a conversion followed almost immediately by a decision to enter the Sulpician seminary in Baltimore and study for the priesthood.

Mrs. Seton and Cooper must have gotten along famously while traveling together, for on 26 August 1808, writing to her sister-in-law Cecilia, Seton confessed an attraction to Cooper. An "involuntary attraction of certain dispositions" was how she later described the experience to her good friend and correspondent Julia Scott in a letter dated 23 March 1809, four months after this first encounter, which suggests that it was still on her mind. "If we had not devoted ourselves to the heavenly spouse before we met", Seton had written to her sister-in-law, "I do not know how the attraction would have terminated; but as it is, I fear him not nor any other. But such a perfect character is a fit offering to the foundation of all perfection. He has my Rosary and little red cross by way of memento of our Georgetown expedition."[13] Cooper remained similarly in mind regarding Mrs. Seton (who was not wearing a religious habit during this fateful journey). Seton's gift of the rosary and cross reminded Cooper and herself that each of them was pledged to walk down a different pathway. Still, Mrs. Seton's frank descriptions of the attraction in her letters to Cecilia Seton and Julia Scott offered suggestions of the warm, loving wife Mrs. Seton had so recently been.

William Magee Seton had been a handsome young man with excellent manners, a bilingual speaker (due to his youthful sojourn in Italy), a pioneer Wall Street banker, a lover of opera and the arts, an amateur musician (he is reputed to have introduced the first Stradivarius to New York), a Christian gentleman—in short, someone to whom Elizabeth Bayley Seton easily devoted herself, body and soul, with the full ardor of youth. Samuel Sutherland Cooper, by contrast, had a sharp nose and slightly concave face that could charitably be described as homely. (Paradoxically, Elizabeth Bayley Seton was sensitive to handsomeness throughout her life, more than occasionally making reference to it, even if the man be bishop or priest.) Coming from a prosperous Virginia family, Cooper was no doubt well-mannered. His experience as a sea captain, moreover, conferred on him a certain manly presence and air of self-assurance. Although he later grew increasingly restless and emotionally unbalanced, that instability would not have been noticeable when he first met Mrs. Seton.

Reaching New York on his journey, Cooper called on Cecilia Seton to inform her of how greatly her sister-in-law wanted Cecilia to move permanently to Baltimore: a self-assignment that suggests the impression Mrs. Seton had made upon him. Or had Mrs. Seton requested that Cooper do something as personal as to call upon her sister-in-law, yet another sign of the intensity of their initial encounter? In any event, Cecilia drank coffee with Cooper and later wrote Elizabeth that she found him "silent and retired". Of course he is, Seton wrote back chidingly. He is about to study for the priesthood. "I should not wish you to know him as I do."

Cooper also called on the Reverend Mr. Louis Sibourd, pastor of Saint Peter's, who had a package he wished delivered to Mrs. Seton. That favor, being accomplished, suggests a second meeting between Cooper and Mrs. Seton before Cooper entered the Baltimore seminary adjacent to the house on Paca Street where Mrs. Seton lived for a year, teaching a few girls and attracting candidates for her proposed order. Neither too much nor too little should be made of the first phase of the Seton-Cooper relationship. How honest and charming for Mrs. Seton to confess this "involuntary attraction of certain dispositions" resulting in an "interest and esteem understood" and to inform Julia Scott that "the only result of this partiality had been the encouragement of each other to persevere in the path which each has chosen."[14] How alive, how human Widow Seton seems in these phrases, how simultaneously connected to her wifely past and vowed religious future.

In an interview conducted and transcribed nearly two decades later, when he was serving as bishop of Montauban in France, DuBourg claimed that Mrs. Seton and Cooper, without consulting each other, had each come up with the idea of establishing at Emmitsburg a boarding school for girls of family as well as a trade school for the local community. Bishop DuBourg was most likely forgetting, perhaps even deliberately, that he had been in constant contact with Seton, then getting established on Paca Street, and with Cooper, then studying for the priesthood on the same campus, regarding the moving of the minor seminary at Pigeon Hall to Emmitsburg. Within a few years, the minor seminary morphed into Mount Saint Mary's College, which by 1812 enjoyed an enrollment of sixty lay and preclerical students. A Sulpician since the opening of the college in academic year 1808–1809, John Dubois, the longtime pastor of Frederick, was also involved in founding Mount Saint Mary's and served many years as its president. It was DuBourg, then—with help from Dubois—who got Cooper interested in the development of the Emmitsburg site, to which Dubois took Cooper for a preliminary reconnaissance. Cooper returned to Baltimore a convinced supporter of the location, not only for the trade school (spinning, knitting, sewing, light manufacture) for unemployed locals but also for Mrs. Seton's boarding school. Cooper did more than approve of these projects (the trade school was his own idea): he talked of pledging between seven thousand and ten thousand dollars to finance them. DuBourg also all but directed Mrs. Seton to Emmitsburg as well, despite the fact that a day school for girls and young women of family would seem to have a better chance of success in Baltimore. In any event, Cooper placed seven thousand dollars or so in DuBourg's hands for purchase of a site and construction of a school and convent under Dubois' supervision. In the summer of 1809, Mother Seton and her sisters arrived at Emmitsburg and made their way to the Stone House in St. Joseph's Valley, which Dubois had made available as their first convent.

Second father superior

Sulpician John Baptist Mary David, the newly appointed second superior of the sisterhood, arrived at St. Joseph's on 1 August 1810. Mother Seton appreciated the three recruits for the sisterhood—Fanny Jordan, Angela Brady, and Julia Shirk—David brought along with him, as she did the three candidates DuBourg referred to her when he returned from Martinique: Louise Rogers, Adele Salva, and Adele's sister Madame Guérin, a widow whose son would join Mother Seton's sons, William and Richard, at Mount Saint Mary's College. Mother Seton, however, did not favor the idea of a religious retreat, to be given by an unknown priest scheduled to accompany Bishop Flaget to Kentucky sometime in the future. She also might have resented Flaget and David's plans to bring to the United States Daughters of Charity from France to mentor the Emmitsburg sisters. French nuns surely would not have approved of Bishop Carroll's decision to allow Mrs. Seton to take vows while retaining custody of her five children, including accepting private gifts of money to help pay for their education. For one reason or another, the three Daughters of Charity failed to arrive; but Flaget and David had brought with them a copy of their Rule of Life. That document was equally incompatible with Bishop Carroll's exemption of Mother Seton from a strict adherence to a religious vow of poverty as understood by the Church since the Council of Trent, which had led to current discussions in Baltimore about replacing Mother Seton with Sister Rose White as religious superior stationed in Baltimore, leaving Mother Seton in charge of the school for girls at St. Joseph's Valley, near Emmitsburg. As the Rule for Daughters of Charity brought over from France was discussed in Emmitsburg and Baltimore, Elizabeth Seton felt herself increasingly vulnerable to removal as mother superior because of her responsibilities to her children.

The forceful Mother Seton, to whom bishops were deferential, was meeting her match in the Reverend Mr. David, who adhered to a conventional view of the role of a father superior: to be in charge. A retreat was held in August, as scheduled by David, and it afforded him a religiously charged opportunity to assert himself as father superior, teacher, confessor, liturgist, and authority figure. A second retreat was held in October, intensifying David's authority over Mother Seton and her fifteen sisters.

A descendant of Breton farmers, born in 1761 in Couëron, a small town in Brittany, John Baptist Mary David was not, like so many Sulpicians, to the manor born. Educated by Oratorians at their college and seminary in Nantes—during which time he became a skilled chorister, organist, and choral conductor—David applied and was accepted to the Sulpicians after a period of teaching, following the completion of his theology course and becoming canonically eligible for ordination upon reaching the age of twenty-four. Assigned to the preparatory seminary at Angers, David became good friends with faculty member Benedict Joseph Flaget, in whose company he was assigned to the United States by Sulpician Father General Jacques-André Emery. David served eleven demanding years in the field as a missioner charged with reviving the practice of Catholicism in rural Maryland before being assigned to the Baltimore seminary in 1804 as professor and, as an additional duty, chaplain to Charles Carroll of Carrollton. Flaget then recruited him for the newly created Diocese of Bardstown.

For a variety of reasons, John Baptist Mary David was not intimidated by Mother Seton. He was a country-born and -bred Celt, possessed of a certain provincial self-sufficiency, as well as a veteran of more than a decade of work among the rural poor. He had little experience with emotional, complex, upper-class Anglo-American women such as Elizabeth Seton. The down-to-earth Sister Rose Landry White, to whom David had ministered through the death of her husband, seemed more congenial and understandable. David was forever entreating Mother Seton to see matters more calmly, more simply, more in tune with traditional Catholic teachings regarding acceptance of God's will.

By contrast, Bishop Cheverus of Boston, Seton's longtime correspondent, wrote her that he looked upon her trials and difficulties "as the stamp of divine favor and protection upon your establishment". Cheverus urged her to remember Saint Teresa of Ávila and Saint Frances de Chantel, foundresses of the Discalced Carmelites and the Sisters of the Visitation, respectively. "Like them, I hope you will become saints and the mothers of many saints."[15] In November 1810, Cheverus visited Emmitsburg. After five years of correspondence, it was the first time the bishop of Boston and Mother Seton had met. Their meeting occurred at the height of discussions of replacing Mother Seton with Sister Rose Landry White. Overcome with emotion, Mother Seton fell to her knees and wept for five minutes upon encountering Cheverus. One cannot imagine Mother Seton weeping in the presence of her current father superior, the Reverend Mr. John Baptist Mary David, priest of Saint Sulpice.

Bishop Carroll also gave advice and counsel to Mother Seton via letters during these stressful months as John Dubois' adaption of the Rule of Life for Sisters of Charity was negotiated and refined by Carroll and the Sulpicians. As he had done when he received Mrs. Seton's vows of religion while she maintained responsibility for the care of her children, Carroll protected the *maternity* of Mrs. Seton's role during negotiations regarding her actual motherhood, her role as mother superior of her community, and her role as *Mother Seton*, the very title he had conferred on her in recognition of her importance as first foundress of an American sisterhood. At the same time, Carroll argued on behalf of an Americanization of the pioneer American nuns, recommending an increase in their powers of self-regulation and autonomy—within limits, of course. After all, it was Carroll who told the cloistered Carmelite contemplatives of Port Tobacco that they must teach school as well as live monastically and who believed that the hospitaller aspects of Sisters of Charity service must be put on hold (perhaps for as long as a hundred years) because of the need for Catholic education in a growing American Republic. Yet Carroll also had confidence in the sturdy and resilient American women who were volunteering for duty alongside Mother Seton, and he did his best—as Saints Vincent de Paul and Louise de Marillac had done their best in seventeenth-century France—to heighten a spirit of self-governance.

Still, as difficult as these months were, they helped transform Elizabeth Bayley Seton into the fully mature foundress and elected mother superior of a full-fledged, canonically established Roman Catholic sisterhood. Even Carroll, who believed her to be a saint, assisted this evangelical, sometimes impulsive daughter of privilege to see herself in a new light—as a new kind of mother, even. This Reverend Mother was steady, stable, patient, accepting on behalf of her sisters. The identity ran concurrently with Seton's actual maternity, which Carroll personally protected by exempting her from the restrictions of a vow of poverty (no personal funds or property to manage, no responsibility for the support of others) while she was raising her children. Meanwhile, Sulpician John Baptist Mary David, her imposed and resisted director, insisted that she master what was perhaps for her the most difficult of the three vows of religion: obedience. Even harder, that obedience was to the directives of a priest superior she had not chosen and with whom she did not share much temperamental affinity. Thus, a European model of sisterhood was brought to the United States. Sisterhoods reported to an ecclesiastical superior, that is, a priest, whose authority was paramount and to whom mother superiors—even saints, for that matter—owed obedience. For someone as intensely attuned to spiritual direction as Mother Seton was, this obligation proved a hardship she learned to accept.

In January 1812 John Tessier, the Sulpician superior replacing François-Charles Nagot, and Archbishop Carroll issued separate statements canonically establishing the first Catholic sisterhood to be founded in the United States, the Sisters of Charity of Saint Joseph. "After having read the constitutions of the Sisters of Charity with great attention", noted Tessier, "and approved of everything contained therein I have presented them to the most Reverend Archbishop Carroll for obtaining his approbation, and at the same time I have confirmed and hereby again confirm the nomination of the Reverend Mr. Dubois for superior-general, in witness of which I have set my hand, on the seventeenth of January 1812." Thus, Tessier established the Society of Saint Sulpice as sponsor of the sisterhood. With comparable brevity, Carroll, in turn, conferred on the sisters canonical status as a sisterhood of archdiocesan standing. "I have read and endeavored before God attentively to consider the constitutions of the Sisters of Charity submitted to me by the Reverend Superior of the Seminary of St. Sulpitius", Carroll stated, signing himself as John, Archbishop of Baltimore, "and I have approved of the same, believing them to be inspired by the Spirit of God, and suitable to conduct the Sisters to religious perfection." Having achieved canonical status, the sisters proceeded unanimously to elect Elizabeth Bayley Seton as superior, Rose Landry White as assistant, Catherine Mullen as treasurer, and Anna Gruber as procuratrix (business officer). Each sister took a temporary vow of one year to the institute, following which they were free to leave or take final vows. All chose to remain, and ten new candidates presented themselves that probationary year.[16]

Accepting direction

Already an experienced chaplain to the Sisters of Charity of Paris from the first years of his priesthood, Sulpician John Dubois, the new ecclesiastical superior, seemed the perfect priest to direct the sisters following David's departure for Kentucky. For some time, Mother Seton had been taking Dubois for granted: respecting him and certainly depending on him for the necessities of life, but not finding in the short, broad-chested, weather-worn executive the quick intuitions and psychological insights of (for all their differences) such former directors as Babade, DuBourg, Carroll, and Cheverus. Yet Mother Seton and her sisters were on the other side of something now that they belonged to a canonically authorized sisterhood. They had become professionals: religious under lifetime vows or novices or postulants aspiring to that status. As such, they were being guided by commitments and by a Rule, by scheduled work and sequences of prayer, not personal preferences based on psychological dependency.

For professionals, vowed religious in an established Roman Catholic sisterhood, the no-nonsense and generalized kindliness and common sense of Dubois would do just fine, thank you. Besides, as ecclesiastical superior, Dubois soon demonstrated a high regard for women as individual personalities. Like Carroll, Dubois recognized Mother Seton as a saint, for one thing, but he refused to be intimidated. While he was doing his best to supervise an upper-middle-class Anglo-American saint, Dubois was also doing his best to recruit to the Emmitsburg sisterhood Mrs. Charlotte Melmoth, an ardent, English-born Roman Catholic convert now living in retirement but in her day (the 1770s, 1780s, and early 1790s) a renowned actress in England, Ireland, and (after 1793) New York. After age and weight gain restricted her to matronly parts and she then retired from the stage in 1812, Mrs. Melmoth kept a school of elocution and a respectable tavern in New York and an equally respectable boarding house and successful school in Brooklyn for the daughters of the leading citizens of that suburban township. This last calling, as a teacher of girls, as well as her Catholicism and good humor most likely confirmed Dubois' belief that Mrs. Melmoth was a suitable candidate for the Sisters of Charity of Saint Joseph. She did not join the sisterhood, but the high regard in which she was held by Dubois (later to become third bishop of New York) testified to that priest's inclusive sense of the various types of women who might make good Sisters of Charity.

The arrival of Little Brother

In 1812 Dubois acquired the assistance at Mount Saint Mary's College of a young Sulpician priest named Simon Bruté de Rémur, a brilliant and intermittently mystical professor of philosophy who was also a qualified physician. Priestly duties at the Mountain were attached to three sites: the parish church of Saint Joseph in the village of Emmitsburg; Mount Saint Mary's College on a plateau at seven thousand feet on the Catoctin spur of the Blue Ridge Mountains; and St. Joseph's Valley, two miles distant, site of the Sisters of Charity's convent and school. Village, Mountain, Valley: Bruté first visited this tripartite rural Catholic settlement in July 1811. At the time, the young priest's pathway of service remained unsettled. He had graduated first in his class in medical school but had entered the Seminary of Saint Sulpice upon graduation, distinguished himself academically, and joined the Sulpicians upon ordination. Bruté was teaching at the restored Sulpician seminary at Rennes in 1810 when Bishop-elect Flaget recruited the talented thirty-one-year-old priest for missionary service in America. Although the Sulpicians of Baltimore persuaded Bruté to accept a temporary professorship at Baltimore, Bishop Flaget persisted in his efforts to recruit him to Kentucky. At the time, Bruté nurtured two other dramatically contrasting possibilities. The first was to return to France in an effort to join the reconsolidation of Catholic belief and practice in the Napoleonic and Restoration aftermath of the French Revolution, in which Bruté as a boy had served as a secret courier to imprisoned Catholics and royalists (Bruté's father administered royal domains in Brittany), laymen and priests who were awaiting trial or, more commonly, execution. Second, Bruté contemplated gaining permission to bring the Sulpician mission, the preparation of clergy, to the French-connected regions of China and Southeast Asia. As it turned out, however, the Mountain, Valley, and Village fifty-two miles from Baltimore would prove to be Bruté's destined service, followed by five demanding years on the frontier as the first bishop of Vincennes, Indiana.

As in most cases, Bruté's destiny took a few years to define itself. In the summer of 1811, Bruté and Mother Seton became friends when Seton helped Bruté with his English pronunciation by reading aloud with him from *The Imitation of Christ*. At the same time, Bruté met and was befriended by Mrs. Melmoth, the retired actress, then summering on a small farm she owned in the area and attending Mass frequently. When Mrs. Melmoth returned to New York, Bruté kept in touch by letter. In the course of his brief stay, Bruté noted the burden borne by Dubois as sole priest on the staff of the college, chaplain to the sisters (which meant saying a very early daily Mass), and, filling in when necessary, parish priest in the Village.

Bruté, however, was called back to Baltimore for the time being. In the summer of 1812, Bishop Carroll—whom Bruté wished would spend more time at the Baltimore seminary—sent Bruté to Talbot and Queen Anne's Counties for missionary work and supervised preaching to improve his English further. That summer, Bruté received a letter from DuBourg saying that he had recommended him to Sulpician superior John Tessier for transfer to Mount Saint Mary's College at Emmitsburg. Bruté's arrival at Mount Saint Mary's allowed this institution to make the transition from a *petit sémi- naire* preparing students for Baltimore to a full-service seminary offering the instruction in philosophy, theology, Scripture, and liturgy required for ordination.

Given the comparable expansion previously put into effect at Georgetown, three major seminaries had surfaced within twenty-two years of Carroll's consecration as bishop. Thus, on 8 October 1812, an aging Carroll journeyed out to the Mountain to confer the tonsure (clerical status) on seven seminarians studying for ordination. Within three years, Mount Saint Mary's had produced one priest, John Hickey, and had a deacon and four clerics nearing ordination. In contrast to the urban environment at Baltimore, the seminarians of Mount Saint Mary's were living a rugged outdoor life in quasi-frontier circumstances, which included continuing work on buildings and grounds.

At long last, with Bruté's arrival, John Dubois had a Sulpician colleague—"Little Brother", Dubois called the young priest—to assist in instruction, chaplain's duties, and parish work (Mass, sick calls, weddings, funerals) when the pastor of the Village church, Charles Duhamel, a priest of the Society of the Holy Ghost, required assistance. Mother Seton and her sisters could now enjoy the spiritual direction of two contrasting but complementary chaplains: the kindly, direct, matter-of-fact missioner John Dubois; and the erudite, ascetic Simon Bruté, whose streak of mysticism was balanced by science, solid learning, and a physician's skills at diagnosis. For the remainder of her life, until her death in 1821, Mother Seton—so sensitive to direction throughout her life—received the guidance she and her sisters required in their Martha-and-Mary lives. On Mother Seton's part, all complaints to Bishop Carroll ceased; and although Bruté was called away from 1815 to 1818 for other duties, he and Mother Seton carried on a steady correspondence that met her requirements for spiritual direction when the Angel of Death reentered her life in full force.

To France and back

Aside from his pastoral and chaplaincy skills, as a Sulpician, Simon Bruté had academic ambitions: not only in teaching future priests, the very purpose of his society, but also in research and writing. Curiously enough, for such an otherworldly figure, Bruté was a proven academic administrator as well. In 1812 John Carroll appointed Louis William DuBourg, president of Saint Mary's College, the apostolic administrator of the Diocese of Louisiana. Secular priest Jean-Baptiste Paquiet, an expert in natural philosophy (science), succeeded DuBourg as president and served for three years until reaching the age of retirement. In 1815 the Society turned to Simon Bruté, a medically trained scientist, as Paquiet's replacement. Bruté likewise served for three years and helped establish a growing science-friendly culture among Baltimore Sulpicians that lasted into the midcentury.

Bruté inaugurated his presidency with a promotional visit to France in the company of young William Seton, for whom Mother Seton had arranged an internship with Filicchi Brothers in Leghorn. Landing in Bordeaux on 22 May 1815, Bruté found the royalist city in an uproar following Napoleon's escape from the Island of Elba on 1 March, which made it impossible for Bruté to proceed to Paris for consultations at Saint-Sulpice, as planned, once he had dispatched Seton to Leghorn under the protection of the American consul. He proceeded to Rennes for a reunion with his mother and, most likely, to prepare his library for shipment to the United States, which failed to happen because funds never became available. Once peace was declared on 17 July 1815, Bruté went on a tour of seminaries in northern and central France, recruiting young clerics for the American mission. He recruited three, and they sailed with him for the United States on the *Blooming Rose* on 17 October 1815.

Not much to show for six months abroad—outwardly, at least. Inwardly, though, Bruté's life was coming into sharper focus and continued to do so as he successfully conducted affairs for two more years at Saint Mary's College in Baltimore. As Bruté served as president of the college, however, his thoughts returned increasingly to the Mountain and its adjacent communities of layfolk in Emmitsburg and Sisters of Charity in St. Joseph's Valley. Bruté had departed for France still attracted to a life of teaching, scholarship, and literary production. Given his distinctive background as priest, theologian, and scientist, a first-rate Sulpician appointment was his for the asking in France, perhaps at Saint-Sulpice itself. The sheer inconclusiveness of Bruté's six months in France, however, intensified his gratitude for finding himself on the American mission in the service of a nascent church that he could serve as a Sulpician educator. American ambition coalesced even further when Bruté and his three newly recruited missionaries arrived in Baltimore in time to be present for the death of John Carroll, aged eighty, Father of the Roman Catholic Church in the United States, on Sunday, 3 December 1815, and to attend the Solemn Requiem Mass in Saint Peter's procathedral the following Tuesday.

Bruté's younger French friend, meanwhile, the priest Félicité Robert de Lamennais, was then entering upon one of the most important writing careers in France in the first half of the nineteenth century: a career that brought him to the verge of a cardinalate in its Catholic phase, then earned him papal condemnation and a place on the Index when he sought to recast the Church in political terms. In 1817 Lamennais urged Bruté to devote himself to writing a foundational and comprehensive history of Roman Catholicism in North America as a guide to the American Catholic future. By that time, however, Bruté—while he continued to write innumerable letters of advice and counsel and journalize his life and times—had left scholarship behind. Upon his return to the Mountain, Valley, and Village of Emmitsburg in 1818, he devoted himself to the education of an American clergy via the ordination program at Mount Saint Mary's College and also helped the Sisters of Charity of Saint Joseph establish themselves in other American places. Saint Mary's Seminary in Baltimore, ran Bruté's line of thinking, served the Archdiocese of Boston and its suffragan sees. The Mount Saint Mary's program, by contrast, would educate clergy for dioceses newly or yet to be created on the far frontier and would devote itself as well to opening the priesthood to young men of less-than-privileged backgrounds, American-born and immigrants alike. Mount Saint

Mary's would refashion itself as a national seminary devoted to a national Catholic ideal; and Simon Bruté would serve there until 1834, achieving the kind of greatness that Benjamin Jowett of Balliol College, Oxford, would later claim comes from being at the heart of a great institution.

Ironically, Bruté would in time become one of the last of the first-generation French Sulpician bishops in America, even as a second generation of Anglo-American and Irish-American bishops (along with the first American-born cardinal) were receiving priestly training on the Mountain.

The Angel of Death visits thrice

Mother Seton, meanwhile, was living out the final years of her life. During this time, the death of two of her three daughters continued that ghastly harvest of loved ones—father, husband, two beloved sisters-in-law—that, like motherhood, had so defined her. Mother Seton's very motherhood, the bedrock of her earthly and spiritual identity, would become a source of pain and loss that tested her faith and weakened her will to carry on.

Americans of the late eighteenth and nineteenth centuries lived with death as commonplace. During the yellow fever outbreaks of 1793, Philadelphia devolved into a City of Death reminiscent of bubonic plague outbreaks of the Middle Ages. In this period, Baltimore suffered outbreaks of yellow fever nearly every other year. Smallpox joined yellow fever in regularity in the first two decades of the nineteenth century. Life spans in general were short, and infant and child mortality rates soared. In many cases, parents—knowing that they might lose a third or half (or even more!) of their offspring—feared bonding with children who might not survive until adulthood. The death of older offspring, then, bore a full weight of sorrow for parents whose children had become beloved family members.

Mother Seton passed twice through the shadow of the Valley of Death with the loss of her oldest child, Anna Maria (Anina), and her youngest, Rebecca (Bec). What we know of these two deathbed scenes comes mainly from Elizabeth Seton's journals and letters, which detail and document her daughters' nobility of spirit and their mother's anguish. Indeed, the emotional suffering so evident in these reports renders them almost intrusive to read, as if one were overhearing an outcry of sorrow one had no right to hear.

Temperamentally most like her mother, Anna had lived side by side with her mother during her father's final days in the Leghorn lazaretto and had herself subsequently almost died of scarlet fever. For the rest of her short life, she remained her mother's confidante and best friend and followed her enthusiastically into the Church. As a teenager, Anna grew into a sociable, attractive young woman (her mother noted with maternal approval Anna's fullness of figure) and wanted everything Elizabeth Bayley had wanted at that age: dancing, a beau, marriage. Yet Anna also shared her mother's religiosity; and when Anna's intended (or, more correctly, hoped to be intended) went back to his home island of Martinique for a visit but did not return, remaining there to marry a local girl, the religiosity in Anna surfaced and took hold of her identity. Moving to Emmitsburg, she became a beloved member of her mother's community, specializing in preparing the youngest children at Saint Joseph's School for First Communion.

Tragedy thereupon built upon tragedy. In early 1811 the Seton family curse, tuberculosis, which had carried off her father and two of her aunts now attacked Anina. To help her daughter maintain her strength, Mother Seton had two horses saddled, and the two of them rode together, side by side, on the roads and pathways of Valley and Mountain. But it was no use. By the fall of 1811, Anna had been moved to a small bedroom adjacent to the convent chapel, fitted with a carpet and a stove against the impending winter. By January 1812, Mrs. Seton was massaging the cold feet of her emaciated, coughing daughter, wracked with pain and drenched in cold sweat. Anna received the last sacraments on 30 January and on the 31st asked to be received into the sisterhood. Following her vows, Anna slipped into terminal decline. "I can no longer look at you, my dear Crucifix", she murmured toward the end, "but I enter my agony with my Saviour—I drink the cup with him—yes adorable Lord, your will and yours alone be done. I will it too. I leave my dearest Mother because you will it."[17] Anna died shortly thereafter and was buried next to her aunts Harriet and Cecilia.

Elizabeth Seton sank into a great grief. When she visited Anna's grave to place flowers on the headstone, a fearsome snake darted from cover and slithered across the gravesite. It seemed as if nature, or Death itself in the biblical guise of the Evil One, were mocking her. Rarely, if ever, would Elizabeth Seton fall into such morbidity. "Oh my dear ones," Seton lamented in her journal, "companions of worms and reptiles! And the beautiful soul *where*?"[18]

John Dubois felt that he would have to be a great saint himself—a Saint Francis de Sales, for example—to deal effectively with such sorrow in such an intensely religious but beleaguered figure. He and Bruté consoled the bereft Mother Seton with Scripture, simple expressions of theology, and encouragement based on faith in experience, on daily life, and, most importantly, on the religious life itself: or, as Bruté formulated this counsel, on faith and hope anchored in humility, patience, trust, and continuing service to others. The advice of one saint to another, perhaps, but in a few short years, he would personally feel the full weight of Mother Seton's loss—feel it as a wrenching in the pit of his stomach, a dagger in his heart, feel it to the point when grief edges into despair—when Bruté would enter into the long vigil of decline and death of yet another of Mrs. Seton's daughters, whom Bruté loved as if she were his younger sister.

Even as Anna lay dying, Elizabeth's youngest daughter, Rebecca, born in 1802, slipped and fell on ice and incurred a serious rupture, which Rebecca concealed, not wanting to distract her mother, who was attending the dying Anna Maria. In the years that followed, Rebecca grew into a sickly, pain-ridden youngster who walked with a pronounced limp. Over the years, Elizabeth Seton—who refused to believe that nothing could be done to cure Bec—had her daughter diagnosed by a number of physicians, but Bec's condition eluded the medical insights of the early nineteenth century. By the time of her First Communion, Rebecca could walk (and not too well at that) only with crutches. Soon, she rarely walked; she remained indoors or was taken around in a hand-drawn cart by Joe, an African American gravedigger. Eventually, even these excursions became impossible. When Rebecca grew unable to sleep through the night, Elizabeth Seton would spend hours sitting in a chair in Rebecca's bedroom, cradling her daughter in her arms.

By the fall of 1816, it was obvious to all that Rebecca's life was drawing to a close. In the aftermath of Anna Maria's death, Simon Bruté had reached out to a grieving Elizabeth Seton. Now the two of them—penitent and confessor bound by affinities of piety and temperament, Rebecca's mother and Rebecca's self-described older brother—entered into the Valley of the Shadow of Death along with John Dubois and the Sisters of Charity community as Rebecca endured her final ordeal. Being away in Baltimore, Bruté kept in touch with Rebecca through notes sent back and forth via the normal traffic between Baltimore and Emmitsburg. Rebecca also kept a portrait sketch of Bruté at the foot of her bed during her final days. Like her sister Anna Maria, Rebecca was received into the sisterhood by John Dubois before her death. Held, as usual, in her mother's arms, Rebecca died slightly before four o'clock on the morning of 4 November 1816. For eight minutes or more, Mrs. Seton—a pietà, silent in grief—held the body of her child in her arms. "*Mulierem fortem*", noted Dubois of the scene.[19]

Brave woman, indeed! And brave daughter as well—to meet death with such faith and courage. Four years earlier, Anna Maria's death had thrown Mother Seton into a dark night of the soul as a snake slithered across the child's grave. Now, as the earth fell over Rebecca's coffin, a Te Deum arose in her heart, "a hymn", Mother Seton wrote, "to the holy spirit [of Rebecca] returning". In the days that followed, she would look from her room, her "snug little nest with a window looking directly on the little woods where my darlings sleep", as she wrote to Julia Scott, and where "it keeps up my heart to look over twenty times a day, first thing in the morning and last at night and think: no more pain now and up, up, up the beautiful joyous souls."[20]

Final years

Simon Bruté returned to the Mountain in the summer of 1818 as professor of theology, vice president of the college, and chaplain and confessor to the Sisters. He also found time to develop a pastoral practice among the laity of the region, based out of Saint Joseph's Church in Emmitsburg. Now ordained, Samuel Sutherland Cooper was assigned to Emmitsburg in 1818. Mrs. Seton initially had great hopes for his success at Saint Joseph's, but the mental instability that Bishop Carroll had earlier noted in Cooper had grown even more pronounced, forcing Cooper at one point to break off his seminary studies temporarily. After a mere nine months as pastor, Cooper left Emmitsburg for Georgia when parishioners of Saint Joseph's rebelled at his monomaniacal advocacy of total abstinence from alcohol and his demands that those who had been publicly intoxicated stand in church as penitents at Sunday Mass. John Hickey, the first graduate of the ordination program at the Mountain (as a young priest, Hickey had the distinction of being upbraided by Mother Seton to prepare his sermons with greater care), replaced Cooper at Saint Joseph's and spent the bulk of his long career of service on the Mountain in one or another capacity.

In September 1820 Mother Seton suffered a serious episode of lung disease. Bruté rushed up from the Village to administer the last sacraments. Mother Seton survived this attack but went into steady decline. When it came to her sons, however, a thoroughly maternal Mrs. Seton allowed no obstacle to stand in her way, not even a fatal onslaught of tuberculosis. To secure son William an appointment as a midshipman, United States Navy, she organized a letter-writing campaign on his behalf by influential friends to the relevant authorities, including Benjamin Crowninshield, secretary of the U.S. Navy, and Daniel Tompkins, vice president of the

United States. When his midshipman's appointment came through, Mother Seton sent William fifty dollars toward the purchase of a uniform and later had the pleasure, shortly before her death, of having William show up at the Mountain for an eight-day visit, looking quite smart in his midshipman's uniform. Second son Richard had considered entering the wholesale grocery business in Baltimore, but his mother had better plans. Turning to Antonio Filicchi, Mrs. Seton placed Richard in the Filicchi countinghouse in Leghorn, where he acquired the skills required to qualify as a supercargo (representative of a ship's owner) aboard merchant ships or a civilian captain's clerk aboard a U.S. Navy vessel. Thus, Mother Seton launched her sons into respectable careers—and was not above pulling a few strings to do so. She pulled these strings, moreover, while in decline, focused simultaneously on her sons' earthly and spiritual futures and the Final Things that awaited her.

On 2 January 1821, John Dubois administered the last rites. On 3 January Simon Bruté opened a retreat for children making their First Communion the following day and invited Mother Seton to receive the Eucharist from him on the morrow as well. Sixteen years earlier, in Italy, it had been the Eucharist, the Real Presence, that had initially and so vividly attracted Elizabeth Bayley Seton to the Catholicism that became her life. But she would not last the night. Mother Seton died shortly after midnight on 4 January. Sensing that the end was near, Sister Anastasia Nabbs, Mother Seton's housekeeper since Baltimore days, summoned Sisters Mary Xavier Clark, the assistant superior, Cecilia O'Conway, Susan Clossy, Josephine Seton, and several others to Mother Seton's room. As they knelt around the bed in which Mother Seton, propped up by pillows, reclined semi-upright against the headboard, Sister Mary Xavier recited the Gloria in Excelsis and portions of the Magnificat in French, as Mother Seton loved to hear these prayers recited. Following her death, Simon Bruté advised the sisters to ensure that Mother Seton's journals and letters be scrupulously preserved. In time, this lifelong record would document a Christian pilgrimage of love—Protestant in its beginnings, Catholic in its culmination—that constituted one of America's finest gifts to the universal Church.[21]

10

Baltimore 1821

The Cathedral of the Assumption reprises the
Roman Catholicism of the Early Republic

On 31 May 1821, Archbishop Ambrose Maréchal, assisted by Bishop Jean-Louis Lefebvre de Cheverus of Boston and Bishop Henry Conwell of Philadelphia and attendant clergy, trustees, and laity gathered in Baltimore for the dedication of an almost completed Cathedral of the Assumption, designed by the recently deceased Benjamin Henry Latrobe, lead architect for the Capitol in the District of Columbia. The dedication ceremonies brought to a triumphant conclusion thirty-one years of dreaming, planning, designing, fundraising, building, postponing, repeated fundraising, and further building since *Ex hac apostolicae*—the papal brief appointing John Carroll first bishop of Baltimore—had arrived from Rome in April 1790, charging Carroll with (among other duties) the construction of a diocesan cathedral. Discerning members of the congregation that May 1821 morning, appreciative of the emergent public architecture of the United States, might very well have aligned the Cathedral of the Assumption with a range of Classical Revival buildings, beginning with the Capitol itself, through which the Early Republic of the United States was defining itself as heir to the ideals and politics of ancient Greece and the Roman Republic. For the twenty-first-century observer, that alignment takes on an even deeper meaning. Fronted by a perfectly rendered Greek Revival portico graced by eight Ionic columns, its interior space protected by a domed basilica hovering over a cuneiform floor plan, with a smaller dome sheltering the sanctuary and the choir, the cathedral was at the same time recognizably Roman Catholic, serving the space requirements and the practicalities of liturgy and worship. It was also in dialogue with other Latrobe-designed structures in its ability to fuse utility with a larger resonance via the Classical Revival idiom that Latrobe and his contemporaries and occasional collaborators Thomas Jefferson, Maximilian Godefroy, and Charles Bulfinch were in the process of developing.

Thus, Latrobe's Cathedral of the Assumption, being dedicated that May morning, reprised and emanated the power of Classical Revival to resonate with and project the Early Republic. When Latrobe in 1804 had presented John Carroll with two proposals, Gothic and Roman Revival, the bishop deliberately chose the Classical Revival alternative as more perfectly expressing not only Carroll's taste in architectural styles but also his entire program for Roman Catholicism in the United States. It was one thing for the Sulpicians to choose Gothic Revival for their seminary Chapel of the Presentation—enlivened by its architect, Maximilian Godefroy, a faculty member at Saint Mary's, with the Romantic Sublime—because the chapel was an academic building, for which Gothic was appropriate, and although open for use by the public, the chapel was primarily a semiprivate institutional building. The Cathedral of the Assumption, by contrast, represented the Diocese of Baltimore, the official and formally established Church in the United States. The American church had come to this position after a long repression, having earned it by fully participating in the eight-year Revolutionary War, which was followed by the adoption of a federal constitution guaranteeing the right to religious freedom. Thus, the See of Baltimore expressed the Church Militant—that is, the Church in American society—at the deepest level of institutional identity in spiritual and social terms. Catholicism belonged in this new Republic. That had always been John Carroll's belief and practice as prefect apostolic and bishop, and American Catholic architecture should do its best to reflect that connection. Spiritually, American Catholicism belonged to the universal Church, whose symbol of unity was the bishop of Rome; but that spiritual allegiance to universality depended on the vitality of American Catholicism as a localized entity brought to fullness by a bishop and diocesan organization. Catholicism, moreover—and Carroll was especially sensitive to this fact—shared the United States with a Protestant majority, a sheer matter of numbers that set the tone for Christian America. Forgive, if not forget, the persecutions of the past. No less than George Washington himself in his first months as president had assured American Catholics of their respected place in this new Republic.

Just a year before Carroll chose Latrobe's Roman suggestion, for example, Boston Catholics had completed the Church of the Holy Cross, designed for them gratis by Charles Bulfinch, the icon-creating architect of the region (the Massachusetts State House, Faneuil Hall, the Tontine Crescent, Harvard's University Hall), in the fused London (St Martin Ludgate), Roman (Santo Spirito in Sassia, Santa Maria Vallicella) style that Bulfinch would also use one year later for the New North Church—like Old North Church, an iconic expression of Boston Protestantism. One fifth of the seventeen-thousand-dollar cost of Holy Cross was raised by a committee of prominent Protestant donors headed by former president John Adams. The Boston Protestant artist Henry Sargent—who had studied with American expatriate artist Benjamin West in London and had received encouragement there from another American expatriate artist, John Singleton Copley—painted an outsize *Christ Crucified* to place above the Church of the Holy Cross altar. So grateful was the Roman Catholic community to Bulfinch for joining its new place of worship with the best of Boston that it presented the architect with that most Bostonian of gifts, a silver tea service, now on display at the Museum of Fine Arts.

An earned patriotism

Despite such hopeful developments, one must recall that John Carroll's patriotism existed between a Court of Rome, with its preference for a Catholic polity of decidedly conservative organization, and a lingering tradition of anti-Catholicism in the United States that would see anti-Catholic legislation remain on the books of some states decades after the adoption of a federal Constitution and Bill of Rights. By midcentury, moreover, massive immigration from Catholic Ireland would fan this lingering distrust into full-fledged paranoia and violence. But that was in the future. For the time being, the Early Republic offered welcomed signs of general acceptance of Roman Catholics, even in Boston.

The nexus, focus, and corroboration of this détente were George Washington's associations and, in some cases, warm friendships with Americans he characterized as South Irish—that is, Irish Catholics—of a certain social standing who conspicuously found their way into his diary before, during, and after the Revolutionary War. Prewar associates included county clerk Edward Barry, John Barry, and Dennis McCarty of Fairfax County, as well as another Barry, William, of neighboring Prince William County. The Barrys were politically active in the immemorial manner of the Irish; indeed, a poll for an election to the House of Burgesses from Prince William County in 1741 shows some twenty-nine unmistakably Irish names politically active at the time, and hence most likely known to Washington, who served in the House of Burgesses from 1759 to 1774. Also before the war, Washington had business relationships with Charles Carroll of Carrollton, who became a close congressional ally of Washington during the war. Charles Carroll's cousin John came to Washington's attention in 1776 when Charles and John accompanied Benjamin Franklin and Silas Deane on a diplomatic mission to Canada. Lieutenant Colonels Stephen Moylan and John Fitzgerald served on Washington's staff during the war, following which Washington was initiated into the Friendly Sons of Saint Patrick of Philadelphia and thereby came into contact with the Irish Catholic elite of that city. Both before and after his presidency, Washington maintained social connections with members of the South Irish community of Alexandria, Virginia; the mayor, Colonel John Fitzgerald, remained a close friend and frequently dined with the former president. During his presidency of Georgetown Academy, Sulpician Louis William DuBourg dined at Mount Vernon on 10 July 1797, thanks to John Carroll's good friends James and Joanna Barry, and met with the approval of his host, who agreed to an appearance at Georgetown Academy.

It is not documented if and when George Washington and John Carroll had ever met before Carroll dined with Washington at Mount Vernon on 11 June 1799, six months preceding Washington's death on 14 December 1799 after a brief illness. We do have, however, the later (1855) testimony of Washington's adopted son, George Washington Parke Custis, that "the late Doctor Carroll was an intimate acquaintance of Washington. He was more, Sir: From his exalted worth as a minister of God, his stainless character as a man, and above all, his distinguished services as a patriot of the Revolution, Doctor Carroll stood high in the esteem and affections of the *Pater Patriae*."[1] Indeed, given Carroll's service during the Revolution, his postwar position as prefect apostolic and bishop, his letter of congratulations to Washington upon the occasion of his inauguration as president as well as Washington's gracious reply, Carroll's extensive connections among the Federalist leadership, and his kinship with Washington's steady political and business ally, Charles Carroll of Carrollton, it is difficult to imagine that Washington and Carroll did not meet earlier—perhaps as early as the mission to Canada in 1776 but certainly within the twenty-three years between then and the dinner of 11 June 1799 that Washington recorded in his diary. Furthermore, Bishop Carroll's brother Daniel Carroll of Upper Marlborough—a former Maryland state senator and subsequent member of the Continental Congress, the Constitutional Convention, and the House of Representatives—was a prominent property owner of Maryland lands designated

for the District of Columbia and from 1791 to 1795 (in an age not excessively both-
ered by conflict of interest) served as commissioner for planning the district and
capital city of Washington. According to the diary, Daniel Carroll's first dinner
and overnight stay at Mount Vernon dated back to 10 January 1773, and this social
connection strengthened in Washington's later years.

In addition, Georgetown and Alexandria were in these years Catholic-friendly
places, not only because of Georgetown Academy but also because of the presence
of such prominent and lively Roman Catholics with Mount Vernon connections as
Colonel John Fitzgerald and his wife, Jane Digges Fitzgerald; the socially active James
and Joanna Barry; and Thomas Law and his wife, Elizabeth Parke Custis Law, Martha
Washington's granddaughter. John Parke Custis, the late father of George Washington Parke and Elizabeth Parke Custis, was of Irish descent. George Washington
himself, their adoptive grandfather, had an Irish family connection. Former Maryland
Governor Thomas Sim Lee, a convert, and his Catholic-born wife, Mary Digges Lee,
spent winters in Georgetown and hence were most likely also part of the Catholic
coterie that in 1794 completed construction of Holy Trinity Church, the first Catholic church in the region, and staffed its first board of trustees.

The fact is, John Carroll, Federalist, enjoyed personal and social connections
with Irish Catholics of his class, among whom access to the company-loving
George Washington was one of their privileges. On a less consistent basis, Washington enjoyed socializing with an Irish sea captain in the employ of Alexandrian
merchants, Sulpician DuBourg, two Georgetown students, and a Spanish officer
of Irish descent by the name of O'Higgins. Artisan employees of Irish descent
enjoyed access of another sort at Mount Vernon. Washington's willingness to hire
South Irish employees underscores his acceptance of the Catholic population of
the Republic—Anglo-American Marylanders, German Catholics, and South Irish
alike—as respected citizens. Sensing this acceptance (which is evident in Washington's letter of reply to Catholic congratulations on 12 March 1790), the Federalist
Catholic elite who dominated the still-small Catholic population made Washington
a welcomed patron and protector as well as the leading non-Catholic authenticator
of their acceptance into the new order now beginning (*novus ordo seclorum*) and celebrated in the national seal.

John Carroll both believed in and desperately hoped for Catholics' love of
country and their support of American political values and protocols, especially in
matters touching upon the separation of church and state. In return for American
Catholics' decisive help in the Revolution, their fostering of the Franco-Spanish
alliance, and their continuing affirmative citizenship, Carroll sought an extension
of Washington's respect, friendliness, and gratitude. Carroll realized the precarious-
ness of this reciprocity, and it disquieted him greatly on those occasions when he
believed this reciprocity and acceptance might face the challenges and restrictions
unleashed by the Puritan Revolt of the 1640s and permanently codified by the Glorious Revolution of 1688. Hence, he was cautious in his dealings with the Court
of Rome whenever Roman interference in American affairs appeared even slightly
on the horizon. And hence the eloquent prayer for the welfare of the Republic and
its officials that he composed in 1791, urging that it be offered in all churches at the
end of Mass on high feasts and national holidays. Carroll's prayer led off with a
hymn of praise and supplication to Almighty God, Who has revealed Himself to the

world through Jesus Christ, followed by prayers for the pope, the local bishop, and clergy, a total of two paragraphs and fifteen printed lines. Three dense paragraphs of thirty lines form the bulk of the prayer, with divine assistance being requested for the president, Congress, governors, members of state assemblies, judges, magistrates, and other public officers, and, finally, the people of the United States. In the sixth and last paragraph, a little more than thirteen lines, Carroll prays for the American Catholic community as a whole, past and present. "Finally," Carroll's prayer ends, "we pray to Thee, O Lord of mercy, to remember the souls of Thy servants departed who are gone before us with the sign of faith, and repose in the sleep of peace; the souls of our parents, relatives, and friends; of those who, when living, were members of this congregation, and particularly of such as are lately deceased; of all benefactors who, by their donations or legacies to this church, witnessed their zeal for the decency of divine worship and proved their claim to our grateful and charitable remembrance. To these, O Lord, and to all that rest in Christ, grant, we beseech Thee, a place of refreshment, light, and everlasting peace, through the same Jesus Christ, our Lord and Saviour. Amen."[2] Many things in Carroll's prayer deserve commentary; but from the perspective of the Cathedral of the Assumption, Carroll's prayer was also for "all benefactors who, by their donations or legacies to this church, witnessed their zeal for the decency of divine worship and proved their claim to our grateful and charitable remembrance".

Carroll wanted American Catholics to pray for public officials and the public realm and to pray for church donors and benefactors as well; for a church and the liturgy it supports constitute the prime expression at the local level of *ecclesia*, community, gathered together for worship and Eucharistic liturgy. From this perspective, a diocesan cathedral constituted the parish church of a diocese as a whole, at the apex of an ascending array of parish churches, just as a bishop embodied the fullness of the priesthood being exercised by his authorized clergy. A cathedral thus was essential to a fully established episcopal governance structure. Along with people, clergy, and bishop, a cathedral played its role in the constitutional quartet underlying diocesan formation. Indeed, in Catholic Europe, the chapter of cathedral canons constituted the electors of a bishop when a see became vacant. Now Carroll was faced with the challenge of bringing this essential component of Church governance into existence. The prospect of such a challenge—raising enough money to do so, first of all—was more than daunting. As Carroll confessed to Charles Plowden in a letter dated 13 November 1795, "I am now turning my thoughts towards a Cathedral Church here; but the greatness of the object terrifies me." The paragraph containing that confession is dominated by financial woes; among other things, the three hundred crowns Propaganda Fide remitted to Filicchi Brothers for transmittal to Carroll for the completion of the Georgetown Academy were two years late in arriving. That paragraph, moreover, is followed by notice of a sum authorized by President Washington himself to support two Catholic priests to be sent out to the Indians of the Illinois Territory as a gesture of friendship by the United States.[3]

Yet as Carroll's prayer for public officials and church benefactors also indicated, "zeal for the decency of divine worship" was also on his mind, which reminded him of the cathedral he was obliged to build. Connected to this cathedral was a transition that Carroll himself, along with Catholic Baltimore, was going through in matters liturgical. Centered in Maryland and southern Pennsylvania, the Roman

Catholicism of the colonial era was a missionary enterprise utilizing private chapels and Mass Houses and ministered to by Jesuits of the Maryland Mission of the English Province, who supported themselves through slave labor on their plantations. Mass and five of the seven sacraments (confirmation and holy orders required a bishop), conducted in private circumstances and restricted spaces, were administered by a single priest on circuit or attached to a plantation chapel. Mass vestments and sacred vessels were canonically correct yet simple enough to fit in a saddlebag. Many chalices, for example, could be unscrewed into two sections for easier packing.

Carefully written out and delivered in a quasi-academic manner, sermons tended to be instructional, keyed to an accurate transference of the faith. Scripture reading outside of the Mass—never a strong Roman Catholic practice—increased in colonial Maryland and Pennsylvania among the literate under Protestant influences. The recitation of the Rosary also supplemented attendance at Mass, which increasingly became a regular Sunday and holy day event in population centers. Manuals of meditation and private prayer—such as Richard Challoner's perennially popular *The Garden of the Soul* (1740)—and an array of emotionally satisfying prayers and meditations were available for private or family usage.

This is the culture of prayer and worship that John Carroll returned to in 1774 and in which, along with his fellow ex-Jesuits, he functioned as a priest on mission in rural Maryland. As ex-Jesuits, moreover, Carroll and his colleagues had not been formed in a liturgically exacting tradition. Although they were clerks regular, and hence capable of living a common life, Jesuits were also missionary oriented—accustomed, that is, to solitary ministries in non-Catholic places. They did not chant the Divine Office in common, as did monks and friars; nor were they fond of elaborately ceremonial Masses, even when they were operating colleges or urban churches in Catholic Europe. For a while, in fact, while serving as prefect apostolic, Carroll grew even edgier in his liturgical preferences. In 1787 he wrote a private letter to the English priest Joseph Berington—whose *State and Behavior of English Catholics from the Reformation to the Year 1780* (1780) had been of use to Carroll in framing his reply to Charles Wharton three years earlier—in which Carroll underscored the irony that small ancient churches in the Middle East, as well as Greek and Armenian Catholics, enjoyed the privilege of vernacular liturgies when such a privilege was denied the English-speaking world. In the United States, moreover, both the lack of books and illiteracy made it difficult to obtain any level of self-instruction in the faith. A vernacular Mass could help the less privileged sectors of the Catholic community, including Roman Catholic slaves, to receive instruction along with worship and Eucharist. As bishop, however, Carroll, realizing the avant-garde nature of such opinions as well as Court of Rome resistance, backed off from his (what seemed at the time) radical proposals. The diocesan synod he convened in 1791, though, allowed for vernacular hymns for benediction of the Blessed Sacrament and mandated vernacular prayers (the Lord's Prayer, the Hail Mary, the Apostles' Creed, and the Acts of Faith, Hope, and Charity) at the conclusion of Mass.

French military chaplains, Sulpicians, and the rise of Baltimore as an American Catholic city imbued with French culture coalesced to create not only in Carroll but also in the larger Roman Catholic American community an appreciation of the full tradition of liturgical worship in Catholicism. During the Revolutionary War, French army and navy chaplains introduced Protestants and colonial Catholics to such ambitious liturgies as Solemn High Mass, Solemn High Requiem Mass in conjunction with a military funeral, and Te Deum services of thanksgiving. Sunday morning visits to French naval ships at anchor, moreover, involved Mass followed by refreshments for invited audiences of Catholics and Protestants alike. The exactingly conducted liturgical services held at Saint Mary's Church in Philadelphia on behalf of the French embassy also introduced the Catholic liturgy to members of Congress and to the general public at times of national prayer, mourning, and celebration.

The Sulpicians, moreover, brought to Baltimore a community of diocesan priests committed to an exacting conduct of the liturgy at its most inclusive as part of their teaching mission on behalf of diocesan clergy as well as their responsibility for the conduct of one of the most prominent churches of Paris, Saint-Sulpice, which served as the largest parish in France. Even as they arrived, Carroll envisioned the Sulpicians as his cathedral clergy. They were learned and experienced administrators, for one thing, and could thus advise him in the manner of the cathedral canons in Europe. Masters of liturgy, Sulpicians also utilized Gregorian chant, the organ, and hymnology in their services. The dedication in 1808 of the Chapel of the Presentation at the Sulpician seminary and Saint Mary's College on Paca Street—with its architecture, organ, choir, Gregorian chant, and liturgies—set even higher standards for Baltimore, which was now the third most populous city in the nation and whose large French Catholic population had helped make it among the most sophisticated, and hence most appreciative of a developed cathedral-based liturgical culture. Carroll was already utilizing his procathedral, Saint Peter's, in an augmented, intensified manner as an episcopal pulpit: as a way, that is, of speaking directly to the people of his diocese as their bishop. Witness his heartfelt sermon upon returning from England, expressing his fears of not being up to the challenge that confronted him and facing divine judgment for such a failure.

Carroll found yet another purpose that a cathedral—even such an unpretentious, temporary cathedral as Saint Peter's—offered a bishop: for religiously reinforced civic statements, as in the *Discourse on General Washington* that Carroll delivered on 22 February 1800, following Washington's death on 14 December 1799. Some 350 funereal sermons, speeches, and discourses in honor of Washington's passing, including Carroll's, made their way into print. Their use of scriptural and classical heroes to evoke Washington's life and character document not only a biography of Washington as a public figure but also a compatible fusion of biblical and classical imagery underway since Dante in the High Middle Ages and thereafter accelerated into the eighteenth century. Ironically, the tribute to Washington destined to last— Henry Lee's "first in war, first in peace, and first in the hearts of his countrymen"— was devoid of classical or biblical imagery. Aside from a single comparison of Washington's youthful experiences as a frontier surveyor to the Spartan training of youth by hardship in Rome, however, and two brief comparisons of Washington's death to Moses on the summit of Mount Pisgah bidding farewell to the Israelites as they entered the Promised Land, Carroll's discourse is also remarkably devoid of biblical and classical ornament. Addressing his audience as his fellow citizens, however, does give Carroll's discourse a classical overtone; and Carroll does cite one biblical text—the Wisdom of Solomon (8:9–18)—twice and at great length. Just like the speaker of the Wisdom of Solomon, Carroll concludes, Washington sought divine guidance at times of crisis and thus became an agent of Providence in terms of the successful outcome of the Revolutionary War and the organization and continued well-being of the Republic. "May these United States flourish in pure and undefiled religion," Carroll ended, "in morality, peace, union, liberty, and the enjoyment of their excellent Constitution, as long as respect, honour, and veneration shall gather round the name of Washington; that is, whilst there shall be any surviving record of human events."[4]

Time's wingèd chariot and two cornerstones

How would he himself be remembered, Carroll might well have asked himself as, at age sixty-five, he prepared his discourse in praise of Washington, who had died so unexpectedly at sixty-seven after a brief illness of two weeks. A decade of his episcopate had already passed. How many years remained? And could he push ahead with the development of a cathedral in those years? How much longer would an overcrowded brick chapel on Saratoga Street be forced to serve as the procathedral of the American church? Would he live to see a sequence of money, land, architecture, and construction be brought to conclusion? Carroll began the money sequence (the most difficult) in 1795 with a subscription program that continued into the new century. A lottery followed in the spring of 1803. By 1805, however, the first site purchased by the trustees for the cathedral at Pratt and Exeter Streets, once the best part of town, had lost its luster as Baltimore moved north. Even worse, preliminary grading revealed that the site had been a Protestant cemetery, and descendants of the deceased buried there objected to its planned usage. Furthermore, the Sulpicians were convinced that another site was better located and, hence, more suitable. And so the trustees, at their urging, sold the cemetery site in favor of two acres atop a gently rising hill in a better part of town, bounded by Charles, Mulberry, and Franklin Streets, with a fourth street, Cathedral Street, planned for a later date. A financial loss on the cemetery site, however, along with the cost of the new location—eventually agreed upon at twenty thousand dollars, payable in five interest-free installments (the owner, Revolutionary War hero Colonel John Eager Howard, admired Carroll)—depleted cash on hand for the project.

Still, Carroll pushed ahead with an elaborate cornerstone-laying ceremony on 7 July 1806. On a very hot day, some twenty priests in cassocks and surplices and a smaller number of seminarians proceeded up the hill in full pontifical regalia. Priests and seminarians antiphonally chanted from Psalm 126:

> *Nisi Dóminus aedificáverit domum,*
> *in vanum laboravérunt qui aedificant eam.*
> *Nisi Dóminus custodíerit civitátem,*
> *frustrà vígilat qui custódit eam.*

> Unless the LORD builds the house,
> those who build it labor in vain.
> Unless the LORD watches over the city,
> The watchman stays awake in vain.

While they chanted, Carroll sprinkled two cornerstones with holy water and offered blessings. Following the singing of "Veni Creator Spiritus" (Come Holy Spirit), Carroll briefly remarked on the importance of the morning's event, as etched on a copper plate affixed to the first cornerstone:

> The first stone of the Cathedral Church,
> To be erected for the honor of
> Almighty God, under the title
> Of Jesus and Mary, was placed
> This 7th day of July, 1806
> By the Right Rev. John, Bishop of Baltimore.

Alea iacta est! The die was cast, or, more colloquially, the dice had been thrown. Now that the cornerstones had been laid, there must be a cathedral, no matter how long the construction would take—or else there would be a grave embarrassment for the American church and the memory of its first bishop.[5]

Dashed Bonapartist hopes

The dedication ceremony over, Carroll returned to fundraising. (The Sulpicians sent him six hundred dollars in honor of the occasion.) Three years earlier, Carroll had hoped to raise a large sum from Napoleon Bonaparte, first consul (meaning virtual dictator) of France since late 1799. By the Concordat of 1801, Napoleon made peace with Pius VII and formally restored the Catholic Church in France on the condition that all bishops resign their sees, diocesan boundaries be redrawn, and new bishops be nominated by the state. Napoleon, in short, wanted the state to exercise influence over the Church as it had before the Revolution. A year later, under the provisions of the unilaterally declared Organic Articles that Napoleon described as a supplement to the Concordat, Napoleon claimed for the state further controls over councils, synods, seminaries, clergy, and papal supervision, while mandating adherence to a Gallican (nationalist) explication of Catholicism in France. Napoleon's uncle, the priest Joseph Fesch, kept his nephew close company in the Gallican distribution of honors that followed his nephew's reconciliation with the Church in 1802–1803 and intensified (if that were possible) after Napoleon's self-coronation as emperor of the French in the presence of Pius VII in Notre Dame Cathedral on 2 December 1804, as Napoleon snatched the imperial crown from the pope and crowned himself. In 1802, Napoleon's uncle was named archbishop of Lyon. In 1803 Archbishop Joseph Fesch was elevated to cardinal, and in 1804 he was named ambassador to the Court of Rome, followed by promotion to senator, count, and grand almoner of France in 1805.

From Carroll's perspective, all these developments, however imperfect, represented an improvement over the persecution of the Church during the French Revolution. Even Napoleon's assumption of the imperial crown—proclaimed by the senate and tribunate in May, then confirmed in a plebiscite—seemed to have Pius VII's approval, or why else would the pope travel to Paris with the intention of placing a crown on Napoleon's head before Napoleon so arrogantly gave him second billing? At the least, prior to the coronation, First Consul Napoleon and his uncle the archbishop of Lyon remained—from John Carroll's point of view—enough within the range of respectability for Carroll to seek a subvention from newly re-Catholicized France for a Catholic cathedral for the most Catholic and French city in the United States. Baltimore was now, since the Louisiana Purchase, the see city of the diocese responsible for the spiritual welfare of the French Catholic population of that vast region.

On Christmas Eve 1803, John Carroll, in a mixed-marriage ceremony held in the bride's home, joined Miss Elizabeth Patterson of Baltimore, an Episcopalian, in holy wedlock with Jérôme Bonaparte, youngest brother of the first consul of France. During the French Revolution, Philadelphia had become the refuge of such present and future luminaries as Louis Philippe, later the citizen king of France; the former bishop and future megadiplomat Charles Maurice de Talleyrand; Mozart's librettist, Lorenzo Da Ponte; the lawyer, economist, and literary gastronome Jean Anthelme Brillat-Savarin; and others of comparable notoriety. By 1803, however, both that era and the years 1798–1800 of undeclared but de facto war between France and the United States had ended via the Franco-American Convention of 1800 facilitated by First Consul Napoleon.

And so it was into friendly territory that Jérôme Bonaparte, a former naval officer turned army captain, arrived in the late spring or early summer of 1803 to call upon his former commanding officer, Captain Joshua Barney, a native of Baltimore, who had served in the West Indies as a commodore in the French navy between 1796 and 1802 before resigning and returning to his home city. By definition a celebrity, the nineteen-year-old Jérôme was enthusiastically received by Supreme Court judge Samuel Chase, leading merchants Jean-Charles-Marie-Louis Pascault, the marquis de Poléon, and William Patterson as well as other French or Francophile residents of that very pro-French city.

Early in Jérôme Bonaparte's visit, he was invited to a dinner party at the home of Louis Pascault. Among the guests were the Pattersons and their daughter Elizabeth, a good friend of the Pascaults' daughter Henriette. At seventeen going on eighteen, the Irish Protestant Elizabeth Patterson was already a noted (and very rich) dark-haired beauty, as her triple portrait painted by Gilbert Stuart in 1804 clearly attests. She was also, according to contemporary reports, more than a mere Francophile in a Francophile city. She wanted, rather, life on a grand scale in France itself.[6] In any event, as Henriette Pascault and Elizabeth Patterson stood looking out the window before the dinner guests arrived (so Madame Elizabeth Patterson Bonaparte told James Gallatin, son of the great American treasury secretary and diplomat Albert Gallatin, one wintry afternoon in Geneva in 1815), they espied the young men in French army uniforms approaching the house. "That man will by my husband!" exclaimed Henriette Pascault, pointing to the future French general Jean-Jacques Reubell. "Very well," proclaimed Elizabeth Patterson, "I will marry the other one", pointing to Jérôme Bonaparte.[7] Later that evening, Elizabeth Patterson found herself entangled—accidentally, it was claimed—in a gold chain that was part of Jérôme Bonaparte's military uniform, and the obliging young captain was forced to disentangle himself slowly from the Baltimore heiress held captive at his side. Observing this scene, perhaps, or other evidence of the couple's mutual attraction, William Patterson sent his daughter to the Virginia countryside to escape further attentions.[8]

William Patterson at first believed that he had the upper hand in the situation. He was, after all, a leading citizen of Baltimore and a financier of the late rebellion. During the Revolutionary War, Patterson had enjoyed close associations with General Jean-Baptiste Donatien de Vimeur, comte de Rochambeau, and Admiral Charles-Hector, comte d'Estaing. The late George Washington had been a friend of his, and he enjoyed friendships with the marquis de Lafayette and Charles Carroll of Carrollton. The Bonapartes, by contrast, were Italian arrivistes from Corsica, only recently (1768) made part of France.

Patterson, in short, thought that he had the advantage when it came to handling his daughter's attraction to young Bonaparte, whom she continued to see clandestinely before declaring to her parents her love for him and their desire to marry. At this point, the Pattersons folded, and on 29 October 1803, a marriage license for the couple was obtained from the Baltimore County Courthouse. Six days later, however, William Patterson received an alarming letter. "Is it possible, sir," queried its anonymous author,

> you can so far forget yourself, and the happiness of your child, as to consent to her marrying Mr. Bonaparte? If you knew him, you never would, as misery must be her portion—he who but a few months ago destroyed the peace and happiness of a respectable family in Nantz by promising marriage, then ruined, leaving her to misery and shame. What has been his conduct in the West Indies? There ruined a lovely young woman who had only been married for a few weeks! He parted her from her husband, and destroyed that family! And here, what is his conduct? At the very moment he was demanding your daughter in marriage he ruined a young French girl, whom he now leaves in misery! His conduct at Nantz and in the West Indies has already reached his brother's ears, and he dares not appear before him! His voyage to this country proves it! He now wishes to secure himself a home at your expense until things can be arranged for his return to France, when rest assured he will be the first to turn your daughter off, and laugh at your credulity!... What is here said may be depended upon, and much more might be said, for, without exception, he is the most profligate young man of the age.... Trust not his honor! there never was any in his family! Yours, A Friend.[9]

At this, William Patterson felt the vulnerability of his situation. Jérôme Bonaparte intended to seduce and abandon his daughter! Since he could not dissuade her from this marriage and preferred not to share this letter with her (or with his wife, most likely), and since the marriage license was already (and publicly) issued, his best course of action, Patterson must have reasoned, was to see his Episcopalian daughter married as quickly as possible in a Roman Catholic ceremony that would be binding in the United States—and especially binding in Catholic France and the Court of Rome—and do his best to keep the newly married couple as long as possible in the United States, bound together in legal matrimony. And so, on Christmas Eve 1803, the *Federal Gazette* of Baltimore reported on 27 December, the Reverend Bishop John Carroll joined in holy wedlock Mr. Jérôme Bonaparte, youngest brother of the first consul of the French Republic, and Miss Elizabeth Patterson, eldest daughter of William Patterson, Esquire, of this city. Performed at the Patterson manse, the ceremony was witnessed by Alexander J. Dallas (subsequently secretary of the treasury), James Calhoun, mayor of Baltimore, and other public officials.[10]

Three weeks after this marriage ceremony—intended by Patterson to lock the young Bonaparte into legality—the beleaguered father received another anonymous letter, this time personally presented to him by a Frenchman, perhaps its author. "Sir," the letter began, "this is to inform you as a friend that you must be aware of your son-in-law, as you may now turn him, *Bonaparty*, for has made his brags and boastings, before his marriage, that he would get married to your daughter, and then he would leave her and go home to his brother in France. This he has told in public company before several; and likewise that when he goes to France, he will still be a single man, and she may then go the devil for all he cares; and I and many others you may be assured must think the same—certainly of such a French fop of a fool. So therefore, as a friend, I warn you of him in time, as he has declared the above. Your friend, A Frenchman".[11] If this letter were valid—and Patterson could not afford to take the chance that it was not—it meant that Jérôme Bonaparte refused to be obligated, even by a notarized Roman Catholic marriage witnessed by the de facto bishop of the United States. Patterson was thus being forced into an even more difficult strategy: to sell the marriage to the Bonaparte family, who would, in turn, sell it to the first consul.

Son Robert Patterson sailed for France to manage this campaign in Paris. Robert R. Livingston, now serving as Jefferson's minister to France, did his best to help in the effort. Once Napoleon became emperor, however, his dynastic ambitions fully surfaced. His older brother, Joseph—who favored the option of Jérôme's becoming an American citizen and continuing to live in the United States with his American wife on a pension from the French government—was made king of Naples and Sicily, and sibling Louis was crowned king of Holland. In early 1805 Jérôme and his pregnant wife sailed for Europe. The plan, Jérôme told Elizabeth, was for Jérôme to plead on their behalf personally before his brother the emperor. Arriving in Lisbon, Jérôme was permitted to land, but an imperial edict against Elizabeth's landing was already in effect, and neutral Portugal was in no mood to defy the emperor. And so, Jérôme departed on his alleged mission to his brother—never to be seen again by his pregnant wife until she accidentally encountered him in a museum in Florence thirty years later. Prevented likewise from leaving her ship at Amsterdam, Elizabeth Bonaparte-Patterson (as she styled herself) went on to London, where she gave birth to Emperor Napoleon's nephew Jérôme Napoleon Charles Bonaparte, an American citizen. Napoleon arranged a state decree of annulment for his brother, who was denied a decree of nullity from Rome. In July 1807 he named him king of Westphalia, part of the Confederation of the Rhine, which Napoleon was in the process of assembling, and arranged for him to marry Princess Catharina, daughter of the king of Württemberg. In 1815 the General Assembly of Maryland granted Elizabeth Bonaparte-Patterson a decree of divorcement. In 1816, following the second and final fall of the empire, Joseph Bonaparte, the former king of Naples and Sicily, took some advice he had offered his younger brother Jérôme and moved permanently with his family to the United States, where the onetime king settled on a 1,500-acre estate near Bordentown, New Jersey, and enjoyed the remaining twenty-five years of his life amid the paintings and sculpture he had shipped over from Europe. Prudently investing the pension she was later granted from France, Elizabeth Bonaparte-Patterson lived on to her death in 1879 at the age of ninety-four, a wealthy woman who divided her time between Baltimore and Europe and never remarried. Her son, Jérôme Napoleon Charles Bonaparte, who bore a remarkable resemblance to his uncle the former emperor of the French, was educated at Mount Saint Mary's College, Emmitsburg; Geneva, Switzerland; and Harvard, where, due to his devout Catholicism, he was exempted from mandatory chapel services.

Choosing an architect and building a cathedral

The collapse of John Carroll's hopes for financial assistance from Napoleon for the Baltimore cathedral occurred while he and his trustees were in the process of selecting an architect, choosing a design, finalizing a site, preparing construction documents, and constructing the cathedral itself. All in all, some twenty years were consumed in the process, with Carroll on hand for fifteen of them; but given the fact that the War of 1812 interrupted work on the cathedral for nearly five years, the project was completed in record time, despite the scarcity of workers skilled in large-scale stone construction in the United States at a time when such workers were otherwise employed on federal buildings in the District of Columbia or banks and other commercial structures.

At the epicenter of such projects, moreover, was the architect whom Carroll and his trustees did select, Benjamin Henry Latrobe, one of the two or three founders of professional architecture in the Early Republic. Born in 1764 in Leeds, England, and raised in the Moravian community of that city—his father was a Moravian leader of Huguenot descent, and his mother was a Germantown, Pennsylvania–born Moravian of German and Dutch ancestry—Latrobe had his horizons further expanded when, at the age of twelve, he was enrolled in a Moravian school in Upper Lusatia, near the border of the German principalities of Saxony and Prussia. Family tradition held that Latrobe spent time as a hussar in the Royal Prussian Army following the completion of his Moravian education, was wounded, and, leaving the army upon recovery, completed an ambitious grand tour of Europe. In any event, Latrobe returned to England around 1786 in his mid-twenties, having acquired strong skills in Greek and Latin and some Hebrew; a mastery of German, which probably began with his mother and continued through his Moravian education in Germany and service in the Prussian army; a comparable mastery of French; and advanced abilities in Italian, Spanish, and modern Greek, most likely obtained on his grand tour. Perhaps, again, through his mother—related on her father's side to the great Philadelphia clockmaker, surveyor, astronomer, and mathematician David Rittenhouse—and perhaps through his Prussian army service as well, Latrobe showed skill in mathematics, mechanical engineering, and surveyorship. Furthermore, Latrobe's Moravianism—a pietist, quasi-mystical development within Lutheranism, to which it remained affiliated—had already sensitized Latrobe to Christianity and the spiritual resonances of beauty. Latrobe's watercolors, for example, parallel those of William Blake in their depictions of spiritualized figures and forces.

Latrobe returned to England and began to study architecture with Samuel Pepys Cockerell, a pioneer in promoting Greek Revival, and engineering with the renowned John Smeaton at a time when English architecture and engineering were in the midst of a golden age of innovation and creativity. Had he remained in

England, if one is to judge from his brief English career, Latrobe would have taken his place among this golden age's notable architects and engineers, then in the process of re-creating the public and domestic architecture, engineering, and landscape and urban design that to this day play roles in determining the infrastructure and appearance of the nation.

In November 1793, however, Latrobe's wife, Lydia, died giving birth to the couple's third child; and Latrobe suffered a nervous breakdown. Closing his London office, he decided to emigrate to the United States and make a new beginning. Settling in Norfolk, Virginia, Latrobe soon reachieved the popularity he had left behind in London. His social connections, moreover, led to commissions, along with an invitation to Mount Vernon in the summer of 1796. His friendship with fellow architect Thomas Jefferson—secretary of state (1789–1794), vice president (1796–1800), and president (1801–1809)—led to two major commissions: a penitentiary in Richmond (1797) and the exterior of the state capitol at Richmond (1800), for which Jefferson served as conceptualist (the penitentiary) and architect (the capitol). When commissions in Virginia declined and urban life beckoned, Latrobe moved in 1798 to Philadelphia, where his Greek Revival designs for the Bank of Pennsylvania (ready for occupancy in 1801) had already been accepted. Latrobe remarried in 1800, and he and his second wife, Mary Elizabeth Hazlehurst, had a large family together. Providing for the children from both his marriages kept Latrobe ever busy in an effort to live in style while keeping the wolf from his door.

By the time John Carroll sat down with him in the spring of 1804 to review plans for his cathedral, Benjamin Latrobe had become the predominant architect and water engineer in the nation: a consultant on improving the navigability of the Appomattox, James, and Susquehanna Rivers; the designer of the Bank of Pennsylvania, the first Greek Revival building in the nation; design engineer for the Philadelphia water system, powered by steam-driven pumps in a Greek Revival pump house; and a growing number of signature residences. Most dramatic of all, on 6 March 1803, President Jefferson appointed Latrobe surveyor of public buildings for the United States at $1,700 a year, responsible for the design and construction of the south wing of the Capitol, to be occupied by the House of Representatives. Within seven years of his arrival in Virginia, Latrobe had become, for all practical purposes, supervising architect of the federal government. Like John Carroll himself, Latrobe belonged to that second and successive tier of American founders, busy creating and diversifying the institutional and material fabric of the Republic handed down from the Founders a few short years before. The fact that Latrobe was Protestant did not bother Carroll. So were the majority of his fellow citizens, including Carroll's late friends Benjamin Franklin and George Washington and his close Baltimore friend, James Jones Wilmer, an Episcopalian clergyman. For his part, Latrobe was more than merely Catholic-friendly. As a Moravian Lutheran Christian, he was open to the creedal foundations and mystical traditions of Roman Catholicism and the aesthetic achievement of those Catholic countries in which he had luxuriated during his grand tour, when he all but committed to memory so many Catholic churches and cathedrals. Latrobe admired the culture of the Francophone Catholic clergy he had met and in 1804 enrolled his son Henry in the Sulpician-sponsored French College—as Saint Mary's in Baltimore was called—where he formed a gratifying friendship with its president, the renowned Louis William DuBourg.

Prior to his meeting with Carroll regarding the cathedral, Latrobe had had an opportunity to review the designs drawn up for the Capitol by William Thornton, an English-born, Aberdeen-trained physician who had turned to architecture as a second career. Accepted in 1793, Thornton's designs for the Capitol had already resulted in the establishment of the overall footprint of the building as well as the construction of its north wing, containing the Senate Chamber. Latrobe cited serious structural difficulties with the already completed Thornton work. Thornton counterattacked vigorously and effectively. For political reasons, President Jefferson kept Thornton on the rolls as architect of record, although some of Latrobe's corrections were eventually implemented.

And so, it must have been with more than a little schadenfreude that Latrobe reviewed and critiqued Thornton's preliminary designs for the cathedral and shared his criticisms with Carroll in a letter dated 10 April 1804. Thornton's design was unsafe, for one thing. Both its dome and tower were inadequately supported. It was also too expensive. The fifty-four thirty-foot-high columns Thornton proposed would cost at least fifty-four thousand dollars, the budget proposed for the entire building. At this point, Latrobe offered—working free of charge—to draft two possible designs for the cathedral. By 27 April 1805, he was ready to submit to Carroll two designs, one in Gothic Revival and the other in Roman. Accompanying the designs was a long letter of explanation in which Latrobe recommended the Gothic Revival alternative, thus revealing the English Romantic streak that led him to design the Protestant Episcopal Christ Church, Washington, D.C. (1807); Saint Paul's Church, Alexandria (1818); and the Bank of Philadelphia (1808) in this style years before Gothic Revival—with the exception of Maximilian Godefroy's Chapel of the Presentation (1808) at Saint Mary's College, Baltimore—made its appearance in the United States. The very nature of Gothic, Latrobe argued, excites veneration. Roman architecture, by contrast, while evident in many temples of the ancient world, is less intrinsically religious and more in line with everyday life; indeed, Latrobe opined regarding the Empire style then in vogue, it is currently being used in "the decoration of our meanest furniture".[12]

Latrobe's letter to Carroll revealed not only his love of the Gothic but also his knowledge of Roman Catholic worship patterns and their interaction with cathedral design. A cathedral of the Latin Church, Latrobe informed Carroll, must be cross shaped, with the head of the cross creating sufficient floor space for altar and sanctuary (the choir) and for the large numbers of clergy and acolytes participating in advance liturgies on special occasions. The size of the choir, Latrobe went on, determines the size of the cathedral in terms of both its length and its width. Having already volunteered to design Carroll's cathedral for free, Latrobe followed up this letter with a brief caveat sent the next day. Free did not mean his employees' salaries, of course, only his own, plus legitimate expenses. All things considered, the cathedral should cost no more than fifty-five thousand to sixty-five thousand dollars.

Carroll took Latrobe's alternatives to his trustees. With the provisions—first, from the trustees—that Latrobe reduce the size of the building and—second, from Carroll—that a semicircular apse replace the square space shown in his preliminary plan for the east end, the trustees chose the Roman alternative. In choosing Roman, following more immediate American trends, the trustees (Carroll included) were making a statement. The Gothic bespoke Catholicity, true; and the design

Latrobe submitted demonstrated a regard for an American-appropriate simplification of walls and fenestration. Latrobe's sheer walls and oversize windows, in fact, possessed a certain modernity in comparison with the complex components of the Roman alternative chosen by the trustees. Either alternative would have sufficed, and even Gothic—as evident in Godefroy's Chapel of the Presentation—could have absorbed American decorative motifs, such as tobacco leaves or cornstalks in place of palm branches. But the trustees viewed the Roman alternative as more intrinsically American in the United States of 1805, as the country was still in the midst of its preference for Classicism, linked to the golden age of English Classicism in public buildings of the late-eigheenth and early-nineteenth centuries.

But did Roman Catholic Baltimore have the resources to compete with the District of Columbia, Philadelphia, or secular Baltimore for contractors and workers skilled enough to follow Latrobe's drawings? For that matter, did it have the money for the great quantities of stone necessary for construction? Latrobe already found himself in a begging posture regarding the length of the building and other details. One can only imagine Latrobe struggling to cope with these compounded difficulties. Twenty feet more, please, dear trustees! All right, then, perhaps fifteen. Even ten more feet would better serve the overall design. I am sorry that you do not wish me to design the cathedral rectory at this time. It should be architecturally compatible with the cathedral. You wish the transept porticoes on either side of the building eliminated? Fine!

A crisis occurred when the cathedral contractor, John Hillen, a trustee, read sections of Latrobe's working drawings upside down and mistook the crypt vault for reversed foundation arches and complained to the bishop. Even when corrected by letters from Latrobe to Carroll, Hillen continued his misreading, complaints, and, worse, adjustments of Latrobe's plans. Latrobe demanded that all plans be returned to him for examination. To his horror, he found further adjustments by Hillen and demanded that Carroll fire Hillen and George Rohrback, the project's clerk of works, who was responsible for maintaining the integrity of Latrobe's designs as they came under construction. (Rohrback remained, and Carroll placed the Reverend Mr. Francis Beeston in overall charge of planning documents.) Although a patient and successful mediator, Carroll, from Latrobe's perspective, could sometimes be part of the problem, as when he and the trustees made a major adjustment to Latrobe's original proposal: namely, the expansion of the crossing dome to the full width of the nave and the aisles, which involved reducing the length of the diagonal wings and removing the four central piers in favor of four diagonal reversed arches that allowed the increased weight of the expanded dome to be transferred to eight adjacent central piers. The result of these adjustments—Plan Seven, by Latrobe's reckoning—rendered the cathedral even more architecturally ambitious. Such a sweeping central dome could no longer be treated as an interior canopy on four pillars. Rather, it now soared over the entire central space, a true vault supported by the same eight piers that supported the entire structure.

Throughout 1809, 1810, and 1811, steady progress was made as walls rose, and Latrobe commissioned Capitol sculptor Giovanni Andrei to prepare Ionic column capitals for the galleries and the apse—and a good thing, too, if John Carroll, now seventy-five, would live to dedicate the building in company with the suffragan bishop of his archdiocese. In the summer of 1811, in fact, August Foster, British minister to the United States, personally delivered to Carroll his pallium, the narrow white wool circular band with strings hanging in front and back that for centuries had symbolized the authority of an archbishop; and so, three years after his appointment, Carroll was fully official as the bishop of a metropolitan see. Yet the United States declared war on Great Britain on 18 June 1812—unwisely, as it turned out. The chance to invade Canada surfaced again and this time appeared successful, but it turned, once more, into catastrophe. In the summer of 1814 a British expeditionary force, supported by a naval blockade, torched the White House and the Capitol, then moved on to Baltimore to do more damage. The attacking forces were turned away following an unsuccessful bombardment of Fort McHenry, leaving the United States with a future national anthem, an economy in chaos, and the Federalist Party in ruins. Work on the Baltimore cathedral ceased for nearly five years, and when it was resumed, Baltimore had a new bishop.

The restoration of the Society of Jesus

As a body, the ex-Jesuits of the United States never lost hope that the Society of Jesus would one day be restored. Witness the declaration that the Select Body of the Clergy extracted from Carroll in 1790 that he had no intention of appropriating ex-Jesuit properties. As far as the ex-Jesuits of Maryland were concerned, moreover, that hope was given a partial and frail vitality in 1778 by the fact that the former English Jesuit College of Liège—where all of them, including Carroll, had studied before ordination—had been returned as the Academy of Liège to an ex-Jesuit faculty by special privilege of Pius VI, who had never been a member of the anti-Jesuit faction. After unsuccessfully trying to persuade Frederick II of Prussia and Catherine II of Russia to enforce Clement XIV's brief of suppression, Pius VI had begun to reconsider the matter, especially after Catherine II established a Jesuit novitiate in 1780 for the replenishment of the Society in Russia. By 1783–1784 Pius VI was talking discreetly about restoration and extended secret approval for the continuation of the Society in Russia. In 1794, during the French Revolution, the Academy of Liège was allowed to relocate to Stonyhurst mansion in Lancashire, donated by Thomas Weld of Lulworth Castle, and this return of a formerly Jesuit college to England seemed hopeful. In the turmoil and divided allegiances of the Napoleonic era, Bourbon opposition to the Society, which had accounted for the suppression of 1773, had begun to divide against itself. Duke Ferdinand of Parma annulled his duchy's prior expulsion of the Jesuits and requested that Catherine II send some Jesuits to Parma. To clarify the duke's request, Pius VII, a former Benedictine monk, on 7 March 1801, issued the brief *Catholicae fidei*, declaring that the Jesuits of Russia—some two hundred of them, under the protection of Catherine II—constituted a true and authentic survival of the Society of Jesus, which had never been fully and finally suppressed. On 8 February 1794, three Jesuits from Russia arrived in Parma. In short order, Parma became a vice province of Russia under the guidance of vice provincial Joseph Pignatelli, who renewed his vows on 6 July 1792 and served as master of novices as well. Issued on 30 July 1804, Pius VII's brief *Per alias* restored the Society of Jesus in canonical union with Russia in both Naples and Sicily. Ninety-three ex-Jesuits rejoined the province. When Napoleon expelled the Jesuits from Naples on 2 July 1806, the Jesuits relocated to

Rome and then were forced to go semiunderground in May 1809 when Napoleon annexed the Papal States. Living somewhat clandestine lives, they remained, however, Jesuits in good standing. The monarch of the Kingdom of the Two Sicilies wished to bring Jesuits back to Naples to counteract the further spread of French revolutionary ideologies. Pius VII shared the king's hopes of restoring the Jesuits as shock troops in opposition to revolutionary ideologies and for the next decade watched and waited for the right opportunity.

An affiliation movement grew up in England and the United States. On 27 May 1803, English ex-Jesuits indirectly but effectively received verbal permission from Pius VII to aggregate themselves with the Russian province. Father Gabriel Gruber SJ, the Russian general of the Society, appointed Father Marmaduke Stone, president of Stonyhurst College, to serve as provincial of these reaffiliated Jesuits, once they had made a retreat and renewed their vows. A year later, a novitiate was opened near Stonyhurst, despite the opposition of the anti-Jesuit Cardinal Stephen Borgia, Antonelli's successor as prefect of Propaganda Fide.

As far as the United States was concerned, John Carroll—who truly mourned and resented the suppression throughout his life—did not have the easy option of group aggrievement and group action in his relations with his fellow ex-Jesuits. Even when serving as a simple priest in Rock Creek, Maryland, following his return from England in 1774, Carroll had resisted the continuation of Jesuit lines of authority in a postsuppression era. As a constitutional theorist and planner during the White Marsh meetings, Carroll had enjoyed the pleasure of once again being part of the group. But when Propaganda Fide chose him as prefect apostolic and his fellow ex-Jesuits freely elected him to be the first bishop of a national diocese, Carroll increasingly experienced the growing distance that accompanied authority, even though those over whom he exercised such authority were by agreement paying his salary and living expenses. His expenses, in effect, were paid by profits from the ex-Jesuit plantation system, and his former colleagues demanded that Carroll sign an agreement that he would not seize it for his diocese. Then the Sulpicians entered the scene—well born, bred, and educated, backed by European resources—and emerged for a generation or more as the dominant clerical group under Carroll's supervision as bishop. They became his cathedral clergy, for one thing, and introduced a new level of liturgy to the nation as well as leading educators (Saint Mary's College, the Seminary, Mount Saint Mary's) while Georgetown languished under the presidency of ex-Jesuit Leonard Neale, the pious but do-nothing auxiliary bishop with right of succession forced on Carroll by the ex-Jesuits. While the ex-Jesuits remained tied to Maryland and southern Pennsylvania, moreover, the Sulpicians accepted frontier assignments and formed an important component of the first generation of frontier bishops. As bishop, Carroll had a special responsibility to develop a diocesan clergy as well as integrate other religious-order priests into the permanent service of his diocesan clergy or, in the case of émigré French diocesan clergy, into licensed temporary assignments pending their return to France.

Still, despite Carroll's need to keep his distance and act fairly on behalf of all clergy, the Society of Jesus in one way or another had been his home for the nearly thirty years he had spent under its formation and supervision as a student, novice, scholastic, and priest. Although never a fanatic on the issue, he, like his former colleagues, looked forward to its restoration, especially after the cryptic but never fully stated pro-Jesuit policies of Pius VI became the more overt pronouncements in 1801 and 1804 of Pius VII, who, as a Benedictine monk, knew what it was to be formed and sustained as a professed member of a great religious order. Carroll, however, remained guarded. Only a formal and explicit papal brief could fully restore the Society.

The briefs of 1801 and 1804, however, made affiliation with the true, surviving Society in Russia possible. The prospect of a restoration of some sort, as well as this early evidence of vocations, galvanized the usually passive Leonard Neale into action, for Neale correctly believed that only a renewed Jesuit presence could save faltering Georgetown. Thus, Neale, on 25 May 1803, joined Carroll in writing a letter to Father Gabriel Gruber, father general of the Jesuits in Russia (whom they addressed as "Your Paternity", meaning the father general of a still-surviving Society of Jesus), requesting reaffiliation for the fourteen surviving ex-Jesuits in Maryland and southern Pennsylvania. On 12 March 1804, Gruber wrote in reply from Saint Petersburg. Yes, replied the father general (not with any undue haste, given the momentous nature of the request and the slowness of correspondence in that era), the fourteen ex-Jesuits could rejoin the Society. Professed fathers should make an eight-day retreat, followed by a formal reaffirmation of their profession, giving place and date. Those who remained nonprofessed at the time of suppression should make a similar retreat of eight days, followed by a renewal of their simple vows. A year later, they should make a month-long retreat, followed by final vows. Those who had never belonged to the Society should make a month's retreat based on the Spiritual Exercises of Saint Ignatius, followed by a period of probation during which they should cultivate humility and related virtues and study the constitution and the rules of the Society—all this under the supervision of experienced older fathers—before being admitted to simple vows. Bishop Carroll, Gruber concluded, should appoint an American superior and master of novices, to whom Gruber would extend interim powers.

Gruber's letter reached Carroll at some unknown date before 21 June 1805, when Carroll appointed Robert Molyneux superior of the restored Society of Jesus in the United States. Carroll's lifelong friend from Saint Omer's days died on 8 December 1808 and was replaced by Charles Neale. When reporting on these appointments, as required, Carroll confessed that he and Leonard Neale had briefly considered putting aside their episcopal status and rejoining the Society themselves, but they had rejected the idea on the basis that strong episcopal support would be required while the American Society was only privately (*foro interno*) reestablished and still awaited the full restoration of a papal brief. As it turned out, the only friction Carroll experienced came from interim superior Charles Neale (the two of them had never really gotten along), who affronted Carroll by transferring Jesuit Adam Brett from Holy Trinity Church, Philadelphia, to another assignment without Carroll's permission, as canonically required until full restoration. When Neale showed signs of continuing this practice, Carroll wrote the new father general in Russia, Thaddeus Brzozowski, to complain. Brzozowski wrote back with an apology and later relieved Neale of his assignment, replacing him with the talented and diplomatic Giovanni Grassi.

In any event, despite these points of friction, the Society of Jesus was once again operative in what was now the United States. Five older ex-Jesuits immediately joined the Society; and Father General Brzozowski sent over five talented non-American Jesuits, including Adam Brett, an Englishman, later to be noncanonically removed. A novitiate opened at Georgetown, with Charles Neale as novice master, and enrolled a healthy cadre of eleven candidates.

Georgetown revived

The Russian affiliation brought to the United Sates a number of talented, energetic European Jesuits. One of them, the Italian Giovanni Grassi, played the key role in the resuscitation of Georgetown by 1817. Like most ex-Jesuits of the time, Leonard and Francis Neale, president and vice president–treasurer, respectively, were pious priests with a restrictive view of the world and no flair for schoolmastering or institutional development. Under the Neales, Georgetown devolved into a struggling institution that more resembled a minor seminary than an academy en route to becoming a college. Prayers were frequent throughout the day, and the Neales measured the success of Georgetown in terms of how many vocations to the priesthood it produced. By the early 1800s, Georgetown Academy had become a local (83 percent of its students came from Maryland and the District of Columbia), undersubscribed (only forty-five students as of 1806), overwhelmingly Catholic (only two Protestant enrollees recorded between 1800 and 1810), and pervasively dreary place forced to board up rather than reglaze its broken windows.[13] Under Sulpician Louis William DuBourg, by contrast, Saint Mary's College in Baltimore, while remaining French and Catholic in tone, grew in enrollment, attracted Protestants (the sons of James Monroe and Benjamin Henry Latrobe, for example), and received a Maryland charter to grant degrees. By October 1805, no less than John Carroll, founder of Georgetown fifteen years earlier, was recommending to Robert Molyneux that the school be closed until that time when educated English and European Jesuits became available to run it. In the meanwhile, Carroll complained, Georgetown was ruining the hard-won reputation of Jesuits as educators.

That very year, the Alsatian Jesuit Anthony Kohlmann, thirty-five, arrived from Europe. Driven by the French Revolution to Switzerland, Kohlmann graduated in theology from the University of Fribourg and was ordained. In 1796 he joined the Congregation of the Sacred Heart, a holding company of Jesuit aspirants that later (1799) united with the similarly organized Society of the Faith of Jesus. As a member of these congregations, Kohlmann directed a seminary in Bavaria and colleges in Amsterdam and Berlin. Assigned to Georgetown as assistant novice master and philosophy instructor for scholastics, Kohlmann was shocked by the poverty (food was in short supply, and the president slept on a folding cot in the library) and low enrollment (a mere twenty boarders occupied space capable of accommodating nearly two hundred), but he was delighted by the large number of Jesuit novices (eighteen by 1808) the academy was developing.

Impressed by Kohlmann's education, teaching, and administrative abilities, Carroll and Jesuit superior Molyneux appointed him vicar-general for New York and assigned four Jesuit scholastics and the newly ordained Benedict Fenwick to accompany Kohlmann and establish a Jesuit presence in New York. Shortly after their arrival in New York in 1808, Kohlmann and his fellow Jesuits opened the New York Literary Institution, a college preparatory school expressive of Kohlmann's belief that the Jesuits should concentrate their efforts on the two major cities of the United States, New York and Philadelphia. Within a year, forty boys, mostly Protestants, were enrolled.

When Bishop Leonard Neale's brother Francis stepped down from the presidency of Georgetown in 1809, the Neales secured the appointment of their nephew William Matthews, thirty-eight, the first American-born priest to be ordained (1800) from the Sulpician seminary in Baltimore, as president. Then serving as pastor of Saint Patrick's Church in Washington, Matthews took only a partial leave from his pastorate and became president and a Jesuit novice the same day. Matthews compiled an excellent record as president in terms of building repair, recruitment of students, and finances. The Neales, however, felt that Matthews was too lenient a disciplinarian, and Matthews was discovering that he preferred to remain a diocesan priest rather than become a Jesuit. And so, after a mere nine months in office, Matthews resigned and returned to his pastorate at Saint Patrick's, and Francis Neale returned to the presidency while continuing as master of novices, pastor of Trinity Church, and supervisor of finance for several Jesuit plantations. Although the new academic vice president, Giovanni Grassi, did his best to keep Georgetown running, he privately expressed shock when he compared Georgetown with his previous assignment, Stonyhurst. Even the novitiate, Grassi complained, was carelessly conducted and was losing novices in large numbers. "I cannot and never will suffer it to be said", Grassi informed a fellow Jesuit in October 1811, "that such a College belongs to the Society." Or, as Grassi wrote to a Jesuit in England, "We are in India!"[14]

Giovanni Grassi would soon have an opportunity to take the corrective action for which his background and training had prepared him. A native of Bergamo, Grassi had entered the Society in Italy following the reaffiliations authorized by Pius VI. Following ordination, he was named rector of a college in Russian-occupied Poland and in 1805 was ordered to China with two other Jesuits to help develop a reaffiliated Society in that country. The Napoleonic Wars, however, prevented him from securing passage from Europe, and Grassi spent the years 1805–1810 as a research scholar in mathematics and astronomy and a student of English at Stonyhurst. In 1810 His Paternity Thaddeus Brzozowski assigned Grassi to the United States. The next year, Brzozowski named Grassi rector (president) of Georgetown and superior general of the Maryland Mission. Dutifully, Carroll—ever sensitive when Europeans made American Catholic appointments—informed the Jesuits that, since Georgetown belonged to the Corporation of Roman Catholic Clergymen authorized by the State of Maryland, Brzozowski had no authority in the matter. Carroll treaded lightly in the matter of his own authority, for with Grassi, Georgetown at long last had an administratively experienced, academically prepared Jesuit at the helm. Grassi himself backed away from challenging Corporation efforts to maintain control of finances. Nor did he push the fact that Brzozowski had appointed him religious superior of American Jesuits. Although initially slowed down in medias res by a fever contracted at St. Inigoes, where he was on retreat prior to making his final vows, Grassi, between 1811 and 1817, turned Georgetown around and made it competitive. Following a review and overhaul of expenses, he lowered fees from $220 to $125 a year for tuition plus room and board, with comparable reductions for day students. Enrollments improved steadily. Students,

Catholic and Protestant alike, began to arrive from up and down the Atlantic sea-board. To offset the expenses of worthy but financially challenged Irish students, Grassi established and developed a tuition fund. At the same time, he began to make inroads in the recruitment of young men from established French families. Avoid-ing the Neales' insularity, Grassi made friends with politicians and professionals throughout Georgetown and Washington. As a result, the sons of such prominent (and often Protestant) fathers as Speaker of the House Henry Clay, mayor of Wash-ington James Blake, banker Thomas Corcoran, Naval Commodore David Porter, and architects Benjamin Latrobe (the Capitol) and James Hoban (the White House) could be found in the student body at various intervals, thereby helping to reestab-lish an earlier cachet that would never again be lost by this institution. Like any reli-gious superior worth his salt, Grassi could play hardball when necessary. By 1813, for example, enrollment at the New York Literary Institution had dropped to forty students. Still, New York was New York, and Grassi resented a Jesuit institution that might someday compete with Georgetown for preeminence. As religious supe-rior of the Maryland Mission, Grassi in April 1814 forced its closure by threatening to reassign the Jesuits working there back to Maryland. In this case, His Paternity Brzozowski counseled keeping the school open, but Carroll, now seventy-nine, had other, more important things on his mind.[15]

On 7 June 1814, having endured four and a half years of harsh captivity by Napoleon, Pius VII returned to Rome. Shortly thereafter, on 7 August 1814, the pope issued *Sollicitudo omnium ecclesiarum* (Out of concern for the entire church), fully restoring the Society of Jesus after forty-one years of near-total suppression. To emphasize the legitimate continuity of the Russian province, Pius VII directed that all states and dominions, including the Papal States, extend the same courtesies and protections of the restored Society as had been extended forty-one years ear-lier by Russia. On 1 March 1815, President James Madison signed into law a bill authorizing Georgetown College to admit students to programs in, and grant tra-ditional academic degrees for, "any degree in the faculties, arts, sciences, and liberal professions, to which persons are usually admitted in other Colleges or Universities of the United States". Two years later, the New York brothers Charles and George Dinnies became the first to receive bachelor of arts degrees from Georgetown. After a quarter of a century of struggle, Georgetown College formalized its hard-won status as an American Catholic degree-granting college.[16]

Problems in New Orleans

As the planning and initial construction of the Baltimore cathedral, the reestab-lishment of the Society of Jesus, and the revival of Georgetown were underway, serious trouble—centered, ironically, in Saint Louis Cathedral in that city—was reaching a crisis point in New Orleans. While Louisiana was under the jurisdic-tion of Spain (1762–1801), it remained under the ecclesiastical supervision of Luis Peñalver y Cárdenas, bishop of Louisiana and the Floridas. In 1801, following the terms of the Treaty of Madrid, Louisiana was returned to France, and Peñalver was transferred to the archiepiscopal See of Guatemala. Before he left New Orleans, however, Peñalver y Cárdenas appointed two Irish priests who belonged to the dio-cese, cathedral canon Thomas Hassett and Patrick Walsh, as vicars-general for the interim. Two years later, the United States purchased Louisiana from France, and, according to protocols established twelve years earlier by Rome, the Mississippi Valley now came under the jurisdiction of the bishop of Baltimore.

For the next two years, the Diocese of Louisiana and Floridas—twenty-one par-ishes in all—remained only nominally under John Carroll's control via vicars-general for Lower and Upper Louisiana appointed by the previous bishop. In two letters, however, dated 20 September and 21 September 1805, Propaganda Fide instructed Carroll to take direct control of the Louisiana diocese through the appointment of an apostolic administrator. At the same time, the Reverend Mr. Patrick Walsh, the surviving vicar-general of the previous jurisdiction, was to be relieved of his duties pending the arrival of the apostolic administrator sent by the bishop of Baltimore. Carroll's problem now became the adamant refusal of the Reverend Mr. Charles Nerinckx—the candidate for apostolic administrator recommended to Carroll by Propaganda Fide—to accept the position, followed by similar turn-downs from other priests whom Carroll contacted.

Why should Nerinckx and others refuse an appointment that would most likely lead to episcopal status? For financial reasons, perhaps. With Spain and France out of the picture, who would pay the priestly salaries these governments had previously assumed? Parishioners throughout this vast region certainly would not, accustomed as they were to regarding the ministry as governmentally sponsored. But the main reason was the intractability, the ungovernableness, of the city of New Orleans. Two generations of Spanish bishops, the Capuchin Cyril de Barcelona and Luis Peñalver y Cárdenas, had tried and failed to bring to New Orleans some semblance of religious observance beyond the conformity of various laity and the devotion of the Ursuline sisters. But New Orleans—en route to becoming the second-leading port of entry in the United States by 1837—was a wide-open town at its widest and most open. Even the city's sinfulness, though, and the ungovernable nature of its nominally Catholic population might have been psychologically overcome by any candidate for apostolic administrator. Sinfulness, after all, was persistent in even the most Catholic of cities. But New Orleans possessed an even more discouraging disadvantage: a boss, a usurper in religious matters, the brilliant, crafty, resolute, antinomian Capuchin friar Antonio de Sedella, pastor of Saint Louis Cathedral. Backed by his loyal cathedral marguilliers (church wardens), Sedella ran Church affairs in the city.

Born in Granada, Spain, in 1748, Sedella arrived in Louisiana ten years after his ordination. That he had already become something of a power in the Capuchins was evident in the appointments he immediately received—pastor of Saint Louis parish, ecclesiastical judge, commissary of the Inquisition, assistant vicar for Louisiana–West Florida—posts that Sedella used to consolidate his position further. In 1790 Bishop Cyril de Barcelona, auxiliary bishop of Havana, had Sedella deported back to Spain as a threat to episcopal authority; but with the help of lawyers financed by New Orleans supporters, Sedella secured a judgment from Charles IV reversing this order, and Sedella had the pleasure of sailing back to New Orleans on the same ship that brought Bishop Luis Peñalver y Cárdenas to his see city.

Returned to his parish post (with the arrival of Peñalver y Cárdenas, Saint Louis now became a cathedral), Père Antoine—as he was called—further strengthened his hold on all classes. Peñalver y Cárdenas might be the bishop, but Père Antoine, held high in the people's affections, was the power behind the cathedra, the throne on which the bishop sat. When New Orleans became an American city, Bishop Carroll named the Reverend Mr. Jean-Baptiste Olivier, a French missionary, vicar-general. Olivier served from 1806 to 1812. Sedella initially refused to acknowledge Olivier's authority and did so, reluctantly and nominally, only to avoid scandal. Indeed, hearing of Sedella's resistance to his vicar and even worse—reports of a previous effort by supporters of Sedella to bribe Napoleon's government to name Sedella bishop to replace Peñalver y Cárdenas when he was transferred to Guatemala— Carroll went so far as to write James Madison, Jefferson's secretary of state, as to whether the United States government would, in the future, recognize the Catholic Church's sole authority to make such an episcopal appointment. Absolutely, President Jefferson replied when shown Carroll's letter by Madison. The United States government does not interfere in religious affairs of this sort. The president, moreover, Madison concluded, had every faith in Carroll's patriotism, and hence every confidence that "in the selection of ecclesiastical individuals" Carroll would "combine with their professional merits, a due attachment to the independence, the Constitution and the prosperity of the United States".[17]

The refusal of Charles Nerinckx, one of Carroll's most able priests, to accept appointment as apostolic administrator of Louisiana, with an episcopal appointment in view, as well as the temporary nature of Olivier's appointment as a vicar-general not on an episcopal track, prompted Carroll to seek out an apostolic administrator for Louisiana and the Floridas, not from frontier clergy, but from tidewater candidates eligible for such a challenging promotion. His search soon brought Carroll to the candidacy of Sulpician Louis William DuBourg, already one of the most prominent and well-connected priests in the nation. So universal was the reply "DuBourg" when Carroll made inquiries regarding the Louisiana assignment— and so self-explanatory did it seem to those making the recommendation—that Carroll grew slightly peevish, as if he were being maneuvered into a decision on the basis of its alleged obviousness, which was reinforced by the fact that DuBourg had relatives in New Orleans. For a while, Carroll entertained appointing either John Baptist Mary David or Stephen Badin of Bardstown or even Louis Sibourd, Jean-Baptiste Olivier's assistant vicar-general in New Orleans; but when all three of these men proved unavailable for one reason or another (Sibourd turned down the job as beyond his abilities, meaning his ability to control Père Antoine and his marguilliers), Carroll yielded to the inevitable and in 1812 nominated DuBourg, employing the power of appointment granted him by Rome in 1808. By mid-1808 DuBourg was busy winding down his presidency of Saint Mary's College, transferring his share of properties to the Society of Saint Sulpice, and struggling to restructure the remaining debt on these properties when Samuel Cooper demanded that the seven thousand dollars he had lent DuBourg for Emmitsburg be returned, all the while dealing as well with debts he had incurred on behalf of Saint Mary's College. Forty thousand dollars of debt, DuBourg's panicked fellow Sulpicians complained (a figure revised downward in later years).

Bishop Carroll, meanwhile, was using every opportunity of personal contact or correspondence with DuBourg to set DuBourg's agenda for New Orleans. It was time, Carroll urged, to re-remind New Orleans that it was a Christian town belonging to a Christian nation and should start behaving accordingly, beginning with a return to Sunday Mass by the Catholic population. Not documented was any discussion of the port town's pervasive prostitution and drunkenness, although, as experienced confessors, perhaps neither Carroll nor DuBourg felt the need to confer on such matters, since vice was not unknown in the tidewater regions of the nation. Carroll's concern, rather, was to encourage the Catholic population to follow a more openly religious style of living, thereby upgrading the entire city through such means as Mass observance, sodalities, public prayer observances, good works, and (a Carroll bugaboo) an avoidance of theaters and dancing assemblies. As to Sedella and talk of schism, Carroll noted, DuBourg should not hesitate to impress upon James Wilkinson, governor of the newly admitted (1812) state of Louisiana, that as apostolic administrator he held the final and legitimate authority regarding religious decisions and associated church affairs, as guaranteed by the Constitution and the Bill of Rights, which meant that schismatic elements, should they surface, had no right to request government recognition of themselves as equal parties in church governance. Lending such assistance would violate the separation of church and state.

Sailing for New Orleans on 18 October 1812, DuBourg arrived on 2 December and quickly grasped the intensity—indeed, the near intractability—of the challenges he faced. Like Jean-Baptiste Olivier and Louis Sibourd before him, DuBourg did not move into the cathedral rectory—much to Carroll's annoyance, possession being nine-tenths of the law. The unfriendly Sedella was lodged there, as were his two assistants, a Dominican friar from Saint-Domingue, accompanied by his mulatto concubine-housekeeper and her children, and a second priest, Jean Koüne, who was also living with his housekeeper and whose children, eating at the table with him, called him "Papa".[18] Not surprisingly, DuBourg (like Olivier and Sibourd) found shelter near the Ursuline convent and celebrated daily Mass in their chapel.

Thus, because of Père Antoine, his two assistant priests, and their families, Saint Louis Cathedral and its rectory became off-limits to the apostolic administrator, vicar-general, and assistant vicar-general of the vacant Diocese of Louisiana and the Floridas. Staffed by Ursulines from Montpellier—who had taken the place of some sixteen French Ursulines who had left in the spring of 1803 when the American takeover seemed a prelude to confiscation of their properties—the sisters were alert to the divided nature of New Orleans and somehow managed to combine the education of daughters of established families with a ministry to girls of color who wished to leave prostitution. Even before arriving in New Orleans, in fact, DuBourg and his sister Victoire had expressed interest in this challenging ministry. In the summer of 1810, Victoire DuBourg had paid the costs of the Montpellier Ursulines' voyage from Baltimore to New Orleans; and DuBourg—a pioneer upon his arrival from France in offering religious instruction to people of color in Baltimore—recruited a young American with a vocation, Susan Johnston, to join the Ursulines of New Orleans. Thus proceeded their dual ministry to the well-off with everything to look forward to and exploited young women of color desiring a better life.

And so, discreetly avoiding (for the time being) a confrontation with Père Antoine, which he most likely suspected he would lose, DuBourg launched a counterministry to Sedella's, aimed initially at reenergizing the religion of the already observant. Fluent in French, Spanish, and English, DuBourg preached effectively in these languages at the Ursuline chapel and on parish visits throughout Lower

Louisiana. In New Orleans itself, he made special efforts at outreach to people of color. DuBourg laid siege to the city on behalf of renewed faithfulness, religious practice, and canonical governance. His headquarters for this campaign was the Ursuline chapel. The center of resistance could be found at Saint Louis Cathedral, where Père Antoine, his cathedral marguilliers, and clergy as well as their dependents held sway, backed by a populace still loyal to the old French and Spanish regimes and generally suspicious of the Anglo-American newcomers who now held sovereignty over their city.

Significantly, Saint Louis Cathedral functioned as the place, prize, and symbol of resistance to the new order. Designed by Gilberto Guillemard, a French military engineer in the service of Spain, the cathedral rose at a nexus of royal patronage and reward. Its patron, Don Andrés Almonester y Roxas, sat in a place of honor when the structure was dedicated on Christmas Eve 1794 (having cost a hefty $100,000); Almonester was named Knight of the Royal and Distinguished Order of Charles II less than two years later. Like New Orleans itself, the cathedral was a somewhat haphazard pastiche: brick plastered over to resemble marble—so Benjamin Henry Latrobe, in town to design new waterworks (a project that cost him and his son their lives), described it—stabilized by iron bars whose anchors defaced external walls, its interior columns clumsily sculpted in stucco. The congregation, Latrobe noted, tended to be largely female, white and black, for the wealthy men of New Orleans tended to let women do the churchgoing. Père Antoine, however, was capable of calling in the male half of his constituency when necessary. When DuBourg first tried to preach in the cathedral, he was greeted with an orchestrated cacophony of coughs, grunts, spittings, and shoe scrapings, which ceased when he finished his sermon.

At this point in his campaign—about half a year into it—DuBourg found himself discouraged by such rejection, by Sedella's deliberate racketeering of priestly authority, by what seemed to be the institutionalized sinfulness of the city, and, because of all this and more, by his loss of self-confidence after a lifetime of facing challenges with optimism and panache. It would take a saint to turn New Orleans around, DuBourg wrote to Carroll on 29 April 1813; and he was not a saint. Nor was he even good bishop material. Carroll should seek another candidate: Jean-Baptiste Rauzan of France, for example. Carroll looked into Rauzan but, as he later informed DuBourg, rejected him on the basis of his close association with Napoleon's uncle Cardinal Fesch, which, should Rauzan be appointed, would bring the emperor back into Louisiana affairs.

DuBourg, in any event, recovered his self-esteem in the months that followed. Most likely he was helped along by the fact that his brothers Louis and Pierre-François, his niece Victoire, and their families resided in New Orleans, with Pierre-François holding the important position of collector of the Port of New Orleans. Turning away from the city, DuBourg had begun to concentrate on the hinterlands to the north on the banks of the Mississippi, where he hoped to establish a Trappist monastery. La Trappe turned down the opportunity, as did the Jesuits, whom he also tried to recruit.

Despite these setbacks, DuBourg felt confident enough in the summer of 1814 to suspend cathedral priest Jean Koüne from saying Mass and administering the sacraments (but not burying the dead), on the basis of his scandalous disregard of the celibacy requirement. From the mayor of the city (a friend of Sedella) to the city's prostitutes (a formidable lobby), New Orleans erupted into massive protest. The city justice was besieged with affidavits in Koüne's favor, and his supporters threatened to escort the suspended priest by force to the cathedral altar. Père Antoine was, of course, behind this resistance, which, following the news of Napoleon's abdication and charges that DuBourg was an avid Bonapartist, included the gathering of large crowds outside the cathedral and threats to drag DuBourg away from the cathedral altar if he dared try to celebrate Mass there in Koüne's place. At this, DuBourg fled the city and remained away for the rest of the summer and the fall, living in the home of another niece, Aglaé, daughter of Pierre-François, and her husband, and enjoying—so he wrote to Carroll—great peace of mind as he visited parishes in the rest of the diocese.

The normality of Catholic life in these parishes, in fact, engendered a bold plan. He would travel to Rome and give the Holy Father one last chance to appoint another candidate for the bishopric of Louisiana and the Floridas. If the pope refused, he would seek consecration in Rome itself, a validation that even Père Antoine had to respect, and then recruit missionaries and money for his diocese.

Fought on 8 January 1815, two weeks after the Treaty of Ghent had ended the war, the Battle of New Orleans afforded DuBourg an opportunity to return to the city and, subsequently, leave for Europe with the highest form of corroboration from General Andrew Jackson and the American government that he, not Sedella, was the legitimate representative of Catholic governance in this rebellious city. The British invasion force—fifty vessels and 7,500 soldiers—under the command of Sir Edward Packenham had nothing less than the entire Mississippi Valley in mind, once the fractious city of New Orleans yielded. Commanding the opposition to the British was Jackson, fresh from his suppression of an uprising of Creek Indians in the Mississippi Territory. Exercising his role as apostolic administrator, DuBourg issued a call for public prayer on behalf of an American victory that specifically referenced Jackson and sought to rally the people of the city on behalf of pro-American resistance.

"While our brave warriors, under the command of the Hero of the Floridas, prepare to defend our firesides and our altars against a foreign invasion, it is for us, ministers of the Most High, and all Christians whom the feebleness of sex or age prevents from taking an active part in this important struggle, to unite under the wings of religion, to implore divine protection for the arms of our defenders. However just, however holy our cause; however well-founded our confidence in the intrepidity of our soldiers and the experience of the chief who commands them, we must not forget that victory, like defeat, is principally in the hands of the supreme arbiter of human destiny."[19] General Jackson loved DuBourg's *Mandement pour prières publiques* and had his adjutant general write DuBourg an official letter of thanks. Jackson was even more grateful when the disparate elements of the city—Americans, French, free African Americans, Choctaw Indians, even local pirate bands—rallied to the defense of the city. DuBourg was saying Mass in the Ursuline chapel four miles outside the city when news of an overwhelming American victory arrived. Following Mass, DuBourg intoned a Te Deum of thanksgiving and then called for the support of the Ursulines, who, at their day school in the city, began to receive and treat casualties. Thirteen Americans died in the battle; thirty-nine were wounded and nineteen captured. The British, by contrast, attacking the well-entrenched defenders, lost 291 dead, 1,262 wounded, and 484 captured. Many of the British casualties were Irish Catholics, an irony most likely not lost on DuBourg and the Ursulines as they ministered to those young men, grateful to find themselves in Catholic circumstances.

The crisis leading up to the Battle of New Orleans elevated DuBourg for the first time as the publicly acknowledged leader of Roman Catholics in this crypto-schismatic Catholic city accustomed to taking orders in religious matters from the Spaniard Antonio de Sedella. This recognition of DuBourg, moreover, came from the highest American sources, led by Jackson, who, on 19 January 1815, formally requested from DuBourg a ceremony of public thanksgiving on Monday, 23 January, in Saint Louis Cathedral, a venue DuBourg had almost dared not enter since his arrival in the city. Observances began with a joyous civic gathering (for which Jackson lifted the nine o'clock curfew) in the Place d'Armes in front of the cathedral, now renamed Jackson Square. Some twelve thousand citizens jammed into Jackson Square for the festivities. The next day, Jackson and his staff rode through the streets lined with military companies offering salutes as they passed. At the center of Jackson Square, the general and his entourage passed beneath a triumphal arch supported by six columns, dismounted, and then entered the cathedral past lines of young women dressed in white, each representing a state or territory of the Union, whose flag they held in one hand. In the other hand, each grasped a basket adorned with blue ribbons and filled with flowers, which they strewed in the general's path as he and his staff proceeded toward the cathedral. There, a vested DuBourg graciously welcomed them with a speech that blended religion and patriotism, in which DuBourg addressed the general personally as an agent of divine deliverance. As the choir intoned the Te Deum, DuBourg escorted Jackson to a seat of honor near the altar for further ceremonies, prayers, and speeches, triumphantly presided over by an apostolic administrator who only a few months earlier had been threatened with assassination as the instigator of resistance.

When Jackson left, however, the indefatigable Sedella proved once again that he was not finished—not yet, at least—by peppering DuBourg with a series of objections to his forthcoming trip to Rome and his appointment of the Reverend Mr. Louis Sibourd as vicar-general in his absence. Playing the canon lawyer, Sedella demanded that documents verifying DuBourg's original appointment be deposited in the city archives. He followed that with an argument that only the pope could order a prelate to Rome (which implied a recognition, however clumsily stumbled into, of DuBourg's legitimacy), and then called for proof that John Carroll had authorized DuBourg's Roman journey (which countered Sedella's pope-only argument)—all this interspersed with requests for more documents. Canonically, DuBourg might have come out best in this final exchange before his departure for Europe on the *Balize* on 9 May 1815. Yet Père Antoine's continuing resistance, as well as the truculent nature of his letters, underscored the danger that DuBourg was risking by leaving Père Antoine in New Orleans while DuBourg spent years away. True, he would return from Europe a bishop with newly recruited clergy in tow. But in the interim, would Père Antoine and the marguilliers grow more powerful, and would Bishop DuBourg ever be able to gain control of his cathedral and govern the church from its throne, pulpit, and altar?

ACKNOWLEDGMENTS

Kevin Starr began his life as a Catholic under the guidance and care of the Dominican Sisters of Mission San Jose who conducted the Albertinium School in Ukiah, California, where he was raised as a child. He continued with the same congregation at Saint Boniface School in San Francisco. Franciscan Fathers conducted the adjacent parish church. In the years that followed, Jesuits and Sulpicians furthered his education at Saint Ignatius High School, San Francisco; Saint Joseph's High School and College, Mountain View; and the University of San Francisco. As a graduate student at Harvard in the 1960s, he studied religion as a social and cultural force under the guidance of Professor Alan Heimert, a preeminent historian of religion in colonial America.

For twenty-seven years Kevin was privileged to be a member of the faculty of the University of Southern California. A sabbatical from USC enabled him to complete the previous volume, *Continental Ambitions*, pursued intermittently as he completed the eight volumes of his Americans and the California Dream series.

I wish to thank Professor John McGreevy of the University of Notre Dame and Professor Emeritus Robert Senkewicz of Santa Clara University, who read this manuscript prior to publication. I am indebted to Melody Lacina of Wilsted and Taylor Publishing Services and Vivian Dudro of Ignatius Press for their masterful and intuitive editing of this manuscript.

Father Joseph Fessio SJ, founder and editor of Ignatius Press, knows the admiration and affection Kevin had for him. Father Fessio has my gratitude for publishing these volumes.

Sheila Starr

NOTES

Preface

1. Michael Clodfelter, *Warfare and Armed Conflicts: A Statistical Reference to Casualty and Other Figures, 1628–2007*, 3rd ed. (Jefferson, N.C.: McFarland, 2008), 142.

1. Quebec City

1. John Carroll to Charles Plowden, 28 February 1779, in *The John Carroll Papers*, ed. Thomas O'Brien Hanley, 3 vols. (Notre Dame: University of Notre Dame Press, 1976), 1:53.

2. Walter Pilling Percival, *The Lure of Quebec* (Toronto: Ryerson Press, 1965), 42.

3. Patricia Bonomi and Peter Eisenstadt, "Church Adherence in the Eighteenth-Century British American Colonies", *William and Mary Quarterly* 39 (April 1982): 274–75.

4. *The John Carroll Papers*, quoted in John Gilmary Shea, *The Life and Times of the Most Rev. John Carroll, Bishop and First Archbishop of Baltimore*, in John Gilmary Shea, *History of the Catholic Church in the United States* (New York: John G. Shea, 1888), 2:137.

5. *The John Carroll Papers*, reprinted in Martin I.J. Griffin, *Catholics and the American Revolution*, 3 vols. (Philadelphia: printed by the author, 1907), 1:246–48.

6. "Address to the Inhabitants of Quebec", 26 October 1774, in Griffin, *Catholics and the American Revolution*, 1:15–17.

7. Adams' letter first appeared in *Familiar Letters of John Adams and His Wife, Abigail, during the Revolution*, ed. Charles Francis Adams (New York: Hurd and Houghton, 1876), 45–46, and is partially quoted in J. Thomas Scharf and Thompson Westcott, *History of Philadelphia, 1609–1884*, 3 vols. (Philadelphia: L.H. Everts, 1884), 2:1372; and Thomas T. McAvoy, C.S.C., *A History of the Catholic Church in the United States* (Notre Dame, Ind.: University of Notre Dame Press, 1969), 39.

8. Martin I.J. Griffin, *Catholics and the American Revolution*, 3 vols. (Philadelphia: printed by the author, 1907), 1:127–29.

9. *Maryland and the Empire, 1773: The Antilon–First Citizen Letters*, Maryland Bicentennial Studies, ed. and with an introduction by Peter S. Onuf (Baltimore: Johns Hopkins University Press, 1974), 188–89.

10. Charles Carroll of Carrollton to George Washington Parke Custis, 20 February 1829, *National Gazette*, Philadelphia (26 February 1829), reprinted in Griffin, *Catholics and the American Revolution*, 2:396.

11. Charles Carroll, *Journal of Charles Carroll of Carrollton during His Visit to Canada in 1776 as One of the Commissioners from Congress, with a Memoir and Notes* (Baltimore: Maryland Historical Society, 1876), 55.

12. Ibid., 76.

13. Griffin, *Catholics and the American Revolution*, 1:177–80; 3:224, 254.

14. Ibid., 1:223–31.

15. Ibid., 3:220.

16. Ibid., 1:108.

17. Ibid.

18. Ibid., 3:341.

19. *John Carroll Papers*, 1:49–50.

20. Griffin, *Catholics and the American Revolution*, 1:181.

2. Valley Forge

1. Robert Middlekauff, *The Glorious Cause: The American Revolution, 1763–1789*, rev. and exp. ed. (New York: Oxford University Press, 2005), 396. Regarding the battles of late 1776 and 1777, see chapter 15, "The War of Posts", and chapter 16, "The War of Maneuver", 340–41.

2. See George Washington's letter to Landon Carter from Valley Forge, 30 May 1778, in *The Papers of George Washington: Revolutionary War Series*, ed. Philander Chase, 23 vols. (Charlottesville: University Press of Virginia, 1985), 15:267–70.

3. Charles Carroll of Carrollton to George Washington, 27 September 1777, quoted in Ellen Hart Smith, *Charles Carroll of Carrollton* (Cambridge, Mass.: Harvard University Press, 1942), 175.

4. Martin I. J. Griffin, *Stephen Moylan, Muster-Master General, Secretary, and Aide-de-Camp to Washington* (Philadelphia: printed by the author, 1909), 8.

5. George Washington to Richard Henry Lee, 29 August 1775, in *Papers of George Washington*, 1:372–76.

6. George Washington to John Hancock, 23 April 1776, in *Papers of George Washington*, 4:112–113.

7. Paul Walker, *Engineers of Independence: A Documentary History of the Army Engineers in the American Revolution, 1775–1783* (Washington, D.C.: Historical Division, Office of the Chief of Engineers, 1981), 219.

8. Smith, *Charles Carroll*, 177, 179.

9. *Papers of George Washington*, 12:127–31; 13:319–22.

10. Paul Lockhart, *The Drillmaster of Valley Forge: The Baron de Steuben and the Making of the American Army* (New York: HarperCollins, 2008), 88, quoting *The Life of Ashbel Green*, ed. Joseph H. Jones (New York: R. Carter and Brothers, 1849), 109.

11. Lockhart, *Drillmaster*, 44–60.

12. Martin I. J. Griffin, *Catholics and the American Revolution*, 3 vols. (Philadelphia: printed by the author, 1907), 1:172–75.

13. Peter Guilday, *The Life and Times of John Carroll, Archbishop of Baltimore, 1735–1815* (New York: Encyclopedia Press, 1922), 81–82.

14. Griffin, *Catholics and the American Revolution*, 3:381–83.

15. *Papers of George Washington*, 14:176–177.

16. Ibid., 14:243.

17. Griffin, *Catholics and the American Revolution*, 3:245.

18. Charles Metzger S.J., *Catholics and the American Revolution: A Study in Religious Climate* (Chicago: Loyola University Press, 1962), 138–76.

19. Griffin, *Catholics and the American Revolution*, 2:193–216; 3:304.

20. Ibid., 2:185–89.

21. Ibid., 3:329–34.

22. *The American Revolution in Drawings and Prints: A Checklist of 1765–1790 Graphics in the Library of Congress*, comp. Donald H. Cresswell (Washington, D.C.: Library of Congress, 1975), 40.

23. J. Thomas Scharf and Thompson Westcott, *History of Philadelphia, 1609–1884*, 3 vols. (Philadelphia: L. H. Everts, 1884), 1:380–81, presenting André's article at length.

24. Middlekauff, *Glorious Cause*, 426–34.

3. Camden, South Carolina

1. Robert Middlekauff, *The Glorious Cause: The American Revolution, 1763–1789*, rev. and exp. ed. (New York: Oxford University Press, 2005), 440–501.

2. A. E. Zucker, *General de Kalb, Lafayette's Mentor* (Chapel Hill: University of North Carolina Press, 1966), 74–77.

3. Martin I. J. Griffin, *Catholics and the American Revolution*, 3 vols. (Philadelphia: printed by the author, 1907), 3:365–66.

4. Ibid., 1:39.

5. Ibid., 1:288.

6. Ibid., 3:223.

7. Ibid., 3:227.

8. Ibid., 3:220.

9. Ibid., 1:322–24.

10. Ibid., 1:37–38.

11. Ibid., 2:100.

12. Ibid., 2:126–34.

13. Francis Cogliano, "To Obey Jesus Christ and George Washington: Massachusetts, Catholicism, and the Eastern Indians during the American Revolution", *Maine Historical Society Quarterly* 32 (Fall 1992): 107–33.

14. Joseph Donnelly SJ, *Pierre Gibault, Missionary, 1737–1802* (Chicago: Loyola University Press, 1971), 57–58.

15. Ibid., 70, quoting *George Rogers Clark Papers, 1771–1781*, 64 vols., ed. James A. Jones (Springfield: Illinois State Historical Library, 1912), 1:231.

16. Griffin, *Catholics and the American Revolution*, 3:394–98.

17. Ibid., 3:397.

18. Ibid., 3:235; Donnelly, *Pierre Gibault*, 74–75.

19. Griffin, *Catholics and the American Revolution*, 3:234.

20. Ibid., 1:257.

21. *The Papers of George Washington: Revolutionary War Series*, 23 vols., ed. Philander Chase (Charlottesville: University Press of Virginia, 1985), 19:323, 361.

22. Griffin, *Catholics and the American Revolution*, 1:298–305.

23. Ibid., 1:306–11.

4. Yorktown

1. Robert Middlekauff, *The Glorious Cause: The American Revolution, 1763–1789*, rev. and exp. ed. (New York: Oxford University Press, 2005), 579–86.

2. John Gilmary Shea, *The Life and Times of the Most Rev. John Carroll, Bishop and First Archbishop of Baltimore*, in John Gilmary Shea, *History of the Catholic Church in the United States* (New York: John G. Shea, 1888), 2:166.

3. Martin I.J. Griffin, *Catholics and the American Revolution*, 3 vols. (Philadelphia: printed by the author, 1907), 1:295–97.

4. Robert Howard Lord, John E. Sexton, and Edward T. Harrington, *History of the Archdiocese of Boston in the Various Stages of Its Development, 1604–1943* (New York: Sheed and Ward, 1944), 1:340–41.

5. Aidan Henry Germain OSB, *Catholic Military and Naval Chaplains, 1776–1917* (Washington, D.C.: Catholic University of America Press, 1929), 23–24.

6. Shea, *John Carroll*, 2:175–77.

7. Ibid., 2:166.

8. Ibid., 2:165–66; Griffin, *Catholics and the American Revolution*, 3:286–301; Germain, *Catholic Military and Naval Chaplains*, 23–31; Lord, Sexton, and Harrington, *Archdiocese of Boston*, 1:340–47.

9. Griffin, *Catholics and the American Revolution*, 2:389–96; 3:365.

10. Lord, Sexton, and Harrington, *Archdiocese of Boston*, 1:342–44.

11. Shea, *John Carroll*, 2:161–62.

12. Robert Emmett Curran, *American Jesuit Spirituality: The Maryland Tradition, 1634–1900* (New York: Paulist Press, 1988), 110–11.

13. Lord, Sexton, and Harrington, *Archdiocese of Boston*, 1:345.

14. Middlekauff, *Glorious Cause*, 583–90.

15. Claude Robin, Letter 12 in *New Travels through North-America: In a Series of Letters*, trans. Philip Freneau (Philadelphia: Robert Bell, 1783), 78–79.

16. Ibid., Letter 11, 64–65.

17. Ibid., Letter 13, 81.

18. "Anna Rawle: Diary, 25 October 1781", in *The American Revolution: Writings from the War of Independence*, ed. John Rhodehamel (New York: Library of America, 2001), 750–51.

19. Griffin, *Catholics and the American Revolution*, 3:225.

20. Ibid., 1:312–14.

21. Ibid., 1:290–94.

22. Ibid., 3:359364.

23. Ibid., 3:222.

24. William C. Stinchcombe, "Americans Celebrate the Birth of the Dauphin", 62–63, quoting "Rush to Ferguson, July 16, 1782", in *Letters of Benjamin Rush*, ed. L. H. Butterfield, 2 vols. (Princeton: published for the American Philosophical Society by Princeton University Press, 1951), 1:279–80.

5. Paris

1. Claude Robin, *New Travels through North-America: In a Series of Letters*, trans. Philip Freneau (Philadelphia: Robert Bell, 1783), 13–14.

2. Ibid., 20.

3. Ibid., 14–15.

4. Ibid., 50–51.

5. Ibid., 35.

6. Ibid., 94–95.

7. Sally Mason, "Mama, Rachel, and Molly: Three Generations of Carroll Women", in *Women in the Age of the American Revolution*, ed. by Ronald Hoffman and Peter Albert (Charlottesville: University Press of Virginia, 1989), 286.

8. Ibid., 245, quoting *Baroness von Riedesel and the American Revolution: Journal and Correspondence of a Tour of Duty, 1776–1783*, ed. and trans. by Marvin L. Brown (Chapel Hill: University of North Carolina Press, 1965), 85.

9. Mason, "Mama, Rachel, and Molly", in *Women*, 287, quoting June 1782 letter of Henrietta Hill Ogle to her uncle John Thomas, now in the Pennington Collection of the Maryland Historical Society.

10. Martin I. J. Griffin, *Catholics and the American Revolution*, 3 vols. (Philadelphia: printed by the author, 1907), 3:253.

11. Rufus Wilmot Griswold, William Gilmore Simms, and Edward Duncan Ingraham, *Washington and the Generals of the American Revolution: With Finely Engraved Portraits from Original Pictures* (Philadelphia: J. B. Lippincott, 1856), 269–71.

12. Martin I. J. Griffin, *Stephen Moylan, Muster-Master General, Secretary, and Aide-de-Camp to Washington* (Philadelphia: printed by the author, 1909), 79.

13. John H. Campbell, *History of the Friendly Sons of St. Patrick and of the Hibernian Society for the Relief of Immigrants from Ireland* (Philadelphia: Hibernian Society, 1892), 52–54, 63.

14. Arthur Granville Bradley, *The United Empire Loyalists: Founders of British Canada* (London: Thornton Butterworth, 1971), 128.

15. Griffin, *Catholics and the American Revolution*, 3:341.

16. Richard Boylan, *Benedict Arnold: The Dark Eagle* (New York: W. W. Norton, 1973), 248.

17. Ibid., 122.

18. Ibid., 129.

19. Ibid., 130–32.

20. Charles Carroll of Carrollton to George Washington Parke Custis, 20 February 1829, published in the *National Gazette*, Philadelphia, for 26 February 1829 and reprinted in Griffin, *Catholics and the American Revolution*, 2:396.

6. White Marsh Plantation

1. *The John Carroll Papers*, ed. Thomas O'Brien Hanley, 3 vols. (Notre Dame: University of Notre Dame Press, 1976), 1:66.

2. Ibid., 1:78.

3. Ibid., 1:71–77.

4. Jules A. Baisnée PSS, *France and the Establishment of the American Catholic Hierarchy: The Myth of French Interference, 1782–1784* (Baltimore: Johns Hopkins University Press, 1934), 117.

5. *John Carroll Papers*, 1:163.

6. Edward Devitt SJ, "Letters of Father Joseph Mosley and Some Extracts from His Diary, 1757–1786", *Woodstock Letters* 35 (1906): 241.

7. Ronald Binzley, "Disaffected Children: The Ex-Jesuits and the Shaping of Early American Catholicism, 1773–1790", *U.S. Catholic Historian* 26 (Spring 2008): 76, quoting Charles Plowden, *A Candid and Impartial Sketch of the Life and Government of Pope Clement XIV, Containing Many Interesting Anecdotes during That Period of Church History: In a Series of Letters From Rome* ... (n.p.: printed by the author, 1785), 1:5.

8. Peter Guilday, *The Life and Times of John Carroll, Archbishop of Baltimore, 1735–1815* (New York: Encyclopedia Press, 1922), 250–51.

9. Ibid., 278–81, 279.

10. Ibid., 309–10.

11. Robert Howard Lord, John E. Sexton, and Edward T. Harrington, *History of the Archdiocese of Boston in the Various Stages of Its Development, 1604–1943* (New York: Sheed and Ward, 1944), 1:391.

12. Ibid., 1:400–1.

13. Ibid., 1:418.

7. Dorset, England

1. "From George Washington to the Hebrew Congregation in Newport, Rhode Island. 18 August 1790", Founders Online, National Archives Original Source: *The Papers of George Washington*, Presidential Series, vol. 6, 1 July 1790–30 November 1790, ed. Mark A. Mastromarino (Charolottesville: University Press of Virginia, 1996), 284–86.

2. John Tracy Ellis, *Documents of American Catholic History*, 3 vols. (Milwaukee: Bruce Publishing, 1967), 1:172–76.

3. *The John Carroll Papers*, ed. Thomas O'Brien Hanley, 3 vols. (Notre Dame: University of Notre Dame Press, 1976), 1:289–96, 570–71.

4. Ibid., 1:282–87.

5. Ibid., 1:361–63.

6. Ellis, *Documents of American Catholic History*, 167–71.

7. C.M. Anthony, "Lulworth Castle", *Catholic Historical Review* 1, no. 3 (October 1915): 250–51.

8. Charles Plowden, "Discourse", in *A Short Account of the Establishment of the New See of Baltimore in Maryland, and of Consecrating the Right Rev. Dr. John Carroll First Bishop Thereof on the Feast of the Assumption, 1790* ... (London: J.P. Coghlan, 1790), 5–9.

9. *John Carroll Papers*, 1:447–48.

10. Ibid., 1:476–78.

11. Walter Hartridge, "The Refugees from the Island of St. Domingo in Maryland", *Maryland Historical Magazine* 38 (January 1943): 109–10.

12. Thomas W. Spalding, *The Premier See: A History of the Archdiocese of Baltimore, 1789–1989* (Baltimore and London: Johns Hopkins University Press, 1989), 23–27.

13. Robert Emmett Curran, *A History of Georgetown University* (Washington, D.C.: Georgetown University Press, 2010), 1:36–38.

8. Baltimore 1808

1. John Gilmary Shea, *The Life and Times of the Most Rev. John Carroll, Bishop and First Archbishop of Baltimore*, in John Gilmary Shea, *History of the Catholic Church in the United States* (New York: John G. Shea, 1888), 2:622–26.

2. Charles G. Herbermann, *The Sulpicians in the United States* (New York: Encyclopedia Press, 1916), 145–46.

3. Joseph M. Finotti, *Bibliographia Catholica Americana: A List of Works Written by Catholic Authors, and Published in the United States, Part I, 1784–1820* (New York: Catholic Publication House, 1872), 136, 176.

4. Ralph Gray and Gerald Hartdagen, "A Glimpse of Baltimore Society in 1827: Letters of Henry D. Gilpin", *Maryland Historical Magazine* 69 (Fall 1974): 267–68.

5. Christopher Phillips, *Freedom's Port: The African-American Community of Baltimore, 1790–1860* (Urbana: University of Illinois Press, 1997), 14–26.

6. John Carroll to Sulpician Superior Jacques-André Emery, September 1801, in *The John Carroll Papers*, ed. Thomas O'Brien Hanley, 3 vols. (Notre Dame: University of Notre Dame Press, 1976), 2:358–59.

7. *1791–1891 Memorial Volume of the Centenary of St. Mary's Seminary of St. Sulpice, Baltimore, MD* (Baltimore: John Murphy, 1891), 14–16.

8. John Thayer, *An Account of the Conversion of the Reverend Mr. John Thayer: Formerly a Protestant Minister of Boston, Written by Himself* (1787), Google digital copy, 20–21.

9. Robert Howard Lord, John E. Sexton, and Edward T. Harrington, *History of the Archdiocese of Boston in the Various Stages of Its Development, 1604–1943* (New York: Sheed and Ward, 1944), 1:454.

10. Leo Ruskowski PSS, *French Émigré Priests in the United States, 1791–1815* (Washington, D.C.: Catholic University of America Press, 1940), 1–3, citing Augustin Sicard, *L'ancien clergé de France*, 3 vols. (Paris: Librairie V. Locoffre, 1893–1903), 3:19–20.

11. Annabelle Melville, *Louis William DuBourg: Bishop of Louisiana and the Floridas, Bishop of Montauban, and Archbishop of Besançon, 1766–1833*, 2 vols. (Chicago: Loyola University Press, 1986), 1:18.

12. Ibid., 1:68, quoting François Blondel, *Cours d'architecture* (Paris: P. Aubouin and F. Clousier, 1675–1683), 1:378.

13. *Elizabeth Seton: Selected Writings*, ed. Ellin Kelly and Annabelle Melville (Mahwah, N.J.: Paulist Press, 1987), 235, quoting Mrs. Seton's "A Journal for Cecilia", 16 June 1808.

9. Emmittsburg, Maryland

1. Annabelle Melville, *Louis William DuBourg: Bishop of Louisiana and the Floridas, Bishop of Montauban, and Archbishop of Besançon, 1766–1833*, 2 vols. (Chicago: Loyola University Press, 1986), 1:192–95.

2. Ibid., 1:194–95.

3. Ibid., 1:196–99.

4. Ibid.

5. Annabelle Melville, *Elizabeth Bayley Seton, 1774–1821* (New York: Charles Scribner's Sons, 1951), 172.

6. Melville, *Louis Wiliam DuBourg*, 1:200.

7. Melville, *Elizabeth Bayley Seton*, 171.

8. Ibid.

9. Ibid., 67.

10. Ibid., 77.

11. Richard Shaw, *John Dubois, Founding Father: The Life and Times of the Founder of Mount St. Mary's College, Emmitsburg, Superior of the Sisters of Charity, and Third Bishop of the Diocese of New York* (Yonkers, N.Y.: United States Catholic Historical Society, 1983), 33.

12. Ibid., 35.

13. Melville, *Elizabeth Bayley Seton*, 135.

14. Ibid.

15. Ibid., 173.

16. Madame de Barberey, *Elizabeth Seton*, trans. Joseph B. Code (New York: Macmillan, 1927), 328–30.

17. Melville, *Elizabeth Bayley Seton*, 186.

18. Ibid., 189.

19. Ibid., 245–46.

20. Ibid., 246.

21. Ibid., 294–99.

10. Baltimore 1821

1. Letter of George Washington Parke Custis to the Rev. Dr. Charles I. White, presented by Peter Guilday in the preface to *Eulogy on George Washington* (New York: P.J. Kenedy and Sons, 1931), xx.

2. John Carroll, Prayer for Government Officials, in the foreword to *Eulogy on George Washington*, xv–xvii.

3. *The John Carroll Papers*, ed. Thomas O'Brien Hanley, 3 vols. (Notre Dame: University of Notre Dame Press, 1976), 2:158.

4. *Eulogy on George Washington*, 24.

5. Annabelle Melville, *John Carroll of Baltimore: Founder of the American Catholic Hierarchy* (New York: Charles Scribner's Sons, 1955), 263–65; Annabelle Melville, *Louis William DuBourg: Bishop of Louisiana and the Floridas, Bishop of Montauban, and Archbishop of Besançon, 1766–1833*, 2 vols. (Chicago: Loyola University Press, 1986), 1:136–39. The Latin for Psalm 126:1 is taken from *The Psalms: A Prayer Book* (New York: Benziger Brothers, 1947), 327, based on a new Latin translation from the Hebrew. The English is from the Revised Standard Version of the Bible—Second Catholic Edition (Ignatius Edition), in which it is Psalm 127.

6. William Thomas Roberts Saffell, *The Bonaparte-Patterson Marriage in 1803, and the Secret Correspondence on the Subject Never Before Made Public* (Philadelphia: published by the Proprietor, 1873), 27, https://archive.org/details/bonapartepatteroosaff, accessed 3 August 2017.

7. Walter Hartridge, "The Refugees from the Island of St. Domingo in Maryland", *Maryland Historical Magazine* 38 (January 1943): 109–22.

8. Saffell, *Bonaparte-Patterson Marriage*, 27.

9. Ibid., 29–30.

10. Ibid., 31.

11. Ibid., 32.

12. Talbot Hamlin, *Benjamin Henry Latrobe* (New York: Oxford University Press, 1955), 236.

13. Robert Emmett Curran, *A History of Georgetown University* (Washington, D.C.: Georgetown University Press, 2010), 1:58–59.

14. Ibid., 1:63–69.

15. Ibid., 1:70–82.

16. Ibid., 1:70–83.

17. Peter Guilday, *The Life and Times of John Carroll, Archbishop of Baltimore, 1735–1815* (New York: Encyclopedia Press, 1922), 708.

18. Melville, *Louis William DuBourg*, 1:282.

19. Ibid., 1:312–13.

ESSAY ON SOURCES

General Reference

Regarding John Gilmary Shea, see Monsignor Peter Guilday, *John Gilmary Shea: Father of American Catholic History, 1824–1892* (1926), from the United States Catholic Historical Society. Monsignors John Tracy Ellis and Robert Trisco's *A Guide to American Catholic History* (2nd edition, revised and enlarged, 1982) and *The Catholic Periodical and Literature Index*, edited by Dana Cernainau (1994), both issued by the Catholic Library Association, proved invaluable, as did Edward R. Vollmar SJ, *The Catholic Church in America: An Historical Bibliography* (2nd edition, 1963), from Scarecrow Press. As a faculty member at the University of Southern California, I enjoyed access through JStor to a multiplicity of titles. I have also built my bibliography through such recent references as *The Encyclopedia of American Catholic History*, edited by Michael Glazier and Thomas J. Shelley (1997), from Liturgical Press, along with the two classic reference tools I am fortunate to own: *The Catholic Encyclopedia* (15 volumes and index, 1913), from Encyclopedia Press, Knights of Columbus edition; and the *New Catholic Encyclopedia* (14 volumes and index, 1967), from McGraw-Hill. Written by the finest scholars of their era, these three encyclopedias are magisterial and authoritative in their content and bibliographical references and are fully acknowledged as guiding my inquiries and interpretations in every instance. Also useful in this regard for content, interpretation, and bibliographical reference is the equally magisterial *Oxford Dictionary of the Christian Church*, 2nd edition, edited by F. L. Cross and E. A. Livingstone (1983); and J. N. D. Kelly's *Oxford Dictionary of Popes* (1986). Invaluable for the interpretation of Catholic doctrine and moral teachings is the *Catechism of the Catholic Church* (2nd edition, 1997), from Libreria Editrice Vaticana. Also of value for concise reference is *The HarperCollins Encyclopedia of Catholicism*, Richard P. McBrien, general editor (1995), from HarperSanFrancisco.

More than forty years ago, I was fortunate to acquire from the Starr Bookshop in Cambridge, Massachusetts, John Gilmary Shea's four-volume history of the Catholic Church in the United States (each published in New York by the author) under the titles *The Catholic Church in Colonial Days, 1521–1763* (1886), *The Life and Times of the Most Rev. John Carroll, 1763–1815* (1888), *History of the Catholic Church in the United States, 1808–1843* (1890), and *History of the Catholic Church in the United States, 1844–1866* (1892). Across four decades, I have lived with, read, and cherished these volumes, and I have used them as guide and inspiration for *Continental Achievement*. I have also read, meditated upon, and used for bibliographical reference a number of histories of American Catholicism, many of them classics.

I began with the works of Monsignor John Tracy Ellis, who taught at my alma mater, the University of San Francisco, from 1963 to 1976, following his retirement from the Catholic University of America. At this point, I wish to acknowledge the total influence of Monsignor Ellis as I read and reread the Ellis canon, which includes *American Catholicism* (Chicago: University of Chicago Press, 1956), *Perspectives in American Catholicism* (Baltimore and Dublin: Helicon, 1963), and *Catholics in Colonial America* (Baltimore and Dublin: Helicon, 1965). In terms of content, interpretation, and reference, I have also profited immeasurably from Ellis' *Documents of American Catholic History* (volume 1, 1956; volume 2, 1967; volume 3, 1987) and have made every effort in my narrative to quote from these selections.

With its pioneering treatment of the relevance of Catholic political theory to the American Constitution and its exhaustive treatment of Catholic intellectual and literary life in the nineteenth and early twentieth centuries, Theodore Maynard's *Story of American Catholicism* (1941) has accompanied me as long as the Shea volumes and remains a comparable source of inspiration. Sydney E. Ahlstrom's *A Religious History of the American People* (1972), from Yale University Press, has also proven to be of continuing value.

Continental Achievement is a selective and narrative history that does not seek to be comprehensive. Nevertheless, I have guided my research and understanding of American Catholic history through the reading and assimilation of such respected and eminently useful histories as Francis Xavier Curran SJ, *Major Trends in American Church History* (1946); Theodore Roemer OFM Cap., *The Catholic Church in the United States* (1950); Peter J. Rahill, *The Catholic in America: From Colonial Times to the Present Day* (1961); Newman C. Eberhardt CM, *Survey of American Church History* (1964); Thomas Timothy McAvoy CSC, *A History of the Catholic Church in the United States* (1969); Philip Gleason, *Catholicism in America* (1970); James Hennesey SJ, *American Catholics: A History of the Roman Catholic Community in the United States*, foreword by John Tracy Ellis (1981); James Hennesey SJ, *Catholics in the Promised Land of the Saints* (1981); Jay P. Dolan, *The American Catholic Experience: A History from Colonial Times to the Present* (1985); Charles R. Morris, *American Catholic: The Saints and Sinners Who Built America's Most Powerful Church* (1997); *Building the Church in America: Studies in Honor of Monsignor Robert F. Trisco on the Occasion of His Seventieth Birthday*, edited by Joseph C. Linck and Raymond J. Kupke (1999), from the Catholic University of America Press; Jay P. Dolan, *In Search of an American Catholicism: A History of Religion and Culture in Tension* (2002); James T. Fisher, *Communion of Immigrants: A History of Catholics in America* (2002); John T. McGreevy, *Catholicism and American Freedom: A History* (2003); Patrick W. Carey, *Catholics in America: A History* (2004); *Catholic Makers of America: Biographical Sketches of Catholic Statesmen and Political Thinkers in America's First Century, 1776–1876*, edited by Stephen M. Krason (2006); and James M. O'Toole, *The Faithful: A History of Catholics in America* (2008). Four collections of essays have also broadened my understanding and added to my bibliography: *The Catholic Church, USA*, edited by Louis J. Putz CSC (1956); *Essays in the American Catholic Tradition*, edited by P. Albert Duhamel (1960); *Catholics in America, 1776–1976*, edited by Robert Trisco, foreword by the Most Reverend Edward A. McCarthy (1976); and *An American Church: Essays on the Americanization of the Catholic Church*, edited by David J. Alvarez (1979). See also Monsignor Francis Weber, *America's Catholic Heritage: Some Bicentennial Reflections, 1776–1976* (1976). Useful for biographical reference is Joseph Taggart, *Biographical Sketches of the Eminent American Patriots* (1907).

Regarding the history and physical details of representative American Catholic churches, I have consulted Francis Beauchesne Thornton, *Catholic Shrines in the*

United States and Canada (1954), and *Famous American Churches and Shrines: Catholic Edition*, edited by Walter T. Murphy (1968). See also Edward F. Rines, *Old Historic Churches of America* (1936).

1. Quebec City

The online *Dictionary of Canadian Biography* is crucial to this chapter and the chapters on French Canada that follow as a source of biographical detail and bibliographical reference. Indeed, it is difficult to imagine how anyone, especially a nonspecialist, could enter the tangled thicket of the history of New France without the constant assistance of this comprehensive research tool, sponsored by the University of Toronto and Université Laval, as a source of biography, bibliography, and research. Articles from the *Dictionary of Canadian Biography* are cited by author, subject, and the designation *DCB*. The following *Dictionary of American Biography* (*DAB*) entries are of relevance to the American invasion of Canada: Ethan Allen, Benedict Arnold, Moses Hazen, James Livingston, Richard Montgomery, Philip John Schuyler, and David Wooster.

Regarding the invasion of Canada, see George McKinnon Wrong, *Canada and the American Revolution: The Disruption of the First British Empire* (New York: Macmillan, 1935). Also of value is *The Oxford Companion to Canadian History*, edited by Gerald Hallowell (2004), online version, 2012. Of continuing usefulness to these chapters are *The Concise Oxford Companion to Canadian Literature*, edited by William Toye (2001); and the *Literary History of Canada*, Carl F. Klinck, general editor (1970), from the University of Toronto Press.

General histories of Canada that have guided these chapters include Joseph H. Schlarman, *From Quebec to New Orleans: The Story of the French in America* (1929); Arthur R. M. Lower, *Colony to Nation: A History of Canada* (1946); Gustave Lanctot, *A History of Canada*, translated by Josephine Hambleton and Margaret M. Cameron (3 volumes, 1963, 1964, 1965), from Harvard University Press; *The Illustrated History of Canada*, edited by Craig Brown (1987); J. Bartlet Brebner, *Canada: A Modern History*, new edition revised and enlarged by Donald C. Masters (1970), from the University of Michigan Press; Kenneth McNaught, *The Penguin History of Canada* (1988); and the eminently useful J. M. Bumsted, *A History of the Canadian Peoples* (4th edition, 2011), from Oxford University Press.

My understanding of the Quebec Act came from Charles Metzger SJ, *The Quebec Act: A Primary Cause of the American Revolution* (New York: United States Catholic Historical Society, 1936). Regarding Edmund Burke and the Quebec Act, see F. P. Lock, *Edmund Burke* (Oxford: Clarendon Press, 2006), 372, 375.

Regarding the anti-Catholic tradition that played such an important role in dissuading Canadians from joining the United Colonies, see Francis Cogliano, *No King, No Popery: Anti-Catholicism in Revolutionary New England* (Westport, Conn., and London: Greenwood Press, 1995); and Brendan McConville, "Pope's Day Revisited, 'Popular' Culture Reconsidered", *Explorations in Early American Culture* 4 (2000): 258–80. See also Owen Stanwood, "Catholics, Protestants, and the Clash of Civilizations in Early America", in *The First Prejudice: Religious Tolerance and Intolerance in Early America*, edited by Chris Beneke and Christopher Grenda, (Philadelphia: University of Pennsylvania Press, 2011), 218–40. Also of relevance is Patricia

Bonomi and Peter Eisenstadt, "Church Adherence in the Eighteenth-Century British American Colonies", *William and Mary Quarterly* 39 (April 1982): 245–86.

Regarding the transformations experienced by the American Catholic community before, during, and after the Revolutionary War, see Thomas O'Brien Hanley SJ, *Their Rights and Liberties: The Beginnings of Religious and Political Freedom in Maryland* (Westminster, Md.: Newman Press, 1959); Robert Emmett Curran, *Papist Devils: Catholics in British America, 1574–1783* (Washington, D.C.: Catholic University of America Press, 2014); Robert Emmett Curran, *Intestine Enemies: Catholics in Protestant America, 1605–1791: A Documentary History* (Washington, D.C.: Catholic University Press, 2017); and Maura Jane Farrelly, *Papist Patriots: The Making of an American Catholic Identity* (New York: Oxford University Press, 2012).

Concerning the military dimension of the American Revolution, I admit a total dependence upon Robert Middlekauff, *The Glorious Cause: The American Revolution, 1763–1789*, revised and expanded edition (New York: Oxford University Press, 2005), a volume in *The Oxford History of the United States*, under the general editorship of David M. Kennedy. Since I have no training as a military historian, I remained dependent on Professor Middlekauff's masterful presentations of strategies, battles, maneuvers, and tactics of the long and difficult Revolutionary War. Middlekauff writes with the assurance of a scholar who is a first-rate writer as well as a veteran of combat service as a Marine officer during the Korean War.

For the social and cultural dimension of the military struggle, see Ronald Hoffman and Peter J. Albert, *Arms and Independence: The Military Character of the American Revolution* (Charlottesville: University Press of Virginia on behalf of the United States Capitol Historical Society, 1984).

I also made extensive use of *The American Revolution in Drawings and Prints: A Checklist of 1765–1790 Graphics in the Library of Congress*, compiled by Donald H. Cresswell, with a foreword by Sinclair H. Hitchings (Washington, D.C.: Library of Congress, 1975). At a time predating photography, the graphic art gathered in this volume from American and English sources offers a continual visualization of the people, places, and events of the war comparable to a photographic record. Compiler Cresswell, moreover, accompanies each image with extracts from magazines of the period, together with his own vivid scholarly commentary.

My focus in these chapters was primarily on personal and social transformations experienced by Roman Catholics as a result of their Revolutionary War service. To that end, I explored the social and psychological causes and effects of the Revolutionary War on the nation as a whole. I began with a book that has been in my library since college days: John C. Miller, *Origins of the American Revolution*, with decorative drawings by Eric M. Simon (Boston: Little Brown, an Atlantic Monthly Press book, 1943). I continued with a rereading of a classic study I read in graduate school nearly a half century ago: Bernard Bailyn, *The Ideological Origins of the American Revolution* (Cambridge, Mass.: Belknap Press of Harvard University Press, 1967). In the late 1960s, I had the pleasure of sitting next to Mr. Bailyn, Winthrop Professor of History, at a dinner party in the Master's Lodgings at Leverett House and receiving his encouragement for my doctoral dissertation in progress regarding— although I did not recognize it at the time—the ideological origins of the California experience. My further reading in Revolutionary War history involved forays into *Essays on the American Revolution*, edited by Stephen Kurtz and James Hudson

(Chapel Hill and New York: University of North Carolina Press and W.W. Norton, 1973), published for the Institute of Early American History and Culture at Williamsburg, Virginia; the volume opens with another instructive essay by Bailyn, "The Central Themes of the American Revolution".

Thus oriented in the most general terms by Middlekauff, Miller, and Bailyn, I got down to my stated topic, Roman Catholics in the American Revolution, through a reading and inventory of a chronically underestimated contribution to the field: *Catholics and the American Revolution*, compiled and edited by Martin I.J. Griffin (printed by the author in 3 volumes; Philadelphia:1907, 1909, 1911). Like John Gilmary Shea, Martin Ignatius Joseph Griffin (1842–1911) spent his life as a Catholic journalist, social activist (temperance, the Irish Catholic Benevolent Union), and protohistorian, founder of the American Catholic Historical Society of Philadelphia in 1884, and from 1886 to 1911 proprietor and editor of *American Catholic Historical Researches*, the first American journal of its kind devoted to the publication of documents of American Catholic history and their interpretation. Griffin is also the author of brief biographies, *History of Rt. Rev. Michael Egan, DD, First Bishop of Philadelphia* (1893), *Commodore John Barry* (1902), *General Count Casimir Pulaski* (1909), and *Stephan Moylan* (1909), studies that he incorporated into his three-volume anthology. *Catholics and the American Revolution* consists of hundreds of annotated primary sources, which must have taken Griffin years to collect. These volumes save the twenty-first-century writer the effort of assembling such sources from scratch. Decades after Griffin's death, any Catholic university press might very well have brought out an annotated edition of this anthology, which is today available online (https://archive.org/stream/catholicsandame01grifgoog /catholicsandame01grifgoog_djvu.txt 11/13/2016). (I, however, also enjoyed the use of the anthology in book form at the Gleeson Library of the University of San Francisco.) Like Shea, however, Griffin was forced to raise money by subscription and publish himself the three volumes that have proven so useful.

For a general, Protestant-oriented treatment of religion and the American Revolution, see Thomas Kidd, *God of Liberty: A Religious History of the American Revolution* (New York: Basic Books, 2010).

Regarding Roman Catholics and the American Revolution, Charles Metzger SJ, *Catholics and the American Revolution: A Study in Religious Climate* (Chicago: Loyola University Press, 1962), proved consistently useful. See also Maggie Bunson, *Founding of Faith: Catholics in the American Revolutionary Era* (Boston: St. Paul Editions, 1977); and Thomas O'Brien Hanley SJ, *The American Revolution and Religion: Maryland 1770–1800* (Washington, D.C.: Catholic University of America Press, 1971), especially chapter 7, "Catholic Emancipation", 171–94. Since the Maryland experience is so important in this regard, see also Thomas Joseph Peterman's information-rich *Catholics in Colonial Delmarva* (Devon, Penn.: Cooke Publishing, 1996). Written by a priest of the Diocese of Wilmington, Delaware, this book overflows with useful information regarding Catholicism on the Eastern Shore of Maryland and Delaware.

For further background, see the sheer tour de force of scholarship and analysis in Ronald Hoffman, *A Spirit of Dissension: Economics, Politics, and the Revolution in Maryland* (Baltimore and London: Johns Hopkins University Press, 1973). See also Aubrey Land, *Colonial Maryland: A History* (Millwood, N.Y.: KTO Press, 1981);

Michael Graham, "Roman Catholics, Not Papists: Catholic Identity in Maryland, 1689–1776", *Maryland Historical Magazine* 92 (Summer 1997): 138–61; and Tricia Pyne, "The Politics of Identity in 18th-Century British America: Catholic Perceptions of Their Role in Colonial Society", *U.S. Catholic Historian* 15 (Spring 1997): 1–13.

Regarding the multigenerational Carroll saga, see Ronald Hoffman, *Princes of Ireland, Planters of Maryland: A Carroll Saga, 1500–1782* (Chapel Hill: University of North Carolina Press, 2000). *Dear Papa, Dear Charley*, edited by Ronald Hoffman, Sally Mason, and Eleanor Darcy (Chapel Hill and London: University of North Carolina Press, 2001), gathers the correspondence between Charles Carroll and his father during Charles Carroll's long European sojourn. Concerning Carroll's entrance into public life in 1773 as a controversialist, see *Maryland and the Empire, 1773: The Antilon–First Citizen Letters*, Maryland Bicentennial Studies, edited and with an introduction by Peter S. Onuf (Baltimore and London: Johns Hopkins University Press, 1974). Regarding Charles Carroll's distinctive childhood, see the chapter on Carroll in Pauline Maier, *The Old Revolutionaries: Political Lives in the Age of Samuel Adams* (New York: Alfred A. Knopf, 1980).

In 1876 Brantz Mayer edited for the Maryland Historical Society the *Journal of Charles Carroll of Carrollton during His Visit to Canada in 1776 as One of the Commissioners from Congress: With a Memoir and Notes* (Baltimore: Maryland Historical Society, 1876). Carroll's *Journal* constitutes the only extensive record of this diplomatic mission.

Further background to the invasion of Canada and Carroll's mission can be gleaned from Don Gerlach, *Philip Schuyler and the American Revolution in New York, 1733–1777* (Lincoln: University of Nebraska Press, 1964); and Martin Bush, *Revolutionary Enigma: A Re-Appraisal of General Philip Schuyler of New York* (Port Washington, N.Y.: Ira J. Friedman, 1969). Regarding the role played by American merchant Thomas Walker's welcoming of Americans to Montreal, see Lewis Thomas' entry on Thomas Walker in the *DCB*.

Benedict Arnold makes his debut in this chapter. See Brian Richard Boylan, *Benedict Arnold: The Dark Eagle* (New York: W.W. Norton, 1973).

As far as biographies of Charles Carroll are concerned, we begin with Kate Mason Rowland, *The Life of Charles Carroll of Carrollton, 1737–1832, With His Correspondence and Papers* (2 volumes; New York and London: G.P. Putnam's Sons, Knickerbocker Press, 1898). A mere 750 copies of this informative biography and anthology of letters were published. The United States Catholic Historical Society issued *Unpublished Letters of Charles Carroll of Carrollton, and of His Father Charles Carroll of Doughoregan*, compiled and edited with a memoir by Thomas Meagher Field (New York: United States Catholic Historical Society, 1902), a University of Michigan Library reprint. This annotated anthology of seventy-two letters written between 1754 and two weeks before Carroll's death on 30 October 1832 is especially valuable for information regarding Charles Carroll's later years and the taking of London by storm by his three Caton granddaughters. Ellen Hart Smith's *Charles Carroll of Carrollton* (Cambridge, Mass.: Harvard University Press, 1942) is well researched, vividly written, and comprehensive. Thomas O'Brien Hanley SJ produced two equally comprehensive volumes: *Charles Carroll of Carrollton: The Making of a Revolutionary Gentleman* (Chicago: Loyola University

Press, 1982) and *Revolutionary Statesman: Charles Carroll and the War* (Chicago: Loyola University Press, 1983). Scott McDermott, *Charles Carroll of Carrollton: Faithful Revolutionary* (New York: Scepter Publications, 2002), represents a briefer but effective treatment.

Regarding the other Carroll on the diplomatic mission to Canada, it was a pleasure in this chapter—indeed, throughout the book—to have access to *The John Carroll Papers*, edited by Thomas O'Brien Hanley SJ, under the auspices of the American Catholic Historical Association (3 volumes; Notre Dame and London: University of Notre Dame Press,1976). Not only are Carroll's extant and available correspondence and other writings reproduced in this work; innumerable persons are identified and annotated. John Gilmary Shea produced *The Life and Times of the Most Rev. John Carroll, Bishop and First Archbishop of Baltimore* (New York, 1888) as the second volume of his four-volume history of American Catholicism. Monsignor Peter Guilday's *The Life and Times of John Carroll, Archbishop of Baltimore, 1735–1815* (New York: Encyclopedia Press, 1922) remains the comprehensive and authoritative biography of the first American bishop. Forty chapters and 864 pages in length, Guilday's biography also serves as a de facto history and anthology of primary sources for the Revolutionary War era and the organizational development of the Roman Catholic Church in the newly founded United States. I acknowledge a continuing dependence on Guilday's biography for not only the history of John Carroll but also the development of the Church under his guidance until his death in 1815. Less comprehensive but brilliantly written and exquisitely detailed is Annabelle Melville's *John Carroll of Baltimore: Founder of the American Catholic Hierarchy* (New York: Charles Scribner's Sons, 1955), awarded the John Gilmary Shea Prize of the American Catholic Historical Association in 1955.

Regarding the Loyalist priest who confronted and outdebated Carroll in Montreal during Carroll's mission to Canada, see Richard MacMaster SJ, "Parish in Arms: A Study of Father John MacKenna and the Mohawk Valley Loyalists, 1773–1778", *Historical Records and Studies* 45 (1957): 107–25. See also Ewen MacDonald, "Father Roderick Macdonnell at St. Regis and the Glen Garry Catholics", *Catholic Historical Review* 19 (1933): 265–74; and Thomas O'Brien Hanley SJ, "The Carrolls in the American Revolution", chapter 7 of *Catholics in America, 1776–1976*, edited by Robert Trisco, foreword by the Most Reverend Edward A. McCarthy (1976), 19–32.

Regarding Benjamin Franklin, Carroll's friend and traveling companion in the Canadian mission, I had recourse to the classic biography by Carl Van Doren, *Benjamin Franklin* (New York: Viking, 1938).

Concerning John Carroll's brother and patron, see Sister Mary Virginia Geiger SSND, *Daniel Carroll, a Framer of the Constitution* (Washington, D.C.: Catholic University of America Press, 1943). See also the extensive entry in the *DAB*. Regarding Maryland governor Thomas Sim Lee, see the entry in the *DAB* and the numerous references in Frank White Jr., *The Governors of Maryland, 1770–1970* (Annapolis: Hall of Records Commission, 1970), 11–14, and numerous other references. Regarding Thomas Attwood Digges, see *Letters of Thomas Attwood Digges (1742–1821)*, edited by Robert Elias and Eugene Finch (Columbia: University of South Carolina Press, 1982). Regarding Thomas FitzSimons and George Meade, see Martin I.J. Griffin, "Thomas FitzSimons, Pennsylvania's Catholic Signer of the

Constitution", *Researches of the American Catholic Historical Society* 2 (1886–1888): 45–111. See as well their respective entries in the *DAB*.

2. Valley Forge

At this point, George Washington enters the narrative, in which he will remain for the rest of part 1. Whenever possible, in military matters relating to Washington, I have made use of *The Papers of George Washington: Revolutionary War Series*, edited by Philander Chase (23 volumes; Charlottesville: University Press of Virginia, 1985). See also *The Diaries of George Washington*, edited by Donald Jackson and Dorothy Twohig (6 volumes; Charlottesville: University Press of Virginia, 1976–1979). Also of relevance to this and the following chapters is William Alfred Bryan, *George Washington in American Literature, 1775–1865* (New York: Columbia University Press, 1952).

Regarding Washington's longtime antagonist Charles Lee, see the entry in the *DAB*.

Regarding Catholic Indians' loyalty to Washington, see Francis Cogliano, "To Obey Jesus Christ and General Washington: Massachusetts, Catholicism, and the Eastern Indians during the American Revolution", *Maine Historical Society Quarterly* 32 (Fall 1992): 107–33.

Concerning Thaddeus Kościuszko, see *Autographed Letters of Thaddeus Kościuszko in the American Revolution*, edited by Metchie Budka (Chicago: Polish Museum of America, 1977). See also David Zabecki, "In the Cause of Human Freedom: Tadeusz Kościuszko Fought for Independence in America and Poland", *Military History* 28 (November 2011): 52–57. See also Miecislaus Haiman, *Kościuszko, Leader and Exile* (New York: Kościuszko Foundation, 1977); and Paul Walker, *Engineers of Independence: A Documentary History of the Army Engineers in the American Revolution, 1775–1783* (Washington, D.C.: Historical Division, Office of the Chief of Engineers, 1981).

A superabundance of studies exists regarding Gilbert du Motier, marquis de Lafayette. For those wishing an exhaustive treatment, see Louis Gottschalk's cumulative biography in four installments. Of relevance to this and following chapters are *Lafayette Comes to America* (Chicago: University of Chicago Press, 1935) and *Lafayette Joins the American Army* (Chicago: University of Chicago Press, 1974). *Lafayette in the Age of the American Revolution: Selected Letters and Papers, 1776–1790*, edited by Stanley Idzerda, Roger Smith, Linda Pike, and Mary Ann Quinn (Ithaca and London: Cornell University Press, 1977), abounds in primary sources and scholarly annotations. Olivier Bernier's *Lafayette: Hero of Two Worlds* (New York: E. P. Dutton, 1983) is a well-researched, well-written, accessible account that serves as a lively guide to the entire Lafayette story and its related text.

Regarding Casimir Pulaski, see Leszek Szymanski, *Casimir Pulaski: A Hero of the American Revolution*, foreword by Brig. Gen. Thaddeus Maliszewski (New York: Hippocrene Books, 1994).

Regarding Baron Johann de Kalb, see A. E. Zucker, *General de Kalb, Lafayette's Mentor* (Chapel Hill: University of North Carolina Press, 1966). See also Thomas Fleming, "The Baron de Kalb, Plotter or Patriot?", *Military History* 25 (February/ March 2009): 58–65.

For information about Frederick William Augustus, Baron von Steuben, see John McAuley Palmer, *General Von Steuben* (New Haven: Yale University Press, 1937) and Paul Lockhart, *The Drillmaster of Valley Forge: The Baron de Steuben and the Making of the American Army* (New York: HarperCollins, 2008).

Regarding George Washington's lifelong association with Irish Americans, see Michael J. O'Brien, *George Washington's Associations with the Irish* (New York: P.J. Kenedy and Sons, 1937). Regarding the prominent roles various Irish Americans played in the Revolutionary War, we will consider them in alphabetical order.

Concerning John Barry, see Martin I.J. Griffin, *The Story of Commodore John Barry: Father of the American Navy* (Philadelphia: printed by the author, 1908); Joseph Gurn, *Commodore John Barry: Father of the American Navy* (New York: P.J. Kenedy and Sons, 1933); William Bell Clark, *Gallant John Barry, 1745–1803: The Story of a Naval Hero of Two Wars* (New York: Macmillan, 1938); and Tim McGrath, *John Barry: An American Hero in the Age of Sail* (Yardley, Pennsylvania: Westholme Publishing, 2011).

Regarding General Thomas Conway, see the entry in the *DAB*.

Regarding Colonel John Fitzgerald, see the various entries in Martin I.J. Griffin's *Catholics and the American Revolution*, especially the entry "Colonel John Fitzgerald, Aide-de-Camp and Secretary to Washington", 2:366–88. See also Richard Purcell, "A Catholic Revolutionary Soldier and Patriot", *Thought* 8 (December 1933): 471–88.

Regarding Stephen Moylan, see Martin I.J. Griffin, *Stephen Moylan, Muster-Master General, Secretary, and Aide-de-Camp to Washington* (Philadelphia: printed by the author, 1909).

John H. Campbell's *History of the Friendly Sons of St. Patrick and of the Hibernian Society for the Relief of Immigrants from Ireland* (Philadelphia: Hibernian Society, 1892) abounds in telling detail about the Irish-American establishment of Philadelphia before, during, and after the Revolution. Regarding the socioeconomics of the Philadelphia that nurtured the Friendly Sons, see Thomas Doerflinger, *A Vigorous Spirit of Enterprise: Merchants and Economic Development in Revolutionary Philadelphia* (Chapel Hill and London: University of North Carolina Press, 1986).

Concerning Irish reaction to the Revolution, see Leo Francis Stock, "The Irish Parliament and the American Revolution", *Historical Records and Studies* 30 (1939): 11–29.

3. Camden, South Carolina

Regarding French émigrés and immigrants to the United States during the French Revolution, see Frances Sergeant Childs, *French Refugee Life in the United States, 1790–1800* (Baltimore: Johns Hopkins Press, 1940). See also Annabelle Melville, "French Contributions to the Church in the New Republic", in *Catholics in America, 1776–1976*, edited by Robert Trisco, foreword by the Most Reverend Edward A. McCarthy (1976), 33–37.

Regarding the Franco-American alliance, see *Diplomacy and Revolution: The Franco-American Alliance of 1778*, edited by Ronald Hoffman and Peter Albert (Charlottesville: University Press of Virginia, 1981). See also Samuel Flagg Bemis, *The Diplomacy of the American Revolution* (Bloomington: Indiana University Press, 1967).

Regarding the Spanish alliance, see James Alton James, *Oliver Pollock: The Life and Times of an Unknown Patriot* (New York and London: D. Appleton-Century, 1937).

Concerning the ambivalent ally of George Rogers Clark, see Joseph Donnelly SJ, *Pierre Gibault, Missionary, 1737–1802* (Chicago: Loyola University Press, 1971).

Regarding French Navy and Army chaplains on duty in the United States during the Revolutionary War, see Aidan Henry Germain OSB, *Catholic Military and Naval Chaplains, 1776–1917* (Washington, D.C.: Catholic University of America, 1929).

4. Yorktown

The saga of the American Loyalists before, during, and after the Revolution can be traced through William Nelson, *The American Tory* (Oxford: Clarendon Press, 1961); and *The American Tory*, edited by Morton Borden and Penn Borden (Englewood Cliffs, N.J.: Prentice-Hall, 1972). Arthur Granville Bradley, *The United Empire Loyalists: Founders of British Canada* (London: Thornton Butterworth, 1971) is especially valuable regarding the evacuation of Loyalists to Canada under the supervision of Sir Guy Carleton (Lord Dorchester). See also Jonathan Boucher, *Reminiscences of an American Loyalist, 1738–1789*, edited by his grandson Jonathan Bouchier (*sic*), with a new introduction by Ralph Adams Brown (Port Washington, N.Y.: Kennikat Press, 1967); and Anne Zimmer, *Jonathan Boucher: Loyalist in Exile* (Detroit: Wayne State University Press, 1978).

Regarding Catholic Loyalists, see Martin I.J. Griffin, "Catholic Loyalists of the Revolution", *Catholics and the American Revolution*, 2:161–82. Regarding Joseph Mosley SJ, see Edward Devitt SJ, "Letters of Father Joseph Mosley and Some Extracts from His Diary, 1757–1786", *Woodstock Letters* 35 (1906): 35–55; see also "Letters of Father Joseph Mosley and Some Extracts from His Diary, 1757–1786," *Records of the American Catholic Historical Society of Philadelphia* 17, no. 2 (June 1906): 180–210. The anti-Loyalist rioting in Philadelphia following the Yorktown victory is chronicled in "Anna Rawle: Diary, 25 October 1781", in *The American Revolution: Writings from the War of Independence*, edited by John Rhodehamel (New York: Library of America, 2001): 750–51.

5. Paris

The English version of Abbé Robin's *Nouveaux voyages dans l'Amérique septentrionale* was published in Philadelphia in 1783 by printer and bookseller Robert Bell in an English translation by journalist and poet Philip Freneau under the title *New Travels through North-America: In a Series of Letters; exhibiting the history of the victorious campaign of the allied armies, under His Excellency General George Washington, and the Count de Rochambeau in the year 1781* ...

Regarding the short, tragic life of Mary (Molly) Darnall Carroll, see Sally Mason, "Mama, Rachel, and Molly: Three Generations of Carroll Women", in *Women in the Age of the American Revolution*, edited by Ronald Hoffman and Peter Albert (Charlottesville: University Press of Virginia, 1989). See also *American Catholic Women: A Historical Exploration*, edited by Karen Kennelly CSJ (New York: Macmillan, 1989); and Michael Graham, "Women and the Catholic Church in Maryland, 1689–1776", *Maryland Historical Magazine* 94 (Winter 1999): 397–418.

Concerning the clandestine relationship between Major John André and Benedict Arnold as well as André's subsequent romanticization, see Brian Richard Boylan, *Benedict Arnold: The Dark Eagle* (New York: W. W. Norton, 1973), 185–219, 247–57.

Regarding the Hessian experience during and after the Revolutionary War, see *Hessian Journals: Unpublished Documents of the American Revolution*, edited by Valentine Hubbs (Columbia, S.C.: Camden House, 1980); and Daniel Krebs, *A Generous and Merciful Enemy: Life for German Prisoners of War during the American Revolution* (Norman: University of Oklahoma Press, 2013).

6. White Marsh Plantation

For general background regarding the post–Revolutionary War Roman Catholic clergy, see Ronald Binzley, "Disaffected Children: The Ex-Jesuits and the Shaping of Early American Catholicism, 1773–1790", *U.S. Catholic Historian* 26 (Spring 2008): 47–77. Regarding the extraordinary career of convert priest John Thayer, see the biography in the *DAB*. See also *An Account of the Conversion of the Reverend Mr. John Thayer: Formerly a Protestant Minister of Boston, Written by Himself* (1787), which was reprinted by Nabu Press in 2010 and is also available through Google Books at https://archive.org/details/anaccountconver00thaygoog.

The ongoing relationship between John Carroll and the ex-Jesuits can be traced through Thomas Hughes, *History of the Society of Jesus in North America, Colonial and Federal* (4 volumes; London and New York: Longmans, Green, 1908). Volume 1, part 2, 695–878, presents extensive fiscal evidence of this relationship.

As background to the Carroll-Wharton debate, see two pamphlets by Charles Wharton in the Gale Group Eighteenth Century Collections Online: *A Letter to the Roman Catholics of the City of Worcester* (Philadelphia: printed by Robert Aitken at the Sign of Pope's Head in Market Street Near the Coffee-house, 1784) and *A Reply to an Address to the Roman Catholics of the United States of America by the Author of a Letter to the Roman Catholics of the City of Worcester* (Philadelphia: printed by Charles Cist at the Corner of Fourth and Arch Streets, 1785).

Regarding John Carroll's close associate during his years as prefect, see James Daley SJ, "Pioneer Missionary: Ferdinand Farmer, S.J.: 1720–1786", *Woodstock Letters* 75 (1946): 105–15, 207–31, 311–21.

For a refutation of France's alleged effort to play a dominant role in the establishment of an American hierarchy, see Jules Baisnée PSS, *France and the Establishment of the American Hierarchy: The Myth of French Interference, 1782–1784* (Baltimore: Johns Hopkins University Press, 1934). See also John Tracy Ellis, *Perspectives in American Catholicism* (Baltimore and Dublin: Helicon, 1963), 93–100.

For background on trusteeism in America, see Patrick Dignan, *A History of the Legal Incorporation of Catholic Church Property in the United States (1784–1932)* (New York: P. J. Kenedy and Sons, 1935).

Robert Emmett Curran has achieved the comprehensive *A History of Georgetown University* (3 volumes; Washington, D.C.: Georgetown University Press, 2010). I have drawn upon chapters 1 and 2 of the first volume, *From Academy to University, 1789–1889*, for details in my condensed narrative of the founding and early years of Georgetown Academy. For earlier background, see Richard Purcell, "The

Education of the Catholics in Maryland", *Catholic Educational Review* 30 (December 1932): 586–88.

7. Dorset, England

The documents connected to John Carroll's appointment as bishop were gathered by Edward Devitt SJ, in *Propaganda Documents: Appointment of the First Bishop of Baltimore* (Philadelphia: American Catholic Historical Society of Philadelphia, 1911).

For background relating to the long struggle to establish an Anglican episcopate in the American colonies, see Arthur Lyon Cross, *The Anglican Episcopate and the American Colonies* (New York and London: Longmans, Green, 1902).

Regarding the influential English careers of Charles Carroll's granddaughters, see Jehanne Wake, *Sisters of Fortune: Marianne, Bess, Louisa and Emily Caton, 1788–1874* (London: Chatto and Windus, 2010).

In 1790, London printer J. P. Coghlan issued the extraordinary anthology edited anonymously by John Carroll's good friend Charles Plowden, *A Short Account of the Establishment of the New See of Baltimore in Maryland, and of Consecrating the Right Rev. Dr. John Carroll First Bishop Thereof on the Feast of the Assumption, 1790. With a Discourse Delivered on that Occasion, and the Authority for Consecrating the Bishop, and Erecting and Administering the Said See. To Which Are Added Extracts from the Different Bills of Right and Constitution of the United States,—That Liberty of Conscience is the Birth-Right of Every Man, and an Exclusion of Any Religious Test For Ever.*

Regarding the history and architecture of Lulworth Castle, see C. M. Antony, "Lulworth Castle: Its History and Memories", *Catholic Historical Review* 1 (October 1915): 250–65.

8. Baltimore 1808

For the long and eventful history of the Archdiocese of Baltimore, see Thomas W. Spalding, *The Premier See: A History of the Archdiocese of Baltimore, 1789–1989* (Baltimore and London: Johns Hopkins University Press, 1989).

Of special importance to this chapter is Robert Gilmor, "Recollections of Baltimore", *Maryland Historical Magazine* 7 (September 1912): 235–42. Regarding the city and people of Baltimore, the following titles have proven invaluable: J. Thomas Scharf, *The Chronicles of Baltimore: Being a Complete History of Baltimore Town and Baltimore City from the Earliest Period to the Present Time* (Baltimore: Turnbull Brothers, 1874); Annie Leakin Sioussat, *Old Baltimore* (New York: Macmillan, 1931); Francis F. Beirne, *The Amiable Baltimoreans* (Hatboro, Penn.: Tradition Press, 1968); and Gary Lawson Browne, *Baltimore in the Nation, 1789–1861* (Chapel Hill: University of North Carolina Press, 1980).

Regarding changing patterns of slavery in Maryland and Baltimore in this era, see Christopher Phillips, *Freedom's Port: The African-American Community of Baltimore, 1790–1860* (Urbana: University of Illinois Press, 1997). See also Cyprian Davis OSB, *The History of Black Catholics in the United States* (New York: Crossroad, 1995).

Useful to this chapter is Moreau de Saint-Méry, "Baltimore as Seen by Moreau de Saint-Méry in 1794", *Maryland Historical Magazine* 35 (September 1940): 225–30. Extensive detail regarding Baltimore's adjustment to refugees from Saint-Domingue is available in Walter Hartridge, "The Refugees from the Island of St. Domingo in Maryland", *Maryland Historical Magazine* 38 (January 1943): 103–23. See also Stuart Sherman, "The Library Company of Baltimore, 1795–1854", *Maryland Historical Magazine* 39 (March 1944): 6–17.

Regarding the influx of refugee and émigré French clergy, see Leo Ruskowski PSS, *French Émigré Priests in the United States, 1791–1815* (Washington, D.C.: Catholic University of America Press, 1940).

Regarding the weekend entertainments of Charles Carroll of Carrollton in his later years, see Ralph Gray and Gerald Hartdagen, "A Glimpse of Baltimore Society in 1827: Letters of Henry D. Gilpin", *Maryland Historical Magazine* 69 (Fall 1974): 256–71.

Regarding the various epidemics of smallpox, typhus, scarlet fever, yellow fever, dysentery, malignant bilious fever, and other maladies that afflicted Baltimore during this era, see the website Medicine in Maryland, 1752–1920 at https://mdhistoryon line.net/?s=epidemics.

Concerning the long and fruitful saga of the Society of Saint Sulpice, see Charles G. Herbermann, *The Sulpicians in the United States* (New York: Encyclopedia Press, 1916) and Joseph W. Ruane, *The Beginnings of the Society of St. Sulpice in the United States, 1791–1829* (Washington, D.C.: Catholic University of America Press, 1935). Regarding the early history of Saint Mary's Seminary, see the centennial volume *1791–1891 Memorial Volume of the Centenary of St. Mary's Seminary of St. Sulpice, Baltimore, MD* (Baltimore: John Murphy, 1891), which features a number of valuable lists of faculty and students. Biographies of eminent Sulpicians include Annabelle Melville, *Louis William DuBourg: Bishop of Louisiana and the Floridas, Bishop of Montauban, and Archbishop of Besançon, 1766–1833* (2 volumes; Chicago: Loyola University Press, 1986), a fascinating, detailed account of DuBourg as an educator and, later, as bishop of Louisiana and, in France, bishop of Montauban and archbishop of Besançon, successively.

Regarding the Chapel of the Presentation of Mary at Saint Mary's College and Seminary, see Robert Alexander, *The Architecture of Maximilian Godefroy* (Baltimore and London: Johns Hopkins University Press, 1974). The recent restoration of this landmark building is chronicled by John Kemper PSS and Tricia Pyne in *Update* (Summer 2012), the newsletter of the Sulpicians, United States Province.

Regarding the Caribbean slave rebellions that brought so many French refugees to Baltimore, see *Slave Revolution in the Caribbean, 1789–1804: A Brief History with Documents*, edited by Laurent Dubois and John Garrigus (Boston and New York: Bedford/St. Martin's, 2006). See also the very important aforementioned essay by Walter Hartridge, "The Refugees from the Island of St. Domingo in Maryland", *Maryland Historical Magazine* 38 (January 1943): 103–23.

9. Emmitsburg, Maryland

For relevant facts and lengthy quotations from archival sources, I am totally dependent in this chapter on two interrelated biographical studies by Annabelle Melville: *Elizabeth Bayley Seton, 1774–1821* (New York: Charles Scribner's Sons, 1951) and the aforementioned *Louis William DuBourg: Bishop of Louisiana and the Floridas, Bishop of Montauban, and Archbishop of Besançon, 1766–1833* (2 volumes; Chicago:

Loyola University Press, 1986). See also Melville's "Writing a Saint's Biography", *U.S. Catholic Historian* 10 (1991/1992): 71–77, for an autobiographical statement by Melville regarding the extraordinary career of John Tracy Ellis' finest student. Indeed, for its sweep and detail, Melville's biography of DuBourg, while dealing with a lesser-known figure, stands alongside Ellis' *The Life of James Cardinal Gibbons, Archbishop of Baltimore, 1834–1921* (2 volumes; Milwaukee: Bruce Publishing, 1952) as a classic of American Catholic historiography. Melville's biography of Mother Seton, moreover, is courageous in its subtlety, honesty, and acute psychological insight into the complex nature of this widowed convert from Episcopalianism who never ceased to be a great and passionate Anglo-American wife, mother, widow, religious under vows, and saint in a thoroughly American idiom.

Also important to this chapter is *Elizabeth Seton: Selected Writings*, edited by Ellin Kelly and Annabelle Melville (Mahwah, N.J.: Paulist Press, 1987). See also the rhapsodic but effectively detailed Madame de Barberey, *Elizabeth Seton*, translated and adapted from the sixth French edition by the Reverend Joseph Code, with an introduction by the Most Reverend Michael Curley, Archbishop of Baltimore (New York: Macmillan, 1927). Especially strong on the Vincentian background is Joseph Dirvin CM, *Mrs. Seton, Foundress of the American Sisters of Charity* (New York: Farrar, Straus and Cudahy, 1962). Regarding the relationship between the Sulpicians and the Sisters of Charity, see Betty McNeil DC, "The Sulpicians and the Sisters of Charity: Concentric Circles of Mission", *Vincentian Heritage Journal* 20 (Spring 1999): 13–38.

For portraits of three priests of importance to Mother Seton in these years, see Richard Shaw, *John Dubois, Founding Father: The Life and Times of the Founder of Mount St. Mary's College, Emmitsburg, Superior of the Sisters of Charity, and Third Bishop of the Diocese of New York* (Yonkers, N.Y.: United States Catholic Historical Society, 1983); Columba Fox, *The Life of the Right Reverend John Baptist Mary David, 1761–1841* (New York: United States Catholic Historical Society, 1925); and James Roosevelt Bayley, D.D., Bishop of Newark, *Memoirs of the Right Reverend Simon William Gabriel Brute, D.D., First Bishop of Vincennes, with sketches of scenes describing his recollection of the French Revolution and extracts from his journal* (New York: Catholic Publication Society, 1876). Theodore Maynard explored Bruté's distinctive piety as well as his tenure as bishop of Vincennes in his highly impressionistic *The Reed and the Rock: Portrait of Simon Bruté* (New York and Toronto: Longmans, Green, 1942).

Regarding John Henry Hobart, Mrs. Seton's pastor at Trinity Church in New York City, see the portrait in the *DAB*. See also George DeMille, *The Catholic Movement in the American Episcopal Church* (2nd edition; Philadelphia: Church Historical Society, 1950).

For a generally correct but highly censored portrait of the Reverend Mr. Cooper, see John Edward McGarity, CSP, "Samuel Southerland Cooper, 1769–1843", *Records of the American Catholic Historical Society* 37 (December 1928): 305–40.

Regarding the Carmelites of Port Tobacco, see Charles Warren Currier CSSR, *Carmel in America: A Centennial History of the Discalced Carmelites in the United States* (Baltimore: J. Murphy, 1898). Concerning Elizabeth Carberry, the first American to join the Carmelites at Port Tobacco, see Rose Martin, "The First Nun Professed in the Original United States", in *Catholics in America, 1776–1976*, edited by Robert Trisco, foreword by the Most Reverend Edward A. McCarthy (1976), 39–41.

Regarding the Poor Clares, see Gabriel Naughten OFM, "The Poor Clares in Georgetown: Second Convent of Women in the United States", *Franciscan Studies* 24 (March 1943): 63–72.

The classic history, begun by Mary M. Meline and continued by Rev. Edward Francis Xavier McSweeny, *The Story of the Mountain: Mount Saint Mary's College and Seminary*, can be accessed electronically at the following link: https://books.google .com/books?id=atpEAAAAYAAJ&pg=PA162&lpg=PA162&dq=the+story+of +the+mountain:+Mount+St.+Mary%27s+College+and+SEminary&source=bl &ots=tnUQjfZVw-&sig=vHeO1QXSGhqU1YXPSc_O73VEodQ&hl=en&sa =X&ved=0ahUKEwit5MrXsvLQAhUB8mMKHTwUBzgQ6AEIRTAH#v= onepage&q=the%20story%20of%20the%20mountain%3A%20Mount%20St.%20 Mary's%20College%20and%20SEminary&f=false.

10. Baltimore 1821

Regarding worship patterns in colonial and precathedral Maryland, see *American Catholic Preaching and Piety in the Time of John Carroll*, edited by Raymond Kupke (Lanham: University Press of Maryland, 1991); Robert Emmett Curran, *American Jesuit Spirituality: The Maryland Tradition, 1634–1900* (New York: Paulist Press, 1988); Joseph Linck, *Fully Instructed and Vehemently Influenced: Catholic Preaching in Anglo-Colonial America* (Philadelphia: St. Joseph's University Press, 2002); and Tricia Pyne, "Ritual and Practice in the Maryland Catholic Community, 1634–1776", *U.S. Catholic Historian* 26 (Spring 2008): 17–46.

Regarding the fundraising for and planning, design, and construction of the Cathedral of the Assumption of the Blessed Virgin Mary, see Benjamin Henry Latrobe, *The Journal of Latrobe*, with an introduction by J. H. B. Latrobe (New York: D. Appleton, 1905); Sidney Fiske Kimball, "Latrobe's Designs for the Cathedral of Baltimore", *Architectural Record* 42 (1917): 540–55; William Rusk, "Benjamin H. Latrobe and the Classical Influence", *Maryland Historical Magazine* 31 (June 1936): 126–51; the comprehensive and beautifully written "Benjamin Henry Latrobe", in the *DAB* (1936); Walter Knight Sturges, "A Bishop and His Architect: The Story of the Building of Baltimore Cathedral", *Liturgical Arts* 17 (February 1949): 53–64; William Hoyt, "Land for a Cathedral: Baltimore, 1806–1817", *Catholic Historical Review* 36 (January 1951): 441–45; and Talbot Hamlin, *Benjamin Henry Latrobe* (New York: Oxford University Press, 1955).

Robert Emmett Curran narrates the near failure of Georgetown College and its recovery under the jurisdiction of a revived Society of Jesus in chapter 3 of the first volume of his *History of Georgetown University* (3 volumes; Washington, D.C.: Georgetown University Press, 2010).

For John Carroll's farewell to George Washington, see his *Eulogy on George Washington*, delivered in Saint Peter's Church, Baltimore, February 22, 1800, with a foreword by Peter Guilday (New York: P. J. Kenedy and Sons, 1931).

The story of the marriage of Jérôme Bonaparte and Elizabeth Patterson did not receive full disclosure until documentation surfaced decades later, when the Patterson family correspondence was discovered in a cache of documents and letters being sold as materials to be recycled into new paper. Historian William Thomas Roberts Saffell had the documents copied and used as the basis for his *The Bonaparte-Patterson Marriage in 1803, and the Secret Correspondence on the Subject Never Before Made Public*, which Saffell self-published in Philadelphia in 1873. See also Clarence Edward Macartney and Gordon Dorrance, *The Bonapartes in America* (Philadelphia: Dorrance, 1939), https://babel.hathitrust.org/cgi/pt?id=wu.8909473 8234;view=1up; and Carol Berkin, *Wondrous Beauty: The Life and Adventures of Elizabeth Patterson Bonaparte* (New York: Alfred A. Knopf, 2014).

The restoration of the Society of Jesus in the United States is chronicled by Guilday in *The Life and Times of John Carroll, Archbishop of Baltimore, 1735–1815* (New York: Encyclopedia Press, 1922), 524–66. Also of value is a series of relevant articles gathered in *Jesuits: 2014 Yearbook of the Society of Jesus*, edited by Giuseppe Bellucci SJ, (Padua: Mediagraf SpA, 2013). Regarding John Carroll and the liturgy, see Ellis, "Archbishop Carroll and the Liturgy of the Vernacular", in John Tracy Ellis, *Perspectives in American Catholicism* (Baltimore and Dublin: Helicon, 1963), 127–33.

Regarding Louis William DuBourg's term as apostolic administrator to the Louisiana Territory, see Annabelle Melville, *Louis William DuBourg: Bishop of Louisiana and the Floridas, Bishop of Montauban, and Archbishop of Besançon, 1766–1833* (2 volumes; Chicago: Loyola University Press, 1986), 1:281–327. For key documents relating to the Louisiana Territory under John Carroll's jurisdiction, see *Documents of American Catholic History*, 1st edition, volume 1, edited by John Tracy Ellis (Milwaukee: Bruce Publishing, 1956): 181–84, 189–92.

INDEX